MR. RED SOX

Also by Bill Nowlin:

Ted Williams: The Pursuit of Perfection
(co-authored with Jim Prime)

Ted Williams: A Splendid Life
(co-authored with Jim Prime & Roland Lazenby)

Fenway Saved
(co-authored with Mike Ross & Jim Prime)

Tales from the Red Sox Dugout
(co-authored with Jim Prime)

More Tales from the Red Sox Dugout: Yarns from the Sox
(co-authored with Jim Prime)

Ted Williams: A Tribute
(co-authored with Jim Prime)

Edited works:

The Fenway Project
(co-edited with Cecilia Tan)

The Russian Tragedy

The Guillotine at Work

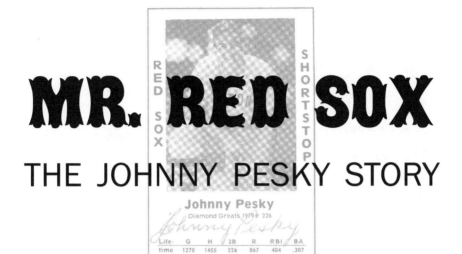

MR. RED SOX

THE JOHNNY PESKY STORY

Bill Nowlin

Foreword by Ted Williams
edited by Jim Prime

Rounder Books
Cambridge, Massachusetts

Published by Rounder Books

an imprint of:
Rounder Records
1 Camp Street
Cambridge, MA 02140

ISBN:1-57940-088-4

Cover design by Steve Jurgensmeyer
Cover photo courtesy of Johnny Pesky
credits for other photographs:
    Nomar Garciaparra & Johnny Pesky, by Bill Nowlin
    Bobby Doerr, Johnny Pesky & Ted Williams, courtesy of Johnny Pesky

Nowlin, Bill, 1945–
Mr. Red Sox: The Johnny Pesky Story
1. Pesky, Johnny 1919— 2. Boston Red Sox (Baseball team)—Biography 3. Baseball—Biography

First Edition

2003098818
796.357'092
[B]
ISBN 1-57940-088-4

Production by Windhaven Press
            www.windhaven.com

Printed in Canada

9 8 7 6 5 4 3 2 1

Contents

Foreword, by Ted Williams 1

Introduction 2

1   Childhood 7

2   Clubhouse Kid 14

3   Signing with the Red Sox 27

4   Minor League Years 37

5   Rookie Season, 1942 47

6   War Years 64

7   1946 74

8   Johnny Pesky & the 1946 World Series 89

9   1947 99

10   1948 108

11   1949 120

12   1950 133

13   1951 142

14   1952 151

15   1953 160

16   1954 165

17   1955–1960, Coach & Manager .169

18   1961–2, Seattle 187

19   Becoming Red Sox Manager 195

20   Manager, 1963 203

21   Manager, 1964 224

22   Johnny Pesky in Pittsburgh 239

23   Broadcaster, 1969–1974 246

24   Coach, 1975–1984 253

25   The Late 1990s 265

26   Mr. Red Sox 272

Index 277

Foreword

Johnny Pesky was one of the nicest guys I ever met in my career. And he was a *damn* good player, a good little hitter. He hit .335 in 1946 playing shortstop and was a career .300 hitter in the big leagues. Oh, BOY, could Pesky run! If it weren't for the war, he might have had 200 hits in each of those lost years.

Johnny could hit a ball past that third baseman harder than I could! POW!—right by the damn third baseman. He could be kind of a slap hitter, but his stroke had plenty of strength to it. It wasn't a big swing, but, boy, he'd power it by them.

He was a great table-setter. He got 200 hits three straight years! Meanwhile, Dom (DiMaggio) was walking all over the place. Some guy will say to me, "No wonder you drove in so many runs. The sons of bitches were on base for you all the time!" And they're right!

Johnny was a spirited little guy, and a winning ballplayer. I think he should be considered for the Hall of Fame.

And Johnny's still out there! Hell, he's been there for fifty years! They ought to put a monument in center field for him. I really have a soft spot in my heart for Johnny Pesky.

But he couldn't fly an airplane for shit!

—Ted Williams

Introduction

M R. RED SOX was inspired by a woman known as "a friend of the Red Sox"—Elizabeth "Lib" Dooley. Lib printed personal cards describing herself as such. A friend of the team. She used to sit in the front row at Fenway Park, about 10 rows in front of me, and had those seats for over fifty years—since before I was born. Once in while, I'd sit with her during a game, and that was a treat.

After Jim Prime and I completed *Ted Williams: A Tribute* (currently available in an expanded edition as *Ted Williams: The Pursuit of Perfection*), Lib suggested to me that I do a book on Johnny Pesky. Well, it took me about five years. My first interviews with Johnny were in 1998. Other matters kept intruding—writing assignments, family, my real job, life. I'm glad to have finished, and before Johnny has finished his life in baseball. I'm pleased the book will come out while he's still on the field before games, and in the clubhouse encouraging younger players.

When I began the book, it seemed like it was going to have a very sad and even poignant ending—this wonderful man, who probably set team records in attending charity banquets and church functions, and may have made more goodwill appearances at businesses and schools than any player in Red Sox history, was denied the pleasure of spending his last years where he most wanted to be: in uniform at the major league park. Mr. Red Sox was banned from the bench in Boston. Instead, he spent more time with Red Sox minor league teams in Pawtucket and Lowell, working with and teaching prospects, and making more friends in the process. It was valuable work—not heroic work, but work he needn't have done save for his unending love of baseball. All he ever wanted was to be around the game, and contribute what he could.

As new ownership took over the team, they thoughtfully (and wisely) welcomed Johnny Pesky back to Boston and, for the last two years, he's been in his element, back at Fenway Park where he belongs. So this book has a happy ending.

I want to thank Johnny himself for all the time he gave me, and for letting me pore over such clippings and materials as he or others had saved. Thanks to Johnny's wife Ruth, who is a remarkable woman in a league all her own. Thanks to the many people who helped me in one way or another; I hope I've not left anyone off my list of acknowledgements.

Jim Prime edited the book at my request, and brought his talents as a writer about baseball and the Boston Red Sox to bear on my manuscript which was at one point far too long and unwieldy.

Thanks as well to Jim's friend Ben Robicheau, who gave it a final lookover and made some nice catches himself!

And of course, I thank Lib Dooley for setting me on the path in the first place. I hope I've captured some of what makes Johnny Pesky so special to Red Sox fans everywhere.

Quite some years ago, Chadwick and Spindel wrote that Johnny "remains a revered figure in Boston, as familiar around Fenway as the Citgo sign." Let's hope this is the case for as many more years as Johnny wants to take the trip to the ballpark.

—Bill Nowlin, September 2003

A NOTE ON SOURCES:

In order to work on this book about Johnny Pesky, I was fortunate to have Johnny's very willing cooperation. I spent perhaps ten mornings interviewing him at his home, for two to three hours at a shot. Johnny was also very generous (and patient) with follow-up questions by phone or in person at Fenway, Pawtucket or Lowell. Ruth Pesky kept scrapbooks for a few years and the various clippings and other items from the Pesky family basement were of great help as well.

On a trip to Portland, Vincent Paveskovich showed me around the family neighborhood and also introduced me to old friends John Bubalo and Dick Benevento. I enjoyed brief research visits to the towns of Bend and Silverton, Oregon.

Mostly, I read newspapers and talked to people who played with Johnny. The players and others who know Johnny are listed with the acknowledgements. I hope I haven't left anyone out. I try to be pretty good about keeping track of anyone who helped. At the Tufts University library, I read every issue of the *Boston Globe* for every game that Johnny Pesky ever in played major league ball, for Boston or the other teams, and relied heavily on the microtext room at the Boston Public Library for the other papers of the day.

There is a lot of primary source information in *Mr. Red Sox*, be it from newspapers or interview. All of the quotations I attribute to Johnny were spoken into my cassette recorder and transcribed. Comments other ballplayers and friends and family made were also transcribed from tape.

I thank the many players and friends who gave of their time to talk with me. All quotes from individuals are from interviews I conducted, unless noted.

When I have taken a quotation from a different newspaper or other source, I have tried to provide credit in a footnote unless the source is clearly noted in the text itself. The *Boston Globe* was my principal reference for newspaper comment, hence my default newspaper source. Any phrases attributed to an unnamed newspaper come from the *Globe*.

I would like to offer general thanks to members of the Society of American Baseball Research (SABR) who often take time to answer research questions posed by me, in Boston, of SABR members who live in places I cannot easily get to.

I would like to offer specific thanks to the following people who helped me in the course of my research:

Larry Abel	Bob Broeg
Marshall Adesman	Dr. John Bubalo
John Alevizos	Steve Buckley
Andy Anderson	George H. W. Bush
Ernie Andres	Bob Carney
Nic Antoine	George Case III
Wendell Antoine	Ken Coleman
Kevin Barclay	Bill Deane
Dick Benevento	Dominic DiMaggio
Sal Bertolami	Bobby Doerr
Arnie Beyeler	Elizabeth Dooley
Wade Boggs	Patric Doyle
Norm Bolotin	Walt Dropo
Thomas Bourke	Bo Duncan
Jeff Bower	Gordon Edes
Jeff Brekas	Mike Emeigh
Dick Bresciani, Boston Red Sox	Eric Enders

David S. Eskenazi
Erv Fischer
Scott D. Fitzgerald
Dick Flavin
Nomar Garciaparra
Bob Gaunt
Eddie Germano
Steve Gietscher, *The Sporting News*
Don Gile
Mike Gimbel
Jon Goode, Lowell Spinners
Lou Gorman
Joe Hall
Rex Hamman
Jerry Hannan
Dan Hart, Pittsburgh Pirates
Ted Hathaway
Fr. John Hissrich
John Holway
Dee Ivison
Dave Jauss
David Kaiser
Al Kaline
Brent Kelley
Johnny Lazor
John Leovich
Frank Lolich
Al Lopez
Tony Lupien
Marty Marion
Ron Marshall
Michael Mavrogiannis
Sam Mele
Joe McGillen
Ray McGuiggin
Rick Miller
Bob Montgomery
Gerry Moses
Dave Mulvey
David Nevard

Rob Neyer
Jim O'Brien
Barbara Ochoa
Sally O'Leary
Cliff Otto
Mel Parnell
Seung-hyun Park
Royce "Crash" Parr
John Pastier
Vincent Paveskovich
Eddie Pellagrini
David Pesky
Ruth Pesky
Eddie Popowski
Jim Prime
Dick Radatz
Jim Rice
Ben Robicheau
Jack Rogers
Mike Ross
Harry Rothgerber
Jim Rowe
Tom Ruane
Guy St. Andre
Tim Samway
Milt Schmidt
Fred Seymour
Dave Shore
Enos Slaughter
Lyle Spatz
Mark Stangl
David Stephan
Glenn Stout
Cecilia Tan
Birdie Tebbetts
Mark Tetrault
Dick Thompson
Kevin Vahey
Dave Vincent
Charlie Wagner

Fred Waugh
Tim Wiles
Jimy Williams
Ted Williams
Earl Wilson
Jake Wood

& Canon AB304486 (microfilm reader) at the Tufts University library

1
Childhood

Johnny Pesky, said to bleed Red Sox crimson, was born to Croatian immigrants in the northwest section of Portland, Oregon. John Michael Paveskovich entered the world on September 27, 1919 in a modest house on Upshur Street, cater-corner from the Blitz-Weinhard brewery.

John was 5th of 6 children born to Jakov and Marija Paveskovich. Jakov had been a cook in the Austria-Hungary Navy before World War I. He came to this country in 1910 from the village of Naglitsa, in the Croatian hills above Split. He told his children that he had been an orphan, and when his service was over, he left to come to America with six of his friends. Still young men, the group landed in New York, traveled on to St. Louis, and finally to Oregon, where they found work in the logging camps and sawmills.

Future Detroit Tigers pitcher Mickey Lolich's grandfather was also part of this group. "Mickey's much younger than I am," Johnny recalls, "but his uncle Frank was my age. There were a couple of Loliches out there. Mickey's grandfather was on the same boat with my father. There was Pete Babich . . . Christ, there's a couple of names I can't even remember. There was another guy by the name of Anthony Vasich. Stepovich. They were all 'viches'—sons of viches, they used to say."

Once established, Jakov brought over Marija Bajama—"Mare" she was

7

called, in the family. She was from Zakucac, a poor area on the coast, just south of Split. Today the area is considered relatively prosperous wine country; however Johnny's younger brother Vincent, now a retired teacher, visited the old country in 1997 and characterized the area as replete with "hovels."

The area of Portland where they settled was a tight-knit community known as "Slabtown." Sawmills, like the Eastern & Western and North Pacific Lumber Mills, provided the livelihood for many in the area. Logs would be floated down the Willamette River and muscled onto a conveyer belt, where the mill workers would begin the process by cutting off the four sides with the bark on. This was referred to as slab wood. There were a lot of Slavs there, too, and the slab/Slav homophone no doubt contributed to area residents being called "slab towners."

"Dad worked in the sawmill when I was a kid," Johnny recalls. "He eventually became asthmatic because of the sawdust. He was working on some kind of a chute where clubs of wood came down. A lot of times, if they turned their back, they'd get hit on the leg. You ought to see his legs. He hobbled. When he became asthmatic, though, he couldn't work anymore."

The leftover wood scraps were made into sawdust at the mill, and provided warmth in winter. "We used to burn sawdust for heat," Johnny explains. Houses in Slabtown always smelled of fresh wood.

There were actually six Paveskovich kids. Marija lost one child, a baby named Marko. First born was Anica (Ann), then Antony (Tony), Danica (Dee), Milica (Millie), Johnny and lastly Vincent—Vinnie. Dee's given name was Danica, but she was called Dee—and actually took the name "Catherine" when she was in school because, as she put it, "it was easier to say." It was easier, too, to describe their origins as "Austrian."

Vinnie is the only one who remained in northwest Portland, and he still lives in the handsome sturdy two story house on Overton Street that Johnny bought for the family in 1942, after his first year in pro ball. Johnny's the one furthest from home, living today in Swampscott, Massachusetts on Boston's North Shore, where he's primarily lived since the middle 1940s.

Johnny described the environment in which he grew up. "My parents couldn't read or write. My dad could read a little of the Slav, but he couldn't read any of the English. Even to this day, I know very few words of their language. My oldest sister could read and write it. Even when she was married, she was home a lot with my folks. They had a language barrier when they first came over here, but one thing they insisted on was school.

"I'd have to say this—we were very well disciplined, mostly by my mother. My dad was easy-going, a nice man. We went to Catholic school. My father was very devout, and my mother . . . we were all baptized, confirmed, and whatever. We had nuns for teachers, and then when we graduated from grammar school we went to public school.

"My mother was a very neat person. She could make a roast, it was great, and she seasoned it well. She used to say that my dad was a better cook than she was, being a cook in the Navy. I remember at Christmas he had a small lamb. He'd stay there and rotisserie. He did it all with a wood stove. A little suckling pig, for Easter. My sisters all were good cooks. None of us were big and fat; we were all kind of thin."

With the father unable to work in the sawmill, the family had to chip in. "They didn't have anything like disability for my dad; in those years they had nothing and the kids just went off and worked. The kids were young, 13, 14, 15. My sister Ann went to work. Dee went to work. Anthony went to work. Vinnie and I, we were the two young ones. My sister Millie, she worked in a candy place. The only one who went on to college was Vinnie. My brother Tony played ball on the Slav team. They called it the Croatian Athletic Club, the CAC. I don't know how much of a player he was. He was always kind of sickly. He was in good shape but he had rheumatic fever as a child and that's what took him. Tony worked at a casket factory when I was still in grammar school, and then he went to work for an electrical company, in charge of a warehouse. He worked at the ballpark, some of the night games. He died relatively young, in his fifties."

Jakov frequented the Blitz-Weinhard brewery. "They made beer and root beer, which we got. Brother Tony had a job there for a while." The three sisters all worked at the True Blue Biscuit Company, making cookies and crackers. Johnny was young enough, though, that he was spared the immediate need to become a breadwinner. He and Vinnie often came home with a sack of goodies from True Blue (and once in a while maybe ran off with a pie set out to cool behind Quality Pie).

"My folks insisted that we go to school. They made sure you were clean, your shoes were shined, you wore clean clothes, underwear and that. My mother insisted on it. She was strict. When she said something, it just was done. Either that or a whack on the behind. There was a big oak tree on the corner of our street, and she'd get that butcher knife and she'd go out and cut these switches. She'd hide them all over the house, in case. She'd get your attention. She didn't hurt you, just whack you across the calf. 'You're bad boy, John,' she'd say.

"My father would just sit and look; he'd never really change his expression. He'd hug you and say, 'Don't do that.' He gave me a real whacking one time, though. I did something I shouldn't have done. He took his belt off. My mother wasn't around. I had a couple of red welts but that was it. Just one time. He didn't have a mean streak in him. My father never laid a hand on us. He didn't have to; he'd just look at you and you better get with it, kid. We ate at 5:30 every night and if you weren't there, you couldn't eat. Of course, she always had something left over which she'd get you. Of all the kids in our family, I think I was the biggest problem, because I had a lot of energy.

"I was like the black sheep of the family. I was kind of an outgoing guy." Johnny remembers. "I hung around the ice rink in the winter, and the ballpark in the summer. I started to play some baseball. I played a little hockey; I was a frustrated hockey player, a left-winger and center ice man.

"Getting a little more mature, we're getting invited here and invited there. If they said you had to be home by 11 o'clock or 10 o'clock, you had to be home. Either that or my brother Tony would come looking for us. He could jerk your arm out of your socket. But there was a lot of love there. My parents had love for us, and my brothers and sisters had love for one another, and that's the way it was in those years."

St. Patrick's was the neighborhood church in Slabtown and the

Black sheep? The self-characterization was intriguing. Asked to elaborate, Johnny offered a story. "They were doing some work on one of the rooms at the school so they put the 4th and 5th grades together. This one girl was big, always grabbing me or pinching me. During lunch hour, we had chores to do and I had to erase the blackboard. She was behind me and a nun was over in the corner doing something. The girl grabbed me and she pinched me pretty hard and I got mad. There was a broom there and I grabbed it and whacked her pretty good. I hit her right along the side of her arm, but just as I hit her, the nun turned around and saw me. 'You go stand in the corner.' Well, I wasn't going to stand in the corner and so pretty soon I slipped out of the corner and went into the bathroom where you could lock the door. Now, it's after noon and school was going to start. The nun knocked on the door, 'Class is starting. You better come out.' 'No, I'm not coming out.' I stayed in there for an hour, an hour and a half, two hours. I kept the door locked.

"She sent a note home to my mother. My mother couldn't understand children attended the parochial grade school. Vincent credits the nuns and priests there for fostering Johnny's interest in baseball. Slabtown not only had a sawmill and a brewery, Oregon Casket and the ESCO Foundry and American Can—it also had the home field for the Pacific Coast League's Portland Beavers, the Vaughn Street ballpark. The park was used from 1901 to 1955, sometimes known as Lucky Beaver Stadium and Recreational Park. The Beavers started playing there in 1903 and Tony worked part-time at Vaughn Street Park as a ticket taker.

"When baseball season started, the nuns at St. Patrick's liked to see the kids go to opening day," recalls Vincent. "In those days, they started the ball game around 2 or 2:30, so we'd get off around 12 or 12:15 and living right in the ballpark area—we were within 8 or 10 blocks of old Vaughn Street. It was natural for us guys to go down. So the good nuns let us go, with the parents' blessing. That's when I really got to see what baseball was like. These were the pros in the old Pacific Coast League."

George Hennessey was a mortician and the man who organized the church choir. "He was a very religious guy, just a nice man," recalled Johnny. "He loved to sing. I did some solos with the choir. There was a lot of kids that had good voices then, but this guy picked me. My voice changed, though. I can remember staying after school and saying, 'Mr. Hennessey, I want to go out.' 'No, no. We've got to get this done.'"

Johnny's sister Millie remembered one incident at St. Patrick's.

what she was trying to say but my brother Tony worked in the casket facory about two blocks away from the school, so she took the note over there. She tapped on the window to get his attention. She said, 'Johnny's been a bad boy, Tony.' Now it's 2:30, quarter to three and I hear his voice, 'Come on out!' 'No, I'm not coming out. I'm not coming out. If I come out, you're going to whack me. If I go inside, the nun is going to whack me. If I go home, I'm going to get whacked.' Now it's 3:30. I've been in there since 12 o'clock. Finally the bell rang and I could hear all the kids leaving and I looked around the corner and it was quiet. 'What the hell am I going to do? I know I'm going to get it when I go home. Well, I better face the music'—because I was getting hungry—so I went home and my mother grabbed me and she used a switch on my fanny and said how bad a boy I was and how she was going to send me to the reform school. But she didn't. The nun, she didn't do anything about it but scold me and made me apologize to the girl. I told her, 'Don't you ever do that again. Next time I won't just hit you on the shoulder. I'll belt you in the mouth.' We became good friends after that."

During one church service, Johnny was marching into church with Mr. Hennessey's choir when one of the nuns noticed he was—as always— wearing his baseball cap. She snatched the cap from the top of his head "and with one quick move, it disappeared inside her long black sleeve."

Johnny talked about going off to play ball, though, a game that took him away from home. "The love we had for each other, it carried on to when we grew up. When I went away to play ball, Jesus, that was something! My father was very emotional. When I first went to play semipro ball, I had to take the train. They all went down to see me off. Every time we'd get to the train, he'd carry on something awful, crying, then he'd have my mother crying, and my sisters."

Their area of Portland was mixed and diverse. "We had Slavs, the Irish, Jewish, Protestants—it was a League of Nations, really. We all got along pretty well. You worked in those days, and all the kids were the same. There was no animosity with one another. You always had a kid that had a little more than some of the others, but a lot of those kids shared it with you. If you had a quarter, you could get a half a gallon of ice cream. You'd each get a spoon and dig it out."

Their dad's asthma forced him to quit work and, in time, the hand-rolled cigarettes he favored. Doc Sharkey told him, "Hey, Jake. You gotta quit." He managed to and, though "sickly," lived to age 75 before dying in 1948, "the day after we played the playoff game with Cleveland. If we'd have won, we would have had to play the Braves in the World Series. He never came east to see me play, but my mother came with my sisters. She and my sister and my brother . . . my brother Vinnie came in my rookie year. I lived in Boston. I was single then. He was in college and I was playing ball."

Even in Portland, Johnny added, his father really never watched him play baseball. "He saw me play one game. My mother's seen me play. All my sisters and brothers have seen me play. My dad, he just didn't understand the game. He played bocce with Lolich's grandfather and the others. My brother Tony and my sister Ann would explain to him some of the game. I remember, I was playing in Silverton and he came to a game with my mother and my sister. He's looking out at the field; he doesn't know what baseball is like. So I hit a ball in the gap and I had a triple. Of course, he knew it was me because he was sitting right near the dugout. I'm running like hell, and he says, 'What's he running for?' She tried to explain to her that it's part of the game. He didn't understand— but he knew I was having fun."

Slabtown stayed with those who grew up in northwest Portland. It wasn't unusual for fellow Slabtowners to show up at major league games when Johnny was playing. They'd be up in the stands and they'd yell out, 'Hey, Slabtown!" Johnny would look up and he'd motion the guys to come down. Then they'd visit and talk about family and friends.

2

Clubhouse Kid

Johnny [Pesky] was the clubhouse boy in Portland in '36 and '37. He was in the visiting clubhouse. I really have a hell of a spot in my heart for Johnny Pesky.

—Ted Williams

I first remember Johnny in 1934, when he was clubhouse boy in Portland. I broke into the Coast League at that time and that's where I first knew Johnny. I was with what they called the Hollywood Sheiks. Sure, I remember Johnny from back then. He was kind of an unusual kid. He and I were about the same age. I broke in quite young in the Coast League and he was in and out of the clubhouse. That's where I got to first know him.

—Bobby Doerr

I certainly do remember John as the clubhouse boy. We'd come up to Portland and John was there and he took care of the clubhouse. Sure, he did. In '37, '38, and I was still in the Coast League in '39. He only spent two years in the minors. When he first came up in 1942, that's when I saw him again. I don't know who spoke first, but I said, "How are you doing? Nice to have you here."

—Dom DiMaggio

I used to pick up Ted Williams' jockstrap.

—Johnny Pesky

14

Johnny Pesky's first baseball memories date back to grammar school at St. Pat's. For Pesky, baseball may have been a God-given talent, but he credits the nuns and good fathers of St. Pat's for supplying the bats and balls to get him going. The Vaughn Street ballpark of the Portland Beavers, just a few blocks away at 24th and Vaughn, was an integral part of the neighborhood. "When we'd get out of school, we'd run to the ball-park," smiles Pesky.

Brother Vince chimes in: "There was one nun called Sister Liliosa, a real taskmaster. You either did things right or she'd have an accounting with you. I think the nuns, God bless them, saw some of the players that were Catholic make the sign of the Cross when they'd come up to bat and figured if it's good enough for those guys, it was good enough for us. Bottom line: God can help you—if you can hit the ball!"

The brothers Pesky and their Slabtown friends also played sandlot ball at Wallace Park, up around 26th Street, just a long fly ball from the Paveskovich house. The kids at Wallace would pick sides. If there were only six of them, three took the field and three hit. If you caught a ball on the fly or on one bounce, it was an out. Johnny explains some of the geographical limitations, "The right field was rather short because the Consolidated Freightline was there—and if you hit a ball over into that area, you got to keep hitting. It was a short right field." Many years later he would become intimately familiar with a major league ballpark featuring a short left field.

When the Beavers went on the road, Pesky and his friends moved into the Vaughn Street facility. "They had a big field right behind the ballpark's left field fence. It belonged to American Can Company. We'd go up there about 9 o'clock in the morning and play into the after-noon. We'd have maybe four on a side and use half the field. You'd have a pitcher, a guy at second, a guy in center field and the other guy in right field. The other four hit. I think we had five outs. You had to hit to one side of the field. They either caught the ball or made the play. If you were right-handed, they would shift to left and they would use third base as first base. I remember one day we went to bat 75 times!

"In those years, you could play American Legion up until the time you were 16½. I had just graduated from the 8th grade and didn't play much my first year. I was like an extra man but I did get to pinch hit a couple of times." *The Sporting News* later reported that Johnny weighed just 95 pounds when he began playing with that American Legion team. "All the summers when I was 13, 14, 15, 16, I played Legion ball. I remember playing with a kid named Joe Erautt, who went to the big leagues with Detroit.

"Actually, we had a couple of different Legion teams. The first year I played, it was for Post Office Pharmacy. We used to go down after the game and get a milk shake or hot fudge as our reward. The last 2 years I played for Jim Kelly's Restaurant."

Meanwhile at Lincoln High School, Johnny was already a bona fide star. "I made the all-star team every year until I graduated in June of 1939. I signed when I was 19. The following September I turned 20 but had already played a season of pro ball.

"Wade W. Williams was the baseball and football coach at Lincoln High, a very disciplined guy. He was the kind of guy that would bark at you, but was really a pussycat. He loved those kids and he worried about whether they went to school or college."

St. Patrick's was about 6 blocks from the Paveskovich family home, on 19th, and there were homes dangerously close to the ballpark. "With a guy like Johnny," Vince remembers, "a left-handed hitter, he could hit one in the street and it could bounce up and break windows. Johnny learned how to become a really good left-handed hitter down at St. Patrick's parish grounds. Across the street from the ballpark, there was a field with craters so big it looked like somebody had lobbed a couple of bombs in there. If an outfielder didn't know how to play when Johnny was hitting, he would go down for a ball and go into the hole and come back out and the ball would be over the kid's head."

Johnny wanted to be a catcher. He was mesmerized by a big placard showing Mickey Cochrane advertising Lucky Strike cigarettes. "It was cardboard and it had a picture of him, catching the ball with the big glove. I was real young and I thought that was wonderful." When the promotion was over, the shopkeeper let Johnny take the Cochrane standup home with him. His older sister Ann bought him a catcher's mitt but Pesky admits, "I wasn't cut out to be a catcher."

Like all born ballplayers, his glove became almost an appendage. "I always had a ball in my hand," he recalls fondly. "There were always a couple of kids around to throw with. Kids now, the parents give them a $150 glove. We had gloves, but not really the best. . . . I got a fielder's glove when I was working at the ballpark. One of the guys gave it to me and even though it was all spread out, I thought it was great. If I was at home, we always had a couple of scuffed up balls. If they got to where the covers were torn, we'd just tape them up. We'd throw against the curb and catch the ball, just practicing. We played handball, too, with that hard rubber ball off the curb. That's the way we went about it, to learn how to play."

Johnny played second base in high school with a left-handed glove he'd found on the street. In fact, he played every position but shortstop—which is where he would eventually make his mark in pro ball—until the day the coach asked him to play the position since he was the only kid who could make the long throw to first.

Johnny's sister Dee remembers helping out: "I'd get out and play catch with them in the streets sometimes. It was pavement, but there wasn't very much traffic back in those days." Dee, as it happens, later married a ballplayer herself, Sam Ivison, who pitched for the Portland Beavers in the late Twenties. Vince points to his older brother Tony as a source of inspiration for Johnny and him. "He's the one who really gave us our start. He was an outfielder who was determined that we learn to play the game right!"

With a professional ballpark a few blocks away, and with support from schoolteachers and siblings alike, Johnny devoted untold hours to a game he was growing to love. The Oregon climate helped. "We had the Japanese current here and it never really got cold. You could be out on the field in February and March. You're playing in drizzles but you still could play."

Johnny and Vince both helped out at the ballpark for a few seasons and in time became clubhouse and bat boys. Rocky Benevento was the groundskeeper at the park, and he told them, "You don't get in here unless you do something." So the kids would either get out the lawnmower or a rake or work in the clubhouse. "We hung up the uniforms on the outer fence so they'd get sun-dried. Not like today—all you've got to do is throw the stuff in the washing machine, time it, and then go back and take it out. I think our day of growing up really was a wonderful era. Today everybody expects to have things done for you."

Richard "Rocky" Benevento was, by all accounts, a wonderfully welcoming groundskeeper. He worked alone and so was glad to draw on the kids for help, but repaid them with friendship and opportunity—and even a little instruction. "When the club was away," Vince explains, "Rocky would tie into a water main and flood the outfield. Johnny and the guys, they learned how to slide." Johnny picks up the story. "It would take about three days for that water to go down. Then we could get back and play on it. We put on a pair of shorts with a jock strap. Nothing up top. We'd slide, and we'd get red welts because we'd slide so much. But you'd learn how to pop up and all that. They used to put a couple of guys outside, ball shaggers. They'd get probably a nickel for any ball they brought back. Boy, you'd see those guys scramble. They'd go under cars. You had to be careful driving up Vaughn Street."

Of course, as today, there was a certain romance about the ballplayers, so big and full of life. A lot of players passed through Portland: Joe Gordon, Mickey Cochrane, Billy Southworth, Roger Peckinpaugh, Fred Haney, Del Baker, Earl Brucker, Bill Cissell and Bob Johnson had all gone on to major league ball. The nuns would let the kids out a bit early for the first day of each homestand, generally a Tuesday. From Tuesday to Sunday, the visitors and the hometown Beavers would play seven games, winding up with the big Sunday doubleheader. Vince remembers being impressed with the lifestyle of the players. "All those guys who came from San Francisco and Oakland, they were a bunch of Italians and whatnot. They'd get a loaf of French bread and have some beer or wine and have a big salami set up. These guys would play cards, smoke the cigars and by the time they got up to Portland or Seattle, hell, they had a good time. That's the way baseball should be, even today."

If Rocky gave you the nod, you could become a clubhouse kid and that could pay off economically, too. "But they didn't go to Vaughn Street to get paid," wrote Guy Maynard in *Portland* magazine. "Something pulled them there: a dream, a hope, a prayer that the game young men played there held some special promise for them, too. They went there to be around baseball. To run in the same grass, to kick up the same dirt as the Triple A Beavers, which was as close as you could get to major league baseball west of Kansas City before 1957." (1)

One of the ballplayers might call for one of the kids and say, "Go across the street and get me a sandwich, or a hamburger, or a chew of tobacco." He'd give Johnny a quarter and Johnny'd run off on the errand. In those days you'd buy something for 15 or 20 cents and the player would often say, "Keep the change, kid." Back then a quarter went a long way. "You had twenty ballplayers," Vince explains, "and we got to be smart and bring Coca-Cola and hope that the guys would take a drink of Coke and put on the calendar, 'I owe the clubhouse boy five cents.' Then when the ball club was ready to leave town, they'd pay up. Say the bill came to about 85 cents, well, then, 'Here's a buck, kid!' "

The chores Rocky doled out were varied. Keep the right field bullpens clean, filling with fresh dirt as necessary. Take a rake after the game and work both mounds, smoothing the area over. Wipe off the seats before games. "If the team went on the road, we had access to the field. They didn't have sprinkling systems so you'd put a gunny sack on a fire hose and just soak an area. But you'd spray the infield. He had an old Model T Ford and he'd drag the field with spikes and then he'd smooth it over, and he did it with home plate."

Being at the ballpark every day, they really got to learn the game. Johnny explained, "We got to see the pros in action. I've shined baseball shoes for some of the guys that I was playing against, in the big leagues when I first got up there. The groundskeeper there was a nice guy, and he'd give us little chores to do so that we could get in. Eventually we worked our way into the clubhouse. The kids before us either grew out of it or left to go onto other jobs. I saw Ted [Williams] in, I guess it was '36 or '37, somewhere in that time. I was just a kid, hanging around the clubhouse, a clubhouse boy. Cleaning up after the players, drying their stuff out, hanging up their sweatshirts and things like that."

Johnny's ego was never a problem. Perhaps his humility is due to these humble beginnings. Even today, he always has a good word for the grounds crew or clubhouse kids, for the staff who work at the ballpark.

"Rocky was real good with us," Pesky continues. "He came up from [San Jose] California [driving all the way in that model T—it took him a week back on 1925 roads] to become the groundskeeper at Vaughn Street. Helped a lot of kids get through school, always made sure you got a couple of bucks somewhere here and there, he'd give you a little pocket money for milkshakes and stuff like that. I never drank a beer until I was older. And I didn't have a drink until I got into pro ball.

"As the clubhouse kid, I had access to the key. When the club went on the road—and in those years they'd start on a Monday and not come back for two weeks—we would get balls and bats and we would go down to the outfield and just hit and play. Hit balls to one another. We had to clean up afterwards, so we didn't leave it a mess."

Benevento was so loved and so appreciated in Portland ("if his name was on the ballot, he'd have been elected mayor," says his son Dick) that the Vaughn Street groundskeeper was ultimately inducted into the Oregon Sports Hall of Fame.

Even though many major league ballparks didn't install lighting until a decade later, Vaughn Street had lighting put in during the mid-1930s. Before the big bulb lighting was put in, games generally started at 2 or 2:30. This presented a problem for the clubhouse kids (not to mention paying customers) on weekdays. With lighting and 8:00 PM games kids could arrive by 4 or even 5 o'clock. "Many a time Johnny and I would come back home at 1 o'clock in the morning," Vince explains. "We'd hang up all the uniforms, we'd knock the dirt out from the shoes. We'd shine those shoes. This is when school's not in session. We'd take them out and hang them on the screen fencing and let the sun rays dry them up. Johnny and I—being clubhouse and batboy—we'd do all these jobs. We'd walk to the ballpark. We'd walk home. In those days, if anybody had a car, they'd become your best friend."

"I had a second-hand bicycle that I paid a couple of bucks for and I parked it outside a drug store on the curb and a goddamned car backed over it. Jesus! That broke my heart. But you know, thinking back, I think that's probably why I could run halfway decent!"

Though they would rather have worked in the home clubhouse, the two Paveskovich boys were given visiting clubhouse duties and were glad to have the chance to get into the games. "Our parents were encouraging, very much so. Mom and Dad, they said, well, if you're going to be away from the home, do something constructive. So we did it either at the ballfield or at the ice arena where we learned to play hockey."

There was street hockey, too. "We used to get these wooden pucks [castaway items used by the brewery]. I'll never forget one time. I'm coming home, coming for supper, and it was still light out. I'm on my skates and I'm on my street. I wanted to shoot the puck into the back yard. Well, my dad had the kitchen door open. He was making a big pot of soup. He more or less stepped aside. When I shot it, I didn't think it would go that far. The thing just kept going and going and going and it went right in the goddamn soup. He come out with that ladle and he had to empty it out and build it all over again. But he was all right about it. Right into the soup. I wasn't very big, either."

Johnny not only helped out as clubhouse kid at Vaughn Street. He was also the "mascot" for the Portland Buckaroos pro hockey franchise. "I was a stick boy and took care of the sticks, and just worked around cleaning up for them. I would just be behind the bench and give them water and stuff."

A couple of newspapermen, L. H. Gregory and Don McLeod, like Wade Williams, influenced Johnny in several ways. One helped provide Johnny with a nickname which matured into a new surname. There were a lot of newspapermen in town who liked to play baseball—writers and others, even older men who worked in the press room. They had formed a Press League. "They would take some of the kids off the field and let us play," Johnny remembers. "I had just started to play. I remember I went up to pinch-hit off of this writer. I must have been 13. He was the sports editor of the old *Oregonian*, L. H. Gregory was his name. He was an older guy, a frustrated pitcher. So they put me up to pinch-hit against him. Jesus, you could catch the ball [he threw] in your hand; it was just like batting practice. He didn't know who the hell I was. He threw me a ball and I hit a line drive over the shortstop's head. He wanted to know, 'Who's that pesky hitter?' Pesky became my nickname.

"When we got into semipro ball, the scouts were around. Vince tried playing pro ball, too. He signed with the Yankees of all people and had two years, playing for Lefty Gomez."

Vince talked about Gregory: "L. H. Gregory was one of these old-fashioned guys. He had a pair of corduroy pants, a sweatshirt and an old glove, and a pair of baseball spikes. His old hat must have gone through forty washings, but he wouldn't part with any of that stuff. His pitches were lollapaloozas. Johnny at that time knew how to handle the bat. He wouldn't dump the ball on the guy and run to first base. He'd lay the ball in between the shortstop and third baseman, or pull the ball down so it would go past the second baseman and first baseman. This used to burn the guy up, and L. H. Gregory used to say, 'You pesky little hitter!' and then eventually he would say, 'You know, Johnny, you're a pretty good baseball player and McLeod and I figure you ought to change your name to Johnny Pesky.'

"Don McLeod pretty much ran everything. He was the head and shoulders, the thinker. He said, 'OK, Greg, we're going to name the kids the Oregonian Orioles.' They called us the Baby Beavers later on."

Gregory takes official credit for the name "Pesky," in a column in *The Oregonian*. He called Johnny a "Vaughn Street rat," admitting that "little Johnny, a slim 'Vaughn Street rat,' slipped into a game in a late inning for experience one day, and made his first hit, a clean line drive to center, off us when we let up a bit at seeing such a little fellow at the plate." He wrote that he told Johnny "you'll get into more headlines with a good, catchy short name." (2)

In glaring contrast to his illustrious teammate Ted Williams, Johnny had close friends in the media, particularly the press, throughout his career. The many hours spent on the ball field with Gregory and McLeod may have helped him feel more comfortable and welcome with newspapermen. He's always been very open with the press. From time to time, this feeling of mutual respect may have paid off for Pesky, just as—perhaps—Williams' respect for umpires occasionally may have paid off for him.

Johnny reflected a bit on college, his brother Vince being the only Paveskovich of Johnny's generation who went to college. "As a kid growing up, you're full of anxiety. I thought about going to college, but it just wasn't in me. I went down to the University of Oregon and Oregon State for weekends, to see how it was—you know how they invite kids down. Well, anyway, I wasn't a great student. My brother was a good student. He went to the University of Portland where they have the Holy Cross fathers, Notre Dame fathers, so he got a good education. He tried to play pro ball after a couple of years of college, then he went back and got his degree and got his master's. He went into education; he just retired a couple of years ago. He was the vice principal of a high school. He went and got the master's. I was away playing ball. I did a lot of reading, but I don't do that much now. Of course, I read the paper, but that doesn't really educate you."

Another Portland boy from their circle who made it to the big leagues, though just for the proverbial cup of coffee, was Johnny Leovich. Vince described him: "Johnny went to Oregon State College and he was a very good linesman. Johnny injured a knee in one or two ball games but he signed a professional contract with the Philadelphia Athletics. That knee today, if it could be operated on, Johnny could have maybe been one of the better catchers in the American League because he was built like a brick shithouse. Wide shoulders, big bottom, strong and very knowledgeable behind the plate. Johnny [Leovich] would always come and visit the house on a Saturday and he'd say, 'Mama Pesky, where's Johnny?' 'He's still sleeping up there.' This is around 8 o'clock in the morning. He'd go upstairs, turn the old mattress upside down and Johnny would yell, 'What the hell you doing?' 'Wake up. You can't sleep your life away.' "

Leovich did hit the big leagues, before Johnny Pesky did, but only for one game in 1941. He went 1 for 2, with a double, for Connie Mack and the Philadelphia Athletics. He recalls playing with Johnny Paveskovich back in grade school: "One game, I pitched. John was playing shortstop and Mike Stepovich—who was later the Governor of Alaska—was playing first. We made a double play, and the play went from Leovich to Paveskovich to Stepovich." Leovich remembers Pesky's work ethic. "I've never seen another person who was as dedicated as John was. He worked hard on everything and tried to excel. Which he did. He was always out there practicing. He'd try everything. Drag bunting, hitting to opposite fields. Just like you would in pro baseball—but he did this as a kid, in grade school!"

Wade Williams was a big influence, and he is remembered by Vincent: "When we went to Lincoln High School, we had a guy that was probably ahead of his time by the name of Wade W. Williams. He was a very, very good fundamentalist baseball coach. He would get on your back if you didn't do things right. He was a disciplinarian. You may get mad at the guy but there was a reason why he disciplined you, and I can recall the time he asked me, 'What's the count on the hitter?' I had to say, 'I don't know.' He come up to me and said, 'Son, when the game's over, bring your uniform in and see me.' Well, I figured, oh God, I'm out. I can't play no more. I take my shower, fold up my uniform and I bring it over. The old man was just finished showering and drying himself off with the towels. I knocked on the door and said, 'Mr. Williams, you wanted me to bring my uniform and come and see you when the game was over.' He turned to me and said, 'Son, do you want to play baseball for me?' I said, 'More than anything in the whole world.' He said, 'Then put the uniform back in your locker and when I ask you what's the count on the hitter, pay attention.' "

Williams also coached the Post Office Pharmacy American Legion team—and was probably responsible for Johnny completing high school. In his sophomore year of high school, Johnny dropped out—according to J. G. Taylor Spink—and started hanging around both the ballpark and hockey rink fulltime. Williams kept on him about finishing school, even going to Johnny's house, telling him he could ruin his own future if he didn't complete high school. "Wade Williams saved me from being a bum," Johnny told Spink. "He made me return to school and finish. On his teams, I learned good, solid baseball." (3)

Al Stump interviewed Wade Williams about Johnny in 1947 and Williams said of his prodigy, "He could think with experienced ballplayers when he was 12. He was a natural right-hander, but at St. Patrick's the right field was only about 170 feet deep and pitted with holes. Left field was long and in the ball game the kids played, you could stay at bat as long as you hit safely. So Johnny switched over—became the left-handed hitter he is today—and would stay up there for hours." Williams died in 1977 at age 86. (4)

Slabtown really produced what seems like a disproportionate number of ballplayers. Vincent drew up a list of Slabtown kids who went on to play baseball outside the neighborhood at one level or another. He came up with 11 players who played professional baseball. Baseball loomed large for these kids. Most of their parents knew little or nothing about the game, and if anything they may have seen it as a waste of time. As Guy Maynard perceptively observed, "For these boys, there were no games of catch with dad, no hands-entangled batting instructions, no frantic, yelling instructions from the sidelines, no expectations, no pressure, no guarantees." (5) The old Vaughn Street Park with its bright lights at night lured the kids, and they found encouragement and reinforcement from other adults around them—the nuns and priests, Rocky Benevento, Gregory and McLeod, Wade Williams and more.

There were a lot of excellent players in the Pacific Coast League and the kids naturally looked up to then. In quality of play, many have rated the PCL of the 20s and 30s as the equivalent of a third major league. "When I was a kid during the Depression, a lot of the players in the Coast League didn't want to go to the big leagues," explains Pesky. "It was not only too far away but a lot of them had jobs in the winter. They had to put food on the table. They paid pretty well. They played more than 154 games, maybe 160 or 170 games but they started in March. They were drawing pretty well. Charging a buck or two, they could fill the ballpark."

Working as a clubhouse kid, Johnny met several players who would make their mark in the majors, Ted Williams, Bobby Doerr and the DiMaggios among them. There was also a man who thirty years later hired, and then fired, Johnny as manager of the Red Sox. "I was out there when Pinky Higgins was the third baseman in '32. I was just a little kid hanging around the ballclub. Wally Berger's brother Fred Berger played for the Beavers. Of course, he [Higgins] was a Texan, about 10 or 12 years older than I was. He finished up his career with us in '46. When he was the GM, we didn't see eye to eye. He didn't have many years of managing. When I got to the Red Sox, I had had five with the Tigers and then I managed the Seattle club in '61 and '62. I tried to tell him what we needed but he just wasn't paying attention to me.

"A lot of those guys were veterans in their late 20s when I was out there as a kid. Joe Becker was a catcher, with the San Francisco [Seals]." Becker had played with the Cleveland Indians for a couple of years, 1936 and 1937. When Johnny made it to the Red Sox, Becker was with Newark. "They had an off day and they came over to Yankee Stadium. Joe Becker knew somebody on the ballclub, and this guy called me over to meet Joe. I said, 'I remember him from the Coast League.' He knew about me, because of coming from the Coast League and being the clubhouse kid. He looked at me and shook hands and said, 'Goddamn clubhouse kids are playing big league ball!' He was a good guy."

Another major leaguer Johnny encountered in this period was Carl Mays, who was destined to achieve a bizarre form of baseball immortality. He had pitched for the last Red Sox World Championship team, in

1918. "Carl Mays, the old submariner. He had a baseball school there in Portland that I attended, Carl Mays Baseball School, located across the river at a place called Jantzen Beach. They had a playoff game at Vaughn Street ballpark. If you were picked as the number one kid, you got to take a trip with the Portland Beavers down to San Francisco and Los Angeles. They picked the top kid of the school, and he picked a kid named Donnie Kirsch who was a second baseman. Kirsch played extremely well. We were about 13 years old, but later on we were the double play combination in Silverton. Donnie Kirsch was a better player than I was at that time.

"Of course, I was still working the clubhouse [while attending Mays' school.] Guys paid maybe 10 bucks or 20 bucks at that time. He did pretty well; he had 40 or 50 kids. I was a freebie, because I worked the clubhouse. When the Beavers were at home, I couldn't leave my job and get across the river, but he understood that. When the ballclub left, he let me come over there when I could. I think he moved up to eastern Oregon." Mays, of course, is remembered as the pitcher who threw the ball that hit Ray Chapman and killed him.

Never shy, Johnny soon developed a reputation as a brash kid. While sharpening spikes and polishing shoes, he chatted up the players. "I used to get into discussions with the players. Sometimes I was a little fresh about it. That's when my good buddy Bill Posedel used to bawl me out. He told me that if I wanted to learn baseball to keep my ears open and my mouth shut. Bill was probably the best influence I had and helped me as much as anybody. About ten years later, I had a strange experience with Bill. We were both in the Navy. Bill was a chief petty officer and I was a junior lieutenant. He had to salute me, which was a strange twist because it was like a father having to salute his son."

Pesky's batting idol in those days was the veteran Johnny Frederick, who had spent six seasons with the Brooklyn Dodgers. "I'd sneak out of the clubhouse just to watch him hit. And how he could hit! He held his feet together, and stood just back of the plate. He stepped into the pitch but delayed his swing until the last split second, and then *swish!* . . . nothing but line drives. He was the picture hitter to me, and I used to rib Ted [Williams] that when he could hit like Frederick, he'd really be something.

"Ted and Bobby Doerr came to town together. I was working in the home team clubhouse at the time so I didn't really meet them. I had my own job to do on the other side of the diamond. I just watched Williams. I knew he was very, very young. He was 17 or 18 at that time, just another player on the team. I think it was '37 because he is just a year older than I am."

Little did this fresh clubhouse kid realize that five years later he would be playing alongside these two future Hall of Famers.

NOTES

(1) Guy Maynard, *Portland*, Summer 2000
(2) *The Oregonian*, October 17, 1962
(3) J. G. Taylor Spink, clipping from Pesky scrapbook
(4) Al Stump, "Pesky, the People's Pet," *Sport*, May 1947, 46ff
(5) Guy Maynard, *Portland*, op. cit.

3

Signing with the Red Sox

Johnny Pesky signed with the Boston Red Sox following a year and a half of semipro summer ball in the mill towns of Bend and Silverton, Oregon. By coincidence, Red Sox owner Tom Yawkey was—albeit indirectly—Johnny's employer a few years before he signed with Yawkey's baseball club. Yawkey's wealth came from lumber mills, largely concentrated in South Carolina but extending as far west as Oregon. The Silver Falls Timber Company, based in Silverton, was one such Yawkey enterprise. Johnny worked two summers at the Silverton mill, playing on the company ball team. His first semi-pro team, however, was the Bend Elks.

BEND ELKS—1937

Johnny played ball at Lincoln High but when school got out in 1937, he joined the semi-pro ranks, playing for the Bend Elks, in the town of Bend, starting late in May. He'd been scouted and signed by Elks' manager Clyde Stokoe, who also signed Portland youngsters John Bubalo and Verne Reynolds. The Bend team had won the Oregon State League championship in 1936 and was hoping to repeat. For Johnny, it was the ideal summer job, working in the mill and playing ball for the company team for the then-handsome sum of $125.00 a month!

"Bubalo, myself and two other guys all lived in a house owned by a

27

lovely lady. She always fed us well, breakfast and supper, all for 5 or 6 bucks a week! We had two rooms upstairs and we doubled up. Everybody treated us well. I got my first Social Security number working at the Shevlin-Hixon Lumber Company mill. They didn't work us too hard and we'd get to playing 2 or 3, sometimes 4 games a week."

The Elks played at O'Donnell Field where admission was 40 cents. League games were always at 2:30 on Sunday afternoons. In between were practices and non-league games. They even played (and defeated) the touring House of David team at one point and, later in the year, played what the local *Bend Bulletin* termed the "colored House of David team"— actually known as Van Dykes House of David—and beat them too, by an 8-7 score.

"It was kind of an open park," Johnny recalls. "They had little stands but if we had three or four hundred people, it seemed bigger somehow. Stokoe, the manager, worked at the mill and he saw that we were taken care of, got a place to stay and a place to eat. We won the league that year."

Stokoe protected his prospect on and off the diamond. "My first year, I was still in high school, and they put me on the saw," he chuckles. "When Stokoe saw that, he swore an oath and told me to go out and stack lumber in the yard. He was afraid I might lose a finger."

As it happens, Johnny was in great demand that summer with Lincoln and Jefferson in a playoff. He missed the Elks' first game, an away contest at Eugene. Pesky's arrival for the first home game was heralded in the *Bulletin* in glowing terms. "John Pesky, outstanding infielder of the Portland interscholastic league, will be here this coming weekend, to remain for the summer." The Elks home opener on May 23, 1937 was a pitchman's dream. A raft of prizes was offered for the first home run (a steak dinner), the first walk ($2 to spend at the Safeway) and the first sacrifice (a subscription to the *Bend Bulletin.*) The Elks won 16-3 over Sweet Home, and the team thereby won a gallon of ice cream at Kessler's. Johnny entered the game late and went 0 for 1, with one assist and one error at second base. An inauspicious debut, but by the following week-end he was up to speed and in a weekend double header against Reedsport, went 3 for 4 with a home run in the Saturday game (the Elks won 8-4) and 4 for 7 in Sunday's game (the Elks crushed the visitors 29-3.) The following weekend John went 2 for 4 as the Elks beat Hills Creek.

The next league game after that was a 10-9 win in 10 innings. Toledo had gone up by one run in the top of the 10th, but then Johnny doubled home Reynolds to tie it and scored a few minutes later on Walker's hit.

John was 3 for 5—all 3 hits were doubles. It was more than a month before Bend lost its first game, a 5-1 loss to Silverton on June 27. The one run was a solo homer by Pesky in the top of the 1st.

Johnny hustled and legged it out. The *Silverton Appeal Tribune* reported, "The Elks drew first blood when Pesky hit what appeared to be a single. However, the ball took a bad bound and rolled clear to the boards for a homer." Another newspaper wrote, "Fiery Johnny Pesky made Bend's only tally with a homer." It seemed that Pesky was becoming as adept with the lumber on the ball field as at the mill.

Shortly afterwards, John hurt his hand and missed a game against the Nippon Giants, an all-Japanese team from Portland. In fact, he was absent from the Elks for a few weeks, playing for the Reliable Shoe team of Portland in the state tournament. An unusual arrangement, perhaps, but Johnny notes that it was sometimes possible to play for more than one team back then. By August 4, though, John sent manager Stokoe a telegram: "Have my mitt ready—I am on my way."

On the 6th, he celebrated his return with a first inning 3-run homer, prompting an 8-column full-page *Bulletin* headline: "HOMER BY PESKY FACTOR IN ELKS' EASY WIN OVER HILLS CREEK TEAM." Johnny was 2 for 4, but still a little shaky in the field, this time committing two errors at second. Still, his home run was "one of the longest ever hit on the Bend field."

Another weekend series saw the Elks beat Woodburn twice as Johnny was 2 for 3 in the Saturday game and 5 for 6 the next day. The following weekend, Boston Red Sox scout Ernie Johnson was reported in attendance. The Elks beat Toledo 16-8 and then crushed Silverton 15-1 in Sunday's contest. Johnny went just 1 for 3 in each game, presumably having walked or sacrificed several times in each game (the local box scores lacked much of today's detail—even omitting RBI figures.)

The semi-pro team mixed younger and veteran players. Star pitcher Fred Roberts had first played for Bend over ten years earlier, in 1926. Before the summer was over and Johnny headed back to resume his studies at Lincoln High, the Bend Elks had won 17 games and lost 2, and again won the Oregon State League title. This was a young but hard-hitting team, with a team batting average of over .400. Johnny Pesky led the league with a .543 average. Naturally, he was named to the all-star squad. Counting exhibition games, Johnny had gone 36 for 75, for a .480 mark and the *Bulletin* concluded, "John Pesky, who played both second and short for the Elks, was one of the greatest infielders ever seen in action on the local diamond." Pretty heady stuff for a high school kid.

SILVERTON RED SOX—1938 & 1939

In 1938 and 1939, Johnny played mostly for the Silverton Red Sox, but there were occasional games for other teams, including at least a game or two for the Portland Babes. He played for Ray Brooks, who ran a traveling team for a local sporting goods store. Johnny recalls moving around to a few different teams: "Joe Gordon was in that group. Ray Cook. In those years, especially early in the year you could play with 2 or 3 teams, in different leagues. One of them would play on a Wednesday, another one on a Friday and then another one on Saturday or Sunday. A lot of times, you'd get a pair of shoes but there was no money around."

Silverton actually fielded two teams, the Silverton Bees and (as of 1937) the newly formed Red Sox, affiliated with the Silver Falls Timber Company, owned in part by Tom Yawkey and Ben Alexander of the Boston Red Sox. This was still the Depression and as late as 1939, team photos show some players wearing Silverton shirts and some—like Johnny—still wearing Silver Falls shirts initially worn by others back in 1936.

The Silver Falls Timber Company boasts another noted former employee—Clark Gable. When in town, Billy Gable (as he was then known) made $3.20 a day working for the timber company and married a local girl—the first of 5 wives.

"Silverton," Johnny remembered. "That's when things broke really good for us. We had a good team. Again, I was near a saw for a few days but then I became the groundskeeper for the ballpark. The same hundred-some dollars a month, but for ten bucks you could do a lot in those years. A banana split was our reward for a win." The team was under the management of William "Mac" McGinnis, superintendent of the mill and for many, many years "Mr. Baseball" in Silverton. A former ballplayer in both the California League and the Northwest League before arriving in Silverton, McGinnis organized the team in 1936. After losing their very first game to the Salem penitentiary team, they ran off 15 straight wins. Orlo Thompson, who covered the Red Sox for the *Silverton Appeal Tribune*, was also the team announcer and was occasionally asked to take the field.

McGinnis Field was a larger facility than the field in Bend, and seated at least a couple of thousand fans. The field was built the year before, in 1937, with WPA matching funds. It featured lighting—a number of 90-foot fir timbers holding 132 lights.

Silverton proved an incredibly supportive town. Mill workers and local citizens raised most of the money for the park and, when construction lagged, about 70 men from the mill installed 1600 feet of 8 foot high board fence around the diamond, all in one day. Area people turned out in droves. Local people recall the town itself as almost deserted during games because townspeople and shopkeepers alike were all to be found at the ball field. For their nearly twenty year run, the average game day attendance for the Red Sox at McGinnis Field (3100) was equal to or greater than the actual 2900 population of the town itself.

The Silverton Red Sox usually played three games a week. Johnny recalled, "On an off day, we would play the Portland Beavers from the Coast League," recalls Johnny. "It was only a quarter to get in, but you couldn't get a seat. The place would be packed. We had the cream of the crop of the high school kids. You were there June, July and August, and the season would be over the first of September. Then we had to go back to school."

Johnny batted .428 in 1938—but the 1939 team was the better team. Johnny was asked back for a second year, at double his 1938 pay. The '39 squad was exceptionally young, averaging less than 20 years of age. "McGinnis was a nice, nice guy. He took the cream of the crop from the high schools, and added a couple of college kids. It was a good mixture. In both '38 and '39 we won the Northwest regionals then we went to Wichita for the national finals. Just imagine. We were still in high school and we went to the Wichita finals as semi-pros! The first year, I think we won one game—it was a double elimination but next year we finished third in the tournament. I don't think we lost 4 or 5 games the whole year. We were all kids, and we played against many players with big league experience.

"We played Kansas City Monarchs, the black team. Then there was the House of David, with the beards. I think we averaged between 50 and 75 games a year. Satchel Paige, Josh Gibson, I played against them all, but then I didn't see the blacks again until well after I got to the big leagues. I know I batted against Paige. I don't remember getting a hit off him, but I did when he left Cleveland and went to the Browns. I'm about 1 for 20 off him. Gibson could hit. They'd take batting practice and they'd put on an exhibition! The House of David put on a phantom infield. It was very cleverly done and it was very entertaining. We had pretty good teams. They didn't beat us 18-3 or anything. We'd score 6 or 7 runs."

The whole team boarded at Rose Specht's boarding house on Fiske Street. Her son Lyle had been on the Silver Falls team a couple of years earlier. Years later, Johnny remembered Mac McGinnis: "Mac was not only a father to all of us, but he kept us out of jail with a little fixin' here and there. When I think of that stadium, and those players, there are a lot of sweet memories." Johnny played just one position—shortstop—for the '38 and '39 teams. Both teams were "Northwest and Regional champions" and both went to the national semi-pro tournament at Wichita; the 1938 team came in 11th place and the 1939 came in 3rd. The '39 team was something special. Five of the members were named All-Americans, and 3 later became major league players—Pesky, Joe Erautt and Dick Whitman. The Silverton Red Sox weren't expected to improve that much on their 1938 performance, but they beat the '38 champion Buford Bona Allens of Georgia only to lose to Mt. Pleasant 2-0. The Halliburton Cementers of Duncan, Oklahoma beat Mt. Pleasant to take the title (and the $5000 first place prize.) As Johnny noted, this was a young team that made it to third place nationally, in a tournament ultimately won by an Oklahoma team featuring some real veterans, some with major league experience.

Local newspapers again ranked Johnny highly. Jim Nutter, the publicity director of the Oregon state tournament, in the program book for the 1939 event, called him John "Warhoop" (sic) Pesky. The 1939 team won 34 games and only lost 2, at one point running off a team string of 96 consecutive errorless innings.

SIGNING WITH THE RED SOX

In 1938, age 18 and about to enter his senior year of high school, Johnny signed with the Boston Red Sox—more precisely their Rocky Mount, NC, farm team. The Portland Beavers were not pleased that Johnny had refused to sign with them. A prospect who'd literally grown up in their own park had been signed out from under them.

This was against the rules of baseball, which at that time forbade major league clubs from signing "sandlotters"—players not already in organized baseball. The Beavers protested to Commissioner of Baseball Kenesaw Mountain Landis but the appeal went nowhere, as Landis determined the practice was a common one, the rule notwithstanding. Sox scout Ernie Johnson had actually signed Johnny to a Rocky Mount contract, not directly to the Boston Red Sox. Landis recognized the subterfuge but could offer no relief. "Boston unquestionably signed the player," he wrote in his opinion. "Rocky Mount was only Boston's instrumentality. The Boston club states that the player had refused numerous

offers from scouts of other major league clubs, but apparently our man
offered him the best proposition and he accepted. Of course, it is, as
Portland states, 'a mere subterfuge' for major league clubs to scout and
sign such players to contracts with minor league clubs which they operate. Even if the scout had been officially designated as a scout for the
minor league club (as sometimes is done, under a mistaken notion that
this successfully camouflages such transactions,) that would have been
only an additional subterfuge in the nullification of the major league's
covenant not to sign sandlotters. However, in this nullification the minor
leagues have acquiesced and co-operated for many years, and therefore
they are about as responsible as the majors for its existence." Landis suggested that the system be reformed to render it more straightforward.

In any event, Johnny did not report to Rocky Mount in 1938, or even
in 1939. In fact, Hall of Fame records list him as "suspended" for the
1939 season—a fact which startled Johnny a bit when he was shown their
records in 2002. His recollection was that he had signed on August 4,
1939. Neither the Red Sox nor the Hall of Fame have documentation.

Johnny thinks what happened was that he agreed to sign with the
Red Sox in 1938, but didn't sign any papers. "In '39 when I got out of
high school, they wanted me to go to Canton. They had a team there. I
think Popowski was playing there and Pellagrini. In the meantime, I had
started to play in Silverton. We had won the tournament in '39 and they
let me finish the year."

In 1939, the Red Sox wanted him to report to their Rocky Mount
club right away but he declined. Sox farm director Billy Evans said, "He
wrote me and said he would like to start from scratch in competing for a
regular berth in professional ball the following spring." Johnny also wanted to finish the season with Silverton. "I signed with the Red Sox, though
I didn't report until 1940. Our team was doing so well . . . in the meantime, I graduated from high school. So it all worked out. 1940 is when I
started playing professionally in Rocky Mount. I got to the big leagues
pretty quick."

When the 1939 baseball season was over, the ice rinks opened up as
usual, and although it didn't freeze in Portland until December or
January, the artificial ice gave Johnny a place to hone his hockey skills.
"Bobby Rowe handled the professional hockey team, but Paul Ail took
over and he took care of us. He was really a concessionaire, and made
a living off of it. We helped out sometimes, and then we had odd jobs
in the rink. We used to scrape the ice by hand, with a sort of snow
shovel. It was before Zambonis. Three of us would go right in back of

each other and you'd scrape it in a corner and it would go down a chute."

At age 16 and again at 17, Johnny had played for coach Danny Edge's Hop Gold team, the Portland city champions. "I was a helluva skater," he admits. "We were just a bunch of kids, but we had some leagues out there, kids leagues. We also had the pros out there. One pro got kind of friendly, and told me, 'Johnny, you ought to try it.' So he got me all set up to go to Hershey to try out with the Hershey Bears—it was a Bruins farm at the time and the Bruins' scout wanted to sign me. My parents wouldn't let me go to Pennsylvania to try out." Had life taken a different turn, Johnny might have wound up as a player on another legendary Boston team—the Bruins.

It was baseball, however, that was to be Pesky's ticket to Beantown. "In those years," he explains, "there was no draft and you could sign with anybody. They signed a lot of players, because you had a lot of minor leagues back then. I had a lot of scouts coming around. I had an offer from the Cubs, the Yankees, the Tigers, both St. Louis teams. And Cleveland." Vince agrees: "Johnny was well in demand. I guess he could have gone with any club, but because this guy was very nice with mom and dad, well, 'let's sign with the Red Sox.'"

One Tiger scout recalled how they would even follow Johnny to the ice rink. "We used to sit around those ice joints with our teeth chattering," he moaned. It was Ernie Johnson's manner and personality that won the day for the Red Sox, even though the offer he conveyed was not at all the best financially. Johnson lived in Santa Monica, California, and had the entire West Coast as his territory for the Red Sox. Johnson was a former major leaguer, with a 10-year career for the White Sox, the Cardinals, the Browns and the Yankees, spanning the years from 1912 to 1925. He'd been scouting for over a decade when he found Johnny. The home office was convinced not just by Johnson, but also by the "constant suggesting" of Red Sox pitcher Jack Wilson, a Portland native who had seen Johnny play. Wilson had apparently bent Cronin's ear on the subject as well.

Ernie Johnson wisely cultivated the family as well as the prospect. In this case, it paid off—and saved the Sox some money. Johnny remembered Johnson's approach. "He would come into the house. We didn't have the best house, but it was always clean. He would bring my mother these beautiful flowers. He'd bring my father a bottle of I. W. Harper, that nice bourbon in those days. My father liked to nip a little bit. He'd savor that for about two months.

"I had another club that was going to give me a little more money, but Johnson got to know my parents. Either my oldest brother or my oldest sister would be there to interpret for them. They had a language barrier. He used to watch our games and kind of latched on to me, you know, being a middle infielder. He liked what I did. I always played shortstop. I didn't play second base until I turned pro. Very little second base."

Johnson's homey approach carried the day, even when at least one other scout offered five times as much up-front money. These were still Depression times and to turn down a full $2500 to sign with the Red Sox for just $500 was a bold decision for the family to make.

Stripped to the waist, Johnny was working as groundskeeper one day in Silverton when a well-dressed gentleman approached him. Louis Butler represented one of the St. Louis clubs and he was sporting a shirt and tie. Johnny had just finished watering and dragging the field. "I was marking the field, getting ready for the game, then I was going to go home and get something to eat, so I'd be ready to play the second game," Johnny recalls. "This was about 4:30 in the afternoon. He says, 'Is Silverton playing tonight?' I say, 'Yes, they're playing the second game.' He says, 'Do you play?' I said, 'Yeah.' He says, 'What?' and I says, 'Shortstop.' He asked me what my name was. He says, 'Jesus, I'm supposed to see you, kid. I haven't seen you play.' That night I got three hits.

"A day later, we've got to play again and he comes back. 'I want to see you one more time,' he said. I had another good night. In fact, I led the tournament in hitting and I got a couple of trophies, one as an infielder and one for the batting championship. He said, 'I liked what I saw, kid. I'd like to sign you' and he made an offer of money. He threw $2500 at me. Jesus. I never saw that kind of money; we'd be lucky if we had five bucks to spend. When the tournament was over, I went home and told my little brother we had a chance to get a few bucks here. My folks sure could have used it.

"Johnson and the Red Sox hadn't said anything yet, just an overture of some five hundred dollars. Butler came and he talked to my parents. My mother just shook her head. She said, 'No. I don't care about the money. Mr. Johnson is the one we're going to deal with.' My mother said to me, 'Mr. Johnson, he was very nice to us. You stay with Mr. Johnson and Boston.'

"Cy Slapnicka from Cleveland was a scout out there. He came in, too, but Johnson came in two or three times and he always went in the kitchen and had coffee with them while I was at school. He looked around; he knew everything was nice and clean. My mother liked this guy. We had this other offer, but anyway, my mother said, 'No, Johnny. Boston. Mr. Johnson, Johnny. Nobody else. He take care of you, Johnny.' "

When Vince talks about it, one gets the sense the family held to other priorities than the dollar. "We didn't have much when we grew up. Today we can count our blessings that we did have parents who provided three meals a day. A good home life and all that goes with it—the love and affection. Really, even today that's still the hallmark of perfection—kids that have loving parents and a good home. This is what we all live for: to have a better life in the future. I think we did well."

Johnson didn't up his offer. "We got the five hundred, but if we stayed in the organization—I was supposed to stay for two years—they'd give me a thousand dollar bonus. After the first year, they gave me the thousand dollars. So really fifteen hundred is what I got. Still a thousand less than the other club. The money could have done a lot for my family but mom said no. My brother and my two older sisters were working; they were bringing money home. They were maybe getting twenty dollars a week, maybe twenty-five dollars a week. That's in the late '30s, early '40s. My mother she said, 'No. Mr. Johnson, he take care of you, Johnny.'

"No one had money in those days. So that's how it turned out. That's why I signed with the Red Sox, and it was the best thing that could have happened. I signed with the Red Sox and I'm glad I did. It turned out pretty good." Marija Paveskovich's instincts were correct. The Red Sox did take good care of Johnny. And vice versa.

A footnote: Vincent Paveskovich also played for the Silverton Red Sox for one year. He graduated from the University of Portland and then went into Yankee chain in 1948. Yes, Mr. Red Sox's own brother signed with the arch-rival Yankees. After a couple of years Vincent doffed the pinstripes and went into teaching.

There could have been yet another Boston connection for Johnny. The city of his birth was named after Portland, Maine, following a coin toss between its two East Coast founders back in 1845 ("Boston" was the other option). "If it hadn't been for old man Lovejoy flipping a coin," Vincent notes, "we would have been named Boston. But because it turned up on the other side of the coin, they named it Portland. Lovejoy came from Portland, Maine. If he had lost the coin toss, we'd have been named Boston, Oregon."

4
Minor League Years

A fter signing his Red Sox contract, Johnny Pesky played out the 1939 season at Silverton and again spent the winter as a rink rat at the Marshall Street Ice Arena. Johnny's first spring training was in 1940. "In those years, they signed so many players, I was just a number as far as they were concerned," Johnny suggests. "They didn't know if I would be a decent player or what. I was supposed to report in March, to Rocky Mount, North Carolina." The scout that signed Johnny also signed Cy Greenlaw and Earl Johnson. Earl went to train with the big club in Sarasota. Greenlaw—who was from Tacoma—met up with Johnny in Portland and they traveled by train across the country, first on the Streamliner named "City of Portland" all the way to Chicago, at that time a grueling 40-hour trip. In Chicago, they switched trains and went on to North Carolina. All told, they were on the rails for four exhausting days.

Further evidence that baseball hopefuls of this era weren't exactly pampered lies in the fact that Johnny brought his own shoes, glove and sweatshirt with him. "We trained right in Rocky Mount. The Rocky Mount Red Sox, Class B, Piedmont League. They'd have the uniforms all made up and you'd just pick your size. They always said, 'If we give you too big a uniform, don't alter it because it may not fit the next guy!' They just threw a number on. I think my first number was 10. Later, at Louisville, it was 6.

"They had a bat rack and you'd go try out different ones and pick the model that was most comfortable. I signed with Louisville Slugger.

37

They would give you either a hundred bucks or a set of golf clubs for your signature. You picked the model and they'd send you six bats. These guys today get hundreds of bats. In the years we were in the minor leagues, you got six signature model Louisville Sluggers, and then when you got down to two, you got four more.

"I used a Heinie Manush bat when I first got down there, but then I broke a couple and I picked this other bat up when I got to Louisville. In spring training that year, we were just down the street from the big club." The Red Sox trained at Sarasota and Louisville trained at Bradenton. There, Johnny found the bat he ultimately settled on, a Tony Lazzeri model, L16. "I said, 'Gee, this bat feels pretty good' and once I found the bat I liked, I stayed with it the whole time I played. My bats were 35 inches long but I choked up about 2 to 3 or 4 inches."

Rocky Mount surprised Johnny in that there were just so many players at the camp, "more than I'd ever seen before. We had over forty players and we had twenty two pitchers." Like Johnny, manager Heinie Manush was a left-handed hitter. "He shined up to me," Johnny recalls fondly. "A Hall of Famer. He was a great guy. He didn't push me. He didn't say, 'Do this. Do that.' He'd say, 'Try this.'

"When I got there, I was holding the bat almost on the end and stood way back in the box, like I was a real slugger. He didn't say anything to me for two or three days. One day we were working out, playing a lot of pepper, and he saw me choked up on the bat and kind of snapping the ball, hitting it kind of sharp. He called me out of the box and said, 'Johnny, you're going to have to go up a little on that bat, and move closer to the plate. The way you hold that bat, these guys are going to knock it out of your hands.' When you're that young you think you're so goddamned strong but I remember thinking 'I'm strong, but here's a guy who hit .330 in the big leagues, a Hall of Famer. I better listen to him.' He moved me a little closer to the plate and a little further up on the bat. He explained to me it would quicken my swing. Shit, I started hitting good and I stayed there. I led the league in hits. I hit .325, right out of high school!

"He taught me how to break fast from the left side on bunts, how to lead off and a thousand other things I didn't even suspect. He made suggestions to me how to approach the ball. I always had a habit of taking that first pitch. He said to me, 'Johnny, once in a while you've got to swing at it.'" The veteran's instincts paid off big on one occasion. "We're in Durham one night, and he's coaching third base. Just before the game, he said, 'Now, Johnny, you've got a guy that's going to try to get ahead of you. When he lays that first one down, hit it!' So, sure enough, first inning, he laid me a cookie and I hit it out of the ballpark. I'm going around third and he was laughing, 'What did I tell you?' "

Roger Birtwell recorded Manush's version of the watershed incident. "It was about the third day in camp and I spotted this kid at the plate. He's standing way back in the batter's box, holding his bat way down at the end, standing there like he was Babe Ruth. I walked over to him and I says, 'Where did you get that stance?' He says, 'In the PCL.' I reckoned I knew what he meant. But I said, 'What's that—a terbaccer?' He says, 'No. It's the Pacific Coast League.' 'You played it it?' I said. 'No,' he says, 'I was the clubhouse boy.'

" 'And who at Portland,' I says, 'hit like that?' 'Johnny Frederick,' he answered right quick, 'and he hit .340.' So I asked him a question. 'How much did old Johnny Frederick weigh?' 'Two hundred and something,' he said. 'And how much do you weigh?' 'A hundred and sixty,' he said. I said, 'Now, son, will you do me a favor and try something? You ain't no big fellow like Johnny Frederick and you ain't goin' to hit no flock of homers like Ruth. Will you just take up on the bat like this?' . . . and I showed him . . . 'and move up here to the front of the batter's box?' So he did what I asked and pretty soon the hits began to drop in."

Johnny hit four home runs that year in the Piedmont League, but he had learned a valuable lesson. "I hit some balls pretty good, but I hit more line drives. I had a quickness. I had quickness for a little guy.

"Rocky Mount was a great experience. We only worked out maybe ten days before the season started, then we played Winston-Salem, Portsmouth, Richmond, and Asheville. All bus travel! We left after one game in Asheville and we had to go all the way to Portsmouth, and it took all night. We went straight to the ballpark. We didn't even check into the hotel. Usually we'd have a two- or three-game series. It was a good growing-up process."

"Manush's Maulers"—as the team was nicknamed—were very much a developmental team, designed more to feed talented players towards higher levels and the parent club than to field a winning team. Bob Gaunt notes that the Rocky Mount team had far more young players and far fewer veteran pros, as a result of their developmental status. By mid-July Earl Johnson was called up to the Boston team, where he joined Bagby, Hash, Dickman and Charlie Wagner—all of whom were former Rocky Mount moundsmen on the big league roster. Other hopefuls were left behind with even more vivid dreams of the Big Leagues

Local papers, as early as May, had noted Pesky's play. "Johnny Pesky was a thorn in the side of the [Charlotte] Hornets by getting three singles and hitting another ball which scored two runners in the eighth when second baseman Guinn failed to handle it." (1) Two weeks later, columnist Dick Herbert noted that both second baseman Al Mazur and shortstop Johnny Pesky were hitting well, Mazur at .320 and Pesky at .333. "No keystone combination that has ever been here has ever done that well." By the end of the month, Pesky had already driven in over 20 runs, exceptional for a leadoff hitter. On May 28, Johnny went 3 for 4 (two triples and a single), bringing his totals in two games against the Winston-Salem Twins to 8 hits in 10 at bats, including three triples and a double.

Teammate Jake Plummer—one of the veteran players on the team—praised Pesky's speed and bat skills, "That kid could bat .300 by bunting in this league." As of June 7, Pesky was up to .352 and the team had won 6 straight. On Independence Day, Johnny hit a triple with two on in the top of the 9th, to give the Red Sox a 2-1 victory against the Durham Bulls. On July 16, teammate Norman Brown—quite a prospect—threw a no-hitter against Portsmouth. Johnny went 2 for 4 and was also named an all-star by the Winston-Salem paper (parenthetically, the game time of the 3-0 game was 1 hour and 16 minutes).

The last weekend of July, in blistering heat, Johnny went 3 for 4 on Saturday and then 3 for 6 the next day. The Rocky Mount team had played the Asheville Tourists in an 11-inning game, then had to travel all the way to Portsmouth for a doubleheader, the bus trip allowing no time for sleep at all. Again the team went straight to the park. One of the Cubs hit a grounder far to the right of second baseman Mazur. He got to the ball, though, and knowing he had no chance to make the pivot himself, tossed the ball to Johnny, who fired it to first in time for the putout. "Stuff like that isn't worked very often in the majors," wrote columnist Herbert, "Johnny and Al practice things like that, though."

"We did that [play] twice that year," Johnny says. "There was one kid at Asheville—and he could run, too. He hit a ball the same way, but this was in Rocky Mount. He didn't run hard. He started to pick up when he knew I had the ball in my hand, but I threw him out by two steps even after he turned it on. He gave me hell. He said, 'Goddamn, what're you doing?' I said, 'Well, for Christ's sake, run the goddamned ball out.' "

By the last day of August, Johnny had been named virtually unanimously to the official Piedmont League all-star team and had already been designated to play for the Louisville Colonels in 1941. The Red Sox ended up in 3rd place, just two games out—a tremendous accomplishment for the "Manushmen," a team that carried only six "class men" (veterans) on its roster. They entered the playoffs and made the cut, losing only in the very final game to Durham. Almost everyone on the team ended up moving up in baseball and Dick Herbert closed the season lamenting that he feared Rocky Mount would never again see a double play combination as great as Mazur and Pesky.

Johnny finished the year—he played in 136 games of the 140-game season—with a team-leading .325 average, accompanied by his 4 home runs and 55 RBI. Ever the table-setter, though, Johnny scored 114 runs. He led the Piedmont League in hits with 187 and triples with 16. He was third in the league in batting average. Johnny was considered the fastest man in the league, but only had 7 steals. "Heinie Manush just didn't let me run much, I don't know why."

It was his only year playing for Manush, the manager enthusiastically declaring Johnny ready for bigger things. In fact, he was so effusive in his praise that he actually thought Johnny had a shot at going straight from Class B to the majors and taking Cronin's job. "This kid was born to be a shortstop," Manush stated. "Even though he is only 20 years old, he knows all the answers about his job. You'd think he'd been playing short for 20 years to see what he can do out there. Nothing stumps him. He's smart. He's spectacular. He can hit .300 in any league, and I include the American. He made plays last summer I hadn't seen made for years."

Johnny laughs, "I had a pretty good year and he had me going to Boston that year. I said, 'Cripes, Heinie, I'm not ready. I've only played one year.'" Manush proved to be the better psychic as Johnny was to serve one more year in the minors before reaching the Bigs.

To jump from Rocky Mount to Louisville was actually to jump three levels. Scranton was a Class A club, but the Red Sox also had a Class A-1 club at Little Rock—Johnny bypassed both rungs on the ladder as he went to Double A. "The next year, I thought I would go to Scranton, but I was given a contract with the Louisville Colonels. I never expected to go to Louisville, but I went to spring training with them in Bradenton, Florida, and had a good spring so they decided to keep me. I thought I'd be there a few days and go to Scranton, but they kept me there the whole year. I played almost every game in Louisville, too and had another good year."

A good year indeed! Hitting in the leadoff position, he hit for precisely the same average as he had in Rocky Mount—.325 and once again led the league in base hits, this time with 195.

The manager for the Louisville Colonels was Bill Burwell. "A

wonderful man. A good guy. He was great with the young players. We
had a good club. We were in the race all year long. I played in the All-
Star Game—just my second year in pro ball. I led the league in hits again
and was chosen the most valuable player that year. By just a few votes, I
beat a guy named Ray Star, a pitcher with Indianapolis who had won
something like 20 games. Columbus had the great pitching staff. They
had a major league club, when you think about it. They had Preacher
Rowe and Harry Brecheen. They had 4 or 5 good pitchers." When Johnny
faced Columbus, he knocked out 11 hits during a three game series.

"The American Association was packed with prospects. Vern Stephens
was such a good player. I played against him when he was a shortstop
with Toledo. In fact, all eight shortstops in '41 went up to the big
leagues—Stephens went to the Browns, Leo Wells went to the White Sox,
Huck Geary went to Pittsburgh. Repass and Klein went to the Cardinals.
The kid from Minneapolis, he went to Cincinnati. Hitchcock was pur-
chased by Detroit, and I went to the Red Sox."

Packed with talent as it obviously was, Johnny still burned up the
American Association and was named MVP, with 40 of a possible 64
points, as *The Sporting News* reported in its story "Pesky Sky-rockets to A.
A.'s Highest Honor." He excelled both at bat and in the field. Louisville
fans had enjoyed the play of Pee Wee Reese just a couple of years earlier
and yet "they almost forgot Reese in applauding the sensational performances of Pesky, who, hitting as Pee Wee never did, made a more lasting
impression on supporters of the Colonels." A subhead in the article read
"Steadiness Almost Belies His Lack of Experience" and comparisons were
drawn with Phil Rizzuto, who had similarly jumped from the Class B
Piedmont League to Class AA.

Al Mazur had come up from Rocky Mount with Johnny and again
their double play combination won praise. They roomed together and
even jointly bought an old jalopy for $150.00. The 5'9" Pesky told the
Louisville Courier-Journal's Tommy Fitzgerald, "Al is the brains of the
combination and I am the brawn. It should be the other way 'round
because Al's bigger than I am. But he's still the brains." It was quite a
double play combination for announcers too. Neither had changed their
names and, though known as Pesky and Mazur, the actual scoring on a
6-4-3 DP would have been Paveskovich to Mazurkiewicz to the first baseman.

As a fielder, Burwell noted that Pesky was awkward in spring training, but that facility had a rough field and Johnny was initially a little
nervous. He pressed too hard and wound up with a sore arm. "I couldn't

say anything about the arm," Johnny confessed to J. G. Taylor Spink the next year. "That would be a fine thing for a little punk to be alibiing right at the start. I was supposed to be showing them something out there and I wasn't doing anything—except to prove I was years away from a big league chance. Luckily, they didn't give up on me, as they should have on what I showed. I was terribly confused and bewildered. I believed I had as good an arm as any shortstop in the league, and yet it wouldn't operate for me. So, no matter how hard I fought myself, I developed a beautiful inferiority complex." After a bit, though, the arm started to get better and Johnny began to hit, and never quit.

As he developed self-confidence with Louisville, he was clearly getting his baseball legs, hitting safely 7 of his first 14 times up and batting .321 after the first 13 games. The lessons he'd taken from his Rocky Mount manager paid off here, too. Johnny said that when he first came to bat, "an old time catcher named Joe Glynn took one look at me and said, 'Here we have a pup out of Heinie Manush' and I really felt proud of that analysis."

The Sporting News commented on his "exceptional speed" and the advantage he had running to first from the lefthand side of the plate, saying he could "beat out bunts with the ease of taking a drink of water." He made a couple of errors in those first 13 games, but improved steadily in the field as well. Fellow ballplayer "Junie" Andres said of Pesky, "It seemed like he got on base the first time he was up almost every time. John was a good shortstop. I played next to Reese one year and next to John one year. Of course, they were both fine shortstops. I think Reese was a little better shortstop and probably had more power, but John was a better hitter for average. They both had pretty good speed."

Manager Burwell took Johnny aside at the end of the season and told him, "Johnny, you improved 100 percent in the last three months" and he wished Johnny well, telling him that if he could hit just .275 in the big leagues, he'd stick with the Boston Red Sox.

Johnny, in his modesty, may have said he was not ready, but he certainly benefited from the Red Sox' faith in him. There was that deal which he had signed with Ernie Johnson, the Sox scout back on his parents' kitchen table in Portland, the one that said he'd get a $1000 bonus if he stayed in the organization for two years. His pay was $150 a month, and the Red Sox gave him the thousand-dollar bonus after just his first year.

Johnny traveled back to Portland after the season. It was there that he learned he'd been selected as the American Association's Most Valuable Player from a neighbor in Portland, a subscriber to *The Sporting News* who received his copy at home in advance of the newsstand edition. The friend called Johnny and asked him if he'd seen the paper and when Johnny replied that he had not, his friend told him to go get it—but wouldn't reveal why and kept any trace of excitement out of his voice. Johnny went to the cigar store and bought the paper, and took it outside before he opened it, expecting to see some nice little story about how he'd hit .325. There it was, though, the story he had been named MVP. "I let out a yell of glee right there on that sidewalk. Boy, did that tickle me! Honestly, it never occurred to me that I had a chance for it."

Johnny already had the personality which would serve him well in the big leagues, and forever afterward. Tony Lupien recalled, "He had a lot of friends in the press." And then added, with a hint of envy, "This is how you become an MVP." Friendships or not, Johnny had won the Triple Crown. As Ted Williams learned in 1942 and again in 1947, you can indeed win the Triple Crown and still not the MVP, but Johnny never put the theory to the test, making friends wherever he went—in the press, with the clubhouse kids, and fellow players.

In the winter of 1941–42, Johnny kept busy back in Portland. Hockey still fascinated, and beckoned. "I was a regular linesman in the Western Hockey League. I was in good shape."

Pesky had drawn the attention of a number of hockey legends, including Bobby Rowe, who owned the local Portland Buckaroos, Vic Ripley, who had been with the Rangers, Bruins and Blackhawks, and Buckaroo "Airtight Andy" Aitkenhead.

"The winter after Louisville, I went on the big league roster and the Red Sox were going to send me a contract. I used to work out with the Portland Buckaroos and I could skate with them. We had Dutch Gainor out there, the old hockey player with Montreal and a couple of guys from the Chicago Black Hawks. I kinda fell in love with the hockey thing and I was doing pretty good. This one guy says, 'Johnny, I think you could play in the AHL.' That was the American Hockey League, a great minor league. So I went home and talked it over with my older brother and my folks, and they all said, 'No way.' About three weeks later I was on my way to Florida."

"I wanted baseball anyway," Johnny allows.

When he had played hockey it was with a pseudonym. "I was going under the name of Joe Fisher. I didn't want to use my name. Andy

Aitkenhead was the one who told me, 'You're better off going to play baseball.'" Wade Williams had agreed. He told Johnny, "Forget this hockey stuff. You'll keep your teeth and be a big man in baseball before you're 30."

When I finally did get to Boston, I had to stop all that. Those hockey guys were tough. No helmets then. About three weeks before I'm going to go to spring training with the Red Sox, I'm working out—there were just 2 or 3 of us just down at one end of the rink. I was skating behind the net and someone yelled, 'Look out!' I turned and I got hit with the puck right under my [left] eye. I had to go and get stitched. It puffed up a little bit. One of the guys shot the puck and it just grazed me under my eye. It was like a glancing blow, just hard enough to break the skin. It didn't bleed much, but I had a couple of stitches.

"When I went home, I'll never forget, my dad was at the stove cooking some soup. My mother and my brothers and my sisters were all in the living room. When I came in, my dad turned around to see who was coming in the door. They all got excited. My mother said, 'You're getting ready to play with Boston. You crazy kid.' My eye was getting black. So she had Vince go to the store and get a piece of steak. By the time I got to spring training it was all cleared up. It just left a little indentation."

But it also left a big impression on the young athlete. The final word on his future in hockey was handed down by Joe Cronin after Johnny had again gone back on the ice, under another name, and had a good game playing with the semi-pro team. With two goals and an assist, he was feeling great, until he was handed a telegram from Red Sox manager Cronin. "Stay off the ice," was all it said. Johnny was astounded he'd been found out and sent a wire back to Cronin, who replied by return: "Our scouts are paid 12 months per year. Pesky, Paveskovich or Smith—stay off the ice!"

Buoyed by having won the American Association MVP award, Johnny tried briefly to bargain with the Red Sox during the off-season. The Sox sent him a contract for $4000 and Johnny decided to ask for $5000. "So I sent it back and said I'd like another thousand dollars. A week or so later, I got another letter back from Collins and he said, 'Please sign the enclosed contract because we don't know if you can play in the big leagues.'" Johnny quickly signed, put his hockey career on ice, and set out for the warmer climes of Florida to prove his worth at spring training.

NOTES

(1) *Rocky Mount Evening Telegram*, May 4, 1940

5

Rookie Season, 1942

P esky was on the fast track to Boston. He had already jumped from B ball to AA and the next leap would be all the way to the majors. His horizons seemed limitless. And then fate intervened, obscuring those horizons amidst the smoke of war.

On December 7, 1941, the Japanese attack on Pearl Harbor precipitated immediate entry of the United States into war in the Pacific. Joe Cronin had already let it be known in the fall of 1941 that Pesky was to be the shortstop in 1942, but after Pearl Harbor all of baseball waited for direction from President Roosevelt. Commissioner Landis had sent the Commander-in-Chief a letter in the first few days of the new year asking for guidance as to whether to schedule baseball during wartime. *Baseball* magazine had written, "The 1942 season may be called off entirely." Roosevelt felt that baseball could help with morale and, in mid-January, the President wrote back, giving baseball a green light.

Johnny was to get his shot at major league ball after all. His first spring training with the Boston team was just a few weeks later, in February. Another cross-country train trip brought him to Sarasota, albeit 48 hours late largely because of the extra traffic caused by war activities. He'd already been assigned his number in the Selective Service draft, a high number assuring him the opportunity to get in most of the season before being called. "Uncle Sam may call me any minute and I'm ready to go," a philosophical Johnny proclaimed to a reporter. He noted that baseball had already been good to him, and that even the minor league pay of the day provided him about four times as much as his brother Tony, who worked as a stock man in the casket factory. Johnny was the main breadwinner in the family.

Ted Williams was also late reporting to camp. He had his own draft situation to sort out first. As late as February 26, it was not known for sure if the Kid who had hit .406 in '41 would even be back.

The field itself was like "an old barn with some lockers in it. And we had only one diamond with a lumpy infield surface and a terrible hitting background. But I'll tell you one thing. We were awfully happy to be in Florida at a major league spring training camp." (1)

Johnny was not confident that he would make the Red Sox. "I had no idea, being a rookie. There were guys who came to be in the big leagues that had better stats. But I came out of the American Association with some pretty good stats. I was hopeful. I said, 'If I play well . . . ' "

Joe Cronin was a player-manager who played shortstop, but he was putting on weight and becoming less mobile. He had held on an extra couple of years, and done well, though in the process taking the spot which would have been Pee Wee Reese's, had the Sox held onto Reese out of Louisville. With Reese gone, Cronin was looking to find a capable replacement and there was a bit of a contest between Johnny Pesky and Eddie Pellagrini, a good player from the Boston area. Cronin said if Johnny didn't make it, or was drafted, that he might play short himself. Indeed, when Johnny hurt his thumb in late May, Cronin did play a few games and did well, pinch-hitting a homer his first time up. Really, though, Cronin had pretty much decided on Pesky and Boston headlines such as "Red Sox Silent on Ted's Case, Cronin More Interested in Arrival of Johnny Pesky" ran prior to the opening of spring training. It was pretty clear that anyone who could upstage Teddy was a sure bet to stick with the club. "Pesky Accepted as Sox Regular" headlined the *Boston Globe* on March 13.

"I fought Pelly," Johnny says, "I think Pelly was older than I was because he started in '38 and I started in '40, so he had two years' experience on me. Cronin was fair to both of us. He'd play him one day and then he'd play me the next. We were going to go play the Yankees and the Cardinals in St. Pete, because they both trained there, and Pelly came up lame. He had something wrong with his leg so he didn't make the trip. I played both teams, and I played well. Now it came down to where Cronin had to get down to your 25-man roster and, really and truly, my stats were a little bit better than Pelly's.

"One of us had to go to Louisville. I played well enough to make the team. Joe called me and said, 'Johnny, I'm going to keep you and I'm going to send Pelly out.' Pelly said, 'Joe, are you sure you're not making a mistake. What do you think those fans are going to say in Boston?'" Pellagrini was a fan favorite in Boston, a local kid, but Cronin chose Pesky. Despite the competition, Pesky and Pelly, both still living in the Greater Boston area, have been friends ever since. "Pelly has been very loyal to me, and I to him. He went to Louisville and I came to Boston. He left in the middle of the year to go into the Navy. Pelly was a different type of player. He was a little guy, but he tried to hit everything out of the ballpark."

Cronin helped Johnny out, the manager advising Pesky that he was lifting his front foot too much. Johnny replied that he'd been watching Musial, and Musial lifted his foot the same way. "Musial?" said Cronin. "Why copy a guy like Musial? Williams is the fellow for you to follow."

Johnny made the team, as Cronin had anticipated. He had come heralded and had made the grade. And he'd known some of the other players on the team. "I knew Ted [Williams] when he was in the Coast League when I was the clubhouse boy. I hung up his jockstrap in the Coast League. I knew Bobby [Doerr]. They remembered me from being around the ballpark."

Even when Pesky made it to his first big league spring training in 1942, he got drafted for clubhouse work. "Johnny Orlando made me help him. We must've had 40 or 50 players in camp and Johnny would have me shining all those shoes, drying sweatshirts. 'You're gonna make it, kid,' he kept telling me, 'you're gonna make it big. Keep brushing.' Bobby Doerr or somebody said to me, 'You're on a major league ball club, what do you think you're doing?' 'Shucks, I'd always lived in a clubhouse,' I told him. 'I got nowhere to go. I like to keep busy.' "

Johnny also remembered Indian Bob Johnson's welcome to him in the bigs. Johnson, too, had been with Portland back in 1932 when Johnny was a clubhouse kid. Now a veteran in his tenth year with the Athletics, he grabbed Pesky: "First time I was near him in the big leagues he picked me up like a fungo and shook me, 'You needle-nosed little creep. Go get me a sandwich.' "

"They welcomed me aboard. Tabor was the third baseman. I took over for Cronin at short. Bobby Doerr was at second. Jimmie Foxx was the first baseman. We had Williams, DiMaggio and Lou Finney. I knew who they were. You studied box scores. In '41, we had played a couple of games with the Red Sox. I met Tabor. And Hughson, I knew Hughson." [Hughson had pitched for part of the 1941 season for the Colonels, winning 7 and losing 1.]

Though it was common for veteran players in those days to make life difficult for aspiring youngsters who threatened their jobs, Johnny experienced none of that personally. Many of the players—and not just those he'd known earlier—were quite nice to him.

"We played some exhibition games—four or five games against Cincinnati coming north. We played a game in Atlanta or one of those places. Vander Meer was pitching. Second or third time up, with a man on, I hit a ball in the gap in right center field for a triple. Then I got another hit. Cronin called me over after the game and said, 'Kid. You just made the ball club today.'"

As soon as Johnny got the word he had made the Boston Red Sox squad, he phoned home. His sister answered the call. "Ann, I've got good news. Mr. Cronin told me I made the ball club." She answered simply, "That's fine."

"Of course, I talked to my mom and I talked to my dad and my brothers," Johnny remembers. "They were all happy for me. They said, 'Take care of yourself. Don't do anything to get them mad at you.' Especially my older brother Tony. He was tough on me. He said, 'You've got to do those things. Be a gentleman, Johnny.' I said, 'Well, I'll do the best I can, Tony.' I got along pretty good. In those years, I was a nice boy [laughs]."

Ted Williams, hardly foreseeing that Johnny was going to hit for the second best batting average in the league, conceded, "Pesky is going to help our defense." Mel Webb, writing the same day, said, "Johnny Pesky has played good ball in the short field . . . While not a driver at the plate, takes a first class 'cut' at the ball." He noted how well Pesky and Doerr combined on the double play.

After playing their way from Florida up to Boston, Johnny feared he was about to get sent right back down again. It was tradition then for the Red Sox and the Boston Braves to face off in a pre-season City Series. In 1942, the game was held at the Red Sox' home park, Fenway Park. The *Globe* wrote, "The initial appearance of Johnny Pesky will be anxiously anticipated." Back on March 13, the same paper headlined another column: "Red Sox Pennant Hopes Rise or Fall with Pesky." Around the same time, Johnny commented on the military draft, "the uncertainty disturbs me a little." It was Pesky's first exposure to big league pressures.

Eight thousand hardy fans turned out for the game. "It's a cold, dreary day," Johnny remembered, "and it started to snow near the end of the game—I made four errors! I only made one good play the whole game. I'm thinking, 'Oh my God, I'm going back to Louisville tomorrow.'

Next day, we had a workout. Cronin didn't say a word." Johnny did go 1 for 4, and Cronin started Johnny Pesky at short on Opening Day. He was given Lefty Grove's old locker.

The season opened on Tuesday. It was a clear, crisp day and Johnny got off to a quick start. "First time up, I got a single. Yeah, my first time up in the major leagues, I got a single. Everybody hits home runs, but I hit singles.

"I got a couple of hits. I hit a triple off Bob Johnson, who knew me as a kid in the Coast League. After the game, he came in the clubhouse and said, 'Cripes, I thought someone was chasing you, the way you run around those bases.' Made me kind of feel good, you know. He says, 'Well, good luck, Johnny. Keep it going. Don't try to do too much.' I think I got 5 or 6 hits in that first series.

"I didn't make an error in my first 18 games. Every ball hit to me, boy, I was right behind it, made sure I come up and take a little crow hop and put something on the ball. It worked out pretty good. I got relaxed, but not too relaxed. I couldn't play that way. I ran everything out, ran the bases hard . . . played hard.

"The big leagues is much more explosive. There's more at stake. Your reputation's at stake. I had good minor league stats, but that doesn't mean anything. There was a guy in the Coast League who hit anywhere from .390 to .400 every year for ten years and never could make it in the big leagues. He went to the Dodgers. Oscar Eckhardt—I never will forget his name. Look him up!"

This was new territory for the youngster from the West Coast, just two years out of high school and experiencing a whole new round of adventures. "You never forget that rookie year. When I came up to the City Series, that was the first time I'd seen Boston. You went into New York, you went in to Philadelphia, you went into Washington, you went into Detroit. This was the first time I'd seen any of these cities."

What was Johnny's first impression of Fenway Park, which was to become his home for most of the next sixty years?

"I thought I was in a museum, it was so pretty. The weather had just changed. It looked like every blade of grass was perfect. I even remember the groundskeeper's name, a guy by the name of Connie Sullivan. There were so many great people around in those years. They knew you were away from home and they made you feel welcome. Barbara Tyler was there, the secretary to Collins. [Switchboard operator] Helen Robinson was there; she's still there. She came in '41." [Helen Robinson died in 2001.]

The first time Johnny went up to the office, it was to request some Red Sox stationery so he could write a letter to his folks. Helen Robinson was out in front, just as she was at the start of the 2001 season. "I go upstairs. I said, 'Hi' and she said, 'Hi.' I said, 'I'd like to see Barbara Tyler, Mr. Collins' secretary.' She said, 'Well, what do you want?' I said, 'Well, I think I should tell Mrs. Tyler.' So she gets her on the phone and Mrs. Tyler comes out from the other office. She says, 'Oh, hi, Johnny.' She was at spring training, so we met down there. I said, 'I want to write a letter to my home but I'd like to use some Red Sox logo stationery.' Next word out of her mouth, she said, 'They sell stationery in the drugstore down in Kenmore Square.' So I said, 'OK' and I left.

"Helen Robinson got quite a kick out of that. She's a great gal. I've had a lot of fun with her through the years. She's always been nice to me and my family. She can be crusty at times. I'll say one thing. If you tell her something and you don't want anybody to know it, you'd have to kill her, cut her neck, to get it out of her. We always had a decent relationship. She was at my wedding and so was Barbara and that whole gang from Fenway.

"We did things together as a group. Of course, I didn't know Ruthie in 1942. I didn't even have a girl friend then. There were a couple of girls I knew at home. We were just friends; we'd go dancing and stuff like that. Go to a movie. That was about all. I was kind of fussy.

"We went into Boston and I went with the single guys. We all stayed over on Bay State Road. I roomed with Joe Dobson until his wife came up and then I roomed with Mike Ryba. Nice man. A veteran. Crusty old guy. He'd get three or four cigars and sit in the lobby after supper. You'd go to a movie and come back a couple of hours later and you'd see two or three cigars in the ashtray, and he'd be sitting there barbing with the people. He was a great guy. I loved him. Ted, myself, Wagner, Dobson. We used the Sheraton. When the Braves come in town and we were going out of town, we'd just flip-flop. The guy there treated us real well. And the food there was excellent. We used to go down to Jimmy O'Keefe's for supper, a ten minute walk down on Boylston."

Johnny wore number 6 with the Red Sox. "When I first came to the Red Sox, I had 16, but Cronin wanted infielders to have single numbers. Tabor was 5, I was 6, Bobby was 1 and Foxx was 3."

Johnny Pesky has an intimate memory of the strength of Double X. "As a rookie on one of our train trips, he was doing what all rookies had to do—climb into the upper berth—when nice guy Jimmie happened to come down the aisle. 'Hey, kid," he said. 'Are you trying to get into that berth?' When Johnny told him yes, Foxx put one hand on Pesky's rear end and hoisted him into the air and then into the bunk all in one motion." (2)

In the home opener, Dom DiMaggio led off with a walk. Johnny reached first on a fielder's choice, and then Ted hit a home run. "Pepper-pot Johnny" went 2 for 4 with a single and triple, handling 8 chances without an error as the Red Sox won 8-3. Within a week, reporters noted, "Pesky is getting right into the hearts of Fenway fans every day." Williams got off to a great start, with 9 RBI after 3 games. Johnny fit right in, even mugging for the crowd. When Ted caught a ball in left and put a little extra on it firing the ball in to the shortstop, Johnny acted like it stung him, took off his glove and rubbed his hand.

Pesky's first big day was April 22, when he went 3 for 5 with 2 singles, a triple and 3 RBI. DiMaggio typically led off, with Pesky batting second—the opening act for Ted Williams. "As it turned out," Dom DiMaggio said in a recent interview, "we were the table setters for Ted Williams. We both had a good deal of speed but they didn't want us to steal bases. If we ran, we ran on hit and runs. John was clever. On occasion, when John saw out of the corner of his eye that I got an extra good jump, he'd swing through the ball. He wouldn't go after it. He'd give me the hit and run signal, but if I got a real extra good jump and he knew the base was stolen, he'd just swing through the ball. He was that great a hit and run hitter. Any time there was a possibility of my getting caught—if they pitched out—he'd throw the bat at the ball. I never remember a time when they pitched out and got me.

"He'd touch his nose. That was our hit and run sign. On other occasions, he'd say, 'OK, today I'm going to touch my nose but don't take it.' Just to throw the guys off. They kept looking and looking and looking, trying to figure out our hit and run plays. They'd think they have it. 'Oh, it's when he goes to his nose!' John was uncanny. He'd say, 'Well, these guys are pretty clever. In this series, I'll go to my nose, but don't go for the hit and run.'

"If the ball was hit to left center field, of course John would be the cutoff. If it was hit to right center, Bobby Doerr would be the cutoff. He made a fabulous difference. Cronin had slowed down. He couldn't move around as frisky as he used to. Johnny could get to balls that were just eluding Cronin."

Johnny was using a Joe Cronin model bat at this point, and "still pursues a boyhood habit of entwining three strips of tape around the handle of his war club," noted *Boston Globe* sportswriter Mel Webb. The

Red Sox got off to a decent start, with the pitching better than expected. Johnny Pesky was given the credit in a number of articles, including one that bore the headline "Pesky's Fielding Key to Improved Red Sox Pitching." Johnny was hitting .318 at the beginning of May. By the time the month was over, he was at .338. Asked about what it was like to play big league ball, the rookie replied, "It's fast, very fast . . . The fielders are quicker, the runners faster, and the throwing harder." He modestly added, "It's hard to get hits." Asked again in late August, Johnny said he actually found it easier to hit in the majors, because "the pitchers are around the plate more and give you more good balls to hit."

Hanging over the entire 1942 season was the war. Virtually every player—indeed, the whole nation—wrestled with the issues of military service. Some, such as Bob Feller, signed up instantly. Others tried to decide what was the best approach. Ted Williams was exempt from service, being the sole support of his mother, but the public pressure on him was so intense that those around him convinced him it was best to sign up. On May 22, Williams enlisted in the Navy, ending the controversy which had swirled about him for months. Asked why he had signed up for a naval aviation program—a combat service—Seaman Second Class Williams said, "I like to hit!"

Johnny was beginning to build up a loyal following around town with his on-field and after-hours work. Red Sox publicist Ed Doherty noted him as one of the best speakers who worked the banquet circuit. As of May 31, Johnny had already accumulated 55 hits, more than half of them "of the infield variety." Time after time, Pesky beat out bunts, sometimes driving the speedy DiMaggio all the way from first to third.

Charlie Wagner, a former batboy for Reading in the Eastern League, was one of Johnny's teammates that year and, years later, he evaluated Johnny's 1942 performance. "He was a good hitter, excellent runner. He could steal a base and he could do a lot of things with that bat. He could bunt! He used to have a little thing with Dom DiMaggio. If Dom could get on as our first hitter, he'd bunt a ball to third base. Well, Dom would go from first to third on a bunt. Johnny was good enough he would draw the third baseman in to make that play. It wasn't just once or twice. They did it often. It was quite a nice play to watch. Sort of a bunt and run. Nowadays they give you the signal whether to hit and run, but in those days they used to have their own hit and run, and bunt and run. Those were the only two guys who did that.

"They had a play where John would call the bunt by touching his right ear or the hit and run by touching his nose. They pulled the play off several times, and finally it got in the newspaper."

Dom DiMaggio remembered, "When the third baseman came in, I would never stop at second. I'd go on to third. One day in Yankee Stadium, I had a great break and I was around second base. No way they could have thrown me out at third base, but all of a sudden I look up and there's [Yankees catcher] Bill Dickey standing at third base. I slide in and he says, 'Got ya!' He had run from home plate. As soon as John bunted the ball, he ran up to third base and he's standing there. They threw the ball back to him and he tagged me out. I said, What the hell are you doing here?' Those are the exact words: 'Got ya!' "

Dickey let Dominic know that he read the newspaper, too.

Red Sox players, Johnny included, were trying to make their own decisions about military service. Should he wait to be drafted, or take a step and enlist? He looked around and considered the options. "Then I got into that V-5 program in the Navy," Johnny says, "and I got to finish the year, as did Ted. Dominic, myself and Ted—the 1, 2, 3 hitters, we all went into the service after the season." Johnny himself signed up for the Navy on June 10, acknowledging that Ted's enthusiasm about the program had influenced him.

The war was on everyone's minds. Reporter Mel Webb floated the idea that balls hit into the crowd could be voluntarily turned back in by fans and sent to the armed forces. From the day the practice was adopted, not a foul ball was taken home. In order to require one less baggage car on the train, Tom Yawkey had individual suitcases made up for the players so they could carry some of their own gear and store them in the sleepers. Servicemen were let into games free and boxscores often announced not only paid attendance but also the 400 or 600 servicemen who had been admitted. Several times, gate proceeds were donated to war relief and over $500,000 was collected throughout baseball in 1942. A couple of exhibition games were played against teams from military bases. Williams took the mound and struck out three at one such competition. Scrap rubber was used in the baseballs, and many hitters felt this resulted in a less lively ball. For the last game of the year, G. M. Eddie Collins announced that anyone bringing 10 pounds of scrap metal to Fenway Park would be admitted free of charge. 3251 fans dropped off 46,850 pounds of metal and got themselves a free ballgame.

On July 13, Pesky and Williams both began classes at Mechanic Arts High School in Boston. Sitting at high school desks, 250 students began the course work—four hours a night, three nights a week—that would

When I was a rookie and playing the Yankees, Spud Chandler was with them. I used to pick up his jockstrap in the [Pacific] Coast League. He was a 20 game winner. He come out there one year, in the late '30s and he was with Portland when I was still working around the clubhouse, and then five or six years later I'm hitting at him. He was kind of a mean guy. He didn't try to hurt you, but he'd throw at your feet or things like that, especially when the situation called for it.

We were playing a game late in August and we're in a 1-to-1 game at Fenway and our big catcher was on first base with two outs and Dominic hit a ball down by the right field line for a double. Henrich, playing the right field wall, got the ball back in and so we had a runner at second and third. I'm the next hitter. Before the game that afternoon, Jack Mullaney of the old *Boston Post* came down into our dugout and he said to me, "Johnny, you don't have a hit off Chandler." I was going for a 200 hit year. I had about 175 hits at that time—we had another three weeks to go in the season—and I guess I was about 0-for-14 off him. I thought I had a hit off every pitcher in the league that year. So Ted was sitting a little ways away and he hears this so he comes over and says, "Yeah, for crying out loud. He throws you that hard sinker. You're trying to pull this guy and all you're doing is hitting ground balls to second base." I said, "Yeah, yeah, yeah. . . . " He said, "For crying out loud, I'm a foot taller and forty pounds bigger and I can't pull him."

So anyway the game starts and the first two times, 0-for-2. Two ground balls to Joe Gordon. Now, we're in a 1-1 ball game in the bottom of the 8th inning. We've got men on 2nd and 3rd with two outs and first base open. Ted grabs me by the sleeve and says, "Now don't try to pull this guy. What the hell's wrong with you? How can you be so dumb? Your stroke is up the middle and to left field. Just try to hit the ball. Go the other way with this guy. If he throws you that hard sinker . . . I've told you before, I have trouble pulling this guy." So I said, "OK, I'll do exactly what you say." Sure enough, I get ready to jump in the batter's box and then he grabs me again and he leans down at me and as a parting shot, he says, "You know damn well they're not going to walk you to get to me."

So I said a quick prayer and got in. Chandler's out there scowling at me. He was mean; he'd throw at your feet. He had a face like a bulldog. I'm up there and I said, "Oh, God, please." Ted told me exactly what he was going to do. He said, "Johnny, he'll throw you the hard sinker away hoping you'll hit it—if you hit it." So ball one, strike one. Ball two. Here comes that 2-and-1 pitch, the ball was right out there. The third baseman Rolfe is playing me in on the grass, maybe about 15 feet in. I hit the ball pretty good. It was by the prepare them for service in Naval Aviation. Williams was called to the front of the class to say a few words. Caught unprepared, he simply said, "I only hope I can prove myself worthy to go through with you. I give you my word I'll do my best." Then Lieut. Donahue asked Johnny Pesky to mount the platform. "We're on a bigger team now—in the Navy—and I know I've got the guts to go through with you. When Ted and I get going in there with you, we'll give 'em hell!"

About midway through the season, King Peter II of Yugoslavia paid a

---

third baseman. If it's at him, it's an out but it happened to be to his left. I hit it sharply and it went by him. Dominic had a good jump from second base and he scores. Now we're ahead 3 to 1, and I'm standing on first base. I'm looking at Williams and he's pointing to himself with a big grin on his face. "Nice hit, Dummy."

Chandler's walking around the mound and he's giving me holy Hell. "You little so-and-so . . . " Now after about two or three minutes of that, he decided to get back up on the mound. He gets into his stretch and he steps off. We never took big leads with Williams hitting. He's getting ready to pitch to Ted and he steps off, and I'm standing on the bag. Chandler was really upset. "Next time, I'm going to stick one in your ear." I said, "Ah, I'll spit it out at you." He gives me another blast and I told him where to go, and I said, "Besides that, you were a lousy tipper when you were in the Coast League." Now he pitches to Ted and the very first pitch Ted must have hit it over 400 feet to right field. Over the Red Sox bullpen. So I'm running like a scalded dog—when there's two outs, you always run hard until you're told to slow down. Anyway, I'm rounding third and then I'm in the dugout when Ted's rounding third base. He gets into the dugout. I'm in the dugout and I'm sitting down next to Bobby. Now here comes Ted, and everybody was, "Oh Ted, you got all of that" and "The sound of that was terrific." "Yeah," he says, "I really got ahold of that. Where is that horn-nose little shortstop of ours?" I'm waiting for him, so he comes over to me and says, "Didn't I tell you how to hit Chandler, Johnny?" I said, "Well, let me tell you something, Ted. He was so goddamn mad at me for getting that dinky little single that he forgot you were the next hitter."

I've told that to Ted a few times and he just laughs, "Yeah, yeah. I remember that."

Bobby Doerr broke up a no-hitter against Chandler in '46. And he broke up two against Feller, and I got the other one. I got one against Feller. I did mine early in the game. I think Bobby did his in the 8th inning.

visit to Yankee Stadium and saw a couple of Slovenian-Americans (Walter Judnich and Steve Sundra) playing for the visiting Browns. Al Milnar, Pete Sudar and Joe Kuhel were others of Yugoslav extraction, but none were doing as well as young Paveskovich, rated as one of the "finest frosh finds of '42."

The 1942 Red Sox got off to a good start, but soon fell 10 games out and never seriously challenged.

Individual players did well, and six Sox were named to the All-Star squad. Pesky was "conspicuous among those not chosen," but with six other Hose on the team, and Pesky—after all—a rookie, this wasn't entirely surprising. On July 1, columnist Jerry Nason judged the Sox near the midpoint and argued, "the only reason the pitching is better is on account of young Johnny Pesky, the skitter-footed shortstop. Pesky covers a great deal of ground. He has zest and fire and a great throwing arm. He's aggressive and game. The Red Sox pitchers are throwing with more confidence when they look out there and see Mrs. Paveskovich's little boy Johnny cutting off what were hits in 1941 but are not today." One time in Washington, Senators fans rewarded Johnny with a standing ovation for his fielding. He even mastered the hidden ball trick, pulling it off twice in 1942. Bill Zuber, a pitcher, doubled to lead off the fifth inning on May 31. Interestingly, Mel Webb's suggestion regarding fans returning balls hit into the stands played a role here. As Zuber was on second, the following batter hit a ball into the grandstand and a fan was reluctant to give up his souvenir. The fans started booing heavily and distracted the players. Pesky took advantage and tagged Zuber as he strolled off second. A few weeks later, Lou Boudreau got picked off base and word spread around the league.

Johnny pulled the hidden ball trick three times in all, the third time coming in 1947. "The best one of all was when Ed Rommel was the umpire. We only had three umpires in those days—home plate, first and third. When they had a man on, the umpire at third would move. It was July 4, 1942. The ball went down the right field line and I was in the middle between second base and third, and I cut it off. Tommy Henrich was on second base, talking to Eddie Rommel. The pitcher was off the mound somewhere. Rommel knew I had the ball. You had to alert the umpire. Boudreau had pulled the hidden ball trick the week before, and Henrich had read about it. I was behind them and he gets off the base about 4 or 5 feet and says to Rommel, 'Eddie, that Boudreau's been pulling that hidden ball trick. This is how far off I'm going to get, so they won't get me.' Just as he got it out of his mouth, I tagged him. Rommel was laughing, and Henrich wanted to kill me!"

Johnny rarely tangled with umpires, but got his first heave-ho on the 23rd of July. Ed Rommel threw him out for protesting too vociferously the safe call on Joe Kuhel's steal of second in the bottom of the 9th at St. Louis. Johnny also was assessed a $25 fine.

The next day, also at Sportsman's Park, Pesky smacked out his first major league home run, off the Browns' Bob Muncrief. A two-run homer, it was apparently quiet a drive. The *Globe* coverage reported that he "blasted his maiden four-master onto the right-field pavilion roof." Right field ranged in depth from 309.5 feet down the line to 354 in right center. There was a concrete wall 11.5 feet high with a wire fence on top. In right center there was pavilion seating, so Pesky's drive must have been a pretty solid smash, more to right center than down the line and would have left the field at least a dozen feet above the playing surface. "I got under it. I was very strong in those days," he laughs. His second and last homer of 1942 was on August 18, a 3-run shot at Fenway against the Yankees, which tied the game at 5-5, as the Red Sox went on to win 8-7 in the 10th. The home run was just inside the right field foul pole, the first of six home runs Johnny hit in Boston—most of which were wrapped around what's become known since as the "Pesky pole." Today it represents the shortest distance to a home run in major league baseball. It's not as though Pesky hit a lot of them, but Mel Parnell started using the name during his years as broadcaster and it stuck.

That kind of power was rare for Pesky. He hit to all fields, though, beat out a lot of infield hits and generally did what he could to get on base or move the runners ahead. By year's end, he had 17 sacrifices but probably beat out as many attempted sacrifices for safeties. The name "Pesky" fit him very well. For most of the year, his average hovered around the same .325 he had achieved in both Rocky Mount and in Louisville. There were no real streaks and no real slumps. His average bobbed up and down, but was hardly ever below .313 and hardly ever above .338. He finished strongly, at .331—an improvement over his minor league average.

On the 22nd of August, Johnny had a remarkable achievement: he hit five singles in five consecutive innings during a doubleheader against the Philadelphia Athletics. Two of the singles were in the last two innings of the "lid-lifter" and then he hit one single in each of "the first three heats of the nightcap." The statisticians of the day couple find no such record in the books and assumed it unlikely that it had ever before been accomplished. Two of the singles were bloopers and one was a bunt. The Sox won both games, by scores of 11-3 and 11-5. Rickey Henderson in September 1991 had five hits in consecutive innings, all in one game—the first four were singles but the final one a home run.

Pesky played hard. Just two days later, against the Indians, the Sox down by one, DiMaggio singled and Johnny bunted to move him over. It wasn't his best bunt, though, and the Indians' Ferrick fired to second, but DiMaggio was called safe. Williams then bounced right back to Ferrick, which could have set up a doubleplay. Surprised that Ted had uncharactersistically provided this gift, Ferrick froze for an instant, then fired to second to force Pesky. But Pesky came in hard and wide open, taking out Boudreau and forcing his throw to first to sail wildly into the Red Sox dugout. Ted took second as DiMaggio scored the tying run. After two walks (the first one, to Doerr, intentional), a hot grounder by Finney was knocked down but there was no play and Williams scored the winning run.

Dom DiMaggio wrote that "Johnny became one of the outstanding contact hitters in baseball, after being smart enough to take the advice of Heinie Manush. . . . When Pesky was breaking in, Manush advised him to be a singles hitter 'instead of hitting fly balls to the other team's outfielders.'" (3)

On September 15, Johnny got his 200th hit—off Ted Lyons in Chicago. Lyons had retired Johnny 13 times in a row before that, so it was a doubly satisfying hit. The only problem was, it didn't count. The game was called in the fourth due to bad weather. "I hadn't made a hit all season off Lyons. But I felt that I was going to hit the guy this time and yelled out to him, 'Lyons, if I get a hit, will you give me the ball?' He said he would and I promptly hit a blooper into right field for a single. He came over to me after he got the ball back from the outfielder and said, 'I'd like to hit *you* with it.'"

A day later, though, in St. Louis, Johnny hit a clean double off Johnny Niggeling of the Browns, which did hold up. Johnny was the first shortstop to achieve 200 hits and only the 13th player in major league history to reach the total in his rookie year. The last player to have done it was Dale Alexander in 1929. The 205 hits Pesky ultimately made set a Red Sox rookie record which held until Nomar Garciaparra hit 209 over 50 years later, in 1997. Fittingly, Johnny had worked with Garciaparra during Nomar's minor league years and in spring training 1997. Purists will note that Johnny played in a 154 game season, and Nomar's 206th hit did not come until the 157th game.

Pesky also led the A.L. in sacrifice hits, with 22. The Red Sox finished the year in second, but 9 games behind the Yankees whose 103 victories easily earned them the AL pennant.

Charlie Wagner talked about Johnny: "John did everything well. He was an aggressive guy, particularly at the bat. Of course, he had Bobby Doerr at second base. Jim Tabor at third. They all worked well together and they caught a lot of my mistakes. That was important as hell. He could always put wood on the bat. He didn't strike out an awful lot.

"He knew what the pitcher was pitching him and didn't try to over-power it. When you know your strengths, well, you should use them. He knew what he could do and he knew what he couldn't do. If you threw him outside, he was hitting to leftfield. If you pitched him in, he was try-ing to pull the ball. If a guy had more than he could handle, he was bunting him and dragging him. And he could run, like someone was chasing him.

"John was everything you'd ask for in a guy. Very aggressive. On the ball. Early at the park, and late getting out. That's a good sign. Working on fielding as well as hitting."

There was no formal Rookie of the Year award granted back then, but baseball historian Lyle Spatz calculated "retroactive rookie of the year awards" and argues that Johnny was the clear winner. Johnny hit .331 and was second in the American League only to teammate Ted Williams, who led the league with a .356 average—Ted's second straight title, hard on the heels of his spectacular .406 season in 1941. Bill Deane did a similar evaluation for *Total Baseball*, "awarding" Johnny his after-the-fact "rookie of the year" honors for 1942. *The Sporting News* named Johnny the short-stop on its All Star Major League team.

The baseball writers would seem to have agreed as well. Johnny came in third in the voting for the Most Valuable Player in 1942. Joe Gordon, who lived in Eugene, Oregon, won the balloting (270 points) with Williams second (249 points, despite having won the Triple Crown!) and Pesky third (143 points.) Two of the 24 writers gave Johnny their first place votes, clearly, de facto "rookie of the year" recognition by the base-ball writers association, beating out, among others, Stan Musial and Vern Stephens. The writers chose Pesky as their All-Star shortstop for the year, besting Boudreau, Rizzuto and the rest.

Tom Yawkey had his own treat for the rookie. In the process, he earned himself and the ballclub a loyal friend for life. "The last week of the season in '42," Johnny tells, "There was a note on my chair to go up and see Eddie Collins. Of course, we were never allowed upstairs. They walk up there now, as if they . . . well, anyway, Ted sees this thing and he says, 'What's that?' I said 'I gotta go up and see Mr. Collins.' 'Well, hurry up.' So I went upstairs. He called me in his office, and said 'Sit down.' So I sat down and he says, 'Well, you had a fine year, Johnny. You played well and you weren't any problem off the field for us.' There wasn't much of that off the field activity in the years we played; you couldn't afford it. Well anyway, he handed me this envelope. So now Ted is waiting for me in the clubhouse. 'What the hell happened?' 'Well, he called me in and gave me this envelope.' So he says, 'What the hell's in it?' So I opened it up and there was a check there for five thousand dollars."

Johnny had been sending money home, as it was, but now he was able to take the bonus—an amount in excess of his entire $4000 salary—and pay off the new house on Overton Street, a house his brother Vince still lives in today. "That money paid for the house. I think the house cost about $4800.

"It has stayed with me, what Mr. Yawkey did. That's why I have always loved the Red Sox—with Mr. Yawkey—because of what he did not only for me but for my family. They were so darn nice. That's affected me and that's why when the ballclub loses, it bothers me."

It's quite possible that Tom Yawkey, looking ahead, knew that Johnny was bound for military service and would not be able to contribute to his family's finances for the foreseeable future. It was unquestionably a very generous act, of the sort that endeared the Red Sox owner to so many who played for him. Nearly sixty years later, Johnny remains grateful—and says with genuine feeling that the most disappointing aspect of his entire career is that he was unable to "win a world championship for Mr. Yawkey." The same feeling has been expressed by Doerr, DiMaggio, Williams and Yastrzemski.

The youngster had made it. His toughest critic, though, was spare in his praise. "My idol was Ted Williams," Johnny remembers. "Towards the end of that season, I was kind of hoping he'd notice what I was doing and maybe even give me a pat on the back. But he never said a word. So finally I went up to him and asked him what he thought. He said, 'You're doing pretty well, but let's see you do it again next year!' The only thing that impressed Ted was consistency."

There followed a three-year gap, due to World War II—but Johnny did come back and did unequivocally demonstrate that consistency.

Johnny had starred in Boston. Back home, though, he was still his mother's son and she was maybe not so impressed. My brother was in college. Every day he'd teach my mother a new word. "She told me to do something and I gave her a snip answer. She didn't like it, and she says 'Ohhhh, big-a baseball player. Big-a shit around here.' " That put him in his place a bit. Still, life was pretty good.

"I played. I was single, twenty-one years old. I thought I was going to last forever. I was 22 that fall, and then I went into the Navy."

NOTES

(1) Johnny Pesky, quoted by Herb Crehan, "Boston Red Sox Spring Training History," unpublished manuscript

(2) Dom DiMaggio, *Real Grass, Real Heroes*, p. 45

(3) Ibid., pp. 261, 262

6

War Years

World War II stole three prime years from Johnny Pesky's career. It may have cost him a place in the Hall of Fame. But it also allowed him to meet the love of his life, Ruth Hickey.

The devastating Japanese bombing of Pearl Harbor in December 1941 propelled America into the war with a certitude of conscience and a clarity of purpose. The surprise attack sent a shock through American society that brooked little debate about the merits of war. What followed was an urgent and unrelenting marshalling of the country's human resources. Within months, physically able young men who were not in the service began to feel a powerful scrutiny, particularly the vital young men of professional sports. Even if one were legitimately exempt, the pressures were intense. "All of us were going through that," recalls Johnny. "If you weren't in uniform, people would say, 'What the hell are you doing out of the service?' Unless you were classified 4-F. Well, hell, there was nothing wrong with me. Dominic wore glasses, but a lot of guys wore glasses. They sent my papers on from Portland to here. It was getting time where I had to make a move, and Ted talked me into joining this V5 program in May."

The Navy was trying to build up its aviation wing and Lieutenant Robert "Whitey" Fuller, at Dartmouth College, had some success attracting a few baseball players into the program. It didn't hurt in Johnny's case that his father had been in the Austro-Hungarian Navy. "He always used to say the Navy was nice and clean. You always got to eat good. The Army was out there living in bad weather—too cold or too hot. In the Navy, you can get in out of the rain or the cold weather. It was either get drafted or enlist. I wanted to get into the Navy anyway." Johnny and Ted Williams both signed up in a government building at 150 Causeway Street in downtown Boston.

"The season was over in September—two weeks later we were in the Navy. We took classes in Naval procedure during the summer, over at Mechanic Arts High School, three nights a week when we were at home. After a week at home with my folks, we went to Amherst and got our uniforms."

Other baseball players joined the V5 program, including Johnny Sain, Joe Coleman and Buddy Gremp. Johnny was enlisted as Seaman Second Class Paveskovich. The first step on the long road to war was more class-room—W.T.S., War Training Service, at Amherst, Massachusetts. There they received instruction, both in schoolrooms and in actual flight situa-tions. "We stayed in college dorms. We stayed in Genung House. Ted, Coleman, Sain, Gremp and myself. The students were still in school, but they just made room for us. We were there for about six months, from October to April 1943. We flew out of Turners Falls. We had so many hours in a Piper Cub and then you soloed in the Piper Cub. Then you went to a Waco, which is a biplane, a little heavier aircraft." Johnny had flown for the first time the year before, as a passenger on his way to the All-Star Game of the American Association, flying from Louisville to Minneapolis by way of Indianapolis.

After about six months at Amherst and Turners Falls, it was time to build up the recruits physically. The group went on to Chapel Hill, North Carolina, April through July 1943. "Hand-to-hand combat. Boxing. Wrestling. Each kid had to play one sport. We played baseball and then in the winter, football came in. It was hot as a bugger down there. One morning I was in the backfield and this one kid was running for a touch-down. I threw a block on him and threw him out of bounds. That after-noon we had a baseball game. By the time we left Chapel Hill, we were in pretty good shape." Sport was clearly seen, both within the military and in American society as a whole, as an important force in strengthen-ing the nation.

The group arrived at Chapel Hill and, the season being right, made time to play some baseball. The base newspaper, *The Cloudbuster*, tracked the games. It was good publicity for the Navy to have celebrity ballplayers in the service and they took PR photographs of Williams, Pesky and

Coleman at their duties and while playing ball. After Chapel Hill they traveled on to Peru, Indiana for primary flight training. Johnny struggled with the actual flying. Ted Williams, in his book *My Turn At Bat*, wrote that Johnny "flew an airplane like he had stone arms" and he recounts one day when Johnny had to make eight approaches to land a Cub he was flying. "It looked like they were going to have to shoot him down. They finally got Pesky out of there. In an airplane he was a menace to himself and everybody else, but he was certainly officer material so they moved him into O.C.S. [Officer Candidate School] and he actually got his rank before I did." In comments for this book, Ted was even blunter: "He couldn't fly an airplane for shit!"

Johnny said he could fly all right, but he had trouble with navigation. "I used to see Ted when we had supper at night. I'd leave him around quarter of seven and go down to get extra work. After two or three weeks, Ted said, 'For Chrissakes, why can't you get this?' I said, 'Well, Ted, I'm not you. Your mind is much quicker than mine.' 'Well,' he said, 'when you get it, you'll retain it.' Which was a left-handed compliment. He worried about me."

Six weeks into training at Peru, Johnny was soloing and working on acrobatics. "I got lost," he recalled years later. He looked at his watch and realized he had to get back to the airport—but he couldn't find it. He had no idea where it was. He'd been out a while now and was running low on fuel, so he picked out a farmer's field to land in ("a good landing, too!" he laughs.) Johnny climbed out of the plane and had tucked his parachute under the wheel when the farmer wandered over. "What's the matter, sonny? You lost?" "Yeah," he admitted. It turns out the airport was straight ahead and just a couple of miles away. Pilot Pesky climbed back into the open cockpit, put his goggles back on, gave it full throttle and pulled up from the farm, returning an hour late. The instructor Bill Barwick said he'd seen Johnny's acrobatics and that he'd done his maneuvers pretty well, but then had to ask why he'd come back an hour behind schedule. "You goddamn ballplayers get every break around here," cracked Barwick.

Flying was obviously serious business, with little margin for error. "When I was getting ready to get into formation flying, we had to take a test in navigation work. Christ, I was 150 miles off-course according to my instructor. He said, 'Look, I could pass you, but suppose you got involved in something. Not only you, but you might take somebody with you. 'I'll tell you what, Johnny, you come down here and I'll give you some extra work.'

"That night flying was a bastard. I was going to stay back two more weeks and try to catch up with my class." A base captain named Roy Callahan steered Johnny toward Operations work. "He was a Yankees fan, of all things," recalls Mr. Red Sox. An Operations school in Atlanta needed personnel, so Callahan selected some of his people for that duty.

"There was a guy from Harvard and a guy from M.I.T., a kid from up in Maine and myself, and the captain wanted us to go to this school. As an Operations officer, you get your commission." Callahan called them in one at a time and told Johnny, "I'd like you to go there and get your commission. You'll learn how to operate a field. We go all over the world."

Johnny understood the need: "We were getting so many kids and so many flyers, they had this program where they needed guys to work on air stations. Casualty units, carrier aircraft service units. They put them into areas where they needed someone with a little rank. I said, 'Yeah.' I just wanted to get my commission. I went to this school and I really bore down. I never left the base. I was doing well. I mean, I wasn't in the top of my class, but anyway, I got my commission. That was one of the proudest things I've ever experienced—I made it to the big leagues as a player, and then I got my commission. Just having a high school diploma."

Johnny was assigned to the Naval Air Station at Gordon Field in Atlanta. Ted was sent on to Pensacola for combat flight training. After two years of training, the two finally went their separate ways. When he first arrived, Johnny met Larry Abel, with whom he has kept up a long friendship into the 21st century. Larry was a chief petty officer then and recalls when Johnny first came in from Indiana: "I was in the disbursing office in Bainbridge, Maryland. He came in and he had no money so I got his records and I got him some money, an advance. He never forgot that. When the ballplayers came through, Bobby Doerr and all those guys, he brought them to me. We've kept in touch ever since."

This was still Cadet Paveskovich, though he used the name "Pesky" while playing ball. "It was always 'Pesky' in high school ball, and in semi-pro. My first year in pro ball, I was still legally Paveskovich. My checks were made out 'Pesky' and they were honoring them. Finally, when I was going into the service, I had to use my Christian name. I was being processed in Bainbridge and the kid who was working in the office is looking at all these cadets going through there for transportation and so forth, and he saw my name. He said, 'Former employer. Boston Red Sox. I don't know anybody by this name.' Finally he realized I was 'Pesky' and we became friends. In fact, I stood up for him when he got married. He came from Revere. Carl Pisano was his name."

The Boston Red Sox did keep in touch with their players in the service. Barbara Tyler, Eddie Collins' secretary, coordinated communications. "She used to correspond with all of us during the war. She used to make up a little four-page flyer. About every other month, they'd send us some news. Helen Robinson was knitting socks for guys in the service, whether in the Aleutians or whatever. I was with Williams, of course, and Sain. Dominic, I think once he got in the Navy, he went out in the Pacific, after training in Norfolk in '43. Joe Dobson was stationed down in Georgia and I kind of kept in touch with him. I read the papers every day and kept up with the team. We lost Dominic, myself, Ted. Mickey Harris was gone. Dobson was gone. Mace Brown was with us then. He got a commission. Charlie Wagner was there; I used to see Charlie when he was at Norfolk. In '44, we got kind of spread out and kind of lost contact with one another. Ted went from the Navy to the Marines. The Marines took the top ten percent of the flyers."

Commissioned in May, 1944 in Atlanta, Ensign Paveskovich could

---

After returning home, Johnny found that a few words learned in the Paveskovich household may well have saved the life of a close childhood friend during World War II.

"We only had one black family in the neighborhood. Billy Bell was a great kid. I was confirmed with him. He went to the University of Oregon, and he got in that ROTC program. I saw him a couple of times that winter. He stayed down in Eugene, Oregon, where the university is. So now I don't see him from 1941 and the war comes on and I lose track of him. I don't see him until after the war. I came back from Seattle, where I had just got discharged and I'm walking down the street. I saw a big Lincoln car coming this way and I see it's Billy Bell and he's got his wife with him. Now he's a captain. He's got fruit salad all over his chest. He was going someplace to make an appearance. A great little kid. He's about my size. He had joined the air force. We talked there for a good hour or more. So I said, to him, 'Billy, where'd you get your training?' He said I went here and there, and then I went to a place in Alabama. I said, 'Oh really? We played a couple of exhibition games there before I went off to the service. Did you ever get in town?' He says, 'No, you know how they treated us. The black situation.' He was down there with a lot of crackers.

"He left there and he went to Texas and he was flying P-47s. He went to now move into officer's quarters as he settled into duty as an operations officer. On receiving his commission, he was asked his choice of duty and he selected aircraft carriers so he could continue to be around planes, but baseball intervened. "The exec there, Hatch, was big in New York. Stocks and bonds. Then we had the captain, a four striper. He was a baseball fan. When I got my commission, I thought I'd be assigned somewhere but the captain of the base called me in and he said, 'We want to get a baseball team together.' He had something to do with Washington. They called me in and said, 'Johnny, can we put a team together?' There were about 6 or 7 minor league players there. Some AA players. Bob Kennedy came through from the White Sox, and he fit the bill for us. I was there and going to work every day.

"I was a station officer, a jack of all trades, master of none. You took watches, you were officer of the day. You'd take inventory. I did just about everything on the base. I didn't have to do much teaching, though I taught aircraft recognition. Planes and ships and stuff like that. I'd have maybe 25 or 30 guys in class. I really got a college education out of all that classroom time. You'd flash them up on the screen and they'd have

England. I think he made something like 25 missions. He says, 'Johnny, I'm flying over Germany. I'm covering for the B-26 bombers and I got hit with flak. Not a spot in the air, a beautiful day out. Now my plane's on fire. I've got to eject. In the meantime, I'm drifting over into Yugoslavia.'

"When he was a kid he came into our home, and he learned a few words of the language, you know. My mother used to bake bread every week, especially on the weekends, and Billy would hang around and he'd smell that bread cooking. Billy was always around when my mother made that bread. My mother just loved him. She'd say, 'Bee-ly. Come and have some bread. Let it cool off a little bit.' He'd sit there and he'd eat two or three slices of that warm bread, with butter on it. He'd say, 'Mrs. P, thank you very much.' She'd say, 'OK, Billy, see you next week. Study hard.' He was a great kid.

"So he says, 'Jesus Christ, I got to bail out. So I bail out and I'm coming down. I've got a .45. I land in this field and here come three guys, two with pitchforks and one with a club.' He says, 'Johnny, I could have pulled my .45 and shot them' but finally he said to one of the three, he said, 'Daime yamaku' [Die-me-yamaku] which means, 'Give me an apple.' They looked at one another. Then he says 'Daime kruva' which means 'Give me bread.' Oh, we've got a black Slav! They got him back to the underground. He went back to England, went on a couple more missions and then come home."

to say what the planes were. B-24. C-47. F4U. F6F. F4F. I got to know those things pretty well. Enemy planes, too, the Messerschmitts and Focke-Wulf."

This was certainly serious business. The ability to accurately recognize friend from foe, and to know the capabilities of the craft in question could be a matter of life and death. Although playing baseball on the bases was a way to instill an element of lightheartedness and maintain morale, winning the war was the mission at hand. Johnny's family did not pass through World War II unscathed. His sister Ann lost her husband, Bill Franciskovich, killed at Anzio in 1944 by a sniper.

"I never met Ruthie until after I got my commission. I didn't get involved in anything until I got that commission. Then we met at the Naval Air Station and started dating in September. There were 5, 10 thousand people there but I saw Ruthie on the line where she was working, revving up planes and seeing that they got checked out. There was a bunch of WAVEs down there. She didn't pilot planes but she liked to fly. A lot of times when the guys were being checked out, they'd put the aileron on the plane and scare her half to death."

She was WAVEs Aviation Machinist Mate Hickey when they met in Atlanta. "Johnny was flying with the Navy and had come to the airport to see a friend off," Ruthie recalls. "Talk about being swept off your feet! We hadn't even been introduced when he lifted me bodily and said to everyone, 'This is the girl for me.' My first impression, of course, was that he was just a bit too sure of himself. I didn't hear from him again for some time, then he called me for a date. Actually, I'd forgotten about first impressions and all that, and I went out with him. That was in June."

Pesky implies with a sly grin that Ruth Hickey even chose him over Tyrone Power! Power was stationed on the base at the time; he was a Marine. "Very friendly," notes Johnny, "but they had to put a guard on his door. All the nurses. . . ."

"One day I was coming up the stairs after teaching the recognition class and when you're the instructor, and you stand, everybody stands up at attention and all this crap. I'm coming out of the room and these guys are coming up behind me, and Ruthie's coming up the stairs and spits water all over my uniform. She thought I was a fathead, anyway."

Looking back, Johnny realized, "I wasn't in the position to get married. I never would have gotten married, but when I met Ruthie, I just flipped, that's all. This is the one. She didn't know anything about me, but we kind of hit it off. Talk about perfect wives, I'd have to say she is.

You really don't realize what kind of a girl you have until she's put to the test."

Johnny settled into regular duty as a station officer. Despite having signed up for aircraft carrier duty, the war was going reasonably well and there was a chance Johnny would serve out the war in Atlanta. "I figured, Jesus, I might not have to leave here." So we got married. Seven months after meeting, on January 10th, 1945, they were married in Lynn, Massachusetts. Red Sox coach Tom Daly served as best man. Ruth says, "We spent a 24-hour honeymoon in Boston, stayed with my folks for a week, then went back to Atlanta. Two days later, Johnny was shipped out. "Three weeks later, I was in Pearl Harbor. I was out there three weeks after I got married."

As a high school softball player, Ruth confesses, "I couldn't hit." She clearly was a hit with Johnny, though, and the feeling was mutual. Even though Ensign Pesky did not rank as high as her Aviation Machinist Mate Third Class standing, the difference meant nothing to her

On their first meeting, at Penn Station, Johnny dressed to impress Ruthie's mother, sporting sharp, crisp khakis with carefully pressed lapels. "I thought I was Admiral Nimitz, for Christ's sake. She looked at me and her face must have dropped a foot. She expected to see a 6-foot-4 blue-eyed Polack. She sees me, with the little beady eyes, little sawed-off guy." Ruthie and her mother were walking along, and Johnny was walking with Ruthie's sister behind them when he heard Mrs. Hickey ask Ruth, "You're not going to marry him, are you?" He thought, "Oh, my God." He took her mother over to the officers' club and that didn't impress her either. "I don't know a thing about you," she said. "You're a goddamn foreigner. You're out there with the Indians, out there on the West Coast. That's all I know about you." Johnny told her, "Mrs. Hickey, I'll take care of Ruthie. Don't you worry about it."

"That was 53 years ago and I still love her to death," says Johnny. "She's not a pretentious, high-falutin' gal who demanded everything." And then he adds with a twinkle, "She also kept me in line pretty good." Nearly sixty years later, it's clear that Mrs. Hickey had little cause to worry.

Johnny was able to pass through Portland on the way to Pacific duty. "The proudest day of my father's life was when I came home with my Navy commission. I told him, 'Pop, I'd trade all this gold braid back to Uncle Sam in a minute for my Red Sox uniform.'

"I was stationed at Hawaii for the rest of the war. I was playing baseball but I still had to do my duties. The war was really heating up. They were moving people into the forward areas. Planes were coming in one after the other, an amazing operation. I was on my way to Okinawa, on the billet with maybe 50 other guys. The orders were all written. I was a junior officer. Then they dropped the Bomb and we never did go.

"Ted came to Pearl before the summer was over, on his way to the forward area. He played in a couple of games. There was an All-Star Game, too, the National League against the American League. I had access to transportation, so I'd go with the admiral to where he was stationed. My bars were almost turning silver with age. Ted said, 'Are you a J.G. already?' I said, 'No, it's my goddamned bars. I'm still wearing the same bars they gave me when I was commissioned in Atlanta, in '44.'

"We were lucky—everywhere we went, we played." In Atlanta in '44 Pesky also got a taste of managing. The team Johnny managed was made up of fellow servicemen, many of them college kids. "We had maybe 15 or 16 guys on the team. We didn't play that much, a couple of days a week. We played in Ponce de Leon Park, where the Atlanta Crackers played. Sometimes the captain would let guys from the base come to watch a game. I made out all the batting orders and all that. We didn't have any kind of name at all. We were just a base team." Nineteen years later, though, Johnny was making out lineups as manager of the Boston Red Sox.

"In '45, I played at Pearl Harbor. Bill Dickey was in charge of the baseball program. We played maybe 30, 40 day games because they didn't have lights then—and it was all darkened anyway due to the war. You couldn't get in the place—sailors, Marines, all service people came and many Hawaiian civilians. They had a separate section for admirals. You got excused from your regular duties to be able to play."

Asked how he fared in wartime baseball, Johnny laughed, "I was a star during the war! I played shortstop. They kept track of averages and standings. We had different teams—ship repair, sub base, Naval Air Station John Rogers. It was well organized, and we had a pretty good team."

Johnny also got another taste of managing in Hawaii. When he first arrived, Bill Dickey was in Washington, but as soon as Dickey got back, he called Johnny in and asked him to take on a program in a location where baseball hadn't yet been instituted. "They didn't have a team there. The Seabees built us a ballpark, just some wooden stands and planted grass—not a real ballpark—just somewhere the sailors could sit and watch the game. If you went a couple of hundred yards, you're almost on the airstrip."

Johnny's brother Vince also came to Pearl Harbor. "He had been stationed in Guam; he took care of fatigued pilots and guys like that. The guy in charge of that program was from Bowdoin College and I knew him. I said, "Christ, my brother's in Guam. Get him the hell back here." They had the same program right there in Honolulu. They just wrote up another set of orders for him, instead of rolling his orders over. He came back from Guam and got duty in Pearl Harbor."

After the atomic bombs were dropped on Hiroshima and Nagasaki, the Japanese quickly sued for surrender, a few months after the Allies saw victory in the European theater. The A-bomb saved a lot of Allied lives. "It saved a lot of us. I was billeted for Okinawa when they dropped that. We missed it maybe by 10 days. When they dropped the atom bomb, that kind of stopped everything." Now it became time to shut down the war effort. Many were kept on duty for Occupation and other duties, but the bulk of the servicemen (and women) were slated to be sent home. A system was formulated to determine the order in which service people were mustered out. The number of months you were in the service entitled you to so many points. So did other circumstances. Everybody was scurrying around trying to get points, so they could go home. Johnny was just a quarter of a point from the cutoff point. "It's a good thing I was married because it gave you ten points. If I hadn't had Ruthie, I'd have had to stay there another six months. Ruthie always told me, 'I got you out of the Navy.'

"I came back on a ship to San Francisco. Ruthie got out before I did and went up to Boston. I went up to Seattle to get discharged, then home to Portland and then I came back east to be with her. I had my ensign stripes. If I'd stayed in just a few more days—29 days or something like that—I'd have become a J.G., but I said the hell with that, I want to get out."

7
1946

"It was a great feeling to be back at Fenway for the opener that year. We had all made it back. A lot of people didn't. We were together again. And we were playing baseball."

—Johnny Pesky, *Boston Herald* April 14, 1986

The war was over and life was slowly returning to normal, though many things would never be the same again. Johnny describes the time:

"We were glad to be back—I was glad to see Ted, Bobby, Dominic. I hadn't seen Ted for almost a year. Dominic, I hadn't seen for close to two. Dave Ferriss, I didn't know anything about him. I'd been reading about him in the papers. Bobby, of course. I'd played at different places I was stationed, but it was different coming back. I was still young and stayed in pretty good shape.

"Eddie Lake played shortstop during the war. They traded him to Detroit for Rudy York. We had about 3 or 4 third basemen. That spring, Rudy York didn't get a hit all that spring! Everybody was starting to worry about him—he couldn't see or . . . he had a little age on him. I think he was the oldest guy on the ball club, 37 or 38. That was considered old in those years. We left camp and I'll never forget this. In Montgomery, Alabama, in the 3rd or 4th inning, he hit a home run. I

74

mean, he hit it a ton. You could sense the thing turning around, and he hit 30 home runs that year. Two grand slams in one game, in St. Louis. He used to laugh at me, he'd say, 'You don't use a bat. You use a tennis racket!'

"Pellagrini was the other shortstop. Pelly always had something wrong with him physically, and Cronin kept me. Pelly, to this day, thought he was the better player. We did a lot of things together when we were with the club in '46 and '47. We went to every Holy Name, bar mitzvah, you name it. We had a great time together. We didn't make much money but we got a lot of rosary beads and prayer books. We always ate well. In those days, for a buck or a buck and a half you'd have 2 or 3 players for a sports night. It was a lot of fun. We had morning breakfasts with the Catholics. The Jews had their thing and we'd go to that.

"I remember one time right after the war. We were all back and G.E. was having a promotion in Fenway and they wanted to honor a player. We had just moved into our house in Lynn. They presented me with a stove, a washing machine and a refrigerator. Jack Riley was the athletic director at West Point. I was in the Navy with him. He said, 'What are you going to say?' 'Christ, Jackie, I have no idea.' So he gave me this line: 'I'm going to be like Marc Antony when he went to Cleopatra's room. I didn't come here to talk.' And I said it! There might have been twenty five thousand people in the stands. Everybody laughed. When you're in some place like that, no one wants to hear a long speech.

"You know, you get acknowledgements from people and they try to portray you as a stud. Well, I was never a stud. I often said when I got up to accept something, 'I wish I could have been a better player.'

"I was very fortunate when I ran into Dick O'Connell in Pearl Harbor. He was in Naval Intelligence, on Nimitz's staff. Eddie Doherty was our PR guy and Joe Comiskey was one of the treasurers of the ball club. Ted, me, Ed and Joe, we all went out to eat one night along with O'Connell. We'd played a game at Barber's Point, which is an area of Honolulu and then we went back early because of the curfew. We got talking. I can still see O'Connell; he never opened his mouth. He was one of the most quiet guys I ever saw. I got to know him when we come back.

"He knew Ed Doherty, so he went to Fenway and there he meets Eddie Collins. They wanted to put a team down here in Lynn, so that's where he started.

"He knew how to operate. He goes into Fenway and he set up a whole new thing for tickets. He improved the ballpark in a lot of areas.

He always had the knack of picking the guy for the job. O'Connell handled things very well. They claimed that when he wanted you to know something, he'd talk with clarity. When he wanted to keep something to himself, he'd mumble. Clif Keane, the old writer, gave him the name 'Mumbles.' Say there's a possibility of a trade to help the ball club. The writers would be after him. The difference between O'Connell and Gorman was that Gorman would go on and on, but a lot of times he wouldn't tell you much! O'Connell handled himself as well as anybody I've ever been around."

There was no doubt that Johnny was the man at short, a solid regular on the team despite having played just one year before missing the next three to the war. A few weeks into spring training, one newspaper report termed Pesky one of the "irreplaceables" along with Williams, Doerr, DiMaggio, York and Wagner. Gene Mack's March 2 cartoon showed Pesky and Doerr solidly fielding both sides of the second base bag, which showed a "No Vacancy" sign posted to ward off other infield candidates. Doerr averred, "Pesky is even better than he was in 1942. He is a little more sure on every play." Cronin said he'd noticed it as well, and attributed it to Johnny's self-confidence thanks to having a full year of major league play—even stardom—under his belt.

A few days later, the team traveled by charter to Havana, Cuba for an exhibition series against the Washington Senators. Johnny tripled in the 9th and drove in two runs. Havana was where Bernardo Pasquel of the Mexican League offered Williams huge money—reportedly half a million dollars—to jump from the American League to his Mexican League in an effort to kick-start the new circuit. Pasquel also courted Johnny Pesky, who was offered a vacation trip to Mexico. He declined. A *Globe* headline said that Pesky had been offered $10,000 cash down against $45,000 per year for three years. Although a written offer, whether it was really $45,000 for three years or $15,000 a year totaling $45,000 seemed unclear even to Johnny, but he "was convinced by Bernardo's charming lady interpreter that Bernardo meant $45,000 a year." Healthy skepticism reigned, and the "fast-talking agent" whose approach Williams described as "bush" did not prevail.

Johnny recalled another approach made to him in New York. "I was rooming with Bobby Doerr at the Commodore Hotel in New York and there was this guy standing outside our door. I didn't know who he was. He dressed well, though; you knew he was a Latin. I don't know whether he wanted to talk to Bobby, but he wanted to talk to me. He offered me

$50,000. I didn't know anything about the Mexican League. I said, 'Well, I've already signed a contract, Mr. Pasquel.' He said, 'Oh, you can break that.' Stephens, he held out with the Browns that year, and he got some money to go to Mexico. He was there about a month and he didn't like it. I was thinking, though, how the ball club [the Red Sox] had taken care of me and my family."

Neither Pesky nor Williams took the bait and the 1946 season was to be a remarkable ride. By March 12, reporters began to express hints of real optimism about the team's prospects. A subhead in the March 12 *Globe* read, "Sox Have Flag Chance."

Reflecting New England caution rooted in experience, Harold Kaese wrote, "The Red Sox, who have won as many pennants in spring training as the Yankees have won in the regular season, have again persuaded on-the-scene critics to pick them as coming champions. We Boston critics certainly rate as the most hopeful, if not the most gullible, in the world." Later, on the eve of the opener, Kaese picked the Sox to finish 3rd (behind New York and Detroit). Gerry Moore wrote that they

"So I got back and in '46 we had a good year. The club contacted me, sent me a contract. Collins was very nice. He treated us exceptionally well. I was looking for fifteen grand. Their offer was twelve. I said, 'Gee, Mr. Collins. I got married.' He was a nice guy. If he'd have said twelve, I'd take it, but I was trying to get some more money. I didn't even have any clothes, for Christ's sake! And I'd gotten married. So he says, 'Well, I'll make a deal with you. I've give you 500 dollars for every 50,000 we draw over 800,000.' We had that great start. We were winning. The park was filled every day and I'm having a hell of a year. So about July, we're nearing the million mark. I ran into Barbara Tyler going into the park one day and she said, 'Hi, Johnny.' I said, 'Doing fine. Keeping up. We got to win this thing.' There was nobody around and so I mentioned the thing about the contract. I told her, 'If I'd been smart, I'd have let that thing run.' I thought the escalations would stop when it hit fifteen grand. I didn't hear anything, but evidently she told Collins. So she says, 'Pesky was asking about his contract, Mr. Collins.' We've got a fifteen game lead in August and Collins calls me up. The first time I'd been in his office, except when I came back from the Navy. He says, 'I understand you've been inquiring about your bonus.' I said, 'Yeah.' In my own mind, I thought maybe I was making too much of this, so I didn't say much. I just said, 'I just want to thank you, Mr. Collins.' He said, 'We'll let it go on.' I made over nine grand extra."

weren't as good as they looked on paper. The team seemed not to be truly settled at first base, third base or in right. Williams didn't hit his first spring training home run until the pre-season was almost over, on April 4.

Johnny had matured, clearly. A story late in spring training even reported "Pesky Tips Pitchers on Holding Base Runners." During drills, Hy Hurwitz noted the "alertness of shortstop Johnny Pesky. He knew just what mistakes the Sox pitchers were making when they were working at holding runners on the paths." This was perhaps the first printed recognition of Pesky's managerial potential.

The team opened the season in Washington. Ted got his first homer in the 3rd inning and Johnny went 1 for 4 (a double), knocking in the 4th and 5th runs of a Sox 6-3 win. In game two of the season, Johnny went 3 for 4 and in the third game he was 3 for 5 with a double, and he was off! "I got off to a good start in 1946, from the get-go. I often thought, if I could stay aboveboard the first month, I'd be in good shape. I always felt that I did better in June, July & August."

In the April 20th home opener, Johnny recorded the first run in the Red Sox 2-1 victory over the Athletics, scoring from second on an infield force play. "I was on second base and somebody hit a ground ball and the As forgot about me—and I went all the way home and slid under Buddy Rosar to score. I went right between his legs. It was a gamble and it paid off." Johnny won the game in the 8th with a homer off Dick Fowler. There were only two hits in the game, both by Pesky, who scored both runs. "Pesky Steals Show" screamed a banner headline on the jump in the sports section. "Little Johnny Pesky, smallest member of the Red Sox, emerged as the biggest giant of all the gigantic persons and proceedings that attended the victorious home opening of the Sox at frosty Fenway Park yesterday."

What Johnny remembers most about the game was a defensive gem. "The A's had filled the bases with one out. George Kell hit the ball near second base. We kind of bunched him up the middle. Bobby Doerr went over to field the ball and it took a bad hop and hit him on the shoulder and came over to me. I reached over and grabbed it with my bare hand. It was laying up there like an ice cream cone. I stepped on the bag and threw it over to first. Double play. I beat the guy by about a step. Game over. He got an assist, and I got an assist and a putout."

Johnny's home run was right down the line in right, maybe 10 feet to the left of the foul pole and three rows deep. There was a wind blowing, but the ball stayed fair. This was his second Fenway four-base hit; the one he had hit back in 1942 was recalled as "almost identical." Reminiscing about the home run nearly 40 years later, Johnny cracked, "I thought I'd hit 60 home runs that year and I hit two." (1)

On the 22nd, Pesky was beaned in the 5th inning by Sid Hudson, the fastball striking him on the back right side of the head. Johnny never lost consciousness, but as a precaution was carried from the field on a stretcher. Clubhouse man Vince Orlando recalled years later, "They loaded Johnny onto a stretcher and as they carried him off the field, I stood there crying like a baby." The Red Sox were down 4-2, but then Eddie Pellagrini filled in for Johnny and promptly hit a home run over Fenway's left field Wall—in his first at-bat in the major leagues—winning the game for the Sox, who had meanwhile come from behind to even the score. Pesky quipped regarding Hudson, "He ain't fast. At least not as fast as he was in '42, if that was his fastball." Hudson was one of the first into the Boston dressing room after the game and he walked with Johnny and Ruth to the car in which team doctor McCarthy drove the Peskys home. X-rays proved negative. Johnny congratulated Pelly and suggested, "Maybe I had better stay out of the lineup."

"Funny. I saw Hudson's pitch coming and I knew he was going to get me. I turned and took it on the back of the head. Now, that Red Jones, the umpire, is a great guy. When I got skulled, he took me aside and said, 'Tell me, what's my name? Who am I?' I said, 'Look, Red, I ain't dopey or daffy. I know only too well who you are.' So Jones laughed and said, 'You aren't hurt, not a bit, but mind your language.'

John Alevizos, who in the 1970s became a Sox VP and oversaw off-season sales work that Johnny did, was there as a fan that day. "Oh, it was horrible!" he cringes, over fifty years later. "To me, the sound, the crack of his head, I could swear he was killed."

Pesky continues, "That was the second time I'd been beaned. The only other time I got hit was in the minor leagues. Ken Burkhart, who was a 21-game winner in the Piedmont League, hit me—in a playoff game. Rocky Mount, in the bottom of the ninth inning on a Sunday afternoon. Two outs, nobody on and he got me two strikes. He's going to brush me back and I just turned my head and, boy, down I go. I started to get up to go to first base, but my manager said, "No, go on in the clubhouse." I had an ice bag on my head. That one stung. There was a big first baseman hitting behind me—a kid named Herm Scheffler from Oklahoma, about 6'4" or 5"—he hit the second pitch out of the ballpark. We win 2-1.

"I always thought I could get out of the way of a pitched ball. You've got to turn *this* way, towards the catcher, being a left-hander. Now if Conigliaro had turned *this* way [demonstrates right-handed batter turning his head away from the ball toward the catcher], he probably never would have gotten hit in his eye. We never had helmets. Christ, if we had helmets, I'd be sticking my head right over the plate—'Well, go ahead and hit me so I can get on base!' A lot of times I used to get hit intentionally. To get Ted up there. My uniform—Christ, I used to wear it out like *that*!" Johnny demonstrated how he would wear his jersey very loosely, pooched out in front in hopes that the ball would strike his jersey and he'd get himself a free pass to first base.

"To win, you'd like to get a base hit but you've got to get that good hitter up there. I used to get hit in the ass by pitches. A lot of times the guys didn't throw very hard, I just turned [into the pitch and took one]. You've got to get right up on top of the plate and you've got to turn. You can't hit that ball, but if it grazes you. . . . I remember one time in Cleveland. Bill Summers was the umpire. This guy looked like he was just tossing the ball. I took the base. The catcher said, 'He didn't even get out of the way, Bill.' Now Williams is up, and I eventually scored. That bat was laying there and I picked it up. Summers asked, 'Johnny, didn't pull a fast one on old Will, did you?' 'No, I tried to get out of the way, Bill.' He kind of laughed. But we were ahead 4 or 5 runs, so it didn't make any difference.

"One day I was shaving at home in my shorts and I had four or five black-and-blue spots on my leg. My wife saw these spots and asked what they were. 'That's where I got hit by the ball,' I explained. 'Can't you get out of the way?' she asked.

"They weren't going to throw at a Punch and Judy hitter like me—not when you've got Williams and Stephens and Doerr coming up . . . They're the guys that can hit the ball 400 feet. I could hit it 320, 340 at best. We had to get on base. That was our job. Dominic and I did it pretty well for a number of years. At one time, they started pitching out a little bit. They thought they had our hit and run. So I said to Dom, 'Pick a pitch. I'll protect you.' I could handle that bat. Unless it's a pitchout or something—but even if it's a pitchout, you could throw the bat at that ball. A lot of times, I could foul that ball off. We could manufacture a run. You always wanted to get to Williams or Stephens or Doerr, because those were the guys who could do the damage."

Johnny was back in the lineup on the 24th, and went 1 for 4 as Pelly moved to third base. The following day, the two teamed up big-time and earned the headline, "Pellagrini, Pesky Lead Sox to 12-5 Win Over Yanks

Before 32,867." Pelly had (in order) a triple, a double and a home run, but his bid for the cycle failed with him striking out and hitting into a double play his last two times up. Pesky hit two doubles, two singles, scored twice and had two RBI. The beaning hadn't made him gun shy and, once more, Pesky showed off his baserunning skills. He'd doubled, Ted walked and they both moved up on a passed ball. Doerr sent a liner to King Kong Keller in left. "Pesky started up the line with the crack of the bat, but hastily back-pedaled," wrote Gerry Moore. "He completely tricked Keller into thinking he wasn't going to try to score. King Kong was still fondling the ball when Pesky suddenly streaked for the plate, which he reached standing up before the startled Keller's belated peg."

What the papers described as a severe groin strain threatened to side-line him for a while—Johnny says bluntly that he'd hurt his balls—but Bob Feller was due to go for Cleveland and Pesky had never faced Feller. Rapid Robert had already led the league for four straight years in strike-outs, but had enlisted immediately after Pearl Harbor Day and Johnny never faced him in 1942. Feller had no-hit the Yankees just a few days before. Cronin suggested to Johnny, "Better sit this one out." "Gee, Joe, I've never batted off Feller," Johnny pleaded. Given the nod, and despite the injury, he smacked out a single in the first and followed with three straight singles, a 4 for 4 day.

The Red Sox got off to one of the best starts in history. By May 7, they had compiled an 18-3 record. It was a team that played as one. Pesky was at the plate with the Red Sox down 6-4 and two on. Pitcher Jack Kramer seemed to be taking a long time. "My eyes seemed like burnt holes up there waiting for Kramer," Pesky said, and so he stepped out. "I instinctively walked over to [Williams]—and he must have seen my expression for he laughed—and at once brought me out of it. The count was two and two—and I didn't know what to expect . . . and you know how The Kid can gauge a pitch or a pitcher. He loosened me up. Ted told me what to expect and I got the ball I wanted, a fast one and gave it a fair ride." Judnich caught it, but here was Pesky, hitting .407 at the time, still relying on Williams. Ted put his arm around Johnny with a "father-like gesture" and got him laughing it off, which Jack Barry said "places Williams deeper in fan affection than ever."

Pesky was on fire at the plate, coming off a string of 9 straight hits. On the 6th, he received a huge ovation when he came up in the 5th looking for his 10th consecutive hit. On the first pitch, he drove the ball back through the box. Up again the following inning, he swung at the first pitch and again hit it safely up the middle. Johnny Pesky was now just the third batter in history to have made 11 straight hits. If he got a hit his next time up, he'd be tied for the record, 12. In the 8th inning, the Red Sox were up 6-3 and George Metkovich was on first. Johnny gave the sign for a hit-and-run and grounded out to Stephens—Metkovich reached second safely, but Johnny was out by a stride. The paper the next day scored it a sacrifice—and also reported that Johnny really had no idea he was working on a record and that, indeed, it was he who signaled the hit-and-run play. Of the 11 times Johnny had reached base safely, seven of those times he scored. Despite being up in the game by 3 runs, Pesky wasn't taking anything for granted and was just playing ball the only way he knew how—as a team sport, trying to move the baserunner into scoring position.

A variation of the at-bat is provided by writer Al Hirshberg. He says that it was Cronin who called for the sacrifice, with Williams coming up next. Johnny did his part without a word of protest and moved the runner along. Later, Cronin was upset and said, "I'd never have given him the bunt sign if I had realized. . . . The little guy didn't even peep." Perhaps neither Cronin nor Pesky realized the moment.

The next day, Johnny went 1 for 7. Then on May 8th, he bounced back and tied a major league record, scoring six runs in one game. Johnny broke the American League record of five which Foxx and Gehrig and a few others held; he tied Mel Ott's six, the N.L. (and major league) record. Johnny was 4 for 5, with a double and two RBI, and helped the Red Sox beat Chicago 14-10. The last of the six runs scored with about one second to spare; he had barely crossed home plate when Doerr was cut down trying to stretch a single into a double, ending the inning. Johnny was hitting .429 by game's end and had already scored 30 runs just a month into the season. In the first inning of the following game, he scored yet again.

The Sox were at this point nearing the end of a 15 game winning streak, during which time they had scored more than double the number of runs of their opponents. Boston had a 21-3 record before finally suffering the fourth loss of the season on May 11. Despite that spectacular start they were just 4 1/2 games ahead of the second place Yankees. By happenstance, in the midst of the road trip, the Red Sox and Yankees flights passed each other in mid-air. Boston was flying from Chicago to St. Louis and New York was traveling the same route the other direction. It was a little bumpy, and few of the players were really used to what was still a novelty—air travel. Rudy York joked, "If my cows could see me now!" York was briefed by Marine aviator Williams on the TWA

Stratoliner's maneuverability, speed and power, "as Johnny Pesky kicked in with his two cents' worth time and again." As the two airplanes passed in mid-air, they each flashed lights. Dom DiMaggio quipped, "They're higher than us, but only in the air."

Safely on the ground, the Sox kept talking hitting. Williams told Pesky, "I think you've been a little too close up there lately, Johnny. Why don't you back a bit away from the plate and get the fat of your bat on those pitches." "OK, Master," Pesky replied. "You're my doctor when it comes to hitting." The next day, Johnny went 3 for 5 with two doubles. Ted hit a grand slam out of the park in right center, across Grand Avenue and into a house on the other side. The Red Sox showed some patience at the plate, accepting 15 walks and winning 18-8. Five days later, Ted hit another house, this time in Cleveland. Two Pete Center fastballs came in close to Ted's head; angry, he stepped in even closer to the plate and banged one off the roof of a house in back of the high fence in right center.

Johnny was hitting well, so well that during a visit to Comiskey Park in early June, a photographer asked him to pose for one of those stock shots of kissing a bat. Joe Cronin called over, "Save that kiss for the end of the season, kid. It's a long way to go." Johnny reportedly took his manager's advice.

On June 11, the Red Sox record was 41-9, an .820 winning percentage. They still had not lost their tenth game of the season. The next day, they did—closing out a 12 game win streak. Pesky was in the midst of a rare 0 for 17 slump, his average dropping to .316. Most players would be happy to snap an unprecedented slump and find themselves batting over .300.

Most of the Sox losses were under the lights, and Pesky was hitting just .143 in night games. On June 16, the Red Sox lost the first series of the year, dropping two out of three to the White Sox, as "lethargy" and "roaditis" struck and the Sox dropped under the .750 mark. Then the Browns (!) swept the Sox, who went 24 innings without scoring. Johnny's average fell to an even .300, then sank further to .291. Hy Hurwitz says that Johnny credited Mrs. Yawkey with bringing him out of the dumps, in a novel fashion. "He broke out in St. Louis, where Mrs. Yawkey expectorated (spit is a horrid word for a lady) on his bat each time he came up. What a fan she has become." "We all had superstitions in those years," says Pesky. "Coming off the field, you would step on the bag—or miss the bag, whichever one . . . I always tried to hit the bag with my left foot."

"When you're on the bases, you don't worry about which foot to use. If you're going to make the turn at first base, you'd try to have your right foot hit the bag. They say your angle is better. I just tried to get there as fast as I could. I had pretty good speed for 6 or 7 or 8 years, and then it caught up with me and I started getting leg pulls. Ted used to tell me that I hit a ball through the infield as hard as he did—which is a lie! I said, 'You're crazy! How can I hit a ball as hard as you? What are you talking about?' 'Well, you do.' My hands had a little snap in them. A lot of guys my size would just try to get the bat on the ball, but you had to have a little force going with it. I could pull a ball when I had to."

"Williams," Hurwitz contributed, "says that he'll be mad if he's beaten out of the league batting championship this year unless it's his little playmate Pesky who does it."

The recent slide aside, this was as strong a Red Sox team as there ever was, and it was reflected in the 1946 selections for the All-Star Game which—coincidentally—was hosted at Fenway Park. Eight Red Sox players were chosen for the team. Williams and Dom DiMaggio were starters in the outfield. Pesky and Doerr started in the infield, and York was also chosen for the team, as were Tex Hughson, Dave Ferriss and catcher Hal Wagner. Ted, as is well known, went 4 for 4, with 2 HR, 5 RBI and 10 total bases. Johnny went 0 for 2 and made an error, but fortunately Ted's accomplishments overshadowed Johnny's shortcomings that day. At the All-Star break, the team was 54-23, and they'd extended their lead to 7½ games ahead of New York. Johnny was hitting .302, with 98 hits, 20 of which were doubles.

Soon afterwards, on July 26 and 27, Johnny broke out of his doldrums with a vengeance, going 4 for 6 and then 3 for 5. The latter finally propelled Pesky back into the league lead for hits. With a 10 game hitting streak, he'd driven his average back up to .320. The morning of the 26th, the *Globe* had run a story on Ruth Pesky headlined "Ruth Didn't Know Beans About Baseball When Johnny Pesky Popped the Question." She'd missed only one home game all year, and sat in Box 23, always with a score sheet in her lap. "I didn't know beans about baseball two years ago, and Johnny Pesky was just a nice kid who asked me for a date. We were both stationed in Atlanta, Georgia, and I'd never seen a professional baseball game. Football was what I liked." A fellow WAVE, visiting the Peskys, chimed in, "When Johnny gave her his baseball cap that he used to wear, she didn't even know what it was." "Everybody tried to borrow or steal that cap," Ruth admitted, "and all I know was that it worked out fine to keep my hair back when I was oiling planes."

On August 8, Johnny blasted a 2-run seventh inning homer over the right field fence off returned Canadian P.O.W. Phil Marchildon, giving the Red Sox a 4-1 lead. Pesky almost personally engineered the first win in the day's twin bill. He tripled in the first on a drive into the wind that reached the visitors' bullpen. Scooting around the bases, he made it all the way home as the relay from the A's second baseman sailed into his team's dugout. All told, Johnny was on base 8 times on 8/8, with the home run, the triple, three singles, two walks and one time having reached on an error. Ted Williams was writing a column for the *Globe* at that time and he noted Johnny's home run: "It isn't often that I have a chance to shake Pesky's hand at home plate, but it's always a great pleasure just to see Johnny carrying that great big grin from third base." The home run was "about three feet inside the foul pole. It lodged seven rows deep."

The Red Sox were doing so well that in mid-August, the team announced their World Series ticket policy—a limit of two tickets per game for each fan. Johnny Pesky's average had climbed, and in the papers on August 29, his three hits from the day before were noted, bringing him up to .3417, just a whisker behind Mickey Vernon's league-leading .3418—about as close to a tie as one could get. Williams was in third place. "Little Johnny Base Hit"—as he was occasionally called, in a reference to a popular song of the day, was described as "the greatest hustler on a hustling ball club. He's always looking to give credit to somebody else for winning a game. All he wants is to win. When he has a good day, 'Little Johnny Base Hit' will simply say, 'I was lucky. The balls dropped safely.'"

August was a spectacular time for Johnny—he hit safely 53 times in that month alone, an amazing total in the heat of summer. Many regular players would be happy to get double that for an entire season and Johnny shares the Red Sox record with Dom DiMaggio, who matched the total a few years later. The major league mark—an incredible 68—was set by Ty Cobb in July 1912, but little Johnny Pesky was in select company.

The Red Sox were 96-40, .706, now 16½ games ahead of the Yankees. Williams (115), Doerr (113) and York (110) were 1-2-3 in RBI. Ted's 34 homers led the pack. By September 8, the team was in a position to clinch, but then lost several straight during a grueling schedule chock full of night games. "I was scarcely able to walk out on the field when we got here Saturday," Johnny remarked. On the 11th, the team lost its fifth straight, the worst stretch of the year, despite Ted going 4 for 4 and passing (for batting average) Johnny who was horse-collared 0 for 3. In all, the Sox lost 7 straight.

A story surfaced on September 12 that Williams had been paid $10,000 *not* to play in any exhibition games after the season. Bob Feller, who was often active in organizing such tours, had offered Williams that sum for his participation and Tom Yawkey matched it, asking Ted not to play. Feller said that, without Ted, he'd not invite any Red Sox to be part of his touring "All-Star" squad, even though the Red Sox had placed 8 players on the real All-Star team. Johnny Pesky was among those mentioned by name as being upset.

On the 13th, the Red Sox clinched the pennant on a first inning Williams inside-the-park home run to left field (!) versus Cleveland. All season, Cleveland's Lou Boudreau had plagued the dead pull-hitter with the radical shift of three infielders to the right side of the infield. The "Williams shift" or "Boudreau shift" has been well documented elsewhere; it is ironic that it was against the Indians that Ted struck the pennant-winning drive in the 1-0 victory.

Johnny remembers the year and the pennant-clincher vividly:

"That year. Everything Cronin did was right. He brought a guy in; he got everybody out. Need a pinch hitter; got a base hit. It was utterly amazing. We should have had the pennant won by the first of September. We really needed one game early in September to cinch. It took us a week to win that one. I'll never forget that. League Park. Williams hit a line drive and Pat Seery's the left fielder. Of course, Williams being a pull hitter, the fielders were way over. Seery tried to make a shoestring catch and the ball rolled away. Ted had to slide across home plate. 1-0. That was the clincher. We got two hits that day off the pitcher, a skinny right-hander named Red Embree. I got the other hit when he hung a curve ball."

The party was a good one, and those present partook of some well-traveled and well-aged champagne. The Red Sox could have clinched as early as September 8 and Yawkey had flown the champagne to Washington for the possible victory party. The Sox lost, though, and the bottles were sent on along to travel with the team to Philadelphia, where they dropped two more games. Packed up yet again, the champagne bottles moved on to Detroit and the Red Sox lost both games there as well. Riding the rails once more, those bottles were shipped on to Cleveland and Feller beat the Sox there. Finally, Ted had to scrape out that freak inside-the-park job to lock up the flag and finally pop the corks.

On the 15th, Johnny reached his second straight 200th hit season, but Cronin was well aware that he was much more than a table-setter. "Johnny is our little sparkplug out there," he said. "He's always hustling.

He and Bobby are responsible for much of our success with that great double-play work."

Saturday, September 28 was Johnny Pesky Day at Fenway Park, an event organized by a group of friends from Lynn. The brief notice in the *Globe* predicted that he would receive an "electrical appliance shower" and indicated "there are a million housewives who'll be envying Mrs. Pesky tonight." Ted Williams' newspaper column the morning after, was entitled "Johnny Pesky Is Real Live Wire, Electrical Gifts of Fans Appropriate." Ted praised his teammate lavishly:

"I thought the people of Lynn made a most appropriate selection in their gifts to Johnny Pesky at Fenway Park yesterday afternoon. They gave Johnny a house full of electrical equipment. Well, Johnny has been electrical for our club all year long. He has supplied the juice which carried us to the pennant. He has been the sparkplug of the Red Sox and has played as great a game at shortstop as anybody I've ever seen.

"Pesky has made some of the best plays of the year. He has caught

---

The Puck Stops Here

Once again, in the off-season, hockey cropped up and once again, Joe Cronin had to caution Johnny. Bruins hockey great Milt Schmidt reminisces about Johnny on the ice:

"Johnny used to work out with us down at the Arena. Both the Boston Arena and the Boston Garden. I went in the service in '42. I have a picture of he and myself in the Bruins uniform. It had to be somewhere in 1946 or so. We got to be very close friends through another friend of mine who was a friend of John's. A fellow by the name of Dick Broadbent. John came and worked out with us quite a few times.

"He took his turn just the same as everybody else did. His shooting workout. He'd skate up and down and take shots on the net. He'd also take part in our line rushes. We always had one line that would be missing a man, so he'd take his turn there. He scrimmaged a few times with us.

"It was unusual, but he was such a close friend of ours and such a close friend of the bosses, they said, 'Hey, let him go'—until Joe Cronin found out about it. Then he put a stop to it.

"John could hold his own. He was a decent skater who didn't look out of place even though he wasn't in the condition to skate. I'm not in a position to say he could have made it, but you never know. You could tell that the guy was an athlete. He took to the ice quite easily."

balls back of third base and out in my stamping grounds in left field. He has caught balls in short right field and at first base. All year long, I've been expecting him to catch a pop fly at home plate. That's the only place on the field he hasn't invaded.

"Besides Johnny's brilliant fielding, he has been terrific at the plate. He is a little magician with the bat. He can spray the ball to all parts of the field. He has a great eye, and is just as fast as anybody in the league getting down to first base. He leads the league in base hits and has the distinction of knocking out 200 or more hits in both of his first two years in the major leagues.

"I doubt if there is a better hustler in baseball than Johnny. All year long, he has picked up extra bases with his daring running. He has helped us win games by going all the way home from second on infield hits. He has only hit two home runs this year but I think each one of them won a game for us."

The Red Sox were so far out ahead of everyone else that they basically killed time while they waited for the Series. The Cardinals and the Dodgers had to undertake a "best of three" playoff series. On the first day of October, Ted was hit in the elbow by a Mickey Haefner pitch during the fifth inning of a meaningless game. It was front-page news in Boston, where they reported "while there were no bone chips of fractures, there is little question that Ted will be at a disadvantage in the coming series. It isn't likely that he will regain normal use of this elbow for about ten days."

Though Williams never really used the injury to excuse his shortcomings in the Series, the papers had actually predicted it. On the 3rd, it was noted that he was unable to complete the swing of a bat, on the 4th, that he was "at a handicap" and would be "sub-par."

Johnny summarized the 1946 season: "Baseball in those years was so much fun. We didn't worry about the money. It was a great feeling to win the pennant. I thought it was the start of something good. It was sad the next year. All those pitchers having sore arms."

Just as in 1942, *The Sporting News* named Johnny shortstop on its All Star Major League team, leaving fans to opine about what the three intervening war years would have wrought.

NOTES

(1) *Boston Herald*, April 8, 1985

8

Johnny Pesky & the 1946 World Series

"Pesky held the ball!" It has become one of the mantras of defeatism that Red Sox fans are fed with their mother's milk. This one innocuous fielding play has followed Johnny Pesky for over fifty years. It has not haunted him, but it has shadowed him. If it had happened in a regular season game, it would be long forgotten, but the Fall Classic magnifies every hit, every catch, every mental lapse.

It was the bottom of the eighth inning in the seventh game of the '46 World Series with the St. Louis Cardinals. The accepted wisdom is that, on a ball hit to left-center, Johnny held the relay a moment or two longer than he should have before firing to the plate, allowing Enos Slaughter to score the tie-breaking, and ultimately winning, run. It was the precursor of the ball which skittered past Bill Buckner's legs in the 1986 World Series, a ball which, had he fielded it routinely, would have been the final out in a Red Sox World Championship. Whereas millions of viewers witnessed Buckner's gaffe on television, only those at Sportsman's Park in St. Louis and those who watched newsreels in theaters—or who have studied the film since—saw Pesky's. There are real questions as to whether Pesky held the ball and questions as to whether it would have mattered even if he did. Circumstances conspired to pin the horns on his head and Johnny Pesky has gone down in history as the goat of the 1946 World Series.

Was that designation merited? It may have been self-effacing Johnny Pesky who perpetuated it.

It was an exciting Series. Boston won the first game 3-2 in 10 innings on Rudy York's home run. It must be said that Johnny was not at his defensive best in this, his only World Series as a player. Over the seven games, he committed four errors—the same number as the entire Cardinals team. Johnny's first error came in Game One, when he kicked tenth inning leadoff hitter Red Schoendienst's ball into left. Clif Keane reported that Johnny was "jittery the eve of the game [and] scared stiff through all ten innings." In fact, the "jittery" label was used to describe a number of Red Sox players—Tom McBride, Dom DiMaggio and Bobby Doerr among them.

Johnny went 0-for-5 at the plate, and followed that with an 0-for-4 the following day. He was glad that Game Three was in Boston and in the first inning singled sharply down the third base line, the ball caroming off the seats to Walker in left. Ted was walked intentionally and Rudy York hit a three-run homer, all that was needed to win the game and put the Red Sox up two games to one. Johnny went 2-for-4 and the sports page cartoon simply noted, "Johnny's himself again." Ted Williams noted in his daily column for the *Globe* that "our leading table-setter" had scored the first run and in effect gotten the team back on track. Johnny was relieved when he made that first hit, reportedly a little perturbed by the well-intentioned pleas of a few too many people to "snap out of the jitters." He allowed, "I was nervous, but it didn't help me too much to have people telling me about it all the time."

In Game Four, he went 0-for-5 again and threw the ball into the Red Sox dugout when the Sox had Harry Walker picked off first. A run scored but Boston lost 12-3, so the gaffe didn't attract much attention. Despite the 0-5 collar, Johnny made good contact, but as Williams wrote, "Little Johnny Pesky hit in some tough luck. Every time he'd crack out a line drive it was straight at somebody."

Game Five saw Pesky commit two more errors, but also hit 3-for-5 with three singles. "Ablaze at bat . . . befuddled afield," wrote the *Globe*. Boston won, though, and was now up three games to two. But the Red Sox were not handling the pressure well at all. "Who would have guessed," writer Jerry Nason asked, "that Johnny P., the quick and agile, and often astounding fielder of the Summer months, would stagger and

stumble at shortstop for four of the Sox's 10 errors?" He noted that
Johnny had only completed two full years of major league ball, with a
three-year gap in between them. Ted Williams was also struggling,
contributing just one RBI while stranding seven. In 18 official times at
bat, he'd only gotten the ball out of the infield four times. One of his few
hits was a bunt.

St. Louis tied the Series in Game Six, with Johnny's first inning single his only hit of the game.

It was Game Seven, though, which broke Boston hearts and resulted
in lifelong goat horns for Johnny Pesky. Boston had scored once in the
top of the first, but St. Louis came back with one in the second and
added two more in the fifth. Dramatically, the Red Sox tied the game in
the top of the eighth when Dom DiMaggio doubled off the right centerfield screen, driving in two pinch-hitters who'd preceded him. DiMaggio
knew his hit had tied the game but injured himself trying to extend the
double into a triple. "I knew if I could get to third base they'd have to be
very careful how they pitched to Ted, because I'd be ready to score from
third on even a passed ball. I tried to dig for a little more speed and I
pulled a hamstring heading into second base." Leon Culberson came into
the game to replace Dominic. The Red Sox failed to score again and faced
the Cardinals in the bottom of the eighth with their second-string centerfielder in the outfield.

Slaughter singled before reliever Bob Klinger retired the next two batters on a botched sacrifice bunt and then a fly to Williams in left.
Slaughter decided to get aggressive on the basepaths. The right-handed
Klinger wound up and Slaughter was off and running for second before
the pitcher released the ball; he was a third of the way there by the time
the ball reached the plate. Harry Walker (a .237 hitter in 1946) hit the
ball sharply to left-center. Slaughter rounded second and headed to third.
The ball wasn't hit that deeply, but perfectly placed; Culberson ran over
to field it, angling a bit deeper in the process. No one would have expected Slaughter to try to score, yet he was almost at third by the time the
Sox centerfielder got to the ball. The proper play was to throw to Pesky,
the cutoff man, who moved out to the edge of the outfield grass to take
Culberson's throw. Pesky would have been expected to look to second
base and then run the ball back in to hold Walker to a single while
Slaughter pulled up at third. There didn't seem to be anything unusual
about the play and, with no particular urgency, Culberson "lofted the
ball" to Pesky. Pesky took the throw, looked first toward second—but
picked up Slaughter making a "mad dash" to the plate. Surprised, he

geared up and threw home—and a perfect bullet might yet have had Slaughter. But Slaughter was too close to the plate, and scored as Johnny's throw went about eight feet up the line. Walker took second base.

Two different films of the play exist and neither shows any clear hesitation on Pesky's part, though some might interpret a slight hitch in his throw. Glenn Stout and Dick Johnson's *Red Sox Century* offers an extended analysis of the play—questioning why Cronin had not brought in the lefty Earl Johnson to relieve Klinger with the speedy Slaughter on first. They concluded, after repeated viewings of the films, that Pesky "did not pause or freeze with the ball, although his bodylanguage exhibits surprise. . . . [Pesky] simply made an average play in a situation that was already lost. Had he eyes in the back of his head and an arm like Bob Feller's, by the time he got the ball Slaughter still would have scored." (1)

None of the principals involved faulted Pesky. If anyone might be to blame for the goat horns affixed to him, it may well have been Johnny himself, so disconsolate was he with the loss of the game and the Series. The press reaction was mixed, but hardly conclusive. Nevertheless, Slaughter asserted in an interview with this author in March 2000, "That was the media that hung that around Johnny's neck."

Slaughter, asked about the play for perhaps the 1000th time, added, "I think Johnny did his job and he did it well. You can't blame him. I blame the second baseman and the third baseman for not letting him know. You can't see nobody out your rear end. He was catching the ball coming in from left field. In an early game, I tripled and Mike Gonzalez stopped me at third on the play. We lost that game, and I could have scored easy. So Eddie Dykes, the manager, told me that if I thought I had a chance to score like that, he said for me to go ahead and gamble and he'd be responsible. When I hit second base, I knew I was going to try to score." In 1962, Slaughter had explained, "I had the play figured out on my way to second. I knew Culberson [in center] didn't have DiMaggio's arm, and I knew Pesky would go out for the relay. His back is to the infield when he takes it, naturally, and that gives the base runner the edge; that and the element of surprise. If I was to blame anybody on that, I'd blame Higgins for not telling Pesky where to throw the ball."

The *Boston American*'s Huck Finnegan said, "Instead of looking for a goat, however, it would have been wiser simply to credit Slaughter with a daring and imaginative piece of base running." (2)

St. Louis sportswriter Bob Broeg feels the same way—with passion; he told this author that it was Slaughter's "mad dash," his daring and his speed which merits attention, not Pesky's play. "I didn't sense any hesitation. It was a run and hit and Slaughter was running. It was a slicing fly ball and [if he hadn't been replaced] DiMaggio maybe would have caught the ball! As he hit second base, he said to himself, 'I'm going to score!' Pesky was surprised and off-balance, his throw was weak and (as it happened) late, but he did not hold the ball."

Broeg remains upset to this day that the official scorers—there were three of them, this being the World Series—scored Walker's looping fly ball in front of Culberson a double. A rookie reporter at the time, he says he told the scorers then and there, "Gentlemen, you know what? By scoring this a double, you've taken the romance out of a great run!" Broeg told this author, "I'm very sensitive about that, because it's not fair to Pesky and it's not fair to Slaughter." In his book, Broeg wrote, "I always resented that arbitrarily, unfairly and unromantically, the official scorers called Walker's game-winning hit a double. Harry, hoping to distract a throw as he watched Slaughter round third under full steam, did reach second. But, as he agreed, it was a single, not a double, as I insisted to the official scorers. They didn't listen. Too bad. Heck, wouldn't history treat the Paul Revere ride of Enos Slaughter more dramatically if, as most certainly happened, the big-butted buzzard from Carolina scored the winning run from first base on a *single!*" (3)

Slaughter agreed. "Pesky turned towards first, saw me, turned and threw home and Walker took second." If Pesky had heard his teammates calling the play, and "if he'd got the ball and turned to the left and throwed home he probably had a good chance of throwing me out. When he turned to the right and saw me at the bend, he throwed off balance and didn't get anything on the ball. Doerr at second and Higgins at third, they see me running and they should have [told] Pesky what to do with the ball." (4)

Doerr was anchoring second and Higgins was planted on third. Roy Partee saw Culberson bobble the ball briefly, then throw to Pesky. He says he saw Doerr shouting at Pesky, but everyone agrees the crowd noise was tremendous. J. Ronald Oakley says that Pesky saw Cardinals third base coach Mike Gonzales give Slaughter the hold sign; he couldn't have known Slaughter would run right through it. Culberson's body language and throw betrayed no urgency unfolding behind Johnny. When he saw Slaughter streaking for home, Partee says that Pesky "tried to reach me on the fly, and he didn't have that kind of arm." (5)

Will McDonough didn't feel that Pesky should be held accountable. "With his back to the play getting the relay from the outfield, he had to wait verbal instructions from his nearest teammate, second baseman

Bobby Doerr, on where to throw the ball. However, Doerr, with a high-pitched voice, could not be heard over the roaring St. Louis crowd." Thus, McDonough excuses any hesitation on Pesky's part. A throw with more on it from Culberson, and a bullet to the plate from Pesky might have cut down Slaughter.

Doerr actually doesn't believe he did shout to Pesky. In early 2002, he said, "I don't know whether I yelled on it. I don't remember. I don't think I did, because I had a play coming in to second base. There was no way that Johnny could have heard me even if I was calling. He was out on the grass and there were 32,000 people yelling. He'd have never heard me. He never would have heard Higgins, either. It was just an unfortunate thing that happened. It's unfortunate that Johnny got a rap on that. It was just one of those things. Slaughter gambled. The ball was handled pretty slowly in the outfield. Dom says if he had been out there, he would have been playing more in left center. And that outfield was so rough. I think Culberson probably played the ball pretty conservative. It certainly wasn't Johnny's fault, for crying out loud. Actually, it was pretty darn good, the play that he made. It would have taken a bullet arm to throw him out."

Dom DiMaggio wishes he'd been in center. "Had I been in center field, maybe John would have never had to handle that ball. I don't see how I would have ever thrown the ball to John. I don't think I would have backed up on the ball. What happened was Culberson had to back up on the ball, to keep it from going past." Though left-handed himself, Walker was a notorious left-field hitter and DiMaggio says the players on the bench tried in vain to wave Culberson over more to left. "Had he been positioned correctly, it would have made a big difference. I maintained from the beginning that I might have even had a play on Slaughter at third base. I don't think John would have had to handle the ball. As it turned out, Leon had to go back a little bit to make sure the ball didn't go through, and John had to run out. John was out beyond the grass, but not that far, so after catching the ball, he turned to run in with it. Everybody's yelling, but he couldn't hear anybody. Then when he finally realized that Slaughter had not stopped, he had to set himself— and then came to home plate. I never blamed John for that. The normal thing for John to do was catch the ball, turn around and start running in. No sense in throwing the ball anywhere. With the guy still running, though, he had to re-set himself." In other words, DiMaggio saw a bit of a hitch—but it was not an error, not a misplay, just Pesky doing precisely what he was supposed to do in the circumstance. Without verbal cues from Doerr or Higgins—or perhaps a visual cue from Ted in left—Pesky may have momentarily been taken by surprise. The films, though, really show no definitive hesitation.

How did it come to be that Johnny has borne the tag of having held the ball? In St. Louis, most of the press focused on Slaughter and his "mad dash." The first printed game accounts in the Boston papers didn't suggest that Pesky held the ball. Newspaper accounts in general were mixed. Some mentioned a hesitation; some didn't mention anything of the sort. Some of the same words and phrases show up in different accounts, in newspapers from different cities, leading one to believe that the newspapermen talked amongst themselves a bit before filing. Many of the papers of the day lacked any allegations at all about Pesky, among them the *St. Louis Globe-Democrat* and the *New York Daily News.* Two accounts (the Associated Press and the *Chicago Tribune*) both say that Pesky turned to his right—but the film is absolutely clear that he never turned to his right. John Holway surveyed press coverage in 17 newspaper reports for *Baseball Weekly* in 1992 and found that, while many writers did mention a "hesitation," it was not something they featured. The *Herald Tribune* story didn't mention it until the seventh paragraph and the *New York Daily Mirror* had it in the fourteenth paragraph.

Reporters flocked to both clubhouses after the game, of course, and what they saw and heard in the Red Sox clubhouse may have colored their reporting. Johnny was quick to assume the blame. He was bitterly disappointed, as were all the Red Sox and he blamed himself out loud for not making the play. He was all too willing to accept responsibility, frustrated with his four errors in the Series, an anemic .233 average and having scored only two runs. This play was never ruled an error, but he knew that if the full relay Culberson-to-Pesky-to-Partee had been executed perfectly, they could have had a shot at Slaughter. The Red Sox had men on second and third with nobody out in the top of the ninth but couldn't tie the game. There was disappointment aplenty and sometimes people assign themselves more blame than might truly be merited.

Johnny took it on: "When Walker hit the ball I didn't think Slaughter would dare to take more than two bases, not even after Culby fumbled momentarily. I went out to meet the throw and had my back to the infield. I heard Bobby [Doerr] yelling at me. He must have been telling me to throw home, but I couldn't make out what he was saying, because of the noise of the crowd. When I turned and saw Slaughter going all the way, I guess I was dumbstruck. He had six or eight steps on me, I just couldn't seem to make myself throw quickly enough, and when I finally did get rid of it, I knew I couldn't hit him with a .22."

Austen Lake, writing in the *Boston Sunday Advertiser* in 1962 recalled the train trip home after that final game, remembering Pesky. "I still see the little buzz-saw as he was when the moribund 1946 Red Sox turned their Pullman-car retreat from St. Loo into a conscience clinic with each player claiming a major share of the blame, on the sound assumption that the Cardinals had not won the global title so much as the Red Sox had bungled it. Ted Williams claimed priority to the wreath of razzberries for not hitting with the runs on the bases and Dave Ferriss asked for a double serving of contumely for throwing custard pies and apple dumpling pitches instead of customary streaks of white light. But Pesky kept insisting that had he taken the common precaution to wheel around promptly after receiving a throw-in from his outfield, as is a shortstop's A.B.C., he would have nipped Slaughter at the plate by the width of a streetcar ride."

Johnny can still remember one moment on that long train ride. Some of the guys were talking in the dining car in the train, and as Johnny was leaving and heading back to his stateroom, he overheard Cronin say— after he'd gotten about 10 feet past his young shortstop—"I hope they don't break that kid's heart." "Meaning me. The next year, I hit .324, played every game. 200 hits."

THE AFTERMATH

John Holway believes the film evidence is unambiguous: Johnny took the throw, whirled to his left and threw home in one continuous, fluid motion. How, then, explain the fact that a number of reporters wrote of a hesitation or "bewilderment"? Holway's theory has much to recommend it. "Six years earlier," he wrote, "in the seventh game of the 1940 Series, Detroit shortstop Dick Bartell really had held the ball on a relay play from center field, allowing Cincinnati's Frank McCormick to score the tying run in a 2-1 victory. The memory of that play was still fresh in many writers' minds.

"In 1946, [Jack] Hand of the AP was emphatic in his story that Pesky "held" the ball. He or someone else may have shouted: 'Did you see that? Did you see that? Pesky held the ball! Pesky held the ball!' The other writers hadn't noticed it, but they weren't sure that they hadn't noticed it either. Afraid of getting rockets from their editors after reading Hand's AP story, they inserted the Pesky play into their reports in some fashion to cover themselves. It might even have been done back at the sports desk."

He points out that there was no instant replay in 1946.

Rather than worrying who to fault, Bob Broeg's initial instinct was correct. This was Slaughter's play, not Pesky's. Forget about positioning and play of the Red Sox defense. Score Walker's perfectly placed opposite-field hit a single and grant him and Enos Slaughter all the credit for the successful play.

The label stuck, though. Pesky "held the ball." For a couple of months afterwards, Johnny admitted he was reluctant to leave the house. He couldn't get away from the story. Even back home, 3000 miles away from Boston, while attending the Oregon-Oregon State football game at Corvallis, nine weeks later, Johnny and Ruth saw Oregon fumble and recover on the very first play of the second half, then fumble and turn over the ball on the next play. A loud, intoxicated Oregon partisan shouted, "Give Pesky the ball! He'll hold it!"

Other fans were more generous and have remained in Johnny's corner. Al Stump tells of six Boston schoolteachers who were brought to Portland by the school board, who wined and dined them, then asked if there were anything else they'd like while in town. The "schoolmams" were all "rabid Red Sox rooters" and replied, "Could we . . . would it be possible . . . do you suppose we might meet Johnny Pesky?" The wish was granted and Johnny dropped by, wearing "a beat-up flight jacket, hob boots, a two-day beard and a large smile. 'Hi, Boston!' he yodeled." The teachers were "goggle-eyed" and Dorothy Lynch, one of the group, exclaimed, "Why, he's just an ordinary . . . well, he's human, isn't he?"

Still today, the legend continues. It won't go away. Dan Shaughnessy wrote that Johnny told him in 1975 he still thought about it sometimes even when he was alone—"but not so much in the last fifteen years." "It's a terrible way to be remembered and I wish I could have done something of importance that was involved in winning the ball game, like a base hit or a good play or whatever. Stealing a base. It just didn't happen in my case and I thought sure we'd be in four or five World Series."

At a Society for American Baseball Research regional gathering in Boston in October 2001, Johnny told a few folks gathered around before his talk, "They're probably going to ask me about the play. I've already talked about that a hundred times. It doesn't embarrass me. Young guys who weren't even born in 1946 ask me about it, but that's all right. The first couple of years after it happened I was kind of sensitive about it—because I didn't think I did anything wrong—but I don't mind talking about it. Most baseball people didn't blame me. If Dom had been there, he would have thrown the ball to third. He wouldn't even have bothered with me. He'd have just thrown ahead of the runner. . . . "

POSTSCRIPT

Johnny may have been hard on himself, but at least one person took
the Red Sox defeat even harder. The October 17 *Boston Herald* reported
"An Andover man who apparently took his baseball seriously is reported
to have shot himself when he heard that the Cardinals defeated the Red
Sox in the World Series. He is John McIntyre, 61, of 70 Tewksbury Street
and although struck in the head by a 25-caliber bullet, his name was not
on the danger list at Lawrence General Hospital where he is a patient." In
fact, McIntyre died of the self-inflicted wound, relatives explained in
2001, but he had suffered from a number of mental problems and while
the Red Sox defeat may have immediately precipitated his action, it was
almost certainly not the primary cause.

NOTES

(1) Glenn Stout & Richard Johnson, *Red Sox Century*, Houghton Mifflin,
    2000
(2) *Boston American*, October 12, 1962
(3) See also Broeg's book, *Memories of a Hall of Fame Sportswriter*,
    Sagamore Publishing, 1995
(4) Rich Phalen, *Bittersweet Journey*, McGregor Publishing, 2000, p. 57
(5) J. Ronald Oakley, *Baseball's Last Golden Age, 1946–1960*, McFarland,
    1994, p. 47

9

1947

Pesky never forgot what Ted had told him at the end of his first year in baseball: "you aren't a good ballplayer until you have shown consistency over a period of at least 5 years." Johnny had hit .331 in 1942, and he followed that with a .335 average in 1946. "And you know what Ted said to me? He said, 'Let's see you do it again next summer.' He still wasn't convinced."

As it happens, in his third season, Johnny hit .324 with 207 hits, and he scored 120 runs. Even Ted was on his way to becoming a believer.

Johnny drove to spring training from Boston. Hope was in the air. There was every reason to believe the team could repeat and maybe, this time, bring home the Series trophy. The team was virtually intact, with Rudy York the only holdout, although York said he "ain't holdin' out— just waitin' to sign up." York and Yawkey soon came to terms.

In Knoxville, the Red Sox matched up once again with their traditional barnstorming partners, the Cincinnati Reds. Ed Erautt, a 22 year old rookie held the Sox to just 5 hits, all singles. Like Pesky, Erautt had started out as a clubhouse boy in Portland. He was one of Johnny's successors, brother to Joe Erautt, a White Sox catcher. Neither Johnny nor Ted got a hit off him. Roger Birtwell wrote, "They must raise pretty good clubhouse boys in Portland, Ore." Another note suggested that the Portland Beavers "might make more money out of peddling clubhouse boys that it does from selling ballplayers or trying to win pennants."

Back in Boston for the first game of the City Series, Johnny got on base four times, but didn't do at all well once there. He was thrown out trying to steal second, thrown out at home trying to score on a double, cut down at second again, and then thrown out going into third in the ninth inning.

Birtwell's column on the eve of the season opener was headlined "Sox, Young and Rich in Reserves, Appear Set for Long Stay on Throne." The subhead read "1947 Team Infinitely Better." Harold Kaese picked the Sox for first but with typical Sox fan foreboding: "The Red Sox are a cinch to win the pennant. This is bad news. A year ago the Yankees were a cinch to win the pennant. The Yankees finished third."

The Red Sox took the home opener on April 15, sacking the Senators 7-6. Johnny went 2-for-5, and reached base a third time on a sacrifice bunt that resulted in fielder error. The Sox won their first four games, lost game 5, and Johnny's error in the eighth cost the Red Sox a win in game 6. An Earl Johnson throw to Johnny—to force Rizzuto at second—was a "perfect" one, but bounced out of his glove and became "Pesky's Fatal Muff" in the next day's sports page headline.

Cronin was trying to find a position for Pellagrini who'd filled in nicely when Johnny got a bad cold in Detroit. Cronin remembered that back in Florida, Johnny had said, "You don't have to look for a third baseman. I can play there." He approached Johnny before an off-day workout on May 1 and asked if he'd been kidding. "No," Johnny answered. "If you think it will help the club I'll move to third." They spent a couple of hours working with Johnny at third and Pelly at short and both looked great. Johnny revealed he'd actually broken in at the hot corner. "As a kid, I wanted to be a catcher. I went out for the American Legion team in Portland. . . . . They had a good shortstop but were shy of third basemen. So I broke in at third. I played second and in the outfield. It was not until I broke into organized baseball with the Sox farm system that I first played shortstop." (1)

Cronin welcomed the move, convinced that Pellagrini was better at short than at third. Having moved himself from shortstop to third in 1945, the Sox skipper had no doubt that Pesky could cope. Anyone who could play short could play third, he felt.

Johnny's first day at third, he singled to left in the first against Bob Feller. It proved to be the only hit for Boston all day. The May 2 game marked the third time that Feller had thrown a one-hitter against the Red Sox. Doerr had broken up both of the previous ones.

Pellagrini's hitting didn't sustain itself and by the end of May he wasn't hitting well at all. Rip Russell was put in at third, and Johnny moved back to short.

Johnny also struggled with hitting early in 1947. As of June 12, he was only averaging .246 and press reports noted that he had put on weight in the off-season. That bad cold set him back in early May, and then he came down with swollen glands at the end of May. At one point, he'd gone an uncharacteristic 0-for-16, but broke out with four straight hits.

The first night game ever played at Fenway Park was June 13, before 34,510. Johnny went 1 for 4. A lot of the games the Red Sox lost in 1946 were night games. "We only played 14 night games. None at Fenway Park. We didn't get lights there until 1947. They had lights in Washington. Philadelphia. Some of those lights were terrible. You should hear me complain—Christ, Williams didn't hit well at night. When we got lights at Fenway, it looked like it was daytime. They were nice and bright."

A couple of days later, the Sox swapped Rudy York to the Tigers for Murrell "Jake" Jones, who came into his first game and hit a ninth inning grand slam for the Sox, capping off a day where he amassed 7 RBI. Johnny went 5 for 10 in the double header, his best day of the year, breaking out of the doldrums.

The Red Sox began to come around in mid-June with a 7 game win streak, lifting them into first by the 17th. The *Globe* noted that Johnny "recaptured his hitting stroke . . . with seven hits in his last three games" adding 18 points to his average.

On the 15th, the team won its eighth in a row, courtesy of a 1:05 AM single by Pesky, his fifth single of the night. In four games his average had ballooned 31 points, on the strength of twelve hits. This last game was a thriller. Tied at 2 after regulation (thanks to a sensational catch by Ted with two on and two out in the 9th), the Browns scored once in the top of the thirteenth and the Red Sox countered with one in the bottom. St. Louis plated 2 in the top of the next inning, and the Red Sox replied in kind: now both teams were knotted at 5-5.

After his game-winning single, Pesky was greeted in the Boston clubhouse "as if he were the greatest ball player who ever lived. Wally Moses, veteran right fielder, came in and planted a kiss on Pesky's smiling countenance. Ted Williams, who doubled two important runs into position in the 14th frame, patted him on the back and then got out of the way as an avalanche of players swarmed Pesky, threw jackets onto the pipes running across the ceiling and grabbed cold drinks."

Johnny finally reached .300—an even .300—on June 29, going 3 for 8 in a twin bill, as the Sox dropped both games to the Athletics. It had taken an 11-game hitting streak to reach .300.

The knock on Williams was that he was indifferent defensively, but the players knew otherwise. During June, Ted spent a fair amount of time taking infield at short, working to improve in the field. He was doing fine at the plate, and had all season long. When it came time for the All-Star selections, Williams was the only Red Sox player to make the roster. Bobby Doerr was later named to the team as a backup. With Joe Cronin managing the team—since his team had won the pennant the previous season—this showing was in marked contrast to the '46 squad, dominated by Boston players.

As of July 1, the first Boston writers began to muse on the possibility that the Braves could win their pennant while the Red Sox failed to grasp theirs. The team lost Dom DiMaggio for a while. Slumps hit Williams, Pesky, York and Doerr; combined with the arm ailments of Hughson and Harris, things looked pretty bleak. By the 4th, Johnny remained at .300—two points above Williams' .298 (though Ted led the A.L. with 15 homers and 48 RBI). The Sox were in fourth place, 7 games out at 34-32.

Mid-season, Larry Doby joined the Indians, the first African American player in the American League. Jackie Robinson had, of course, been playing for Brooklyn throughout 1947.

Johnny remembers Doby's arrival. "He was a nice kid. We never had a black player when I was there. The Browns had two. We kind of accepted them. I had Doby in a rundown one time. He tried to run over me. He did, but I hung onto the ball and I got him out. I called him a black son of a bitch. Spur of the moment. He just looked at me, but color didn't mean anything to me. I liked the guy and to this day, there's maybe one or two black guys [I didn't like]. Doby was a good guy. Easter was a wonderful guy. Satchel Paige. They were good players!"

Pesky's calling him a "black son of a bitch"—as Johnny tells the story over fifty years later—comes across as though he'd called him a "dumb Mick" or whatever other ethnic slur passed for male humor in those days. In effect, Johnny treated him just like he might treat anyone else, not being overly sensitive about political correctness and certainly not being racist.

Not all the players were as tolerant as Johnny. "There were some guys who were pretty rough. That north/south stuff was ridiculous. Robinson looked like a hell of a player." Enos Slaughter was pretty vocal against black players in baseball, but has since apologized, and publicly stated that he felt he had been wrong. "Well, that's something you learn in your family background," Johnny says. "The blacks would sit in one section. That's what I didn't like. That's all changed. They were way out of line." Later, as a minor league manager in the south in the late 1950s, Pesky had to contend with problems arising from the Jim Crow laws of the day.

Certainly, Mr. Paveskovich knew what it was like to be a minority, in his case an immigrant family in another culture. It was in 1947 that Johnny finally, legally, changed his name to Pesky. It wasn't because of discrimination. It had been Johnny's baseball name for more than ten years. It made perfect sense to change the longer name to the shorter one by which he was known. "I changed it. They had to put it in the paper and see if somebody objects, and my parents found out about it. They didn't like it at all. When I went home that year after I changed it, I was still getting my checks as Pesky. My parents were upset. 'Are you ashamed of your name, John?' 'No, Ma, but you're in a new country . . . A lot of people do that. I still say my prayers every night. '"

Johnny Pesky still holds the Red Sox record for pulling off the hidden ball trick, tied with Marty Barrett who did it three times between 1985 and 1988. Pesky did it twice in 1942 and now on July 6, Pesky pulled the hidden ball trick on Buddy Lewis. Johnny would stick the ball inside his glove, in his hand under the glove, but hidden from view so the glove showed empty. "The ball would come from the outfield and I would put it in between my glove and my hand, and cover it up. I'd pound my glove a few times. I'd walk and kick around at the dirt.

"Mickey Harris was pitching and he had the bases full. No outs. I got the ball from the outfield and I think I'd already made an error in that inning—screwed up a ground ball or something. Lewis was on second base. I wound up with the ball. Lewis didn't even look to see where I was. I had to alert the umpire, 'I've got the ball.' He knew that I had the ball, but he didn't say anything. I was bluffing him a little, getting him to go back to second, then I tagged him with the ball. The next batter— ground ball, double play and the inning's over. I got three of them. All three were at Fenway and all three were unassisted. I had another one, too. Red McQuillen. I tagged him out but Bobby Doerr had called time out. I'd have had four."

Johnny went 5 for 9 in a doubleheader on July 13, but Boston dropped both games to the Indians and Clif Keane termed them "a completely washed up team." He had pushed himself up to .313 by the 23rd. He was hitting incredibly well against Feller. Rapid Robert was already in the military during Johnny's rookie year, but in 1946, Johnny hit three singles and drew a walk the first time he faced Feller. He had a 4 for 4 game later in the season, and a 2 for 4 outing, winding up the 1946 season batting .409 against Feller! Johnny added two more hits in his first six 1947 at-bats. Feller commented to writer Ed Rumill, "Frankly, I didn't realize Johnny had done so well against me. But, after all, he makes over 200 base hits a year, so he must hit everybody pretty good. Johnny, however, is the type of hitter that would give me trouble. He has a slight crouch at the plate, with his bat held high and ready, not leaving you much strike territory. He guards the plate pretty well. And he has good eyes. You've got to get the ball over. Sometimes if you get behind him, maybe you have to take a little off your pitch to get it over, and that's the ball he'll hit. I'm not taking anything away from him, understand. I'm just saying that he makes you pitch that way to him. And when the ball comes in there, he slaps at it—pokes it into left field or pulls it to right." Feller added with a grin, "Another thing. Johnny probably bears down a little harder against me than some of the other pitchers."

In these years, there was an astonishing number of doubleheaders. The last thing today's owners want is a single-admission twin bill, but in the 1940s they were a proven crowd-grabber and really drew fans. Kaese noted that "Most Sox regulars . . . have contracts which call for bonuses based on home-crowd figures for the season", so the players were content with the practice.

By the first of August, the Red Sox were 12 games behind the first place Yanks and the papers began to talk football. On the 7th, Johnny beat out two singles in the same inning—the fourth—as the Sox scored six runs against the Senators' Early Wynn, a game they won by a gridiron score of 12-2.

By the 11th, the *Globe* noted Johnny's home/away splits.

	AB	R	H	AVG
HOME	217	37	70	.323
AWAY	214	30	64	.290

Johnny had worked his way up to 145 hits by August 22, the date Ted took the lead for the batting title, in fact leading in all three Triple Crown categories. Johnny's average was now .305 but to get his 200 hits, he would have to average 1.5 hits per game for the entire rest of the season—a daunting task.

On the 24th, he began his bid going 4 for 5 (with 3 RBI) in game one of a double-header and following with a 2 for 4 in game two, picking up six of those 55 needed hits in one good day.

On the 28th, facing Hal Newhouser, he went 4 for 5 again, this time with 5 RBI! He'd booked only 18 RBI for the season before the current road trip, but he'd busted out and collected 26 hits and added 10 RBI on just one trip away from Fenway. Having nearly halved the needed 55 safeties, suddenly 200 didn't look quite so unattainable.

Back home, on the final day of August, he nearly managed an inside-the-park home run as the ball caromed off the fence right by the right field foul pole and skittered around toward center hugging the wall. He was cut down by a perfect relay. The Sox won 5-1 and when Williams made his last at bat, Jack Benny got up to leave as did hundreds of others.

The team, though, was 12 ½ out, just two games ahead of the Tigers. This was not 1946 redux. The pitching staff had just fallen apart. "It was awful. We thought we were going to have good pitching for the next 4 or 5 years. Hughson came up lame. Dave Ferriss came up lame. Mickey Harris, he come up lame. We had a terrible time with our staff. It was a shame."

Pesky had made up all the lost ground in his personal stats. By September 4, he was batting third in the league at .320, with 172 hits. A classic contact hitter, Johnny struck out only 22 times in 1947, in 638 at bats. In fact, once he wrapped up his major league career, Johnny had only struck out a grand total of 218 times in a full 4745 at bats. He had more doubles (226) than strikeouts.

The Red Sox began to worry about holding on to second place, losing two to the As on the 7th, despite Pesky going 2 for 5 twice. Johnny was on a tear, hitting in 24 straight games. On the 17th, he got 5 more hits in another doubleheader, bringing him to 197 hits and a .326 average. Only a serious injury was going to keep him from collecting three more hits with nine games remaining.

"Sure, I'll get 200 hits," he'd joked to Bob Holbrook he day before, but Holbrook noted his resolve. "Confidence. That was it. Pesky, the smooth-working, stocky Red Sox shortstop, has all the confidence in the world, but it must be related that there was a time this season when he wasn't the least bit sure he would reach the 200-hit circle."

Holbrook talked about Pesky's style. "Pesky objects to being called a 'banjo hitter.' It might be best to describe him as a spray hitter. That's what he does. Somehow it seems that he envies the big, hulking, free-swinging individuals like Joe DiMaggio and Ted Williams. Slugger Jake Jones says he [Pesky] has a 'seeing-eye' bat. Pesky laughs at this. But he doesn't laugh when talk revolves around the age-old subject of hitting. If you think Williams gives thought to his hitting, then Pesky is in the same class." (2)

Three days later, on the 20th, Johnny got two hits each game in yet another doubleheader, going 2 for 4 twice. This put Johnny over 200 hits, and set an all-time Red Sox mark of hitting in 26 straight games. In those 26 games, there were seven twin bills, including back-to-back-to-back doubleheaders on the 15th, 16th, and 17th. Johnny played in all six of those games, gathering thirteen hits.

Ray Scarborough of the Senators finally shut him down on the 21st, but not before Johnny had climbed back into third place in the league with a .327 average. He led the league in hits. Johnny was "horse-collared" in the next two games as well, not collecting a single hit in the last three home games of the year.

Closing out the season on the road, Johnny added a few more hits, going 2-for-3 with a double and two singles on the 27th, for a total of 207 on the season. In the final game, he did nothing, and the Red Sox did nothing either, losing the last game of a lackluster season. They wound up in third place, 14½ games out. Ted Williams won the Triple Crown, leading in average, home runs and runs batted in. Johnny Pesky came in third with his .324 average.

The evening of the last game, Cronin announced that the Red Sox had signed Joe McCarthy to skipper the 1948 Red Sox.

Johnny had reached 200 hits for the third straight season. "Little Johnny Pesky" had accomplished something only two other players had ever done. Wee Willie Keeler, who "hit 'em where they ain't" had done it on the cusp of the modern era, from 1899 through 1901. Chuck Klein, also in the National League, had done it his first four years with the Phillies: 1929, 1930, 1931 and 1932. As with so many ballplayers who lost time during World War II, one wonders what Pesky might have accomplished during the three years he missed. "If I hadn't gone into the service, I could have got 1000 hits in five years. That's never been done." Had he made 200 hits each of his first six years in the major leagues, there is every reason to believe he'd be in the National Baseball Hall of Fame today.

Would he have accomplished this? Well, there's no way to know. John

Pastier of SABR ran a projection which attempted to "fill in" the missing years by looking at the year before and the years afterward—and Johnny (had he not suffered any major injury during the seasons he missed) might well have come very, very close. John qualifies his projection by terming it "reasonable math, but not necessarily reasonable science." The figures he came up with were: 202.96 hits in 1943, 203.58 hits in 1944, and 199.50 in 1945.

Pesky described himself mid-season as a "lucky hitter" to the *Globe*'s Bob Holbrook. "I'm a lucky hitter. I'm not a good hitter, just lucky." Holbrook wouldn't accept the characterization. "Pesky is no average hitter. And he is not lucky, either. . . . He is a spot hitter and has made at least 200 hits every year that he played professional baseball. He led his league last season when he cracked out 208 hits . . . when a player fashions 200 bingles every year you can throw out most of the luck element." Holbrook did comment that Pesky hit better while playing shortstop and that it might well have been more than coincidence that his hitting improved when he moved back from third to short.

When pressed, Pesky notes that his speed afoot helped. "A spray hit-ter, that was the way I like to be described, remembered. But listen, I got some cheap hits, too. I got my share. Williams used to make fun of me. I hit a ball in Chicago one time. Hit it on the end of the bat and the pitcher goes up and it goes off the top of his glove. The ball could have hit in there and it wouldn't have even made a dent, but he lost track of the ball. The ball stopped between second base and the pitcher's mound. Williams went wild. 'JEEZUS, WHAT A STINKIN' HIT!' You know how he was. I said, 'Well, Ted, you gotta go with the grain.' I got a lot of infield hits. If I had a ball to the right of the shortstop . . . I had that kind of speed. Especially going from home to first."

NOTES

(1) *Boston Globe*, May 2, 1947
(2) *Boston Globe*, September 17, 1947

10
1948

Johnny first met Joe McCarthy in January, in Boston, when the new manager was in town to be introduced at the annual Baseball Writers dinner. In 1942, Johnny had broken a game against the Yankees wide open with a solid hit. Almost six years later, as Cronin was showing McCarthy around the park, they ran into Pesky, and Cronin introduced the two. Johnny smiled, "How are you, Mr. McCarthy?" to which McCarthy replied, "Oh, yes! The fellow who knocked us out of a ball game!"

One might expect positional stability after three seasons of 200-plus hits, but when 1948 began, Johnny Pesky had no idea where he'd be playing. With McCarthy in charge, and with a couple of new infielders for him to juggle (the Red Sox had acquired Vern Stephens from the Browns and Billy Goodman looked like he might make the big league club), Johnny asked as he boarded the train for Florida, "Where am I going to play?"

Indeed, it was an open question, and Johnny had already demonstrated his willingness to play third if it might help the club. There was no question he preferred shortstop, and had played better there.

Stephens and Pesky roomed together in spring training and became

108

very good pals even though they were both vying for the shortstop slot. Johnny joked, "Listen, I'm going to catch and Vern is going to pitch this season." The guessing was, though, that Stephens would play third, since Pesky and Doerr formed "a tailor-made combine around the keystone cushion." McCarthy had both players work out at short.

On March 3 McCarthy announced that he would put Pesky at third and Stephens at short. In the 21 games Johnny had played at third in 1947, he'd made just one error in 67 chances. "He can't miss as a third baseman," said McCarthy. "Pesky should be able to make plays at third that the others couldn't." Essentially, though, McCarthy was being diplomatic, as Harold Kaese noted, portraying the positioning of Stephens at short as a promotion for Pesky. He was really saying that Stephens was the better shortstop; Johnny received the news "with an outward grace, although it must have jarred him inside."

Publicly, Pesky took it in stride, quipping, "It should add two years to my career, because now I won't have to walk so far to my position." Johnny claimed he'd wanted to stick at third in 1947, but when the ball club didn't do as well during that stretch, "I got a bit down on myself. So I went back to shortstop. If they told me to go to right field, I'd have played out there. As a kid, we used to try to play all over the place. All my years as a pro, though, I had played shortstop."

What McCarthy may not have fully realized was that Johnny's hitting had suffered markedly in 1947 during those games he'd been positioned at third. His average was a paltry .249 for the 21 games. The Red Sox reportedly had tried to trade Pesky for Stephens back in 1946, but the deal was called off because St. Louis felt that Stephens had a stronger arm from the hole and a better move throwing to third from short. The Sox now had them both—forcing the hard choice. McCarthy, for his part, reportedly concluded that "the more agile Pesky was the superior at coming in on balls and making the snap underhand throw." (1)

Johnny laughed it off, "Well, here I am, just a rookie again." He had, characteristically, never assumed he had anything locked in place. He took double fielding, with both the first string and second squad players. Confidently, and diplomatically, he commented, "I believe I'm going to be a better third baseman than I was a shortstop. I think it was highly complimentary of Joe McCarthy to pick me as his third baseman. I'll do anything he says, even if he wants me to be a bat boy again."

A few rocky days in the field followed, though, and neither Pesky nor Stephens were hitting. "All he asks is that people leave him alone for a while and give him an opportunity to become accustomed to his new position," reported Bob Holbrook, essentially underscoring a Pesky plea for patience. One of the most serious players in camp, flubs bothered Johnny. He said he'd never had any really tough plays at third in '47 but now all sorts of fluky plays had developed. He hadn't handled them fluidly, and it was getting to him. "My main trouble is that I am too impatient," he acknowledged. "I try to learn everything in one day and that can't be done."

As the 1948 season unfolded, it offered the potential to be the greatest year in Boston baseball history. Doc Cramer—at the time a player-coach for the Tigers—indicated in late March that he thought the Braves had a chance to win the pennant and the Sox were dramatically improved on paper. Late in the month, Pesky's hitting started to come around slowly and he was looking better in the field; he was said to be genuinely enjoying playing third. It wasn't until April 7 or 8 that he really started to hit. It was around that time—early April—that Bobby Doerr said the Sox had as good a team as any he'd been on.

Harris, Dobson, Kinder, Ferriss and Kramer were named as starting pitchers, Hughson still uncertain.

For the first time since 1915, there began to be some serious talk about an all-Boston World Series. Harold Kaese acknowledged the talk, chiming in with typical local cynicism: "Only the formality of winning 85 or so ball games between now and the end of September faces the Braves and Sox."

The young Mickey McDermott—only 19 years old—was boarding at the Pesky household as the City Series began. Johnny remembered how lonesome he'd been in his own rookie year in Boston and invited the engaging Sox pitcher. Johnny had an RBI triple in the first game of the series, and his ninth inning hit in the second game gave the Sox a 2-1 win. It seemed he was poised for another big season. Would the traditional Braves/Red Sox pre-season series prove a precursor of post-season play, pitting the two Boston teams against each other come October?

Then came Opening Day, a doubleheader, and Johnny went 0-for-7 as the Sox lost both games to Philadelphia. He may have been affected by stories that hit on the eve of the season, that he was going to be traded to Washington for Early Wynn. This was a player who'd made 200 hits three years in a row and finished in the top 3 batters in the League each year. Now he was being shuffled around on the field and had to suffer trade rumors as well. On top of that, though not widely known at the time, the Red Sox had actually cut his salary by 12.5 percent. Some reward for excellence!

Johnny got a single and a double in game 3, but the Red Sox lost that one, too. The three game opening home stand at Fenway Park was a bust. Within about a week, the Braves had opened the season with a 1-6 mark and the Red Sox were only marginally better at 1-5. The next day both teams shut out their opponents.

Then Johnny had one of the worst days of his career, making an error which allowed the fourth and fifth runs to score in a Yankee 5-4 win. To make matters worse, he struck out with the tying run on base in the ninth. Afterwards, McCarthy denied the Pesky-for-Wynn story still circulating. Johnny, after his first seven games, was batting .194.

The Red Sox first won at home on May 1. Johnny was 2 for 4. On the 4th, the Sox evened the year at 6-6. In early May, WBZ broadcast the first televised game from Fenway Park.

On May 16, Pesky went 2 for 3 but pulled a muscle in the rear of his thigh and missed several games. Then he came back for a few and did OK but had to be taken out for a few more with a charleyhorse. He missed eleven games in all—the most he'd ever missed as a major leaguer—and, as of the end of May, had just 31 hits, batting .261 with 7 RBI. The team was showing a miserable 14-23 record, 11 ½ games out. Losing a lot of one run ballgames, the Sox limped home from a 4-12 road trip. It was beginning to look like 1947 all over again, but worse.

Johnny came back to pinch-hit on June 2 and singled for Hitchcock in the 9th but Boston still lost 3-1. He first really got back in the lineup on 6/6, but just managed 1 for 8 in the doubleheader. The Sox took both games, though, from the Tigers. With those two wins, they'd notched five straight. "I'll have to hit some to get my 200 hits, won't I?" asked Johnny.

Clark Griffith of the Senators spoke up as the June 15 trading deadline approached. He wasn't about to trade Wynn for Pesky, he said, though he'd gladly pay $100,000 for Pesky. "Offering money to Tom Yawkey for Pesky, however, would be an insult to Tom. He already has half the money in the world."

On June 11, the Boston Braves slipped into first place in the N.L.

The Red Sox headed out for a 16-game road trip on the 18th. For the first time in years, Boston headlines and coverage featuring the Braves began to outpace the Red Sox. Nevertheless, the Sox began to climb, winning twelve of their next fifteen games.

Johnny hit a home run in the fourth inning on June 19, as the team reached .500. It was his first homer since August 8, 1946, the fifth of his career, a two-run drive off Tigers pitcher Hal White. Like all table-setters, Pesky remembers it vividly. "That was the longest one I ever hit, into section 93, in right-center field. The wind must have been blowing out that day and it carried up into the seats."

In late June, he'd put together ten or twelve very good games in a row, but then disaster struck. "I really fielded well. I was awfully proud of myself. We were starting a series in New York and somebody asked me . . . how I liked third base, and I said I liked it great and felt that I had about mastered the position." That very day, the first of July, Gus Niarhos hit one down the third base line in the first inning. Bill Johnson was on second, with two outs, and three runs had already scored. Pesky snared the ball on the high hop, stepped on third and fired to first. Trouble was, there was no force play at third, and because he took the time to step on the bag (failing to tag the runner Johnson) Johnny's throw was late—a double "skull." Had he simply made the play to first, or tagged the committed runner, the inning would have been over. Both players were safe, though, and the next man up walked. The pitcher was up next—Frank Hiller—and he helped his own cause with a 3-run double. Johnny had done well in the batter's box that day, going 2 for 5 with a double and a home run off Hiller into Yankee Stadium's lower right field extension. He batted in two, but the Red Sox lost 7-3. Joe McCarthy was understanding. "Don't let it get you down, Johnny. Red Rolfe had the same trouble when he first went over there. Just don't quit on yourself."

Johnny revered McCarthy, and when he became a manager in later years he often talked about doing things "the Joe McCarthy way." "That man . . . " he told Red Smith when he took the reins as Red Sox manager in 1963, "He'd make me sit next to him on the bench, and sometimes the other guys would give you the business for that. Joe heard one of 'em making a kissing sound one day. 'Never mind, kid,' he told me. 'Greater men than you have sat in this seat.' He could make you feel like Ty Cobb, and you know something? I never was a Ty Cobb."

On July 4th, Johnny singled twice in the seventh inning as the Red Sox scored 14 runs. Pesky drove in 4 runs in the inning. He'd already contributed an RBI in the second with a sacrifice fly. There weren't too many days Johnny had five runs batted in. The next day, the Sox took two from the Yankees.

Five Braves were selected for the All-Star Game, and 4 Red Sox: Ted, Bobby, Stephens and Birdie Tebbetts. Vern Stephens had been a good acquisition. He'd done well during the talent-depleted war years, leading the majors once in home runs and once in runs batted in. In 1947, he had 15 home runs and 83 runs batted in, decent but not spectacular stats. With the Red Sox, however, Stephens would turn in RBI figures in

1948, '49 and '50 of 137, 159 and 144—the latter two were league-leading figures.

Meanwhile Stephens' road roomie, Pesky, had sunk to the .260s—but on the eve of the All-Star Game went 6 for 9 in a doubleheader with a home run and two doubles. The homer was a 3-run shot over the Athletics' right field wall in the seventh of game two. The Red Sox won the first game in 10 innings, and had climbed back from a 6-1 deficit in the second capped by Johnny's home run but Philadelphia's blue laws forced the game to be halted at 6 PM on Sunday, and the Red Sox lost 6-5, not even able to complete the 8th inning.

After the All-Star Game, on July 15, the Red Sox played a "Branch Rickey Special" (as day/night doubleheaders were sometimes called—Rickey having devised them for the extra revenue) and beat the Tigers twice, 13-5 and 3-1. Johnny had two RBI in the first game and one in the second, 3 for 7 on the day. He went 2 for 4 the next day. Another doubleheader followed, and Johnny went 5 for 7 with 3 RBI, and also made the "play of the day" with a "Pie Traynor" stop of a wicked skip-ping grounder that Gerry Priddy had hit deep behind third. Now he had reached .292, the first time he'd risen that high.

On July 22, the Red Sox were within two games of first place. Then they beat the Indians twice, their third consecutive doubleheader sweep. They did this even without The Kid. Williams had torn some cartilage, suffered while rough-housing with young Sam Mele on the train.

During the doubleheader on the 24th, the Sox won without both Pesky and McCarthy, as both were thrown out of the game during the third inning of the "lid-lifter" (first game)—thrown out for the day, not just for the game, for arguing when Pesky was called out on strikes. "The goddamn ball was two inches outside. I started to walk away. We were always told just walk away, have your say and go. He followed me, the umpire, and I turned and I got in his face. One word led to another and he kicked me out. Now here comes McCarthy and he runs McCarthy. Billy Hitchcock goes in [in my place] and I'll be goddamned. He gets the base hit in the first game that ties the game, and in the second game he gets the base hit that wins the game. I went to McCarthy after the game and said, 'Maybe it was a good thing I got kicked out, Joe.'

"I was steaming and so was owner Tom Yawkey. Finally we composed a letter to Will Harridge, president of the American League. We said we thought it was unfair to keep a star out of an important game because doubleheaders were considered as one game in the case of ejection. We thought the doubleheader should be considered two separate games, with a man being out of only the game from which he was chased. We asked Harridge to poll the owners about changing the rule. Will wrote back that he did not have to take a vote because this was not a rule in the book, merely a league regulation. He would change regulations, he said, and he did." (2)

The Red Sox climbed into first place for the first time on July 25. It had been a long, hard climb but this was not the 1947 team. They had won thirteen in a row, 15 of 16—though only batting .274 as a team over the stretch. Johnny was at .278. The Braves and the Red Sox were both in first place for the first time since 1916.

Having reached the top, the Sox promptly lost three in a row, tumbling to fourth place in a tightly packed field. Over the next few weeks, the team hung in there and the lead seesawed back and forth. The game on August 24th was a terrific one, against the Indians at Fenway. The pitching matchup was Joe Dobson against Satchel Paige and an estimated 20,000 fans were turned away. Had the Red Sox signed Paige as they well could have a year or two earlier, they might have won themselves a pennant in 1948 (he was 6 and 1 for the Indians with a 2.48 ERA). They might have also been the team to break baseball's color line and spared themselves a full half-century of criticism for perceived racism. This August game was incredibly dramatic, the Indians scoring twice in the ninth to take an 8-6 lead, only to have Vern Stephens come back in the bottom of the inning with a three-run homer.

September opened with Johnny's bases-clearing triple to right center sealing a 10-1 win over the Tigers as the Red Sox closed out a 12-3 homestand. Riding a seven game win streak in early September, the Bosox opened a 1½ game lead with twin bill triumphs over the Nats in D.C. on Labor Day. Johnny scored the winning run with a bunt in the second game (a 2-1 affair), scoring on a Billy Goodman single. The Red Sox had now won 22 of their last 26, but the Yankees kept pace, winning 21 of 25.

Bookies were now reported as favoring both Boston teams. Fans camped out as early as 4:30 AM for bleacher tickets to the September 8 home game against the Yankees. Of Pesky's play at third, Doerr said, "He's getting to like it there better than he ever liked shortstop." They won that game and the resulting 2½ game lead was the largest they'd had all year. Pesky made the final putout, catching Joe DiMaggio's "bullet-like smash." It must have been quite a play; one reporter wrote, "He leaped high. The ball bounced out of his glove but the alert Pesky re-caught it on the way down" with his bare hand. Johnny had a double and sac fly in the 10-6 win.

With another victory on 9/9, the team was 3½ up on the Yankees and five ahead of Cleveland. The lead was soon cut to a single game, though, with 15 left to play. Five of those games were against New York, however, and Dizzy Dean predicted the two teams would beat each other up and the Indians would sneak in and snatch the flag. The Braves were breathing easier, with a 5½ game lead.

Then Mele hurt his ankle and Doerr reaggravated the ligament injury. Billy Hitchcock—who had twice filled in capably for Doerr—was himself on the injury list with a charleyhorse. The Indians took two from the A's and the Senators snapped an 18-game losing streak beating Boston and bouncing back to 39½ games out of first.

In Cleveland, Feller beat Dobson on a three-hitter, 5-2 and 76,772 pennant-starved fans saw the Indians enter a tie for first place.

On September 24, both the Indians and the Red Sox boasted 91-55 records, and New York was at 90-56. The Sox lost to New York, and the Indians lost their game, and the morning papers on the 25th reflected a three-way tie for first, all three teams knotted at 91-56 with just seven games to go.

On the 26th, Feller and the Indians won again and took over first place when the Red Sox lost to New York. The Red Sox had now dropped eight of their last fourteen games. Meanwhile the crosstown Braves finally clinched the National League flag.

The 27th was an off day and most of the Red Sox regulars stayed home. Predictably, Pesky came in for a lone workout.

On the 28th, the lowly Senators again beat the Red Sox 4-2 while Cleveland won 11-0. Johnny was 0 for 4 and the Sox slid to two out with just 4 games to play. The Sox won their next game, but so did Cleveland, up by 2 with just 3 left.

Johnny led the way on the last day of the month. He singled and knocked in Parnell in the 2nd, and beat out a hit and later scored in the fifth in a 7-3 Sox win which saw him go 3 for 5 with 2 RBI. The Indians lost the next day and their lead was cut to one.

On the 2nd, playing the Yankees, Ted's 25th homer, with Pesky on base (he'd walked on four pitches) provided the margin for a 5-1 Red Sox win. Johnny walked again and scored again in the 3rd. Johnny wound up the season with 99 walks, up from the 72 he'd taken in '47. For each of his first 6 years, Johnny's walk totals increased. Williams had already led the league four straight times in walks, and David Kaiser reports that "McCarthy and his coaches began ordering the rest of the team to take more pitches, and Johnny Pesky, in particular, remembers that he was no longer allowed to hit on 2-0 and 3-1 counts." It worked; the 1947 Sox had walked 666 times whereas the 1948 model earned 823 free passes. (3)

The Yankees had lost to the Red Sox and were out of the race at last, but still had the final game to play the role of spoiler for the Sox who had to win while the Indians lost. That's just what happened. The Sox beat New York 10-5 and the Tigers took care of the Tribe, 7-1. Both teams finished the regular season at 96-58. Never in the 48 year history of the American League had there been a tie. The Red Sox had won all four of their final games, while the Indians lost two of their last four.

Any single game playoff is going to provide endless "what if" fodder for the loser, and for over fifty years the Boston faithful have debated McCarthy's decision to start Denny Galehouse, wondered whether Kinder and Parnell had really begged off. Asked about the scuttlebutt in the clubhouse when Galehouse was named, Johnny replied, "We never questioned McCarthy. He was the manager. We thought Parnell was going to be the pitcher, but he only had two days' rest or something like that. I know Mel wanted to pitch that game. I was hoping he would have. Kinder would pitch every day! Galehouse had pitched a big game earlier on. McCarthy was pretty good about his pitchers."

The day before, Pesky had worn his Navy dress uniform, since he was attending a friend's wedding that night. Kaiser writes, "As he began to leave, several teammates demanded that he wear it the next day, too, for good luck. After some resistance, Pesky—yielding to the chronic superstition of athletes—gave in to please his mates, but he hardly cared one way or another." Johnny got the game off to a solid start, doubling in the first inning and scoring on Stephens' single. He was thrown out bunting for a hit in the third, made an out again in the sixth and struck out in the eighth. The game wasn't close; Galehouse was hit hard, Boudreau hit well, and the Red Sox lost both the game and the pennant. Cleveland beat Boston 8-3. Pesky "angrily climbed back into his naval officer's uniform and swore off superstition for life." (4)

The *Globe* the next day headlined "No Subway Series"—though a subway wouldn't really have been needed. It was just a 1.3-mile stroll between the two parks. The Indians were rated 13-5 odds to win the Series, and did, denying Boston fans any satisfaction at all.

POSTSCRIPT

Why did Johnny Pesky's average fall so dramatically in 1948? He'd come into the season with a lifetime average of .330, third among active players (only Ted Williams and Joe DiMaggio had higher marks.) He'd led the league in hits three years in a row, with over 200 hits each season. Then in 1948, he only hit .281 (the next three years each saw him back over .300 again) with 159 hits. He played fewer games—143—but had only 60 fewer at bats. There must have been reasons for the anomaly.

Johnny reported that after the 1947 season he took a $2500 pay cut. Astonishing, given that he'd hit .324 and led the league for the third year in a row with hits—207. "I was amazed when I was told I was going to have my pay cut. They asked me how many home runs I hit and how many runs I had knocked in. I wound up playing the next season for $2500 less."

"I really never had any prolonged batting slumps. If I hadn't gone into the service, I might have done it four, five years in a row." Yet when he went in to talk with Joe Cronin, he was floored with the reception he got. "Cronin told me I was a lousy shortstop for the first two months of the season. I got 207 hits that year. It sounds ridiculous." One can only guess that Cronin was trying to shave payroll and leaning on those he thought he could intimidate. He cited Pesky's lack of power—not a single home run in 1947. "I got 207 hits, but how many home runs did I hit?" Johnny's good nature—and loyalty—carried him through, and Cronin may have realized this about him. Had there been no reserve clause, and had Johnny had an agent, nothing of the sort ever would have occurred. But, as Johnny admits, "our values were different in those years. I thought I would play ball forever."

Furthermore, he was enthusiastic about Boston's prospects. "We made a big trade. We got Vern Stephens, Jack Kramer, Kinder. We could have won the pennant the next three or four years. I didn't give a shit about the money. It all boils down to this: what Mr. Yawkey did for me and my family. I've never forgotten that. I needed money to live, but as long as I had enough to live . . . And I went to work in the wintertime. I sold cars one year. Dominic was making $35,000 or $40,000 but he was a better player. He had the golden name."

Asked whether he still retained the clause he'd had in 1946, tying salary increases to attendance, it seemed clear he did not. "I'm sure some of the other players had those clauses in later years. Ballclubs didn't like those. In the years we played the reserved seats were a dollar eighty. Ted was worth a lot more money. There's an old saying, To Thine Own Self Be True. I wasn't a Ted Williams. I wasn't a Bobby Doerr. I wasn't a Vern Stephens. I thought what was happening to me was nice, and I was working for the greatest owner who ever lived. I think every player has that one outstanding year. I had mine after the war."

"I wanted to play in the World Series. I figured I deserved at least a $2500 a year raise. Now I made $20,000 the year before. I went up thinking I'm going to get at least a $2500 raise. $2500 in those years was a lot of money for me. I kind of held it against Joe. I wouldn't sign. I said, 'Joe, why are you doing this?' Christ, I played every game. I had 200 hits. How could I be a lousy shortstop?

"So finally I signed for $17,500. I just wanted to get in the World Series again. Naturally, like anybody, I wanted as much money as I could get. But I figured I could get along here. Luckily, I had a good wife. Other wives would have raised hell. I went from shortstop to third base that year. I played there for two years and then I went back to shortstop when McCarthy left the ball club.

"The way the Red Sox treated me when I was a kid, that's always stuck with me. I could have really held out and probably have gotten the money. But years ago, you got a beer for a dime. A coke for a nickel. The hot dogs are $2.75 now."

Johnny got the $2500 back, eventually, but it left a sour taste. "He made it up to me. He gave me a bonus. But he was adamant. I always thought he liked me, but maybe he didn't. I wasn't a home run hitter. There was a lot of guys like me playing—Nellie Fox, Rizzuto. Winning was the thing. If you were a player that could help your team, you don 't necessarily have to hit home runs.

"I'm in the Red Sox Hall of Fame now, though. That's good enough for me!"

The *Providence Journal* ran an article by F. C. Matzek in 1951 entitled "Pesky's Tops as Team Man But It May Be Time for Him to Think of Guy Named John." Stephens was probably making more than double "and part of the reason . . . is that Junior was tough about signing." Pesky "was never one to quibble with the Socker front office brass . . . Maybe he should have been." Dom DiMaggio, too, was receiving twice as much as Johnny. . . . "(H)e is aware of what some of his mates are getting. Says Li'l John, 'Arrgh, they're probably better ball players than I am.'"

Though he won't say so, it's possible that this treatment by the Red Sox after three great years—was demoralizing in '48. The constant concern about where he was going to play—even *if* he was going to play— had to wear as well. Concentrating on mastering a new position in the field—moving from shortstop to third base—must have taken away some of the focus he otherwise might have put on his hitting.

Did Johnny go to watch the Braves, the only Boston team which did make it to the World Series? Yes, he did, but "it was miserable. It could have been a city series, but it wasn't. I went to the first game. My wife was with me. We went down to Jimmy O'Keefe's. We got a phone call at Jimmy O'Keefe's, that my dad died that day. Ruth and I took the plane the next day. Tony Martin, the singer, was on the same plane."

NOTES

(1) Harry Grayson, NEA Sports Editor, undated publication
(2) *Boston Globe*, May 16, 1963
(3) David Kaiser, *Epic Season: The 1948 American League Pennant Race*, University of Massachusetts Press, 1998
(4) Ibid., pp. 235 & 253

Johnny did get some extra work in the off-season, thanks to sportswriter Gerry Moore of the *Globe*. Johnny served as a "personal aide" to the governor of Massachusetts. Governor Robert Bradford (a Republican) served from 1947–1949 and that winter Johnny was on his military staff, a sort of color guard featuring one representative of each of the services. In early February, Johnny had to tell the four-striper in charge, "You're going to have to get someone else to do that. I've got to go to spring training."

11

1949

In February, Bob Holbrook of the *Globe* caught up with Pesky before he drove south to Sarasota. Johnny had been working out at both the Harvard and Tufts cages. Down in weight from where he'd ended the '48 season, Johnny was confident and full of enthusiasm. A year earlier, he'd not known what position he'd be playing. Now he knew he was set at third base.

Holbrook wrote, "It's no secret that he assumed his new duties with a feeling of apprehension. But orders were orders and he stumbled and sputtered through the first six weeks of the season. In spite of that dismal start, Pesky finished the season confident he had mastered the position. Right now he knows what McCarthy expects of him." Those six weeks had been rough. "Holy Cow! I was awful!" People who followed the ball club felt Pesky had been "swinging too lustily"—perhaps going for a few more of those home runs Cronin had complained were lacking. "That's right. I was swinging too hard. I was trying to hit the ball farther than I ever had before when I was always hitting above .300. This year I'm going to pop them out there like I used to."

Johnny noted that a .285 hitter who can knock runs in is better than someone with a high average who doesn't. Johnny only hit .281 and drove in just 55 runs. Mitigating his lower average, however, were those 99 walks and the fact that he scored more runs than ever before (124) despite missing eleven games. His OBP was actually up a point over 1947, .394 to .393. The 124 runs scored tied him with Ted Williams for third in the league.

Pesky felt good about his 1949 teammates. He envisioned better years from Hughson (who'd hardly pitched in 1948), Mickey Harris and Kinder. Harris came in 22 pounds lighter. Hughson had a full year to recuperate from his two arm operations. Ferriss had gotten married, and Pellagrini said that might help him settle down and become more effective. They were hoping McDermott could get better control of his pitches. There were hopes for two bonus babies—Stobbs and Quinn. Quinn had pitched an entire season for New Britain and posted an ERA of 0.00, with 8 or 9 complete games. The next year his ERA was 0.4 something. He'd gone 5-2 for Birmingham in '48. Parnell (15-8 in '48) looked solid, as did Kramer (19-5) and Dobson (16-10) and Earl Johnson (10-4.) As long as the Sox could start the season decently, they had a good shot at the pennant. The bad start in '48 cost them badly. "I wasn't hitting. Dominic wasn't hitting and Doerr wasn't hitting. Stephens and Williams were and except for them there's no telling where we might have landed. You can't expect Ted to do everything. We'll have to give him help and I think we will this Spring." This team fully expected to take the flag.

Joe McCarthy, for his part, came up with a colorful metaphor for the new spirit he planned to demand in 1949. "We're not going to have a ball club that looks like a tired burlesque show at the end of a long hard road season. You know how the girls just barely seem to be able to make it. They act like they can't wait until the show is over, their costumes are tattered and their dancing is lousy. Well, we're not going to have that kind of a ball club. Everybody moves when they're out there on that field. Nobody stands around. We want to keep the show moving. We want people to come out to the ball park an hour early to see us go through infield practice."

Pesky was still feeling good as March drew to a close. Hy Hurwitz said the infielders practiced with so much zest that they "almost had to be chased off the field by Coach Kiki Cuyler." Pesky handled himself at third "like a seasoned performer." Johnny was quoted: "A year ago, I wore myself out trying to learn third-base play. I believe that's why I couldn't put on my usual late season drive at bat. But I'm saving my hits and my stamina for the regular campaign in 1949."

Johnny had an unremarkable spring training but still the *Globe* suggested "Sox Picked to Win Flag Because of Pesky and Hughson." Picked to win in a walk. In a national poll of 112 baseball writers, 70 of them picked the Red Sox for the pennant.

Pesky was now comfortable at third. "I never want to be a shortstop again," he crowed, "I walked over there today and took a look around. Boy, there's a lot of territory to cover there." Joe Cashman called Pesky and Matt Batts the "most improved players" of the spring in an April 6 column. He quoted Pesky as saying, "I won't be worrying as much about making mistakes as I did last year. I know what the job is all about now. And I've come to enjoy it so much I hope I never again have to play short or anywhere else. Wait and see, I'll play hell out of it."

Johnny was happy to be starting a new season. "What a lucky guy I am," he allowed. "Instead of wearing these shoes, I'd probably be shining them for some other guy in the Coast League." Humility aside, though, he did admit, "What burns me is during the winter, whenever some writer is a little short on fact, he is always trading me—in fiction—to some other club. I'm very happy in Boston and want to stay there as long as they want me. I suppose the boys have to write something, but I wish they'd pick on somebody else." All in all, though, he was very pleased to be with the Red Sox: "I guess you got to be lucky to get the breaks in life . . . And the best break of all is working for Tom Yawkey."

The Red Sox lost the first game of the year, in Philadelphia. They lost the second as well, 3-2, in 10 innings on throwing errors by Pesky and Kinder. Johnny had been 2 for 4 at the plate but his error in the 3rd had set up the second run. He made another bad throw in the 10th, on Fain's bunt. In game 3, Parnell pitched a shutout. All four of the Red Sox runs scored in the top of the 9th, one of them pushed across by Pesky. Johnny hit in his first 5 games, but the team found itself with a 5-6 record at April's end. The Yankees were 10-2. This was not the start Boston had hoped for.

To kick off May, Ted hit his first grand slam since 1946, at Yankee Stadium while Johnny went 3 for 4 and also homered—a two-run shot— off Allie Reynolds. "As I'm running by Phil Rizzuto," Johnny told John Drohan of the *Boston Traveler*, "little Scooter didn't ask me how it felt, but grinned and said, 'How many is that, Johnny?' I had three last year, so I told him, 'Four.' After all, he didn't say how many years."

Only Parnell seemed to be predictably good among Boston pitchers. He doled out just 6 earned runs over his first five starts, every one of which was a complete game. Parnell alone stood between the Sox and the cellar.

Johnny had a shot at pulling off another hidden ball trick in a mid-

May game, but Sox pitcher John Robinson—who only ever pitched 4 innings in major league ball—stepped off the rubber, thereby balking in the runner at third whom Pesky was prepared to put out.

Johnny had cooled off at the plate, and by mid-May he was back down to .280. By the end of the month, Pesky had built his average up to .285, with 43 hits and 18 RBI. The Sox were in second, 4½ out.

The team slacked off a bit in early June, dropping back to 4th and then 5th place as Johnny's average also swooned. Boston was now under .500. When Johnny sank to .264, a June 12 *Globe* story headlined "Pesky and Stephens Seen Battling to Hold Sox Berths." They weren't playing well in the field, either. Balls were squirting between them.

Boston then traded Sam Mele and Mickey Harris to the Senators for pitcher Walt Masterson. They'd recalled McDermott from the minors, but refused to give up on Ferriss. McCarthy had never forgiven Mele for damaging Ted Williams in horseplay aboard that train in 1948, even though it was Williams who prompted it. Johnny recalls, "McCarthy never cared for Mele for some reason, even though Sam was a pretty good player.

"Yeah, he [McCarthy] had a drinking problem. He was a fine man, though. He knew about music, the great stars of Broadway, baseball. To me, he knew more baseball than anybody I was ever around. I used to love to listen to him tell stories. He used to wear those long sleeves. He didn't wear cutoff sleeves. He was always moving around. He might be behind the batting cage and then a moment later he might be out in right field.

"When my mother came to Chicago to visit her sister—her sister was sick, and my mother didn't have the greatest health—my oldest sister was with her to make sure everything went all right. After the game, it was a hot day and when they went into the bar to get something to drink, McCarthy came in the bar. I introduced him to my mother. She understood some English. He leaned down and shook my mother's hand, 'How are you?' 'Hello, Mr. McCardy'—you know, with her little accent. He didn't say too much. She always felt embarrassed when she talked in English. He leaned down to her and said, 'You have a nice boy'— meaning me—and of course she understood that. She beamed and said, 'Thank you. Thank you, Mr. McCardy.' He was a class act."

The Red Sox were a sorry lot. "Heck, there's nothing wrong. We're in a slump," McCarthy noted, as the team dropped to 6th place, 9 out, on June 16. On the 18th, the Sox won 7-5 on the strength of a six-run 4th inning, the big blow being Pesky's bases loaded triple into Fenway's right field corner in a tie game.

Johnny wasn't the only Boston batter who had been struggling. Ted Williams' average was 100 points below his 1948 mark—of course, with Ted, this meant he was "only" hitting .315 instead of the .415 he'd sported the previous year at the same point in the season! He'd kept up his RBI production, though, and had 77 by June 24. The Red Sox reeled off 6 straight victories and a story that day reported "Pesky is aflame in the field, and is hitting as good as he did in '46." He'd come alive, and went 3 for 4 in a 21-2 win over the Browns, followed by a 13-2 win on the 25th wherein Johnny went 4 for 5. In that lopsided 21-2 win on the 24th, the Red Sox had already scored 19 by the 8th inning—and then decided to pull a double steal. Williams was on first and Pesky on third, when Ted broke for second (Ted's only stolen base of 1949) and a moment later Pesky scooted home with run #20.

The next day, the 26th, Johnny added three more hits and finally cracked .300. The Sox were in third place, and he was hitting .302. A Gene Mack cartoon depicted Johnny helping a bandaged and bewildered St. Louis Brownie leave the hotel. "Is Pesky Sorry To See Him Go" said the cartoon, and the balloon coming out of Johnny's mouth had him solicitously saying, "Take good care of yourself and come back soon won't you? Just a second and I'll call a cab—Now is there anything else?"

Jack Barry's story said, "The play of Johnny Pesky has been a big factor in the Sox surge, which has seen them win 10 of 14 games at home. Pesky is hitting as he did in 1946 when the Sox rode to the pennant. And the improvement in Pesky's play at third base has silenced his critics." He'd hit safely 25 times in 57 at bats during the homestand.

Their fortunes turned, however, when Dom's big brother brought his Yankees to town. Just off the disabled list, Joe D showed no mercy and clobbered four home runs in 3 days as his team swept the Sox. The A's then swept the Red Sox at Shibe, too, before Boston hobbled into New York and dropped a twin bill. In a sequence which Roger Birtwell wrote was "the play that killed the Red Sox hopes for a pennant," Pesky was tagged out at home on a close play. It was a freakish dark stormy day, with sudden bursts of wind that resulted in several capsizings and drownings in New York waters. The Sox were down 3-2 going into the 9th in the first game. Pesky singled and went to third on Ted's single. Raschi walked Stephens to fill the bases. Al Zarilla, hitless his last 14 times up, stepped into the box but play had to be halted as a tremendous dust storm turned the infield into the Arabian Desert.

When play resumed, Zarilla banged the ball into right. It was "still almost pitch dark" and Johnny thought the ball was going to be caught. So had Rizzuto, it was later reported. "Instead of running for the plate, Pesky was doing a 'wrong-way Corrigan.' Johnny headed back to tag up at third. He was apparently blinded by the dust." Williams was "yelling like mad" at Pesky to run home, as the ball bounced three feet in front of Cliff Mapes who fired a perfect one-hopper to Lawrence (of Arabia?) Berra at the plate. Johnny stumbled trying to reverse direction, then collided hard with Berra, knocking him down. But he was forced out. Cuyler, the third base coach, had urged Johnny to play it safe. "I've never seen anything like it," Johnny lamented. "We just can't seem to win. . . . We've gone through this roller-coaster and in six weeks we hadn't picked up a game."

The Sox then won 7 games in 6 days, but they were still 8½ games out of first place, in fourth. The team was nonetheless optimistic. Pesky was .302 at the All-Star break. Ted had 85 RBI and Stephens had 86. The Sox regulars were hitting just .259 on the road, but a sterling .330 in their home park. Ted had cracked a rib just before the All-Star Game, but played and was credited by manager Boudreau as having made the play that saved the game with a spectacular running catch,

After the break, Johnny's average continued to climb to .316 as the team returned to Boston on July 26 for a 23-game do-or-die homestand.

In a comic interlude, the St. Louis Browns offered to trade Bob Dillinger to the Red Sox for Johnny Pesky plus $200,000. The Red Sox should have taken Dillinger after the 1947 season, and not Stephens, the Browns declared. Stephens knocked in 137 runs in 1948, was closing in on 100 of the 159 RBI he'd achieve in 1949 and was going to post another 144 in 1950. Dillinger did have 207 hits in 1948, but only 44 RBI. He hit well in 1949, too, winding up at .324 (he'd hit .321 in '48) but the Sox needed a slugger, not another table setter.

"Right now, Pesky is starting to arrive," wrote Holbrook on July 26. Had he not gotten off to such a slow start, he might have made that year's All-Star squad, as he'd intended. "His play in the field has improved immeasurably over the last two months. Sunday he made one of the best tags of his career when he scooped a throw from second baseman Bobby Doerr to erase an over-enthusiastic Brownie baserunner. He's right up there with the league-leaders in hits. . . . " Johnny had started thinking of 200 hits again. "Little Pesky is more valuable than it appears sometimes," continued Holbrook. "He's an ideal second hitter, because of his ability to bunt and the number of hits he gets over the course of a season."

July 30 saw Johnny go just 1 for 6, but he made that one hit count, driving in 3 with a triple in the 8th which tied the game at 6 all. Pesky doubled to left-center off Satchel Paige scoring Goodman and Zarilla, but umpire Bill Summers ruled that Dale Mitchell threw his glove at the ball—creating an automatic triple and sending in Lou Stringer with what was then the tying run in the game. Doby had gone for a shoestring catch but missed and Mitchell tried to trap the ball. Mitchell said the glove fell off his hand. "He went after the ball and it looked like he threw his glove at the ball. I don't know whether it hit the ball or not but Bill Summers called it," Johnny recalls. Paige then walked Williams and got Stephens swinging. The Indians scored four unanswered runs in the top of the tenth and won. (1)

On the final day of July, Dom DiMaggio's hit streak in progress reached 27 games, eclipsing Johnny's 26-game club-record streak that he'd set in 1947. Before it was over (brother Joe caught his fly ball in the 9th inning of the final game) DiMaggio stretched it to 34 games, and by the time it ended the Red Sox were 17-8 since the All-Star Break, though still 6½ games out, in third place.

In early August, Johnny was still hitting well. He bunted safely in back-to-back-to-back games on the 1st, 2nd and 3rd, getting three hits in each game. Pesky and DiMaggio pulled off a double steal on the 3rd, while the Browns' highly-touted Bob Dillinger was napping at third.

On August 12, taking two from the Senators that day, the Red Sox reached second place for the first time since June 4th, just 5 games behind the Yankees. The wins were by 15-7 and 13-11 margins, hardly tightly-pitched contests, but Pesky went 5 for 7 with 5 runs scored and 4 batted in, and made "a horde of standout defensive plays" according to the *Globe*. Winning 18 out of 22 games, the Bosox pulled to within 4. Maybe there was hope after all. Then Johnny pulled a muscle in his left side during a game.

An ashen white while he was being taped up by trainer Eddie Froehlich, Pesky said: "I feel awful sick. I've never had anything like this. I'll have to get some relief from this pain pretty soon." He'd hurt himself swinging at a Paul Calvert pitch in the first and doubled up with pain. He got taped up and jumped back in the game, grounding out. He singled in the 6th but just as he scored, following singles by Williams and Stephens, he felt it again and was taken out. "I haven't missed an inning all year long. I wanted to play every one this year. But I couldn't stand the pain any longer. . . . It feels like somebody stuck a knife in me," he said in the trainer's room after being lifted in the 7th of game 2. "I hated to get out of there." By this same date, James W. Bailey of the Boston

Evening American, had declared that "Little Jawn" has really settled down at third. Now he was out, and it was feared he might be out two weeks. They could ill afford to lose his services.

In a 7-week stretch, beginning July 5, they had won 32 out of 47 games. After a long climb back, reminiscent of the 1948 season, the Sox found themselves just 2½ games back. Casey Stengel was said to be looking over his shoulder as Boston crept closer in the race. Pennant talk began to bubble up again in the Hub. "Don't say it," piped in Pesky to an ebullient Kramer, who was talking to a reporter. "You were just about to claim the pennant. Remember what you told Parnell about popping off. But if we keep on going like we're going, we're going to be tough to beat. Here I am sitting out these games when things are getting hot. I'm almost going crazy sitting on the bench. . . . The Boss, J. R. McCarthy, is feeling good these days. He was full of pep on the bench with the Senators. I even started to kid with him and he had a grin from ear to ear."

Johnny's mother came to Chicago to see her sister—her first trip out of Portland in 45 years—and see her son play in the majors for the very first time. Pesky got into town a day early and went over to Comiskey Park to get in a little workout. He borrowed an Athletics uniform and took some batting. Cat Metkovich of the White Sox saw Johnny in the A's uniform and went over to ask what was up. "Oh, they got me on waivers yesterday," Johnny said with a straight face, to his 1946 teammate. Johnny was able to get back into his proper uniform that night and collected a hit, but the Red Sox lost the game. The next day, though, they took two, Johnny going 5 for 9. The Red Sox won 3 of 4 from the White Sox, but then suddenly dropped four to the Indians, dropped from 1½ to 4 back, and now the Tribe was nipping at their heels.

The Yankees had the easier schedule by far, as far as home field advantage goes. As of the 4th of September, Cleveland only had 3 home games remaining and 18 away games. The Red Sox had 9 at home and 11 away, but the Yankees had 21 at home and only 4 on the road.

On September 9, at one of those New York home games, the Red Sox won 7-1, in part fueled by Johnny's 2-run homer in the 3rd, twelve rows up into the lower grandstand corner in right. "The Red Sox don't need to lug their left field fence around with them, after all," wrote Roger Birtwell. "Pesky finally found a pitch to his liking and drilled a low liner to right. It some parks, that probably would have been all it is. But Pesky had his sights trained on the right spot. The ball cleared that low right-field fence for a two-run homer."

Johnny's mother had traveled on to Boston and on the 13th saw him make a couple of fine fielding plays at home. She also, unfortunately, saw him embarrassed—in the bottom of the 3rd, there were two outs and Johnny was on second. Tigers centerfielder Hoot Evers snuck in behind Johnny and he found himself picked off second, ending the inning. A *Globe* writer remarked, "According to Johnny, she doesn't know much about baseball but she knows when he gets a base hit and makes an error."

The heart of the Red Sox, Pesky loved to play hearts. Joe Kelley of the AP reported that Pesky was an inveterate player, usually with three scribes while on the road. The writers passed the Queen of Spades to Johnny so often that he became known as the Black Widow Spider. "Pesky's blood pressure mounted with every visit of the ebony Queen, a fact which tickled his tormentors." So the writers enlisted Cleveland third baseman Ken Keltner's help. In a custom which we find bizarre today, back at this time players left their gloves on the field as they headed back into the dugout for their ups. Keltner slipped the black queen into Pesky's glove between innings. When Johnny took the field in the bottom of an inning at Cleveland, he shoved his hand into his glove and found the black queen there. The press box, watching expectantly, convulsed at Pesky's reaction. On to Detroit. There, Tigers third base coach Dick Bartell was enlisted. When Johnny took the field in the second inning, the Black One was back again. Johnny shook his fist at the press box and stopped talking to the two writers he believed responsible. Some time later, the A's came to Boston. Someone got a black queen and had it autographed by every Boston writer and mailed it to Johnny, but they had tipped off Al Simmons—who somehow managed to gather a lot of the Philadelphia players around to witness Johnny opening his mail.

The papers of the 26th showed the Red Sox tied for first place with a win over the Yankees. After another terrible, slow start, the Bosox seemed to finally have peaked at the right time. "Pesky's 2-run single, Ted's 43rd Pace 4-1 win," headlined the *Globe*. Johnny was 3 for 4, and "was terrific around third." The Sox had found themselves on the 21st two games behind with only eight to play. The Yankees still had ten to play.

The very next day—the 22nd—Johnny was injured by a Ted Williams pitch. "It was an off day, "Johnny recalls. "We were hitting. He'd pitch to me and I'd pitch to him. He was pitching and he hit me right in the elbow. My right elbow." A bystander remarked, "There goes the pennant." Johnny continued, "I played, though. Jackie Hickey, my pal, was with me that day shagging, and a couple of clubhouse kids—Vinnie Orlando and Frankie Kelly." Hy Hurwitz reported under the headline "Williams' Pitch Injures Pesky, But He Will Play" that Pesky was "painfully injured" and walked off the field and put an ice pack on his elbow, soon wise-cracking about this "pitching duel" with Ted.

On the 24th, Johnny played well again, with three hits and a "fine game in the field." He rubbed a bruise on his chest, saying, "That grounder that Hank Bauer hit down to me in the last inning jumped and stung a little. I'm getting to be a pretty good glove man, aren't I? So don't try to trade me after the season is over like the boys have for the past few years."

So the Red Sox had tied for first on the 25th. Then both teams left Boston and entrained to New York where they resumed the battle on the 26th before 66,156 rabid Yankees fans at the Stadium. Boston won again, this time by a 7-6 margin, coming from behind, and earning Boston sole possession of first place. The dramatic winning run was scored by Pesky, safe from third on a squeeze in a Sox 4-run 8th inning. With one out, the bases loaded, Williams on first, Bobby Doerr bunted on his own; Pesky had no idea it was coming. Doerr's leg was taped and he didn't think he could drive the ball far enough for a sacrifice fly. He knew he couldn't beat out a close play, but he knew Johnny well enough to know that Johnny would be poised and ready for anything.

Pesky, ever alert, "saw Doerr's hand sliding down the bat as the ball left Joe Page's hand." The ball went about 10 feet and stopped, on resodded grass. Tommy Henrich grabbed it and fired perfectly to catcher Ralph Houk at the plate, in time. But "Houk seemed to freeze for just a moment," JP explained. "He didn't slap the tag on me. Just seemed to tighten up. I caught the base under him and after I crossed the plate, he tagged me on the hip. He didn't have the plate blocked."

It was a hotly disputed play, a "$200,000 decision" by plate umpire Bill Grieve. Grieve called Pesky safe, but Houk exploded, actually slamming his mask off Grieve's shoulder. Stengel bumped Grieve as well. Mapes yelled, asking Grieve how much he'd bet on the game—which cost Mapes a $500 fine from the League.

Everyone in Yankee Stadium could see that the throw beat Pesky to the plate, and photographs confirm it.

The New York press ran the photos the next day, but Grieve—in perfect position—said the pictures didn't tell the whole story—and that they didn't run all of the photos. One that didn't run may have shown Pesky's foot across the plate before Houk tagged him. "I know that umpires, like ball players, occasionally miss plays. I know that I didn't miss this one," said Grieve. "Sure, I could have made the easy call," Grieve added, "giving it to the home club, but in my heart, I know I made the right call."

Red Smith wrote, "the Yankees did not lose because of an umpire's decision. They lost because they played bad baseball and booted away a three-run lead." This was the Sox' 10th straight win.

Bill Grieve figured in another play the next day. In a story intriguingly titled "Ted Beats Pesky In Foot Race; Costs Sox Run" the question was asked, "Can Ted Williams sprint from first base to second faster than Johnny Pesky can race from third to home plate?" Ted was on first, and Johnny on third, with one out when Vern Stephens lined to left. Washington's Ed Stewart caught the liner and fired to second. Both Ted and Johnny had tagged up, but Ted was tagged out at second a moment before Pesky scored. Ted may have assumed the throw was heading home, but he was caught out in a double play and the run didn't score. Grieve was the second base umpire. The Red Sox won, anyhow. With five games to play, Johnny had said, "We've got to beat the Yankees to win the pennant. If we don't beat them, we don't deserve to win."

They lost on the 28th as Stobbs faltered in the 9th, prompting Parnell's appearance in relief, and the Senators scored two times to win the game, the final one on Parnell's wild pitch. Both New York and Boston now sported identical 95-56 records. There were just three games to play.

Both Boston and New York had their next games postponed by rain. On the 30th, the Red Sox beat Washington by the score of 11-9, on just 5 hits! The game featured 14 free passes given to Boston by uncommonly generous Washington pitching. The Yankees lost to lowly Philadelphia, so the Red Sox were up by one game, with just two to go. A Red Sox win on the 1st could seal it, since there were only two games left, both New York–Boston match-ups. "If we can't win one out of two, we don't deserve it," affirmed Tom Yawkey.

The Yankees had so far taken 11 of 20 from Boston. Fans who had lined up 36 hours in advance at the Fenway ticket office saw the Red Sox jump out to a 4-0 lead, only to lose 5-4. On the 2nd, in New York, the Yankees won again, 5-3, and the season was over. The Red Sox had put in their patented last-minute scare, pushing across all three of their runs in the final frame but it was just too little. Time had run out. Kinder had won 13 games in a row, but now his streak had snapped, too. Neither Williams nor Pesky got a hit, as Raschi held the Sox to just five hits on the day. Ted even lost the batting title to George Kell, .3428 to .34275.

One more hit would have given Ted the title, but he'd only managed one hit in the final five games. The Red Sox had come from 12 back, only to lose on the final day of the year, another heart-breaking last-minute devastating disappointment for the Boston faithful.

For the second year in a row, the Red Sox had lost the pennant on the final day of the season. In 1946, they'd lost in the final game of the Series. Three out of four years, then—1946, 1948 and 1949—they had gone right to the last game, and lost every time.

Post-mortems didn't call for any trades, recognizing that the Sox already had a truly great lineup. "We'll Be Back Next Year . . . They Made A Good Fight" was the reported reaction of Red Sox rooters. The team, dispirited, packed up and went their separate ways.

Thus was born the spectre of Sisyphus that has haunted the Red Sox ever since—the struggle to play out a full 154-game season, to battle on the road and to best the visitors at home. To come so close but then just miss three out of four years forged a powerful image in the hearts and minds of New England fandom, of a team maybe destined to always fall short. They came close again in 1950, but then were nowhere until 1967. The Game Seven losses in three later World Series (1967, 1975 and 1986) only reinforced the same notion. The Red Sox have now lost four consecutive World Series Game Sevens.

Ben Walsh, contributing to a SABR chat list, wrote, "The Boston faithful have endured a fate worse than any the Greek Gods came up with. Sisyphus forever rolling a boulder up a hill, only to have it roll down again at the summit. Tantalus, eternally tempted and tortured by cool water and fruit just out of his reach. These guys have nothing on the Red Sox fan. It didn't even take Ulysses 83 years and counting to get home. That's why it's a Curse—it's far more than just not succeeding. Any team can fail. It's failing when the prize is so close you can touch it that is the mark of the Curse."

For his part, Johnny has never forgotten the 1949 season. Speaking with a sportswriter in 1990—more than four decades later—Johnny said, "I don't think there's a day goes by I don't think about losing that last game of the season in 1949 to the Yankees. That will stay with me forever . . . the feeling I had that we let Mr. Yawkey down again. That's why anything I can do, the smallest of things with just one of these kids, if it results in helping the Red Sox win it all some day, this will all be worth it. That would be my pay back to Mr. Yawkey."

NOTES

(1) Johnny remembered another story as well, of the time a clearly foul
    ball was declared a triple. It was hit foul and "the fielder took his
    glove off and hit the ball. The batter was given a triple. Cal
    Hubbard was the umpire. Luke Sewell was the manager of the
    Browns and he came out screaming, and Cal Hubbard recited the
    rule, verbatim. It was in the rule book, and the rule book didn't say
    the ball had to be fair. They changed that rule the next year."

12
1950

How does a team recover from crushing, disheartening defeat? How do they mentally and physically rejuvenate themselves, survive yet another meaningless spring training schedule, and slog through nearly six months of play? How does a team do this when it's lost and then lost, and then lost again—each time when victory was within their grasp?

It can't have been easy, but Johnny had a ready reply when posed the question years later: "Was it hard getting up for spring training after what the ballclub had been through in '46, '48 and '49?" "Yeah, but we figured all we had to do was win one more game than the other club and it wouldn't have happened." His attitude was refreshingly simple. It didn't focus on the negative, the ultimate disappointment, all that hard but futile work. The way he saw it, just win one more game and the flag would be yours. That's taking baseball a day at a time, and the Red Sox felt they had a good shot at the pennant again in 1950.

1950 looked promising for Johnny from the start. He'd rebounded from his off year (1948) with a solid .306 average in '49. He traveled to Florida early and reported to camp about a week ahead of schedule. Even Ted Williams showed up a day early—prompting a newspaper headline. Vern Stephens, though, was a holdout—reportedly seeking $50,000, up from the $25,000 it was said he'd received in 1949. Stephens' argument was that he was at least half as good as Ted Williams, who was thought

to be making $100,000. The minimum at the time was $5000. Power hitting has always been rewarded disproportionately, both financially and in
terms of celebrity status. A solid, versatile performer like Johnny Pesky
was less likely to reap big rewards, no matter how well he played his position and regardless of his talents as a table-setter. To his credit, Johnny
has always understood this and bears no ill will to those stars—even
though it was Pesky getting on base which provided many of the runs
which a Williams or a Stephens batted in.

The Red Sox were very loose in spring training, "the most carefree
club in Florida," according to a United Press dispatch. There was no
weeping over spilt milk on the squad, though at least one fan grumbled
that "Pesky's baserunning boner cost them the pennant" in 1949. That
was a reference to the early July game in New York when Johnny, his
vision obscured, ran back to tag up at third rather than heading directly
home. Never mind that there was still half a season to play at that point,
or that the team lost 58 games in all.

The very first game of spring training, Johnny injured his left side,
reaching for a ground ball. It was the same muscle pulled in August 1949
that cost him eight games. Johnny quipped, "I ought to come down here
20 pounds overweight. Nothing ever happens then."

Red Smith felt the Red Sox were the best team in baseball, but little
things cost them in '49. The question in 1950 was: were the Red Sox getting too old? McCarthy may have been pushing them a little too hard—
he decided to make all the veterans play all nine innings of every game in
spring training, to try to counter the slow start they'd had in 1949. The
players didn't complain, though. Smith wrote, "As long as he has been in
the game, the notion of finishing second has filled McCarthy with
loathing. Twice . . . his team has broken tardily and finished second." In
1950, 22 of the first 30 games Boston played were at home—affording
them a real shot at getting off to a strong start.

WON-LOSS RECORDS BY MONTH

	1948	1949
April	5-6	3-5
May	15-10	11-18
June	15-15	18-6
July	18-12	25-9
August	24-8	19-10
September	19-5	18-10
October	0-2	2-1

Grantland Rice saw the Sox, the Yanks and the Bums as the only three standout teams in the "bigs" in 1950. New York bookmakers made the Red Sox 7-5 favorites. Whenever Casey Stengel talked about Red Sox players, he always singled out Johnny for praise. Papers made it clear he thought it was a mistake to play Stephens at short, and that had McCarthy kept Johnny at short and had Stephens play third, they might have taken a pennant or two.

Johnny Pesky felt that the '50 Sox were going to be a great team. Doerr was in fine shape, and Pesky predicted Stephens would hit 45-50 home runs. But recalling events of '48 and '49, Johnny hedged his bets: "You can't get too cocky in this business because anything is apt to happen."

Boston opened at home against New York. The first four batters reached base safely and the Red Sox were up 9-0 after four innings. It looked like a laugher and both starter Parnell and Ted Williams were taken out of the line-up. The Red Sox lost the game 15-10! Johnny went 2 for 5 that day, and made a standout play of a Joe DiMaggio smash, but the Yankees roared back to win. The Yanks beat the Sox 16-7 a day later, after losing 6-3 in the first game of that day's doubleheader. By the end of April, Pesky was leading the majors in runs scored with 17, five more than the next closest hitter. He was batting .360.

After nine games the Sox had only three victories to show for their efforts. Then they reeled off six straight wins.

On May 9, the Red Sox finally climbed into first with a 6-1 win over the Tigers, Parnell over Trucks. Johnny was hitting .346, as was Ted. Jerry Nason reported that Dom DiMaggio and Pesky were getting on base so often the umps were striking traffic poses. The Red Sox, Nason wrote, had two 20-game winners, two top sluggers and "probably are the only club in baseball with two 'leadoff' men." By that time, with the season only three weeks old, they had between them already reached base 76 times.

Though they were in first on the 9th, on May 11th the Red Sox lost two to the Tigers and plunged to fourth place, one game out. Williams made two errors—and also made some vulgar gestures to the fans. Johnny pulled another muscle, this time a leg muscle, and was expected to be out a week—this at a time when he was still .333 on the young season. He missed eight games, coming back on the 16th, and went 4 for 6 with 2 RBI in a 13-12 victory over Detroit—then 2 for 4 in the next game.

At 35 games into the season, it was clear that the Red Sox had not achieved the stronger start McCarthy had hoped for. They were four behind the Yankees, in almost exactly the same spot they'd been a year earlier.

Johnny had a nice 5 for 6 game on the 25th, boosting him to .356, as the Red Sox beat the Browns 15-12 on Walt Dropo's grand slam. Two days later, Johnny's single beat the Senators in the 10th, 4-3. The day after that, he knocked in three but the Sox lost 7-6. On the 30th, Johnny went 4 for 9 but Boston dropped two to New York. The Red Sox closed out the month at 24-18, in third place, five games out.

Boston downed the Indians 11-5, then 11-9, and then walloped the White Sox 17-7 and 12-0 before dropping one to Chicago 8-4. When the Browns came to town on June 7, Johnny banged out four hits in a 20-4 win. As if that lopsided victory weren't enough, the Red Sox set a couple of batting records the very next day. Boston rang up 29 runs (Pesky went 5 for 7 with 3 runs and 2 RBI) and annihiliated the hapless Browns 29-4. The Sox set the record for the most total bases in one game (60) and the most extra base hits in one game (17). Chuck Stobbs cruised all the way for the Sox. Talk about run support! In a one-week stretch, the Red Sox scored 104 runs. They boasted ten hitters batting over .300: Goodman, Zarilla, DiMaggio, Dropo, Tebbetts, Williams, Wright, Pesky, Rosar and Stephens—with Vollmer (.296) and Doerr (.287) not far behind.

On June 11, Hal Newhouser held Johnny 0 for 5 in the first game of a doubleheader against Detroit, but in the second game he went 2 for 3 with a rare Fenway homer in the first, into the "right field pavilion"—to the right of the visitor's bullpen. By the 18th, the Sox were 9 1/2 out of first, after dropping five straight. Joe McCarthy was sidelined with pleurisy and flu leaving the team manager-less for a few games; then McCarthy resigned and Steve O'Neill took over as manager.

Under O'Neill the Red Sox won their first seven games, all on the road. Pesky, though, pulled another leg muscle and Billy Goodman took over at third. The ultimate utility man, Goodman started the season at first base, then spelled Doerr at second when Doerr was hurt. Displaced by Doerr's return, Goodman had to warm the bench until Pesky's injury. He played capably, which presented a problem—where to play him. By June, Goodman had already played every infield position.

When Johnny returned, Jack Fadden replaced Eddie Froelich as Red Sox trainer. Johnny's hitting had declined in the weeks before the All-Star Game, before and after his injury. At one point before the muscle pull, he'd hit a 1 for 17 stretch on the road. By the break, he was down, but to a still-desirable .317. The All-Star Game saw Ted Williams break his elbow crashing into the left field wall to snare a Ralph Kiner liner. Despite the pain, he played out most of the game. "Red Sox Chances Slim" headlined the *Globe*. With Ted out, Clyde Vollmer filled in with a home run and two doubles in his first game, but before long it was Billy Goodman who assumed yet another defensive role: Boston's leftfielder.

The Red Sox played in the annual exhibition game at Doubleday Field in Cooperstown on July 24, and Johnny hit a home run as they beat the New York Giants 8-5. First up in the seventh, Johnny's drive tied the score at 5 all "by propelling Hansen's initial pitch to the top row of right field bleachers."

In all of 1949, the Red Sox only lost 16 home games. By July 17, they'd already lost 17 home games, with 34 yet to play. The team was playing better under O'Neill, 19-9 in the first month. By the 24th, they crept back up to 6½ games behind but were heading out on a 22-game road trip, still without Williams.

The Sox were so far back—and with Williams, Zarilla and Tebbetts all injured—Bob Holbrook wrote, "There is not too much point in worrying about the Red Sox and their pennant aspirations now"—a premature prediction as it turned out.

Boston's pitching was coming around, not only from Kinder and Dobson but from a trio of rookies—Willard Nixon, Dick Littlefield and Jim McDonald. Parnell was returning to form. By mid-August, the Red Sox were 29-17 under O'Neill. On the 15th, they took two from the A's behind Parnell and Nixon, as Johnny went 5 for 9. Walt Dropo hit a home run off Hank Wyse, then Wyse hit him in the head his next time up, denying intent after the game by explaining that Dropo was a low ball hitter and he was "throwing him a sinker ball—high." Now the Sox were without Dropo as well. Goodman moved to first, and Vollmer to leftfield. At this point, the Red Sox had won 16 straight home games against the A's, and they won two more the very next day, by scores of 11-3 and 12-7, and won again on the 17th, 10-6.

Williams was beginning to take some batting practice but there was some feeling, even among his teammates, that the Red Sox were doing better without him. They were 42-35 when he went down, 44-19 afterwards. A *Globe* headline credited the chemistry fostered by O'Neill: "Sox Do Better With Ted Out, But O'Neill May Be Answer." O'Neill was closer to the players, not remote as McCarthy had been. McCarthy was rarely even seen by his players on the road or on the trains. As to the new skipper, though, "Why, he had me laughing for three hours one night on a train," Pesky reported.

Dropo came back on the 19th, and Goodman—now the league's leading hitter (.354)—shifted back to left field. Foreseeing Ted's imminent return, the question of where to put Goodman was foremost. "Johnny Pesky is a rock of strength at third base," wrote Clif Keane. Doerr was also having a great year, and Vern Stephens was leading the league in RBI. Dom DiMaggio was hitting .330 and covering center like a blanket. Zarilla was back and hitting .340. The team was beginning to jell; they won seven in a row, but despite that only picked up one game in the standings. At Fenway, the team was hitting a spectacular .343.

Pesky's Fenway average was .363, a full 81 points higher than his road mark. In 1949, he'd hit .349 at home and .259 on the road. Why would this be for a spray hitter who specialized in singles and who rarely took advantage of the left field Wall? When Al Dark asked Williams about hitting, Ted turned his attention to his table-setter, "There isn't much I can tell you about hitting, but if you want to see a great hitter, come out and watch the fellow who hits ahead of me. Yes, Pesky. There's a fellow who hits close to .330 year after year and never hits a 3-and-1 or 2-and-0 pitch. He doesn't hit the cripple, because he's supposed to get on base ahead of me. He's in the hole most of the time, but he still gets his hits." Pesky did get a lot of hits the hard way, and beginning in 1948 he began to earn a lot more walks (99, 100 and 104 in each of the next three years.) Johnny said it was McCarthy who taught him patience at the plate. "He was always on me when I hit a bad ball. He kept telling me, 'Make the ball be over.'"

The Boston writers consistently credited Pesky's infield play. On the 25th, after Stephens won a game for the Red Sox 6-2 with a 9th inning grand slam, the closing paragraph remarked on Johnny's work. "Johnny Pesky had a brilliant day at third base . . . 'I was a leather man all right,' admitted Pesky, 'but we won the game, so my going hitless didn't hurt.' "

Boston fought to within 3½ games of first place and when Stephens was sidelined with an injured Achilles tendon, Johnny moved to short, and Goodman filled in at third. Fourteen Red Sox were hitting over .300, two of them pitchers. The loss of Ted certainly didn't help, but the Sox were now 33-14 without him. Down 12-1 in one game, they came back to win 15-14. Pesky booted a ball on his first play at short, throwing wild into the dugout. "I wanted to make that throw real good, and I held the ball so long that I threw it away. I knocked Mel Parnell plum off the bench," Johnny explained. He took some riding from the Indians' benchjockeys. "When we scored eight runs, the Cleveland players were as quiet as church mice," Pesky exulted.

L to R (back row): Jakob Paveskovich, visiting Yugoslav priest, Marija Paveskovich, Ann, Tony; (front row): Vince, Johnny, Millie, Catherine. Courtesy of Vincent Paveskovich.

Ann and Johnny Paveskovich at First Communion. Courtesy of Vincent Paveskovich.

This 1937 American Legion team representing Post Office Pharmacy in Portland won the Northwest regional tournament. Members of the tournament squad included Franklin Roberts, Bill Carney, Stanley Robinson, Harold Ogden, John Bubalo, Vince Javoric, Bob Patterson, John Granato, Jim Ellis, Stewart Fredricks, Bob Signer, Wesley Hoyt, Frank Lolich, Joe Erautt and Bill Timmons. Their coach (back row) was Wade Williams. The guy in the front row, far right, is Boston Red Sox legend Johnny Pesky.

Post Office Pharmacy team, Portland 1937. Mike Ryerson Collection. Courtesy of Vincent Paveskovich.

Young, but mighty amateur hockey players are the two shown above. They are members of Danny Edge's Hop Gold team, Portland city champions, who will face Eba's Grocers here tonight in the first half of a home-and-home series for the Northwest championship. Left is Johnny Pesky, 17-year-old winger, and right is Tommy Walker, defense man. Both are playing their second year for the team.

Portland newspaper clipping, courtesy of Dave Eskenazi.

Silverton Red Sox, 1939. Note Silver Falls jerseys on some players. Courtesy of Jeff Brekas.

Johnny with Silverton Red Sox, 1939. Courtesy of Vincent Paveskovich.

Mazurkiewicz to Paveskovich (Mazur, 2B to Pesky, SS), Rocky Mount, NC, 1940.
Courtesy of Johnny Pesky.

Pesky slides into third for a triple, August 28, 1942 at Fenway Park. Chicago's Dario
Lodigiano lunges in vain for Luke Appling's wild relay, and Johnny ran home to score.
Collection of Bill Nowlin.

Johnny and Vince at Vaughn Street Park, Portland. Early 1940s. Courtesy of Vincent Paveskovich.

Johnny Pesky & Bobby Doerr, 1942.

Bill Franciskovich, Ann & Johnny.

Ted congratulates Johnny on home run, 1946.

Emerson Field dugout, Chapel Hill, NC, 1943.
L to R: Buddy Gremp, Joe Coleman, Johnny
Pesky, Ted Williams, Johnny Sain. Courtesy of
Orville Campbell and the *Chapel Hill
Newspaper.*

1946 MVP ballot, with Ted
Williams #1 and Johnny
Pesky #2 in the American
League. Collection of Bill
Nowlin.

Ruth and Johnny pack for the drive to spring training, probably 1947. Courtesy of Johnny Pesky.

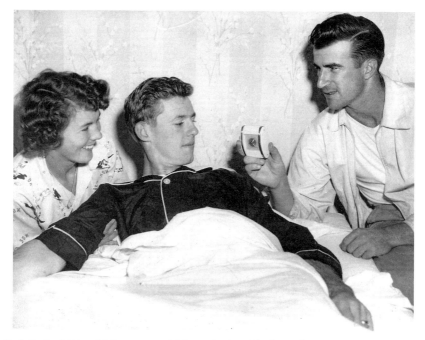

Ruth Pesky, Mickey McDermott and Johnny Pesky with alarm clock, waking up boarder McDermott, circa 1949. Courtesy of Johnny Pesky.

Rhubarb at home plate, 1948 or 1949. L to R: umpire John Stevens, Joe McCarthy, Birdie Tebbetts, Johnny Pesky. Courtesy of Johnny Pesky.

Pesky Day poster placemat, July 24, 1951. Courtesy of Johnny Pesky.

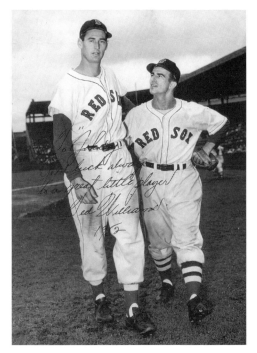

Ted and Johnny, inscribed by Ted: "To Johnny. Good luck always, to a great little player, Ted Williams 1952." Courtesy of Johnny Pesky.

Johnny as manager, Seattle Rainiers 1961-62. Courtesy of Johnny Pesky.

Pesky as Pirates coach. Courtesy of Johnny Pesky.

Ted Williams and Johnny Pesky at Jimmy Fund event, 1986. Photograph by Mark Tetrault.

Sal Bertolami and Johnny Pesky, The Window Boys, working for JB Sash & Door. Courtesy of Sal Bertolami.

Ted and Johnny, instructors at spring training. Courtesy of Johnny Pesky.

Gene Mack sports cartoon depicting a Pesky Pole homer, April 20, 1946.

Johnny with Angel at LeLacheur Park, Lowell, MA, on Angel the Chimp Day, July 6, 2000. Courtesy of Lowell Spinners.

Johnny at the Pesky Pole, May 1998. Photograph by Tim Samway.

Johnny with his fungo bat, late 1990s. Photograph by Tim Samway.

Cooper, Scott - Has been steady since I've been here. Do think his M.R. out put will be better. Great arm - below ave. runner. Fine young man - likes to play.

Kutcher, Randy - has done an outstanding job Could help our big Club in any capacity. Has played SS here - he's no Aparicio - but gets the job done. Does all the little things to help you win. Very good with the young players. Love to have him around.

McDougal J. has been a pleasant surprise Can play SS & 2B. Switch hitter. Could be a good extra man. Has a fine arm Erratic at times.

Vaughn, Mo Great looking hitter - very good power. Has played 1B very well. Takes ground balls every day. Has improved in every department If this young man doesn't do it I'll get out of the game. Very good aptitude & attitude. Great kid!!

Lancellotte - Robidoux - am sure you know about them. Have been very good on this club and give them both an A. Plus

Page from evaluation report sent by Johnny Pesky to Red Sox General Manager Lou Gorman, late 1980s. Courtesy of Johnny Pesky.

Johnny working out infielders
at Fenway, Summer 2002.
Photographs by Bill Nowlin.

The A's were patsies when they came to Fenway. For two seasons, they failed to win even one game from Boston. Connie Mack's A's last beat the Red Sox on September 12, 1948—they were unable to win a single game in Boston in either the 1949 or the 1950 season. Philadelphia was 40 games out of first place.

By the time the Red Sox left home for a 12 game road trip, they were just one game out of first and feeling confident and relaxed. Even rumors of a Johnny Pesky for Bobby Brown trade didn't hurt the team. Williams returned and in his first two plate appearances was walked intentionally by Stengel, and then by Mack. Finally, in his third pinch-hit role, he got a ball over the plate and banged it out, where it nicked the screen and bounced back into play for a double.

On September 15, Ted rejoined the regular lineup and Goodman took over Pesky's third base slot. A banner headline in the *Globe* read "Benching of Pesky on Ted's Return Hard Job for O'Neill." The story then emerged that Johnny had actually gone to O'Neill a few weeks earlier and volunteered to take himself out of the lineup when Williams came back so the hot-hitting Goodman could contribute. In Ted's first full game back, The Kid got 4 hits including a 3-run homer. Now O'Neill decided to go for the long ball, and so he wanted Doerr, Stephens and Dropo in the lineup, along with Goodman. Pesky was odd man out, hitting .310 to Stephens' .350.

Goodman ultimately won the 1950 A.L. batting championship with a .354 average, and much of the credit could be ascribed to Pesky's selflessness. *The Sporting News*, in its 1984 obituary for Goodman, commented, "Ironically, he got to the plate enough times to qualify for the batting title in 1950 only because Williams had fractured his elbow playing in the All-Star Game. Goodman became the Bosox' regular left fielder, but when a healthy Williams returned, he lost his job. There was some question as to where to play Goodman; the other Boston regulars were hitting well and Manager Steve O'Neill was loath to bench one of them in favor of Goodman. Third baseman Johnny Pesky then benched himself voluntarily in order to give Goodman the necessary 400 plate appearances."

Bill Cunningham confirmed Pesky's sacrifice in the *Herald* the day after the season ended, "It was a deliberate gamble with his job in order to give a teammate a break, and he eventually lost the job. The sporting part about his gesture is that he made it for the man who took the job away from him."

This was in a profession where there are only a very limited number of full-time jobs on each team and most players guard their jobs jealously. Goodman clearly needed to be in the lineup on a regular basis, both for the sake of the team and so he could obtain the requisite number of at bats to qualify for the title. Manager Steve O'Neill recounted the story five years later. "One night Johnny and I were out having dinner at the Maryknoll Seminary in Jamaica Plain. Johnny had been out there before and they liked him so much they asked him to come back again. He asked me to go along, so we went out after a game. There were 54 priests there who had just taken their vows and a few others who were on their way to China. We had a very nice time. The priests threw a turkey dinner for us.

"Finally, Johnny got up and gave a little talk about baseball and the Red Sox. Then he looked over towards me and said, 'This part is for you, Steve. I want you to know that you don't have to worry about a place to use Billy Goodman. Any time you're looking for a spot for him, just tell me. I'll be glad to drop out for him, so don't hesitate to tap me if you have to move Billy around.' I think it was one of the nicest things I've had happen to me in baseball. At the time we had no idea when Ted would be back. Johnny was going good, but he had no chance of winning the batting title. Billy had a good chance. In baseball, it's hard to give up your position. Not many people would do it. That's why I think it was a great gesture." (1)

Later in the season, Pesky benched himself yet again, to help get Ted back in the lineup, according to the *Boston Globe* on September 16. "I'd bench my mother if it would help the club win the pennant," Johnny Pesky said.

To the *Herald* the same day, Johnny had laid out the story, "Nobody likes to play baseball more than I do, but we've got a great chance to win the pennant and we've got to have Ted in the lineup every day to do it. I figured I'm the logical one to come out. The kid [this time he meant Goodman] can't be benched. He's hitting and has a chance for the batting championship. Bobby [Doerr] can't come out and neither can Stevie [Vern Stephens] because they can give you that long ball. I wasn't kidding when I told Steve [O'Neill] two weeks ago that I'd be willing to step down when Ted came back."

Some of the St. Louis Browns found the idea humorous. "Here we haven't one .300 hitter and they bench a guy who's up around .320." In the process, though, Johnny earned another accolade among baseball people. In 1985, the *Lynn Sunday Post* editorialized that Johnny Pesky led the majors in "Most Friends." What Johnny did for Billy Goodman in 1950 shows why.

"The most important thing was winning," Johnny said years later. "It meant so much to us. Ted would have given half his salary if he could have won a World Series."

By the morning of September 20, it was suddenly quite a race. And Boston was in the thick of it. Just when they reached for the golden ring, it slipped away. They lost two to the Indians that day, while both Detroit and New York won. This left Boston two games out, with just ten games to play. Williams hadn't regained his stride. Hank Greenberg, Cleveland's GM, said, "The guy isn't himself." The whole outfield hit only .098 over 5 games. Pesky, though, came back in at short in game two and got a couple of hits and made some plays. As the Red Sox headed to New York, they were two games behind the Yankees and 1½ behind the Tigers. The Sox lost, then lost again. Now with just 8 games remaining, they were four games out and it was just about over. Boston swept a doubleheader the next day—but so did New York. The season sputtered to a finish as the lowly Senators swept a final doubleheader from Boston.

The Red Sox had played just .506 ball on the road and Bobby Doerr expressed the team's frustration: "Goldang it, it's terrible to lose out when we made such a fight of it. Seems after every season we have a terrible letdown and everything happens in the last week." Birdie Tebbetts griped that two of the Sox pitchers were "a couple of juvenile delinquents and moronic malcontents. . . . I don't play ball to win friends. I play to win games." With a record out 94-60, the Bosox finished four games out of first place.

The 1950 Red Sox infield knocked in 457 runs and fell just five runs shy of matching the 1934 Tigers for the most runs batted in by an infield: Dropo (144), Doerr (120), Stephens (144) and Pesky (49). Johnny Pesky scored 112 runs in 1950. Pesky and Williams are the only two players in ML history to score 100 or more runs in each of their first 6 years in the majors. Both Earl Combs and Derek Jeter have achieved this six or more years in a row, but both played a few games the year before their streaks began. The average number of runs scored over the first six years of Johnny's career was 112.

NOTES

(1) *Boston Post*, September 16, 1955

13
1951

With characteristic springtime ebullience, Johnny felt bullish about the upcoming season. Spring training had a circus atmosphere. Parnell mailed back the same contract five times, wanting at least a token raise after going 18-10 in 1950. Sammy White was robbed in Sarasota and again in New Orleans. People were asking "Is Yawkey's money jinxed?" and some suggesting O'Neill was too lenient. Others said the team was getting too old. The regular infield was set: Dropo, Doerr, Stephens and the ever-eager Pesky, who reported four days early.

Yawkey had signed Lou Boudreau from Cleveland and the *Globe* reported, "Boudreau, who couldn't even make his own team last year, while managing the Cleveland Indians, is to be the Red Sox shortstop both at home and on the road." Johnny had hit .312 in 1950, despite being shuttled around a bit. He earned 104 walks and he posted a personal best .437 on-base percentage. Boudreau had managed 260 at bats, batting only .269 with one home run, same as Pesky. He'd walked just 31 times and his OBP was .349. The acquisition of the older Boudreau made little sense.

Initially, the plan was to have the right-handed hitting Boudreau play third at Fenway. Given Pesky's historically high Fenway average, this was puzzling. So was the fact that Boudreau played short in spring training. O'Neill had coached for Boudreau at Cleveland, and before that managed him at Buffalo in 1939. With Boudreau jobless after nine years as the Indians' manager, did O'Neill hire him out of sentiment?

To Boudreau's credit, he sought no special privileges. Later in spring training Lou and Johnny had even roomed together. Johnny took it gamely, at least on the surface. "Lou Boudreau will have to hustle to beat me out," he proclaimed on the last day of February. The United Press noted that after six full seasons Johnny's .316 lifetime average ranked fifth among all active major leaguers; only Williams, Musial, Joe DiMaggio and Mize had higher lifetime figures. "The way I figure it, the job is mine, and if Boudreau or anybody else can beat me out they're entitled to it, and that will be a good thing for the team and that is what counts. The big thing is we've got to win the pennant this year for Tom Yawkey and Joe Cronin, after all they've done for us. We just can't let them down again. Williams said over in Miami the other day that a lot of the younger guys on the club just didn't realize how hard they have concentrated on getting us a winner, and that's right."

When Boudreau made a few nice plays at short in a squad game, one of the scribes asked Johnny what kind of competition he had. "From whom? Scarborough and Wight?" No, from Boudreau, replied the writer, saying he'd put on a good show at short. Johnny relaxed a bit at the news Boudreau was at short, and not at third. Another writer chimed in that it was Fred Hatfield who put on the real show. "Gee," Pesky responded, "why are all the rookies third-basemen? They've been burying Doerr for years and they never come up with a second-sack aspirant . . . it gets me." He continued, "Every year, I'm either traded or someone is getting my job. I get my 180 hits and seem to do all right . . . hit .300 but each year it's the same." "Well, John," the writer came back, "You always wind up holding the job and playing about 145 games a year. So why worry?" Still, it had to be disappointing, and at least a trifle aggravating.

The newspapers often reported talk of trading Johnny. One paper announced a deal as imminent soon after Johnny arrived in Sarasota and while Ruth was still home closing up the house. She rushed to call Johnny, sobbing over the line according to Al Hirshberg. Johnny reassured her that just that very day he'd been told by the Red Sox that they would not be getting rid of him. "But it's right here in the paper," Ruth said. "Do I play for a paper?" asked Johnny. However reassuring that may have been for Ruth, Johnny could never quite relax until after the June 15 trading deadline.

Johnny played fairly regularly in spring training, but he always had a good word for Boudreau. "You bet it's the best ball team ever put together," he boasted. "Name me a better one?" Then he added, "There's the fellow who is going to make the difference," pointing to Boudreau. "Just having that guy around helps a ball club. Oh, I intend to be playing third base. But if you need someone to spot in there, or one of us gets hurt, where could we find a better man than Lou to fill in? What a hitter he is."

Jimmy Piersall was a rookie in spring training; he later joined the team in September and appeared in six games. Dom DiMaggio ranked Piersall that spring as the best defensive centerfielder in the business— quite a tribute, considering the source. Both Pesky and Williams gave Piersall advice. Williams' was to "go up to the plate and get mad. Get mad at yourself and mad at the pitcher." Pesky talked to him about hitting 'em where they ain't: "I know what you're doing wrong. You go to bat looking for the curve ball. Don't do it. Go up there and wait for the fast ball. If you do this, they can't throw the curve past you."

Joe Reichler wrote that the Red Sox had finally gotten some good pitching lined up—maybe the best in the league—to go with their "raw power and superb fielding." He picked them for second, behind New York, noting, "everyone hits over .300 including the batboy. But we're through picking them for first. . . . They're strictly homers. They're harmless on the road." O'Neill countered, "I don't see any club which can beat us." Red Smith sided with Reichler, picking New York first and Boston second. A poll of 168 baseball writers saw 103 choose Boston for first place. Grantland Rice asked, "How can the Red Sox possibly discover a new way of blowing the pennant? . . . It will take a master mind or a set of master minds to find a new way to lose this time. But it can happen."

O'Neill felt the Sox were poised for a "fast getaway"—hoping to build up a lead early on and avoid some of the late season catchup work that had plagued them the last couple of years. In the clutch on April 4, on an easy play, Pesky threw the ball wildly to the plate from third, allowing two runs to score and the Senators to win by a run. It was this one play, executed badly in a game where Boudreau had shined at short, which sealed Johnny's fate. That and the reported $45,000 salary being paid to Boudreau meant Johnny was to start as a utility infielder. Boudreau would play short with Stephens moving to third. O'Neill scoffed at the idea they'd trade Pesky. He was capable of filling in at third, short or even second—and everyone knew he could hit.

Used only sparingly, Pesky was slow to get off the mark. As of May 11, Johnny only had 8 hits on the season, in 32 times at bat. Mid-May and into the end of the month, all the Sox pitchers were struggling and the bats were quiet, too. As late as May 21, Ted was at .226, but broke out with three hits off three different pitchers (every one of them to left), including a home run into the net and a double off the Wall. He raised his average some 26 points, and then added three more singles the next day.

Pesky was so discouraged about getting playing time that he even acquired a catcher's glove. Stephens looked to become permanent at third, and Boudreau was still favored at short. Johnny was ready to catch, if need be, and the Sox were short a decent catcher. "Sure, I was going to catch. I want to play. I want to get into that lineup. Do you blame me?" As a young kid, Johnny had been a catcher (remember that Mickey Cochrane was his first baseball hero) and Harold Kaese reported that O'Neill had actually given him the word that he could catch once the Red Sox returned home to Fenway. But then the Red Sox sent Matt Batts out and acquired Les Moss. Pesky's plan to play behind the plate fizzled out. "If Pesky now wants to become a regular," Kaese wrote, "it looks as though he should turn pitcher—preferably relief pitcher."

The Red Sox dropped as low as 6th place before Ted went on a spree, passing Johnny—who was now up to .279, with 17 hits. Boston won 14 in a row, some by big scores. As soon as they left home they lost 8 of 11. Dom DiMaggio had a 27-game hit streak, but Johnny was hitting an anemic .260 in limited action by June 9. Then Boudreau hurt his leg and Boston writers began to remember what it was like to have Johnny in the regular lineup. Writer Jerry Nason noted Johnny's speed, a commodity which had been lacking. DiMaggio and Doerr could both still run, but both had trouble with quick stops and starts. Ted and Dropo lacked speed. "It is a team on which Pesky, like an irrepressible juvenile, can still run. It is a baseball team on which he belongs." Nason felt Pesky showed the "fire and dash and the willingness to gamble" which had gone by the wayside in a team built around power, as too many players just went from post to post, hoping someone would drive them in. "The rumor has been rampant that it took a triple to score a Red Sox runner from second base."

Kaese's column the day before presaged a move a year before it came about. The Tigers had been talking trade, and Kaese mentioned Dropo and Pesky, Evers and Wertz. Bob Holbrook, under a banner headline "Will Pesky Ride Bench Again When Lou Returns?", said that the Sox needed speed on the basepaths. Boston had already hit into 75 double plays by mid-June—the record for a full year was 155—and Holbrook felt they could benefit from playing Johnny more, him being "one of the fastest men on the Red Sox." Pesky covered more ground defensively than Boudreau.

Holbrook was a Pesky booster. He took some time out to reflect on the treatment accorded Johnny. "For nine years Pesky has been a maligned performer. He's been 'traded' more often than any other player on the team, and he never liked it." Designated the goat of the 1946 Series, Johnny "never alibied or tried to toss the blame in someone else's lap when he could have. He took it." Looking ahead to the recently announced Johnny Pesky Night to be held later in the season, Holbrook welcomed it as a fitting tribute and concluded, "Now, if he only knew where he was going to play for the rest of the season everything would be just dandy."

On the 18th, Johnny hit his first homer of 1951. It was at Fenway, and the Red Sox unfortunately lost the game 9-7. Johnny also made the last out, when both Goodman and then Pesky made outs with the bases loaded in the bottom of the 9th. Johnny'd been 3 for 5, with 2 RBI on the

---

With his second home run in August, Johnny Pesky had hit his last home run at Fenway. It wasn't his last homer at home, since all four of his home runs as a Tiger were hit in Detroit.

It only took six home runs in Boston, though, to transform a somewhat undistinguished and previously anonymous yellow foul pole into an institution—the Pesky Pole. The dates of Pesky's pokes were:

August 18, 1942 vs. Yankees
April 20, 1946 vs. Athletics
August 8, 1946 (first game) vs. Athletics
June 11, 1950 (second game) vs. Tigers
June 18, 1951 vs. Indians
August 2, 1951 (first game) vs. Browns

Johnny Pesky: "Where it got the Pesky Pole name, Mel Parnell referred to it as that. I only hit 2 home runs the first two years, and both of them were down that line. 49, 50, 51, Parnell was there and I know I won one game for him around the pole, late in the game. When he started broadcasting, they talked about it, I guess, and it's kind of stuck. Joe and Jerry have taken pretty good care of me on that!"

In Saint John NB for a CYO event in December 1961, JP was asked what his greatest thrill in baseball was. "Hitting a home run. I was just a singles hitter. I left the home run hitting to guys like Williams and [Dom] DiMaggio."

day. The home run was in the 7th, with Goodman on board, "a well-stroked drive into the deep curve of the grandstand." It was a shot, off Bob Feller, a "line drive into the wind which had enough behind it to sail into the grandstand a good way beyond the foul pole." A brief bit in the *Boston Globe* was headlined "Ted Greets Pesky After Latter Makes His Annual Homer." It was reported that "Ted 'No Shake' Williams was there [at home plate] with a hearty handclasp and a big smile for the little guy."

"Sure, it was a thrill," Johnny acknowledged, "but it would have been a bigger thrill if we had won the game. There's no bigger thrill in baseball than being on a winning club. We didn't win today. So everything was canceled." A couple of days later he said it was the hardest hit ball of his career.

The next day, the Sox did win, 9-2, and Johnny went 2 for 5, with a double and a triple, and 3 runs batted in—enough for the margin of difference. The following morning, the *Globe* ran an 8-column headline "Pesky Clinches Berth At Short With Brilliant Play" and the subhead noted "Hustling Johnny on Hit 'Spree.' " Bob Holbrook wrote that Johnny Pesky "has suddenly blossomed into a long-ball hitting threat." O'Neill announced that Johnny was the shortstop now, as long as he continued to hit and the team kept on winning. "Day after day," Holbrook wrote, "Pesky is proving that both Joe McCarthy and O'Neill mishandled him. McCarthy never should have moved him from short to third and O'Neill shouldn't have benched him when Boudreau came on the scene." On June 24th, Johnny's average passed the .300 mark for the first time.

The Red Sox, despite a disappointing start, were three games out of first, in better striking distance for their typical second half surge than in earlier years. On July 1, Johnny homered again, this time off Eddie Lopat, in New York. Mapes almost caught the sixth inning drive to right field, but it was deflected off his glove into the seats for a home run.

Bob Feller, a few days after tossing his third career no-hitter, was asked to name the four toughest hitters he's faced. Three of them were Red Sox. The four he named were: Joe DiMaggio, Ted Williams, Johnny Pesky and Bobby Doerr.

On July 12, the Red Sox arrived in Chicago and took a twilight-night doubleheader from the first-place White Sox (winning game two in 17 innings), vaulting the Red Sox into first place. Johnny's average had slipped to .275 and Ted hurt himself in the second inning of the night game, sliding into second base. Boudreau and Pesky both began playing. "Johnny's play was the factor that saved us," Boudreau exclaimed following a tough win over his former team, the Indians. There had been men on second and third with one out in the fifth, and Luke Easter "drilled a liner over Pesky's head and slightly to his right. He speared it backhanded and turned quickly to double up Doby at second." Pesky returned the compliment and credited Boudreau: "Lou told me that Easter hasn't been pulling the ball as much lately and we decided that I should play him a few steps toward third base. When that ball was hit I had just enough of a margin to get over and grab it."

Tied 8-8 after 9 on July 21, Johnny doubled to left and drove in two runs in the tenth, and then the Sox held the Tigers to just one run in the bottom of the frame. A very successful road trip over, they came home to settle in for a very long homestand.

July 24, 1951 was Johnny Pesky Night at Fenway Park. Gene Mack pointed out that the choice of date was fortuitous. Though he'd been relegated to a utility role earlier in the season, Johnny had firmly established himself at short on the western road trip. "Pesky Night Pays Tribute to Scrappy Sox Veteran" read the front-page headline in the *Globe*. "The kid used to spend all his time at the park, shining shoes of budding stars like Bobby Doerr and Ted Williams," wrote Holbrook. "His real purpose in being a clubhouse boy was to be near the ballpark where he could work out as often as possible, because he swore that some day he'd be a ball player too. Tonight at Fenway Park two of the guys he used to shine shoes for will be among a group of Red Sox players gathered at home plate to watch the former clubhouse boy receive a Cadillac car."

The half-hour pre-game ceremonies were hosted by Curt Gowdy and "Swede" Nelson, under chairman Rev. Francis J. Dolan. The "most touching gift" came from the clubhouse boys, presented by Johnny Donovan— a sterling carving set. Pesky was presented a two-tone Cadillac. Ruthie received a sterling silver set. Dom DiMaggio presented a plaque from the players.

Johnny went 1 for 5, "a perfect hit and run single to left" which sent Dom DiMaggio to third. Williams followed with a broken bat single through the hole vacated by the second baseman on the shift. Dom scored, and Johnny did a few moments later on Stephens' single. The Sox beat Chicago 8-3.

On the second of August, Johnny hit his third home run of the season, matching his single season high. "I hit so few, I should be able to tell you I remember every one, but I can't." This homer was off Al Widmar of the Browns, with a man on, in the first game of a doubleheader, into the right field grandstand.

Then the Tigers swept the Sox in a doubleheader and Boudreau broke his hand. The Red Sox lost five in a row at home, a 11-10 home-stand, and dropped to 4½ out. With a 16-game road trip looming, they faced the prospect of having to win most of their remaining home games and to split on the road. Their chances were rated slim. Doerr and Boudreau were both out. Stephens injured his leg. Mickey McDermott hurt his leg muscle, and developed an infection. Leo Kiely was possibly going to be taken into the service.

In an unusual game on August 22, the Browns walked 16 Red Sox batters as the Red Sox stranded 22. Johnny Pesky went 4 for 6, with three doubles and a single—and the Red Sox won by the slight score of 3-1, on walks in the thirteenth. The very next day, Sox batters culled 12 more walks while Pesky fattened his average, going 3 for 4. The day Stephens came back, he reinjured his thigh and was out for three more weeks. Doerr came back, and re-injured his back. With all these players out, even though Pesky had been "hotter than Jesse James' six-shooter," the Red Sox lost the chance to gain on the Indians as the White Sox swept Boston in Chicago.

Johnny had reached base in 21 straight games, but September 9th was a bad day. The A's took two from the Red Sox as New York swept the Senators and Cleveland won as well. One of the losses was prompted by Pesky's error in a tie game—Pesky was playing second base, never a comfortable position for him—and he missed a fairly routine grounder. A run scored, and before the inning was over the Athletics scored six. The Red Sox were 5½ games back, and it was getting late in the season. They had to pin their hopes on a 12-game homestand.

The Red Sox took the first two, winning the second game when Johnny tripled, then scored in the tenth inning to win the game 2-1.

Johnny was in the headlines again on the 14th, this time with an infield single—again in the 10th, driving in Dominic DiMaggio with the winning run for the Red Sox 5-4. "When I came to bat, [St. Louis pitcher Ned] Garver moved Jennings over toward third. So I made up my mind to hit the ball through the box so that Jennings wouldn't have a chance to field it. I didn't hit it as good as I had hoped but I don't believe I ever ran faster."

The Red Sox won again the following day, and took 6 of 7 to kick off the homestand—but as of the 18th, they still had eight games to play against the Yankees to close out the season, and two more against the Indians. They lost both games to Cleveland, and dropped the first to New York.

Bobby Doerr announced his retirement from the game, at the young age of 33, and Johnny played second base for the rest of the campaign.

Even the lowly Senators swept the Red Sox, who thus were mathematically eliminated. The next day, the Yankees swept the Sox, the first game being a no-hitter by Allie Reynolds, his second of the season as the Yankees clinched. The no-hitter was the first time Boston had been held hitless since 1931.

Boston dropped 12 of its last 13 games, the fight apparently gone out of them, and they wound up an ignominious 11 games behind, deep in 3rd place, though just a bit more than two weeks earlier they'd been in contention.

As it turned out, Johnny did get to play. He played in 131 games with 480 at bats, to Boudreau's 82 games and 273 at bats. Pesky hit .313 and Boudreau .267. Williams edged Johnny for the top average on the Red Sox, but not by much, hitting .318. The glory days of the Red Sox were over.

14
1952

The core of the team—together since 1942 except for the war years—began to dissolve after the 1951 season. Bobby Doerr had now retired and Dom DiMaggio was nearing the end. Ted Williams left for war again—recalled at age 33—and this time feared he'd not come back. And before the '52 season was halfway done, Johnny Pesky would become a Detroit Tiger.

The biggest hole the Red Sox had was the second base slot vacated by Doerr. Johnny offered to move to second, prompting Joe Reichler to define him as a real team player. He was the top shortstop in the league his first three years, Reichler wrote, "yet each year Johnny has to battle for a regular job. Each Spring there are about four rookies who are rated over him. But along about April 15, Pesky is a regular. He's never missed playing 125 or more games. Every club in the league wants him. The Yankees offered two players for him in 1950 and Cleveland offered Ray Boone for him last year."

Nonetheless, despite Pesky's proficiency at short, he'd been shoved over to third base to make room at short for Stephens. He led all third basemen in double plays his first two years and made the most assists and putouts another year. He clearly made the best of the situation. Now he was ready to play second, since that was what his team needed most.

Johnny was going to have to compete with Billy Goodman for second, and young Ted Lepcio was waiting in the wings. Reichler was right—Pesky never had it easy, every year was a battle. "That job [second base] is wide open as far as I'm concerned," stated Boudreau. Johnny did say he thought the move to second would be easier for him to handle than the one from short to third under McCarthy. It looked to be Fred Hatfield at third, Stephens at short, Pesky at second and Dropo at first. Before the season began, though, there was more talk of trading Pesky, maybe for more-established second baseman Gerry Priddy of Detroit.

Managers will often allow that spring training games don't count, that it's just a time to tune up your players and get a look at some of the youngsters who might be able to earn a roster slot. Boudreau didn't take that approach. He declared he wanted to win *all* the spring training games. On the eve of the first game, he announced, "We might as well get into the habit of winning. There's only one way to play this game and that's to hustle and play to win all the time." Boudreau was still looking for that elusive fast start.

"Dominic didn't care for him but I thought Boudreau was a reasonable guy. You had to play and give up yourself more than some of them do today. We didn't want a day off, because the guy that took your place, you might not get it back. That's the way it was in those years. All the writers in Boston were trying to make out the lineup. Stephens outweighed me by 25, 30 pounds. He was a much better player, really, a home run hitter."

Boudreau was planning to play some infield, but had his nose broken when his face was pressed up against the cage watching batting practice and a Gus Niarhos foul caught him flush. He was knocked out, and taken to a nearby hospital but was back on the bench within a couple of hours.

Pesky's first spring training game was on March 10, and he went 3 for 4, then a couple of days later had a 4 for 5 game—but the Sox still lost their first four games and Johnny was said to have "looked poor at second base." In fact, the Red Sox were really hurting at second. At least one article—by Harold Kaese—suggested that Doerr (who'd retired due to back problems) could play second better in a plaster cast than Pesky, Goodman or Lepcio could without one. Johnny had always liked second base as a kid, but in spring training he played a couple of games there, fell down on a relay, and muffed a throw on a double play, and Lou Boudreau moved him back to third—in the 7th inning of the fourth game.

Pesky felt he needed more time than just those few days at second to truly get his feet under him and begin to master the position, but it was denied him. Reporters said that Pesky "looked more natural"—even "slick"—at third. But the 28th was not a slick day; Johnny made two errors, on consecutive batters, in the 6th. At the plate, though, he went 3 for 5, with a homer and knocked in three. Boudreau continued to experiment, playing Jimmy Piersall at short for a while. He came to think of Goodman as his second baseman and Pesky for the hot corner.

The Pesky for Priddy trade never came about, and the Red Sox broke camp looking lackluster, scarcely resembling the sort of winning club they'd appeared a year earlier.

This year, Boudreau was featuring what he called the "youth movement"—Piersall playing brilliantly at short, Ted Lepcio at second, along with Faye Throneberry and Sammy White with Ike Delock and Bill Henry on the mound. This commitment to youth came across so strongly in the papers, it must have felt to the 32-year-old Pesky that he was an afterthought. Piersall, Johnny said, "as good a centerfielder as ever played the game—was playing shortstop. He was just a highly nervous kid—but he could play! Opening Day of 1952, you know who was sitting in the dugout? Dom DiMaggio, Walter Dropo, Vern Stephens, myself and Freddie Hatfield. And Don Lenhardt. The year before, we were regular players. Boudreau had this preconceived idea—Gene Stephens was going to be the next Ted Williams. Gene Stephens couldn't be a pimple on Williams' fanny."

Johnny kept getting called on for pinch-hitting duties—never an easy role—and he kept failing. "You'd just use an imaginary ball and swing. We didn't have those nets to hit into or all that stuff." Johnny was batting just .050 (1 in 20) when he finally got another chance to start, on May 6. That day he went 1 for 4, a single in the eighth—meaning he'd actually sunk as low as 1 for 23 before he collected that second safety.

The Red Sox were 14-5 on the season, though. The Bosox were winning, and Johnny acknowledged the fact. "How can I complain when the team is winning? Perhaps this two-platoon system is the right answer. If it wins, I'm all for it. What's the good of finishing second or third even though you play every day? Maybe it benefits some players to be rested." Clearly, Johnny had never agreed that he was helped by rest—if anything, he was sharper when he played regularly. Ever the booster, Johnny added, "Boudreau has done a great job with this team. He deserves credit. . . . I'm telling you, I'm tickled with the way the team's been going, especially the rookies."

The next few days weren't good for Johnny. On the 9th, with the Sox and Yanks tied at 2, in the 6th, in New York, Pesky (who went 0 for 4 in the game) made a "weird throw to the plate" on a Bob Cerv grounder.

When Sammy White shouldered the blame, Johnny corrected the young catcher. "It was my fault, a lousy throw," Johnny said. Boudreau didn't mince words: "I don't care what White says. It was a punk throw home. It cost us the game. . . . "

On the 12th, Honochick tossed Piersall out of the game for protesting a bad call, and the Sox lost 1-0. It was thought by some that, had Piersall remained in the game instead of his replacement Pesky, he would have stabbed the Bauer single which eluded Pesky, one of two hits which provided the lone run. Pesky didn't have Piersall's range.

After losing the series to New York, Boston was now in third place. They lost the next two games as well, a six-game skid. Detroit was in last place, already 10½ games behind. Tigers manager Red Rolfe seemed on the block after four seasons, soon to be fired. The *Detroit Free Press* reported that the Sox were "known to want Kell or Evers or Groth" and "in return, the Tigers would be offered either Vern Stephens, Johnny Pesky or Walt Dropo."

Johnny by this time was showing only three hits in his first 45 at bats, his worst start ever (.063) but sympathetic *Globe* reporters never noted the fact. The Sox themselves were slumping, and had in fact only tallied nine runs over their last eight games. Finally, on May 18, Clif Keane mentioned that Pesky "hasn't even come close to getting a hit as of late."

The Sox headed to Detroit, and the same trade rumors continued to fly, mentioning Pesky or Dropo, for Evers or Groth. "There's not a thing in the wind," Cronin stated. Boudreau rested Lepcio and Piersall, starting Pesky—leading to suspicion it was to showcase him as "trade bait." He'd gone 23 straight at bats without a hit, but playing third, and leading off, he went 2 for 5—though there were two plays the *Boston Globe* reporter felt he should have made. The two teams talked trade, but Boston reportedly refused to trade Stephens and the Tigers similarly refused to trade Kell. There was no question that Rolfe was interested in Johnny. He said, "Pesky was a good shortstop last year in my book. One of the best in the league."

On the 27th, Johnny pulled a thigh muscle in the 3rd trying to beat out a grounder, a shame because he'd been playing some and was now 10 for 67, .149. "I just tore my hamstring. I was all black and blue. When you're in your thirties, you don't heal as fast. I could hardly walk. I couldn't get my goddamn leg into my pants. That took a long time to heal."

Boudreau had stopped using Johnny as much. "In those days, the playing cycle used to be every 6 or 7 years, maybe ten. Now it's anywhere from 3 to 5 to 6. We never had any weight equipment. Not even a barbell. The only thing we had was a squeezeball. We had a whirlpool. You got in there just to lose a couple of pounds. I was a quick healer. I wasn't a heavy drinker, but the brandy was getting to my legs, I guess. Like everything, you've got to give certain things up and that was one of them." The team had rebounded and was playing well, and on the second of June the Red Sox regained first place.

Johnny didn't get to savor the satisfaction for very long. The next day, June 3, the Red Sox pulled off one of the biggest player trades in history, sending five players—a full 20% of the 25-man roster—to the Tigers for four Detroiters. The Tigers sent outfielder Hoot Evers, third baseman George Kell, shortstop Johnny Lipon and pitcher Dizzy Trout to the Red Sox and received in return Johnny Pesky, Walt Dropo, Fred Hatfield, Don Lenhardt and pitcher Bill Wight.

"Cronin called the house and said, 'I've got some news for you.' He didn't say 'bad news.' 'We just traded you to Detroit.' I asked, 'Who'd you get?' He said, 'George Kell.' That's all. Well, hell, I'd have traded me for George Kell at that time, too! I didn't object to that. I understood that." Walt Dropo was staying with the Peskys that year, so Cronin asked, "Is Dropo there?" "I said, 'Yeah, he's outside.' He was building a house in Marblehead and he had the architect there and they had the plans out on the back of his car. So I went out in the driveway and I said, 'Cronin's on the phone. He wants to talk to you. We both got traded.' We're supposed to pick up the Detroit club in Philadelphia. So we were driving in and at the first stoplight, there was the news: Red Sox and Tigers Make Big Trade. Nine player trade. We finally found out [the whole story] when we got to the ballpark. They decided to go youth. Boudreau must have had a lot of influence, but you know, you're not going to win with just a bunch of kids."

For publication, Johnny said, "I've been traded from one good organization to another. I have no complaints. The Red Sox organization treated me fine, from club owner down to clubhouse boys. I think I've been lucky to be with the Red Sox as long as I have. The only kind of ball players who generally spend lifetimes with the same club are home run hitters and 20-win pitchers. My kind of player gets traded around regularly. If the Tigers can't win the pennant, I hope the Red Sox do." Johnny traded in his #6 Boston uniform for a #7 Detroit one.

Beantown cynics sneered, "The Red Sox were in first place, so they had to do something." The very night before the deal, Don Lenhardt's grand slam off Ken Holcombe beat the White Sox 6-2. That was the win which propelled the Red Sox into first. The day after the trade was announced—they dropped out of first; they briefly returned back to first on the 9th and 10th but essentially lost their hold on the top spot for the rest of the year. "Hit Grand Slam, Traded" was the headline on Lenhardt.

Harold Kaese wrote, "They didn't merely change their lineup. They tore it down and rebuilt it." Why did the Red Sox make the trade? Because they had to? "Hardly," wrote Kaese. "They were leading the league. They were in first place. But they couldn't believe it. They thought it was too good to last. Maybe it was. So they traded their leading home run hitter [Don Lenhardt], their leading producer of runs [Walt Dropo], the new Pie Traynor [Fred Hatfield], everybody's pal [Johnny Pesky], and a winning pitcher [Bill Wight]." The consensus, though, was that the Red Sox got the better of the deal. Salarywise, Tom Yawkey came out ahead, too. The combined salaries of those he took on were said to be $200,000 to $250,000 less than the salaries he traded away. Boudreau said he was pleased that he could now have a "set" ball club. "I don't believe in the two-platoon system. You have too many moves to make. This way you know who is going to play every day and so do the players." "I hated to part with all five players," Boudreau concluded, "especially Pesky and Dropo. But in order to get something you've got to give up something. I needed speed, defense and some batting. . . . I never thought I could get both Kell and Evers."

Nearly fifty years later, Johnny joked, "Detroit was always a great place to play. I always said to Cronin, 'If you ever trade me, trade to Detroit.' Well, he did!"

It was actually a rather bold move to trade Johnny Pesky, since he was extremely popular locally. In May of 1952—the month before the trade—Al Hirshberg had written in *Sport* that "Pesky is an important personality around Boston, where he has become a fixture of the same general magnitude as the sacred codfish than hangs under the gold dome of the State House. The result is that he bounces all around New England, accommodating local organizations. . . . There is a legend around nearby Lynn, where he owns a modest home on one of the main streets, that neither he nor his lovely blonde wife, Ruth, knows where the keys are. The door to their little white frame house is always open."

Hirshberg also added, "No Red Sox rookie can ever be lonesome when he first arrives in Boston. The Peskys take it upon themselves to make any and all visitors completely at home. They are the world's undisputed champions at entertaining ballplayers. Literally hundreds of big-leaguers and would-be big-leaguers have 'dropped by' to see the Peskys. . . . Most of them have stayed for dinner. Many have spent the night. Some . . . have taken up semi-permanent residence in the house." Hirshberg allows that both Johnny and Ruth are there with advice on subjects ranging from loans to love affairs. To trade a player as beloved as Johnny Pesky could not have been easy. Fortunately, the mutual admiration between New England fans and the Peskys was only interrupted and never severed.

The trade was a reality, though. After all the rumors over the preceding years, Johnny Pesky was—in 1952—no longer a member of the Boston Red Sox.

As it happened, the move may have proved beneficial for Johnny in the long run. It was the Detroit organization which was to ask him to manage in their system just a very few years later.

Many fans worried that the Sox had really weakened their bench losing both Pesky and Hatfield. Some fans felt it was like giving up five players to get one (Kell.) Professional gamblers liked the trade. Instead of being 6-1 shots, the Red Sox were now rated 3.5 to 1.

Johnny, still suffering from the thigh pull, didn't play for days but Dropo started drilling home runs. On June 6, the Tigers came to Boston and beat the Red Sox 4-2, with Dropo and Lenhardt knocking in four runs. The *Globe* put a photograph of Ruth Pesky in the paper, waving a Detroit banner, happy with the win. The Red Sox, though, took the next three—and regained the A. L. lead.

Then the Tigers and the Red Sox began to drop in the standings. Johnny was now playing consistently at short but unlike some players who, once traded, prove a nemesis to the club which traded them, Johnny never really seriously damaged the Red Sox over the next couple of years. On June 24, however, the Tigers beat Boston in Detroit, dropping the Red Sox into third place. Johnny hit a home run in that game. It was his first game in the leadoff slot for the Tigers and he went 2 for 5. The home run was in the eighth, a high drive into the lower deck, producing runs 6 and 7 of a 7-1 win. Johnny went 3 for 5 a couple of days later, then didn't play for a full week, due to yet another leg pull.

Five weeks after the big trade, Kaese argued that the trade had not worked for the Red Sox. It hurt them in their home park and hadn't helped them on the road. Before the trade they were 24-17, and in first place; after they were 15-19. The Tigers hadn't done any better. Not very good to begin with, they still weren't. Johnny's first appearance at Fenway in another team's uniform was in a pinch-hit role in the ninth of the final game. He got a tremendous ovation, but grounded out. The applause he received his first time back at Fenway moved Johnny. "The fans always treated me great. One thing about the fans—they can say what they want about all these other places—and I've been to a lot of places—but the fans in Boston are great. They like the guy who gives everything he has." Johnny played shortstop, third and second for the Tigers. Johnny was batting .151 before the trade, but with some regular playing time was hitting .274 afterwards.

Speaking of his former team, Johnny told Jimmy Cannon, "Personally, I think they leaned too much toward Ted Williams. I did it myself. You'd be in a ball game and need a hit and say Ted will do it. Personally, I think he's one of the greatest ball players I ever saw. But the whole club leaned on him. No one could do it every time and when he didn't we'd get disappointed."

Johnny told Bob Holbrook he'd gone to get his eyes checked. "I went down to the eye doctor and said, 'Doc, I'm not hitting the way I used to. There must be something wrong.' He examined me and told me I had 20-15 vision. Imagine that! Ted had 20-10 vision. The doctor told me it couldn't be my eyes, must be something I've been doing wrong."

Near the end of August, Virgil Trucks pitched his second no-hitter of the season (the first had been on May 15 against the Senators), shutting down the league-leading New York Yankees 1-0 at Yankee Stadium. Johnny helped out with three putouts, two assists—and an error. It was early in the game, bottom of the third, and Rizzuto hit an easy grounder to Pesky at short. The official scorer was John Debringer of the *New York Times*. He charged Pesky with an error, since it appeared to him the ball had popped out of Johnny's glove. Johnny recovered, but too late and Rizzuto scooted across the bag beating the low throw. Debringer changed his ruling to call it a hit, but other reporters told him he got it right the first time—so he phoned Johnny in the Tigers dugout just as the Tigers were coming to bat in the seventh. Johnny told him, "I had the ball and it squirted loose from my glove just as I reached up to take it out. I messed up the play." The scorer thus changed the hit back again to an error and the New York fans cheered their approval of the revision. Matt Batts also made an error back in the first inning, but Trucks had his no-hitter.

"I said it was an error," Johnny explained years later. "Even if it was a hit, I'd have said it was an error. I mean, a guy pitching a hell of a ball game. It was a little high-hopper. I had that screwy glove, that had that webbing and my finger got caught in there and I couldn't get the ball out. All I do is throw the ball and I've got him. I was late getting there, and even Virgil said to me, 'I thought the guy was out.' 'I just screwed up the play, Virgil.' Now he goes and pitches a no-hitter. Of course, the writers were around him. They didn't say anything to me. They went to him and I was sitting over there. Virgil came over afterward and said, 'I want to thank you, Johnny.' I said, 'Shit. What the hell's an error for me? I made a lot of them in my time. What's one more? Instead of having 20, maybe it's 21. So what?' " Despite "Fire" Trucks' two no-hitters in the same season, he finished with just five wins against 19 losses, a measure of how bad the 1952 Detroit team really was.

New manager Fred Hutchinson inherited a last place club from Red Rolfe. Rolfe was really ill and Hutchinson had taken over mid-year. Detroit hadn't markedly improved their club, though, either with the trade or with Hutchinson—they were 36½ games out at the time. The next day they lost their 94th game, the most games ever lost by the Detroit club.

Around Labor Day, George Kell was out for the rest of the year with a broken finger and a dislocated disc. The Sox had just finished dropping nine out of ten games, and were almost in sixth place, 9 ½ games behind. The Tigers weren't that knocked out by Johnny Pesky. They'd really been after Vern Stephens, but still felt Pesky would be an improvement over their own shortstop Johnny Lipon. Three months after the trade, it looked like Lipon was faring better than Pesky and the Tigers turned to what a *Globe* typist rendered as "a young collegian named Harvey Juenn." That was, of course, Harvey Kuenn—and a great addition for the Tigers. Kuenn was only 21 but appeared in 19 games, hitting .325—the start of a fifteen-year career, with a lifetime .303 average.

The season ended disappointingly for both the Tigers and the Red Sox. Boston was 24-17 before the trade (.583) but only 52-61 (.460) afterwards. Detroit lost 104 games in all, but their winning percentage was the same dismal .325 both before and after the big trade.

There were a number of negative comments about Pesky's fielding throughout 1952. It was a sub-par year for him but not dramatically so— a .953 fielding average compared to lifetime .964. Johnny had his very best year in 1953, a .991 average over 103 games. Of course, reporters also questioned Johnny's range—as a fielder, if you can't get to the ball, you can't get charged with an error in the first place. It does appear that Johnny's range had diminished, but that his ballhandling had not.

15

1953

In 1953, the Boston baseball demographic changed as the Braves abruptly departed the city and relocated to Milwaukee.

Johnny's personal demographic had changed as well, with the arrival of a son: David, born in December 1952. The timing wasn't great. He joined the family just as the '53 season opened—and Johnny was playing for Detroit. "We wanted a baby so bad, so finally someone talked to us about adoption. We went to the Catholic Charities. We said we would take the first child, and this child became available. We got him when he was five months old. It took us over a year. The priest that married us helped us get David. The minute we saw David, we just loved him. Everywhere we went, David went with us. We were never apart more than two weeks. From what we understand, they matched our background. His parents were Irish, and he might have been born in Canada. Just a girl that probably got in trouble. He has my father's coloring. Ruthie was always there for him. We told him he was adopted. I remember just after we moved in up here, there were two girls over from next door and they were in the backroom talking and evidently he told the two girls that he was adopted. We were kind of shocked but [their mother] said he was quite proud of it. Since he was five months old, he was just a big bundle of joy, a good looking kid. A beautiful boy."

Not much was expected of the Red Sox in '53; Joe Reichler of the AP picked them to finish in the cellar and most writers saw them as a second division team, quite a comedown from the glory years of the post-war era. "The Red Sox are different from the old days," wrote Bob Holbrook. "No Williams, no Doerr, no [Vern] Stephens, no Pesky—no thump." Ted Williams, off at war, spoke up from the hospital ship *Haven* off the Korean coast, predicting a Yankees vs. Dodgers World Series.

Boston's Opening Day itself was postponed due to snow, as was the second scheduled game of the season. Detroit should have postponed its opener—the Tigers lost 10-0. Detroit's second game was indeed called off, due to cold weather.

Even though Walt Dropo banged in five runs the next game, the Tigers lost 11-8. Pesky was used as a pinch-hitter and came up with nothing but outs in his first four at-bats. Finally, on the 22nd he singled. Johnny then singled his next two times at the plate as well. The Tigers, though, lost twelve of their first fourteen games, including two to the Red Sox in Detroit. Johnny wasn't called to play in either game.

Cleveland G.M. Hank Greenberg was said to be interested in trading for either Johnny Pesky or Joe Ginsburg to improve his club. Hy Hurwitz wrote that the Tigers "would use Pesky in a trade if they could make a satisfactory one. Pesky is in great shape. He's down to 165 pounds, his best weight in five years." Pesky himself commented, "I owe it to Jack Fadden, the Sox trainer. He gave me some before-going-to-bed exercises which took off all my extra weight." Johnny had reached base safely five times in a row after the 0 for 4 start—three hits and two walks.

The same day's paper gave front page coverage to Ted Williams' airplane being hit by flak over Korea. In February, Ted had been hit badly and crash-landed his F9F Panther jet, barely escaping with his life from the burning wreckage.

With Hatfield at 3B, Kuenn at short and Priddy at 2B, Johnny didn't see much action until mid-May when he started to bat in the three hole for the first time. "It was nice to get back into the lineup," he remarked, adding a bit sardonically, "Guess we reached the bottom of the barrel."

Pesky, Dropo and Matt Batts, all Red Sox alumni, were playing for Detroit at this point. Priddy had broken his leg in July 1952 and it was still affecting him. Detroit writer Sam Greene wrote, "Pesky looks like the best combination of hitting and fielding that we've had at the job." But then Hutchinson stopped using Johnny again and he didn't even appear in back-to-back 15 and 11 inning games of a May 30 doubleheader, which was swept by the Browns. The Tigers lost 15 straight games yet kept playing Priddy. Owen Friend was used at second base in several games. Pesky finally made an appearance, against the Red Sox, and tripled early in the game—but it was rained out before becoming a regulation game.

On June 30, in a 6-4 Tigers loss, Johnny had a home run and three runs batted in, in a 2 for 3 game. Both Al Rosen and Dale Mitchell hit 2-run shots for Cleveland, though, and Johnny's production alone wasn't sufficient. The Tigers were now 27 games out of first place. The next day, Johnny doubled and began to play on a regular basis, being platooned with Priddy who played the second game of doubleheaders. Johnny evaluated Priddy: "He was one of the best double play makers in the game. Great defensive player."

July 12, Johnny banged out a three-run double and then shortly afterward hit another home run in the second game of a twin bill against the Athletics, which was called due to darkness at 8-8 after 11 innings. On the 25th, he hit yet another homer.

Despite this brief power surge, Johnny had a basically lackluster August and was out altogether the first half of September, not even playing in twin bills. Harvey Kuenn was having a great year and on the 16th got his 200th hit. The last American League rookie to hit the 200 mark had been Dick Wakefield, in 1943—the year after Johnny got his 205.

On September 20, Johnny pinch-hit in both games of a twin bill. He singled for Marlowe in the 8th inning of game one, and singled for Branca in the 6th of game two. Both times Johnny came around to score. It was more or less his last hurrah for 1953. He started another game but went 0 for 3. The next time he got a shot, he singled again in another pinch-hit role. The season ended, one that must have been dispiriting—Detroit finished 40½ games out of first place. Boston did better, but nothing to crow about; they finished 16 out.

Pesky finished with a respectable .292, reversing the horrid stats of 1952 but still below his career-to-date average of .310. He'd only had half as many chances as in his peak years, with 308 at bats, yet he'd mustered a very respectable 22 doubles—he'd averaged 24 the previous eight years getting typically twice as many at bats. It was a decent showing, and one suspected if he'd had more opportunities to play regularly he would have responded as he had in the past. Why he didn't play more is a little unclear. Priddy didn't appear in as many games as Johnny did. He hit only .235 and 1953 was his last year in the majors. Owen Friend only hit .177 during his 31 games with Detroit before he was traded. Fred Hatfield hit .254, with just three home runs. Looking at offensive statistics, it's hard to understand why Johnny didn't get more of a chance at the plate and at either third or second. One suspects the clue rests in the occasional comments about Johnny's range as an infielder; his defensive stats are no worse than Priddy, Friend or Hatfield—in fact, they were distinctly better (.991 as compared to .978 for Hatfield, .977 for Priddy and .947 for Friend.) Johnny just may not have been getting to as many balls. Asked about this while this book was being written, Johnny remarked, "They were saying I was horseshit, right? That could be true."

There's no question why Kuenn and Ray Boone played regularly. Harvey Kuenn had 209 hits and batted .308; Boone hit .312 for Detroit with 22 homers and 93 RBI in a partial year.

"I didn't help myself," Johnny continued. "I thought I should have been playing. I got kind of ticked off. When I went to the plate, I always bore down, though. I said, 'I'm going to hit the ball.'" He never lost his positive mental attitude, and there wasn't much to be done about it in any event. "I went along with what management wanted."

This year saw Johnny mentor a couple of young Tigers, and Johnny's interactions with the two did not go unnoticed. Both Harvey Kuenn and Al Kaline were just starting out, Kuenn having his first full year with the team and Kaline his introductory thirty games; he first became a regular the following year. Kuenn was named Rookie of the Year for 1953 and the following March praised Pesky to Arthur Daley of the *New York Times*: "I'll be forever grateful to Pesky," said Harvey appreciatively. "He re-styled my fielding completely. He changed my stance; he taught me how to charge a ball; he showed me how to get the throw away quickly and he gave me some polish."

Asked about his memories of the two developing stars, Johnny answered, "Harvey was another one of my boys. He was young. He had good control of his bat. A big tall rangy kid. Great strength—a good hitter. He made the All-Star team as a shortstop and then he went to centerfield later on. I spent a lot of time with him. Kaline went into the Hall of Fame. I was with him when he was just a kid. Fred Hutchinson told Al, 'When you're not playing, I want you to sit between these two guys'—Pat Mullin and myself. Al would sit there and we'd talk about situations. One thing I told Kaline, 'Al, let me tell you something. When you play, and you play every day, sometimes it's tough to get out on that field. Your ass is dragging. I want you to remember this: when you go to your position, you don't walk out there. You jog out there. A little sprint. When the inning's over, same thing into the dugout.' I sat with Kaline . . . down the left field line. On days off, I'd throw batting practice to him."

John McHale noticed. Johnny had known McHale in 1947 and '48 while McHale was playing with the Tigers; now McHale was the farm director for the Tigers and they became reacquainted at spring training. McHale saw how Pesky interacted with the young ballplayers and realized that Johnny had good coaching potential.

Both players expressed their appreciation for the help Pesky had provided. Johnny remembers this fondly. "When Harvey was with Milwaukee and they played in the '82 World Series, I was coaching with the Red Sox. When they clinched the pennant, they gave Harvey this automobile. His mother was there and all that. They had the microphone out there and Harvey gets up to accept this automobile, and in his talk to the people, he says, 'I want you fans to know a fellow who was instrumental in my career, Johnny Pesky.' I hugged his mother and shook his hand. That was really a highlight."

Kaline, early in 2002, confirmed Johnny's role: "I was told to sit next to Johnny on the bench. He taught me how to be, around the game, how to bunt . . . He was a very important influence on me. He took a lot of his time to work with me and was a big, big help." Johnny appreciated Kaline's recognition, expressed when "Mr. Tiger" was elected to baseball's pantheon: "Now, Kaline goes into the Hall of Fame and now I'm coaching for the Red Sox, and a guy comes into the clubhouse and asks to see him—a writer. The writer asked him, 'Did anybody influence your baseball life when you were a young player?' He said, 'Yes, Johnny Pesky and Pat Mullin.' When I see him even today, he gives me a big hug and says, 'How are you, Johnny?' I know his wife and his kids. It's been a good association. Kaline is a peach of a kid. Kaline and Kuenn. They played the game like it should be played."

16

1954

1954 was Johnny's last year as a major league ballplayer. In his 10th spring training, and now sporting the threads of the Detroit Tigers, he damaged the Red Sox in a March 16 exhibition game, his eighth inning single driving in the sole run in the 1-0 Tiger victory. "Johnny Pesky, one-time Boston favorite, played the villain's role," wrote Bob Holbrook. Of course no one could buy it. Casting Johnny Pesky as a villain would surely go against any Hollywood director's instincts.

In 1954, the Tigers were counting on a youth movement—led by future stars like Kuenn and Kaline—to carry them into the first division. A lengthy analysis of Detroit's prospects in '54 by the *Boston Globe*'s Hy Hurwitz only mentioned ex-Soxer Pesky in one fleeting sentence near the end of the story: "For spares, Hutchinson has a couple of Red Sox castoffs in Fred Hatfield and Johnny Pesky. They're also good left-handed pinch hitters."

The Tigers got off to a decent start, but Johnny didn't collect a single hit in April, nor did he in early May, despite 6 or 7 pinch-hit appearances. He nonetheless made himself useful, contributing in ways that foreshadowed his later work as coach and instructor. The Tigers signed a 19 year old bonus baby named Reno Bertoia and Johnny spent time working with him. "I knew I was eventually going to get into [coaching]. I learned from good players and managers. Heinie Manush was all by himself." Fred Hutchinson and Birdie Tebbetts would ask him to help out a Kuenn or a Bertoia, and he seemed to be a natural teacher.

By May 9, the Tigers were in first place, but Johnny still hadn't had a hit. Frank Bolling was playing second in most of the games, with Kuenn at short and Boone at third. On May 19, the Tigers used 18 players in a game they won 4-3 in the 9th inning, but Pesky rode the bench.

On May 25, Johnny—coming off an 0 for 9 slump to start the season—had another chance to pinch-hit, and this time he homered batting for Herbert in the eleventh inning. It was a 3-3 game against the Orioles after nine. Baltimore scored once in the eleventh to take the lead, but "Slugger Pesky" tied it up in the bottom of the frame, launching one into the right field stands. Bill Tuttle's triple scoring Kaline from first finally won it for the Tigers in the twelfth.

Unfortunately, even this contribution didn't seem to impress and he continued to be relegated to the role of pinch-hitter, where he tended to come up short.

On June 5, the Tigers played a double header against the Red Sox, in Boston. Pesky didn't play in either game, and "says he feels like an old man around the Tigers," according to a Boston sportswriter. "Imagine," he said, "they [Kuenn, Frank Bolling, Kaline] call me dad." Pesky had just one plate appearance against the Sox in the 4 game homestand, and reached safely on a base on balls.

Pesky hit pinch singles in back-to-back games on June 11 and 12. The next day the Washington Senators dealt for Pesky, sending infielder Mel Hoderlein plus $20,000 in cash to the Tigers. It was the "first ballplayer to cost the Washington Senators hard cash in a trade as far back as anybody can remember," according to Neal Eskridge in the *Baltimore American*, June 20, 1954. Hoderlein had only been used in 14 games that year, with a .160 average, and in fact he never played in a single game for the Tigers—or any other major league club—after the trade. Johnny was only hitting .176 for the Tigers. He'd only had three hits all year long. On the surface, it was not a momentous trade, but baseball insiders could see the significance of the deal.

Sports writer Joe Williams suggested that "Any time old Clark Griffith puts out dough for a shopworn ballplayer with no trade-in value, something's cooking, so don't be surprised if he makes Johnny Pesky his next manager in Washington." The notion that he was being considered as a big league manager by Griffith seemed unlikely to Johnny. In fact, he wasn't at all ready to quit playing baseball.

When someone at the time questioned whether he'd rather play a couple of innings of utility ball a week, Johnny almost shouted, "Are you crazy? I can't do myself or the ball club any good sitting on the bench.

I've got to play!" "So what are you complaining about?" "Who's complaining? Not me. I'm just getting old."

Johnny did pick up his play once he became a Senator. "Maybe I'm a hypochondriac," said Johnny, "but there's no use kidding anyone. I just don't get around anymore. I can't run like I used to. This is no game for an old guy like me." But in his first five games he "covered second base like two infielders" according to game coverage in the Boston papers. His first time at bat in a Senators uniform he rapped out a base hit. He played second base on June 15 (there was no game on the 14th) and went 1 for 4, scoring. On the 16th and 17th, again he had one hit per game, and on Friday the 18th, he singled and scored the first run, then later in the ninth bunted the tying run to second. The next day, the 19th, he singled in the first run and drove in the tying run in the 9th.

He again tattooed the ball in a June 20 doubleheader against the Orioles, going 4 for 7 (with a double in each game) with 2 RBI. He was playing second regularly, hitting in the two slot in the lineup behind "The Walking Man", Eddie Yost. It was a team with a lot of decent players—a typical lineup was Yost, Pesky, Vernon, Busby, Runnels, Sievers or Wright, Umphlett, and Tipton or Fitzgerald. When given the chance to play every day, Johnny managed a modest hitting streak.

Washington was battling Detroit for 4th place. The Red Sox were in last place as of June 26. Johnny was hitting pretty well when he played. He got into 40 games and hit .253, with a few productive games including one on August 2 when he went 4 for 6 (all singles) against the Tigers who'd traded him about six weeks earlier. (At season's end, the Sox were 42 games out of first place, the Tigers 43 and the Senators 45 games behind.)

For some reason, though, the Senators kept playing Wayne Terwilliger, who was batting around .200. He'd never hit much better than the mark he ended his career with, .240 and he didn't have much power, either—but he seemed to keep getting the call and Johnny did not. Still, Johnny was respected for his baseball acumen. That same month, August, Burton Hawkins of the *Washington Star* reported that Pesky was indeed being considered as manager for the Senators.

By late August, Harmon Killebrew began platooning with Terwilliger a bit, though "Hammerin' Harmon"—who was to rack up 573 home runs—didn't show much sign of this in his early years with the Senators. It was an odd start to a tremendous career; in his first five years with the Senators, Killebrew only got a grand total of 254 at bats.

Asked about the late-blooming slugger, Johnny revealed, "I roomed with Harmon Killebrew when he came out. I was his first roommate. Senator Welcker from Idaho saw this kid when he was 18. Harmon had intended to go to the University of Oregon. The coach there was a kid I had played with—Donnie Kirsch. He got beat up awful bad in the war. When we were kids, he was a better player than I was. Donnie told Harmon, 'Tell Johnny.' The traveling secretary Eymon told me, 'We have this kid coming in from Idaho and Senator Welcker seems to think he's got a chance to be a pretty good player. I'd like you to room with him.' I'd never laid eyes on him. I met him, shook hands, took him out to eat, talked to him about the game. We became pretty good friends." After Johnny left Washington and was managing in the Southern League, he ran into Killebrew again; Harmon was with Chattanooga.

Then the Senators began playing Pete Runnels at second and Jerry Snyder at short (Yost still on third.) Runnels had been with Washington since 1951 and batted well, though not yet showing signs of the maturity at the plate which earned him A.L. batting titles in 1960 and 1962 for the Red Sox. He was hitting better than Johnny, though not by a lot.

Johnny saw no action in the first two weeks of September. In one doubleheader, even though five pinchhitters were used, Johnny Pesky was not among them. Finally, on the 19th, he appeared in a 15-inning game against the Red Sox. Johnny was 0 for 0, but reached base and scored. He filled in at short briefly on September 24 but again had no official at bat. Johnny's major league playing career had just petered out and now was over. His second baseball career was about to begin.

17

1955–1960
Coach & Manager

A fter ten years at the same job, Johnny Pesky's resume was about to expand rapidly. In fact he was to move from player to coach to manager in a single calendar year. Released by the Senators after the '54 season, he wasn't ready to walk away from the game he loved. When Paul Richards offered him a playing role, he signed with the Baltimore Orioles on December 16, 1954 and began the 1955 season with the Orioles, hoping to make the team. It just didn't work out. Richards gave Johnny a month's pay and his unconditional release on April 10 and he went back home to Greater Boston. For the first time since World War II, a major league season opened without Johnny Pesky. Then he got the break he needed to launch the next phase of his baseball life.

1955 DENVER BEARS AAA,
AMERICAN ASSOCIATION

Yankees GM Lee McPhail called, explaining that Ralph Houk needed help out in Denver. "Ralph knew about me," recalls Johnny. "I went out there—and it was the best thing I ever could have done. It was a real young team. Bobby Richardson was there, Tony Kubek, Marv

Throneberry, Darrell Johnson was on that club. Don Larsen was on that club. Whitey Herzog. They were all kids, too. Woodie Held. Skizas. It was a good young club. I went out there in May of '55 and they were in last place. They were 8 and 18 or something like that. You could see the improvement every week. They were getting better and better. We were knocking on the door within two months. We had a team!"

So Johnny was hired as a player/coach for the Denver Bears. Denver had just joined the American Association as a New York Yankees Triple A farm club. Some Red Sox fans may find it ironic, if not outrageous, that Mr. Red Sox actually spent time helping develop future Yankees. "I was hired as a player-coach. I had to do everything myself. Shit, I threw batting practice three times a day. Hitting infield. Hitting ground balls. Keeping charts. Just helping Ralph out. Just the two of us were out there. I was the first base coach; Ralph was at third. And Ralph caught. He was a player-manager. Later, when he became manager of the Red Sox, I was one of his coaches. Ralph was very, very good to me.

"One thing about Ralph, he was very regimented. I don't ever remember Ralph being late for anything. I'd played against him when he was in the big leagues—he was Yogi's backup—but I got to know him as his coach. He was the guy who really started me on the other end of the business. We talked over things. Ralph did the discipline, but he had no problems out there. Those players realized where they were—they were only a step out of the big leagues and they bore down and they played very hard. I don't recall any incident we ever had with any of the players. He was a no-nonsense guy."

As a Bears coach, Johnny had his own hotel room for the first time in his baseball career.

The Bears had the youngest infield in the high minors. Woodie Held and Buddy Carter were both 23. Richardson was 19. Throneberry was 21. The club had a 5-15 record at the point Pesky joined them on May 5. Right away, things began to improve. Marv Throneberry was a good example of where Pesky's help paid off quickly. "Marvelous Marv" hadn't earned his nickname yet. *The Sporting News* said Throneberry "had his troubles afield last year after switching to first base [from the outfield] and was still having them in the early stages" of 1955. "Pesky must have hit 50 ground fungoes a night at the willing Throneberry for week after week, giving little pointers as he went along. Now Throneberry has perhaps the widest range of any first baseman in the league on ground balls and has developed into an accomplished fielder." Bobby Richardson was cited as coming along well, too, also due to Pesky's influence. (1)

As Pesky got more into the swing of things, and when Houk occasionally got run from a game, he got a taste of managing. They weren't always moments to savor. "A funny thing happened one night in Omaha after Ralph had been thrown out of the game. The clubhouse is right next to the dugout in the Omaha ballpark. Well, Ralph Terry is pitching for us and he's got a two-hitter going in the ninth inning when he loads the bases with two walks and an error. Houk yells to me out the clubhouse window, 'Go get him, John. Get him out of there.' So I start out for the mound and Terry sees me coming [and he] starts backing off towards second base and I've got to go after him.

"Terry doesn't want to come out. He pleads with me to stay in and it's rough because I'd never had to lift a pitcher before. Terry keeps pleading but I know what I gotta do because when you're working for Houk, you're working for Houk. So I finally talk Terry into coming out and the relief pitcher comes in and a double play saves the ball game for him. Still, I'll never forget that first experience and how Terry didn't help me a little bit."

As a player, Johnny appeared in 66 games and had 143 at bats. Johnny's last home run as a player—the only one he managed in 1955—was one of 153 hit by the team, which batted a strong .284 to lead the league. The thin air in Denver may have helped some of the other players, but Johnny's hits were mostly, as always, singles. He hit a healthy .343 but the fielding statistic was probably the telling one: as a third baseman, he appeared in 30 games and made seven errors. His fielding average was a disappointing .905.

Darrell Johnson was catcher for the Bears and hit .306 with 49 RBIs. Johnson went on to become an active coach and even manager of the Boston Red Sox in 1974, 1975 (taking the team into the World Series) and part of 1976. In 1975, he selected Johnny as one of his coaches—the player became the manager and the coach became his coach.

First place Minneapolis under Bill Rigney swept Denver in the playoffs, taking four games to none, but the Denver Bears drew 426,248 fans during the regular season, by far the most in the league. "We played good baseball and the fans reacted to it. It was a learning experience."

After one year as a coach, Johnny became a manager. In 1962, shortly after being named manager of the Boston Red Sox, he talked with Bill Liston of the *Boston Traveler* and credited Ralph Houk. "You know, if it hadn't been for Ralph Houk, I'd probably be peddling shoes or doing something else right now. He's the guy who first got me interested in being a manager. It was seven years ago when Ralph was managing the

Denver Bears and I was finishing out my playing career. When I first reported to Denver, I started going out to the park mornings. The first thing you know several of the other players were out working out with me. We had fellows like Bobby Richardson, Woodie Held and Whitey Herzog on that club. I'd try to help any way I could and usually I'd pitch batting practice for the extra hitting. One day Ralph calls me aside. He tells me that I obviously had a good touch with young ball players and he urged me to continue those extra workouts in the mornings. He also asked me what I was going to do when I was through as a player. Now, I didn't have the slightest idea of what I'd do. I wanted to stay in baseball but I hadn't been thinking of being a manager. Ralph wanted to know why I didn't try to get myself a job managing in the minors. The more I thought about it the more I was convinced I'd give it a try if I could find a spot."

Johnny joked that he himself was actually was "the only unbeaten manager in baseball" in 1955. "Houk got himself thrown out of five games that season. When he was run off, I ran the ball club." And the Bears won every one of those games.

"That winter, I had an offer from the Yankees to go down to Winston-Salem in the Carolina League and manage. Then Detroit offered me the manager's job at Durham in that same league. I liked the Detroit organization because I figured I had a chance to advance, so I took it." (2)

"I didn't know what kind of manager I would be. When I first managed, I was kind of a screamer. I raised my voice a few times. I had my say. When I first managed, I was a little strict. The first two years, I wasn't very vocal but then to get my point across if the kid made a mistake, I would bring it up to him. Remember Mike Shannon? I had him on my club in Seattle in '62. I still considered myself a young manager at that time. Mike came to me and he was a young player, about 19, 20 years of age. I'd seen him play before and I made a trade for him. He went a whole week and he didn't get a hit. I didn't say anything to him, but I brought him out for extra hitting. Bobby Doerr was our hitting instructor at the time; he spent a few days with us and he pointed out a few things to Mike Shannon. So we're going along. Maybe he's there about ten days or two weeks and he made a throw to the wrong base, and it set up an inning for the opposition. He came in and we were in the dugout and I kind of jumped him a little bit and I said, 'Jeez, Mike, I wanted you to go to third base with the ball.' He didn't say anything. He just took it in stride, but I remember barking at him.

He came to me the next day and he said to me, 'You're a funny little guy. You give me hell for making a lousy play and I haven't got a base hit here all week.' I said, 'Well, Mike, this is a learning process for you, too.' He went along with it and he wound up having a fine year, and then a couple of years later he's a World Series hero. I don't think you should browbeat. I go by how I was treated myself. I did some screaming once in a while just to make a point, but I couldn't stay mad. I could never stay mad at a player. If I didn't like a player, I would just try to stay away from him and try to handle him the best way I knew how, and if it was too much, I'd try to move him. You could do that at the minor league level much more so than you can at the big league level. It's a whole different ball of wax at the big league level. It sounds like a simple thing, but it's not.

"I didn't have too many rules. I didn't believe in telling people how to run their lives. Get to the park on time."

1956 DURHAM BULLS
CLASS B, CAROLINA LEAGUE

Johnny's first position with full managerial responsibility was with the Durham Bulls. At the end of the 1955 season, the Tigers' John McHale called offering the job, and Johnny signed to manage Durham on December 10. "It took me three years to forget I was a player. What I mean, you can't be too good a guy. If you were a player, you can see the player's side, but if you've got 18 boys there'll always be two or three sharpies who take advantage. I let them run all over me that first year. Then I learned, you mustn't get too close to a player."

Johnny really appreciated McHale, who later became the Tigers' G.M. McHale admired Pesky as well. Later in life, he told Ed Callahan, son of the police chief in Lynn, that Pesky was "the best instructor we ever had in our organization."

Managing in the low minors was not lucrative, and the Tigers didn't have Tom Yawkey's deep pockets. "The most I ever made managing in the Detroit organization was $10,000." Still, it was a job in baseball and Johnny knew he needed to work his way up. In 1955, the Bulls under Frank Skaff had finished in fourth place (in an eight team league), eleven games behind with a record of 69-69. In 1956, under Pesky, the team rose to second place. This was a team that played to an annual total of 41,934 fans, a far cry from Denver—but this was class B and, more importantly, it was Johnny's first job as field manager. The club finished just 6½ games behind repeating league leader High Point/Thomasville.

Durham led the league in hitting, runs, walks, intentional walks and sac flies, but lost in the playoffs to fourth place Fayetteville, 3 games to 1.

"I didn't have a coach," recalls Pesky. "I threw batting practice, threw infield, kept the pitchers' charts. I did it all by myself for five years. In those years, you didn't have coaches, except maybe at the higher level you'd have a player-coach. I never had a player-coach until Seattle in 1961, when I had Harry Malmberg. I didn't get a coach until I got to Triple A.

"We had spring training in Lakeland. They had a complex down there. I could live 'off the base' but once a week you stood duty—what they called a night guard. Somebody had to be there, to answer the phone for the whole complex in case of an emergency. I had my wife and son with me so I lived off the base, but then I'd come back and do my night guard duty.

"They gave you a group of players and you just started to work with them. You're looking at players and then you'd talk about them when you'd have the meetings. They'd say, 'Well, this kid is going here and that kid is going there.' Someone would be dropped from the team above you, and you'd get him. You'd ask questions. You've got your list, and you presented them to the farm director. A lot of times when you're a young manager, you're looking at AA and AAA players, and you're in class B or A—and you've got to take a step back.

"The organization would say, 'We'd like you to . . . '—they didn't push guys at you. If you liked a kid, they went along with you. If a kid was really great, then he went higher. You were always working for the development of your players. That takes time and effort."

Though it might seem like a logical card to play, Johnny never really used his own playing career as a point of reference in talking with his players. He could have cited his own successes, trying to motivate the players but in effect patting himself on the back at the same time, but he says he did not. "No. No. You didn't do that. They'll ask questions. Maybe their parents read about me. I never approached it that way. I didn't like that."

He wasn't a strict disciplinarian, either. "I don't like a lot of rules. I never did. I've had to discipline a couple of players. I could have fined them, but they weren't making any money. What I'd do, I wouldn't let them dress for one day. I'd punish them, make them stay up in the grandstand. I did that with one of my better pitchers one time, a helluva

kid—a kid named [William] Mitchell. He was about 6'4" and he gave me
some sass one time on the mound, and oh, I blew my stack. But I didn't
want to embarrass him on the field. I waited until I got in the dugout
and I told him to take the uniform off and I said, 'And don't you leave
here!' He got the message. We got together and he became one of my
better pitchers.

"Sometimes you've got to do something to a kid that kind of hurts
you a little bit, but you do it for a reason. You try to get back to him. I
would never ignore a player. Never. I don't care whether he liked me or
disliked me, or I disliked him or whatever, because you try to get the
most out of him. That's what you're there for. You don't have to go home
and sleep with him."

Johnny had learned from his own managers, of course, and he was
most impressed by Joe McCarthy. McCarthy wouldn't get on a player and
show him up. If you made a mistake, he'd call you over later—maybe
even the next day—and explain it to you. When Johnny had begun working for Detroit, he asked McHale if there was any particular system he
wanted his managers to employ. "McHale was wonderful to me. He put
me on my own." McHale let him try out his own approach, learning on
the job to find out what approach suited Johnny Pesky the best.

"I let the kids run a little bit, but I didn't have any 1 o'clock curfew.
If you want to abuse yourself, that's up to you, I told them. The only guy
you're hurting is yourself. Ninety percent of the kids I dealt with
responded well. I was never a boozer or a chaser. Some guys are different.
When you're a young guy and you're single, you've got to run and play a
little bit. I could understand that. I'd just say, 'Just don't get into trouble.'

"I had very few problems. Drinking wasn't a big problem in those
years. We stayed in hotels. I think I had maybe two or three bed checks
the whole time I managed. I just didn't believe in it. The air conditioning
was bad and those kids would wake up at 1 o'clock or 2 o'clock in the
morning and it was so damn hot they'd go out to one those White
Towers and get a cold drink or a hamburger."

There were incidents, though—things Johnny had to deal with as a
manager. "My first year managing we had a terrible time in Greensboro.
We got into a fight over something and this one guy hit my pitcher—
Harry Coe—with a beer bottle and he had to take six or seven stitches in
his head. Oh, what a mess that was! He was one of my better pitchers at
the time. It was a Saturday night. There was a fan who was on my big
first baseman, Jim McManus. Jimmy was a pretty good kid. He should
have been in Triple A, but they had a backlog of players and they

wanted him to play every day, so they just moved him a half a step back. I was very lucky to get him. This guy called him 'yellow' and all this. The kid told him, 'You come down and we'll see how [yellow I am].' The game was over and this guy came down to our clubhouse and a fight started. This fan and the guy that was with him, they'd been drinking and they had beer bottles. In the melee, Harry Coe was just trying to help out. By the time I got there, it was pretty much over and then the cops got there and they took the guys away. Jesus, it was a mess. When Jimmy hit this guy, he broke his hand. That's how bad it was. In the meantime, my pitcher got hit over the head with a bottle. We had to appear in court. They preferred charges. Next time we came to Greensboro, we had to go to court. We were fined fifty dollars.

"That was part of my job [to appear with my players in court]. When the dust had settled, the freshman skipper earned the distinction of being named 'Manager of the Year' in the Carolina League. I was lucky at Durham. I had some wonderful kids. All I had to do was to fit them together like a puzzle," he told *The Sporting News*. "A few of the kids had problems. I'd get them out about 3 or 4 o'clock in the afternoon and work with them. The kids began to improve. Soon, others who wanted help came out voluntarily. It was a compliment to me. Sure, it was hard work but everything I ever gained was only after a lot of hard work."

Johnny actually played some in Durham, too. He put himself in at second base once in a while, and amassed 35 at bats but only got 6 hits, for a disappointing .171 average. Two doubles and just one RBI. He struck out twice. In the field, he made 26 putouts and had 31 assists, with two errors and a fielding percentage of .966. He helped turn nine DPs. Hitting just .171 in class B, after a solid .343 in AAA ball the year before, it was clearly time to stick with the fungo. Those were his last at-bats in professional baseball. "I had no intention of playing," he explained. "The only reason I played was because of injury." He'd not even been taking batting practice, but filled in a few times when necessary.

Every single year he was with the Tigers, from 1956 through 1960, Pesky was moved to a different club. That was apparently Tiger philosophy: the Tigers asked Johnny to manage the Birmingham ball club in 1957, a couple of steps upward—a double A club in the Southern Association. He visited Birmingham in the wintertime, spoke to the Rotary Club and made a couple such appearances, then readied himself for spring training.

1957 BIRMINGHAM BARONS
CLASS AA, SOUTHERN ASSOCIATION

In their first year as a Detroit Tigers affiliate, the 1957 Birmingham Barons placed sixth in the eight-team league. They had gotten off to a strong start but faded quickly after mid-July, and wound up a losing ball club at 74-79, failing to make the playoffs. After two straight trips to the post-season, this was a disappointment to manager Pesky.

"The worst I've ever finished, I think, was that year in Birmingham. We were leading, doing pretty well, and I lost my two best players to Detroit. I lost my best hitter [Bobo Osborne] and I lost my best pitcher [Harry Byrd]. Then things started to go bad and I think we finished fourth instead of first. I had a general manager who was tough to work for. Eddie Glennon. He thought you should win every day. He was gung ho. Instead of blaming the players, he blamed the manager. But he can't say anything about my work, because I had them out on the field. I used to get them out at 11 o'clock in the morning. I was a little bastard. I says, 'If you guys don't want to do this, I'll move you. If you're not happy here—not that happiness is the key here—but it's a job and it isn't that difficult. It's a day-by-day process. If I don't have a little regimentation here, you guys would go helter-skelter. I'm not going to follow you around. But you're my responsibility. I'm responsible not only to the ball club, but I'm responsible for you.' "

Johnny had just one year of managerial experience under his belt when the Tigers advanced him from Class B to AA. He was in no hurry, feeling he needed at least a couple more years managing in the minors, and then a couple of years coaching at the big league level before he would be ready to undertake what had now become his goal: big league managing. As fate would have it, Johnny spent six more years as a minor league manager, before then hopping directly to the "bigs" as a manager.

In July they were within just a game of hosting the All-Star game. They were in the hunt but Atlanta won the pennant. The best players for Birmingham were Dick Camilli (50 RBI, .269), Steve Demeter (13 HR, 79 RBI, .268), Jack Dittmer (15 HR, 55 RBI, .309), Ed McGhee (8 HR, 48 RBI, .267) and Jim McManus, whose broken hand had healed (17 HR, 60 RBI, .261).

"There was a lot of player movement. At the AA and AAA levels, a lot of movement is made during the season. Of course, you give a lot of players playing time. We didn't have 25 players! You'd have your nine regular players, and you'd hope when you had a day off, they'd catch their breaths. In case of an injury, you'd have one or two extra men— maybe an outfielder, maybe an infielder, maybe a catcher. That's the way you operated. You didn't have all these luxuries that you do today. Now the minor leagues, they'll have guys on the D.L. with a hangnail. The days of barking at players are gone. You can't do that anymore. They'll tell you to go shit in your hat, or buy up your contract and get you out of here."

Glennon did not invite Johnny back, and he made the announcement during the World Series. "A nice man," recalls Johnny, despite their differences. "Very devout Catholic. I liked him personally, but sometimes we couldn't agree on players. I think the year after I left, he said he thought I was too easy with some of the players.

"If I make a mistake, I'll admit it. If you make a mistake, why not admit it? You say you like a kid and then you report that to the powers that do the assigning of these players and they'd say, 'How can you feel that way?' Well, I'm not God. I just like what he does."

1958 LANCASTER RED ROSES
CLASS A, EASTERN LEAGUE

Under Pesky's leadership, the expansion Lancaster Red Roses blossomed to a first place finish with a record of 75-57 and, in a war of the Roses, beat the York White Roses in the first round of playoffs before finally bowing to Binghampton.

On paper, Johnny was dropping back a rung on the managerial ladder, from Double A to Single A ball. "It was where there was an opening. A lot of times the general manager in a town might ask for someone. I think that's why I went from class B right to double A with Glennon. The farm director got together with his staff and says, 'Well, we got to put this guy here. They tried to move the manager with some of the players, especially if you advanced to a higher classification.

So what appeared to be a demotion was actually the Tigers showing confidence in Johnny's ability to launch a new team. The facilities left much to be desired. "It was like a semi-pro ballpark with wooden stands and the clubhouse was . . . . it was awful. It was a good league, though. We were filling that park pretty well.

"Joe Schultz was the manager over at York, a Cardinals farm team about eleven miles away. He must have got run out of ballgames twenty five times! He was always in the umpire's face."

Popowski, who'd managed Greensboro for the Red Sox against Pesky in 1956 was now managing Boston's Allentown farm club. Don Gile and Bob Tillman were on that club, players Johnny would end up managing, when he returned to the Red Sox. He coached Pagliaroni in Seattle.

For Lancaster, shortstop Gordon Figard finished second in the batting race, with a .309 average and the Red Roses led the league with a .271 mark. First baseman Alfred Benza, who also put in quite a few innings at second, had 76 RBI and 15 homers. Third baseman Manuel Diaz contributed 66 RBI. George McCue 51 RBI and Wycliffe Morton 57. Ronald Shoop an even 50. Al Paschal was on this team, too—36 RBI. There were no huge standouts on the club—their accomplishment really was a team effort.

"Figard, he got some kind of religion two or three years later. I couldn't believe it. Good little shortstop. Manny Diaz, he was from Nicaragua. Wendell Antoine was a big six foot two handsome black kid. He made a tag at first base and the runner ran into him and they hit so hard that his arm came right out of the socket. It was so bad he had to have it operated on, and after the operation he just lost all of his strength."

Wendell Antoine was on a comeback in 1958 after an injury the prior year and first met up with Johnny in spring training. "He treated me great," Antoine recalled more than forty years later. "Straight up. Man to man. I broke my finger there the last week of the season but we won the championship that year. He was a fun loving man. He liked to tell jokes and sing along with the guys. We used to sing a lot and drink beer together on the bus. He liked the way I'd sing a song. It was a ditty. A ditty. I was supposed to go with him, to Knoxville, but I went with the Minnesota Twins."

On October 6, Johnny was named manager of the Knoxville Smokies for the coming year, 1959.

1959 KNOXVILLE SMOKIES
CLASS A, SOUTHERN ATLANTIC LEAGUE

In '58, the Smokies had placed fifth in a six-team circuit under manager George Staller. In 1959, under manager Pesky, the team finished in first place, winning 78 and losing 62. Jim Proctor was the league's best pitcher with a 15-5 record, 2.19 ERA; he made it to the majors in mid-September, but only appeared in two games, ever, pitching $2^2/_3$ innings and giving up 8 hits.

Knoxville lost to Charleston in the playoffs, three games to two. The evenly-matched teams had split the season series, each winning ten games.

Years later Johnny would recall Knoxville fondly, "Bill Meyer Stadium was a beautiful little ballpark, right in the Smoky Mountains." Pablo Rivera was the batting leader for Knoxville, hitting .292, third in the league. He played second and short and batted in 37 runs. Al Benza did well here, too—this year driving in 77 runs, with a little more pop (14 homers, 17 doubles.) First baseman Donald Lumley had 75 RBI, hit .275 and 11 HR. Shortstop Frank Kostro had 52 RBI. Bucky Luck had 62 RBI and catcher Bob Rodgers had 55. Again, this seemed to be team play with no one hitter really dominating statistically.

Dick McAuliffe was on the team briefly, collecting 26 at bats but just four hits. Dick joined the Tigers in late 1960 and played for Detroit and Boston right into the 1975 season, where Johnny coached him in his final 7 games in the majors. "I had him early but we needed a player at Durham—and they wanted him to play every day. I could have kept him as an extra man, but. . . . I brought him back and he was on our team when we won our championship.

"There was a lot of player movement. You try to set your ball club . . . the organization always wanted at least to be in contention. My third and fourth years managing, we were pennant winners. In the Texas League, we were in the middle of the race, but the other teams were just better.

"Sometimes you can outsmart yourself. You leave a kid in there and that's his position. If he is struggling at that position, and we're in May maybe you try to find a place for him because you might like him personally—but the reason he's on your team is because he's assigned to you. We're trying to get something across to the player and the only way you're going to do this is to bring him out early. Extra hitting. Extra fielding. I remember when I managed in Knoxville, I had a kid named Jake Wood. He was probably the worst fielder I ever saw. My general manager was a bastard. I'm playing this kid every day and he's shafting me. I finally told him, 'You're the general manager. You call Mr. McHale and you get him out of here.' The more he barked at me about getting this kid out of the lineup, the more I told myself I'm going to play this kid every day—and he'd make two or three errors. So finally I brought him out in the morning and I'd hit him ground ball after ground ball. He had a habit of looking up—I don't know what it was—but I got so exasperated, I kicked him right in the ass. It's a wonder he didn't turn around and hit me. He had every right to. A real quiet kid and a wonderful kid but I knew he could hit and I knew he could run. I would have kept him all year because that's how much I liked this kid. I had a good feeling about him but, then again, I could have been wrong. I had to send him out because I was getting some help. He got to the big leagues. [Wood made the Tigers in 1961 and had a seven-year major league career, with a .250 career batting average and a .963 fielding average.]

"We did have some racial problems. That happened in the Carolina League and certainly in the Sally League. I didn't have a black player at Birmingham. But I had them at Durham and I had them at Knoxville. I was there before the color line was broken. That used to break my heart. Jake Wood. Wendell Antoine was a wonderful kid. Jim Proctor. He was our best pitcher. A kid named Jesse Queen [Jackson Queen]. He was a pretty good little player. You should have seen when we got into Macon and places like that how some of the people in the stands got on those black players. I had to drive them over to the black section and drop them off at the hotel there. Then we'd go back and pick them up and take them to the ballpark. I remember one time my wife was watching a game in Macon. Jesse Queen was one of my better players. Those fans were all over him. David was just a kid, 6 or 7 years old, and Ruthie would be sitting in the stands with him, and say, 'Come on, Jesse! Get a base hit!' They'd look over and they'd use a bad word—you lover of the black. They'd use the 'n' word.

"I had good luck with the black players and I'm quite proud of that."

Mickey Lolich, family friend of the Paveskovich clan, was born in 1940 and in 1959 he joined the Smokies. He started eleven games for Knoxville, and earned a 3-6 record. He had some control problems, walking 53 while striking out 42. He did boast a 2.55 ERA, though, and certainly progressed through the system to a very good career, breaking in with the Tigers in 1963. Lolich eventually won 217 games for the big league club.

"His father and my brother were very good friends. They all went to St. Patrick's. I knew Mickey was just one of those kids that hung around the park but I knew he was good. I took him to Knoxville with me. He was a little wild when he was a kid. I took him, even though I don't think he had any pro ball when he came to Knoxville. I always liked him. You knew he was going to be a good player, but it was a little too much [for him at that level at that time]. I think I sent him back to B ball."

This year Johnny led a pennant winner. "Knoxville—we won by

taking the first game of a doubleheader in Charlotte. We won the first game 5-3 and my leftfielder Bucky Luck hit a three-run homer. After they clinched, the kids threw me in the shower—but we only had the one uniform each and then everyone had to get ready for game two. I called them all together. Proctor was going to pitch, and he was having a great year—in those years, they were seven inning games. I said, 'Well, boys, we've gotta get this win for Jimmy. Bust your hump.' I had no uniform. I was in street clothes then, so I went up in the radio booth with our guy. Proctor shut them out 1-0. He had a good arm, and he looked like he was going to be a good major league pitcher but I think he hurt his arm a couple of years later."

The next day, the last game of the year—the game on the day following the doubleheader—everyone was joking about how they wanted to play different positions. So Johnny let them. Pitchers played in the outfield. Johnny let the trainer run the team. The Knoxville G.M. didn't like it, though. "Bob Bonifay. His son Cam is the general manager with the Pirates now. Cam was a little young kid hanging around Knoxville while I was there. The president of the league fined me $25.00.

"There's only been one place where I really didn't get along with the general manager and that was in Knoxville, the year that we won the pennant. He got involved with his secretary and it was a mess. But he was a strange guy. He'd been in the organization a number of years and every place he'd been, his team won. Well, my team won but we won it in the last half of the season. We won it in August, won 26 out of 30 games to win the pennant by two games. I remember early in the year, maybe June, we'd lost three or four games, and he came in the clubhouse, 'No beer! No beer! No beer!' I had a little office there, and I heard him and came out and said, 'Get your ass out of here. This place doesn't belong to you anyway.' I chased him out of the clubhouse. I asked him to leave. I said, 'I don't go into your office and tell you what to do.'

"Some of the players didn't like him, and I sensed it. Maybe they didn't like me either, but I was still the manager. So I got him out of there. I went into his office the next day and I said, 'Bob, don't ever do that again. I don't come in here and tell you how to run the office. The players belong to me when they're in this ballpark.' He said, 'OK' and then we got along pretty well from that time on."

In terms of the hierarchy of clubs, this was a lateral move from one A ball club to another. He'd gotten Lancaster off to a wonderful start in its first year as a franchise, coming in first. Now he'd taken a fifth place club all the way to first place. This back-to-back success had to look good

to Detroit management—and probably drew notice in other organizations
as well.

INTERLUDE: WINTER BALL IN NICARAGUA

After the 1959 season, Johnny had the opportunity to work in winter
ball. He was asked to manage the Cinco Estrellas (Five Stars) team based
in Managua, Nicaragua. "I learned very little Spanish. They used to make
fun of me: *muy poquito* [very small]. I knew how to order ham and eggs;
they treated us pretty well. The guy who was over us, he was a major
down there, he didn't speak any English, but I had an interpreter from
Bluefields, in Nicaragua, a coach, a very fine man, a black man named
Stanley Cayaso. I had a lot of natives on the team. I had eight Americans
and the rest were local kids. I would bring them out in the morning and
we would work out. I was teaching, just let them play and see what happened, and they did things like they'd run bases ass-backwards. Luckily I
had Stanley there to explain things to them, this is what you've got to do,
like running on two outs, scoring position on second and third. We won
the second half. The thing that the major liked was that I was bringing
the natives out and giving them some routine, about the way we trained
in the States, and he liked that.

"Being in a foreign country, I didn't want to overstep my bounds.
We had already started the season and we were in about the third or
fourth game and my catcher got into a hassle with the umpire. I go
running out to get between him and the umpire and I get in the
umpire's face. I don't know what the hell he's saying and he doesn't
know what I'm saying. Finally, after I was standing there yakking at him
for a while he turns to the press box and goes like this—[back and
forth motion with hand]. What he was doing, he fined me fifty
cordobas. Now I have to sit in the dugout and not do anything. I
couldn't even go out on the lines. We got beat that night and I came
in the clubhouse, and the major comes in—Stanley was always with
me—and he's smiling. So I said to Stanley, 'What the hell's he smiling
about?' He says, 'Well, he's glad what you did tonight. He's happy with
what you did.' I said, 'How the hell could he be happy?' He said he
thought you were too soft. That I was too easy on the players. He was
a military guy, with the army, with Somoza. He was like an adjutant
there, one of the head honchos in the military. He probably was a general a few years after I left.

"The umpire was a nice guy, name of Rodriguez, I'll never forget him. I grabbed ahold of Stanley a couple of days later and I said, 'Tell him the only reason I went out there was so he wouldn't throw the catcher out.' He said he understood that. He said, 'Nice man' [about Pesky]. He probably didn't mean it, but I accepted it. With those guys you have to be careful. Here we are down from the United States. I told the American players, 'Lookit, just back off.'

"They'd shoot off guns down there; they'd have guns up in the stands."

I went down about a week ahead, to see how things were, and then Ruthie and David flew in later. We were always together. I liked having them around. David, by the time he was ten years old, he was in Florida, Texas, Carolinas, Tennessee, the West Coast, Hawaii . . . by the time he was ten years old. He likes to travel."

David Pesky retains memories of Nicaragua. "I was seven. It was a fun time. There's a big volcano right near Managua and I remember going up into the mountains. One of the ballplayers took me up there in a Jeep. The poor guy wanted to get out and take a leak. It was on a steep road and there was no place to pull over. So he just stopped and he put the hand brake on, but he was still worried that it was going to slip, so he told me to sit in the driver's seat and press on the brake. And I was so scared! It wasn't going to slip anyway. That's one thing I remember, the kind of thing a kid would remember."

"Anyway," Johnny continues, "it was a good experience. The only thing I was afraid of, David might get hurt, somebody might grab him. He's very light blond, blue-eyed. Those Latins down there loved him, they were chasing him all over the place. They treated us real well; I really had no complaints. They called me and wanted me back, and I would have gone back but in 1960 I got into the Texas League and then the next year I came back to the Red Sox."

1960 VICTORIA, TEXAS ROSEBUDS
CLASS AA, TEXAS LEAGUE

The arrival of the sixties is remembered primarily by Red Sox fans as Ted Williams' Boston swan song. Few people recall that it was also Johnny Pesky's debut with the Texas Rosebuds (what is it with all these flowers?)

Under manager Pete Reiser, in front of 86,040 fans, the 1959 team came in first, with an 86-60 record and a team batting average of .283—but lost two games to one in the playoff.

Rio Grande Valley made a strong first place finish, a full 8½ games ahead of second place San Antonio. Gaylord Perry had the best league ERA at 2.83 but, despite pitching for the first place team, only managed 9 wins against 13 losses. Victoria came in fourth in 1960, nine games out (the second, third and fourth place teams were all bunched, with winning percentages of .531, .528 and .527.) In the first round of the playoffs, Victoria swept all three games from Rio Grande Valley, but then lost out, being swept in turn by Tulsa in the final round.

Raugh was Victoria's best pitcher, 11-4, 3.33 ERA. Proctor, who had played for Johnny in Knoxville the year before, went 15-8 with a 3.91 ERA and batted .305 to boot.

"Victoria, Texas," Johnny recalls. "They were great down there. I had a guy named Mac Davenport [as G.M.], a wonderful guy. The owner was a fine man. Beautiful ballpark, big league ballpark. There was a huge locker room—hell, big lockers, they looked better than Fenway Park."

Johnny's son David has an early memory of his dad at a ballpark. "One time they lost a tight one and he has the whole team assembled, and he was giving them hell and ranting and raving the way he does. He's funny that way. He'll rant and rave and then he turns around five minutes later and he's laughing. He's not a grudge holder, but he was tough. He was a tough manager in the minor leagues. I forget where this was. I wasn't even watching the game and I came in right in the middle of the ranting and raving and said, 'WHO WON?' Everybody laughed. All the players broke up. He thought that was great. He probably laughed, too. I ruined his theatrics."

An interesting feature of the season were the games Victoria played against some of the Mexican League teams. An early form of interleague play, the Rosebuds played several games against the Mexico City Tigers, the Mexico City Reds, Monterrey, Puebla, Poza Rica, and Veracruz. Monterrey was actually a farm club of the Kansas City A's.

"We played in Mexico City and two or three other places. We didn't play the Mexican teams very much. The Mexican teams would come to our place, too. Bobby Avila came from Veracruz. We flew in to Mexico City and then we traveled by bus from there. Ruthie and David came in one time to Mexico City."

If Johnny had taken Sr. Pasquel's offer, he could have been a player himself in the Mexican League. Now he was managing games against some of the Mexican League teams.

Victoria was Johnny's last team in the Tiger organization. The following year he left the Texas/Mexican border and headed north, close to the border with Canada.

NOTES

(1) *The Sporting News*, July 20, 1955
(2) *Boston Traveler*, October 8, 1962

18

1961–2 Seattle

1961 & 1962 SEATTLE RAINIERS
AAA PACIFIC COAST LEAGUE

Less than three months after Ted Williams struck the ultimate walk-off homer in September 1960, Johnny Pesky was back home with the Red Sox. The Sox had hired him to head their new Triple A franchise in Seattle, having just moved the franchise from Minneapolis. In 1961, the new Seattle Rainiers won 86 while losing only 68, finishing second behind Tacoma.

"My '61 club was the best I ever had, and that includes the big leagues," insists Johnny. "I taught the sliding, had them take their pants off and put on these canvas britches so they wouldn't hurt themselves. Once they did it, they got in the habit of sliding. This stuff with the headfirst shit, we never did that."

Bob Tillman (14 homers, 67 RBI) and Paul Smith (4 HR, 54 RBI) platooned at first. Harry Malmberg played second and Toft third. The shortstop hole was filled by Jenson (69 RBI). Lou Clinton (102 RBI, 21 HR), Tom Umphlett (83 RBI, 12 HR) and David Mann were the primary outfielders, with Paul Smith and Toft both seeing time there. Kenneth Wolfe and Don Gile (78 RBI, 15 HR) were behind the plate. Most of the pitching duties were handled by Borland, Cisco, Palica, Radatz, Ritchie, Schwall, Spanswick and Earl Wilson.

187

"Earl Wilson I adored. Big black handsome guy. I used to call him 'Rafer Johnson' and he'd smile. I loved that guy. Radatz. Earley. Jenson. Coughtry. Tillman . . . I could name all of them."

Wilson had been floundering with wildness when he first arrived in the majors and was sent down to Triple A. Under Pesky, his career turned around dramatically. "I wouldn't say I had anything to do with it," argues Johnny. "Higgins told me, 'John—here's a real fine boy with a great arm. Have some patience with him and he'll be a good pitcher for you.' " He didn't pitch well at first and Pesky could see that he was down. "I called him into my office and said, 'Earl, I don't care what you do out there, you're going to be one of my starting pitchers. I don't care if you throw every ball to the backstop or walk the ballpark, you're going to pitch every four days for me.' " Wilson's responded to Johnny's vote of confidence and returned to the parent club in '62, this time for good.

"If I had a guy on the club I didn't want, I tried to pacify him as much as I could but if he's hurting the club, we tried to move him. I took what I was given. In '61 I lost my three best pitchers in July— Schwall, Cisco and Earley—to the parent club. I thought I was going to lose Radatz, too, but he went up the next year. He was utterly amazing, the Goose Gossage of his time. We wired in on one another and we had a great relationship.

"I loved Tillman like he was my own son. We were leading the league most of the year until Boston took three of my best throwers. Earley was a project. He was a left-hander with a great arm, a starting pitcher. I saw him when he was in the Carolina League, four or five years before that. So now we're in Daytona and now we're setting up our staff. Neil Mahoney, who was our farm director, I said to Neil, 'I'm going to try this kid in our bullpen.' 'Oh, Johnny, he's too wild.' 'Well, goddamn. He's here. Let me try something with him. I've got a whole year to see what he can do.' "

With Tillman, Pesky exhibited the sort of faith he had shown in Earl Wilson. Bob Montgomery recalls, "He had a lot of respect for Tilly. Bobby was having a tough time. He was scuffling and after he'd struck out a couple of times . . . left a couple of people on base . . . he went up to John and said, 'Oh, Geez, John, I'm really trying. I really just can't seem to get it done.' John told him not to worry, he was going to be his catcher anyway, because he liked the way he caught. I believe it was the following year that Tillman went up to the big leagues and John was the one who took him there."

Johnny also sold Radatz on becoming a reliever. "I had about seven guys that were used to starting. It took some convincing—convincing Radatz, and convincing Neil Mahoney, too. Once Dick got used to the idea, he liked it. Now I had a left-right situation coming out of the bullpen. I didn't have Earley the whole year so I used Radatz all the time. For six years he was as good a pitcher as there was.

"I used him once five days in a row and, you know, we have to send the scores back to Boston. I said, Jesus, people in the office were saying 'Radatz in there again. Radatz in there again. Radatz in there again.' We're winning 2-1, 3-2. I don't think we ever beat anybody 10-2. We had good pitching and good defense. So I said to Radatz after the fifth game, 'Don't even come to the ballpark tomorrow. Take Sharon and the kids, go have dinner and I'll pick up the tab.' So I come to the ballpark the next day, and guess who's there? Radatz. I said, '*Jeezus* Christ, what's wrong with you?' He says, 'Well, Sharon was on my ass. The kids were screaming. I had to come get some peace.' I said, 'Well, OK, but stay in the goddamn dugout.'

"The game's going on, and he's up and down. The fifth inning I look around, and he's not in the dugout. So I send the clubhouse kid into the clubhouse. You're supposed to be out on the field. I was always a bastard about that. If you don't want to be in the game, all right, get dressed and do whatever you want. I told him to get his big ass down here. The sixth inning, I look around and he's not down here. He's out in the bullpen! The seventh inning, our other catcher Joe Tyce comes in and says, 'Johnny, Radatz wants to throw.' 'Tell him to sit down!' Well, we're ahead 3-2 in the eighth and finally I say. 'OK, tell him OK, but just easy.' The top of the ninth, we've still got a 3-2 lead but the tying run's on first with one out. When you were ready, we had a sign—you take your glove off and put it on top of your head. I knew I was going to get that from Radatz. He comes in and throws 3 pitches to the first guy. Strikes him out. He got a quick strike on the next guy and then—I can still see him, his ass flying out and he hit a little ground ball to second base and the inning's over. I saw him after the game. I said, 'You big bastard. You're going to get me fired.' He said, 'Oh, Johnny. That's like warming up.' He struck out Mantle something like 60 times!"

"The Monster" credits Johnny with his success: "The first time I played for Johnny was in Seattle but it really goes back farther than that. I was aware of Johnny Pesky when I was 10 or 11, 12 years old, back in the '40s. My dad was a big baseball fan and we used to go to Briggs Field, which became Tiger Stadium. Back in the Briggs days, in the middle '50s, I was aware of Johnny Pesky and that whole ball club. My dad used to watch two people play; he used to love to watch Ted Williams hit and Bob Feller pitch. So I knew the Cleveland and the Boston lineups probably better than any kid in Detroit. I was well aware of Johnny Pesky in those days. To this day I can still name that lineup for the Red Sox.

"Of course, he was with the Tigers, too. I was a Tigers fan. Born and raised there. I had a tryout with them and they didn't think too much of me, and consequently I ended up elsewhere.

"I met him in '61. That was the first time that I formally met him. He was the manager of the Seattle Rainiers then. I had played at Minneapolis and Raleigh the year before, Raleigh being B baseball then. Yaz and I broke in in '59, in Raleigh. I got off to a great start; I was a starting pitcher then. I think I was 12-3 or something there at Raleigh and they brought me from B ball right up to Triple A, which was quite a jump. I was 3-0 up there as a starter. '61, I went down to spring training with a sore arm. I had hurt my arm playing touch football during the winter. I just asked Johnny for a couple weeks of semi-throwing around—I just wanted to get my arm up—and he said fine. It came time to cut the team down and he said, 'Dick, we've got to pitch you.' My arm hadn't gotten much better, but I didn't tell him that. So he took us over to Daytona to play Rochester, which was the Orioles Triple A farm club and he started me that day. The Good Lord was on my side. I started the game and struck out 11 of the first 12 batters. I pitched the four innings and Johnny called me in after the game and said, 'Dick, we're going to take you to Seattle with us. I was very impressed with what you did today.' I said, 'Gee, that's great, John.' And he said, 'Well, we're going to take you as a reliever.'

"Back in those days, that was a demotion. I said, 'Don't do me any favors. Send me back to Allentown'—which was A ball—'I'd like to start every fourth day.' He said, 'No, I'm going to take you with me and teach you how to pitch every day!' I said, 'I can't do that.' But as they say, the rest is history. It was his decision. It was the best thing that ever happened to me.

"Harry Dorish was down there and I worked with him. Because of the fact that I was a one-pitch pitcher, and that being the fastball, they taught me how to warm up rather quickly as opposed to maybe taking 15 minutes. That transition wasn't very hard. It was the warming up to come into games on a minute's notice that was . . . and that took me maybe the first half of 1961 to learn how to do that. You had to be ready again the next day. And the next day, and the next day.

"I had a good job in '61 in Seattle. I think it was 5-6 or something record-wise but that's not always indicative of a closer. I had a number of saves and, although our record didn't indicate it, we had a pretty doggone good club. Arnold Earley and I—he's passed away since—he and I were sort of the right-handed and left-handed closers down there. We did pretty good between the two of us."

Radatz was elevated to the Boston club and won the *Sporting News* relief pitcher of the year award in 1962. Then Johnny was promoted as well, and they joined up once more.

"By 1963, Johnny was up running the Red Sox and I was a happy man! Not only was he responsible for my good fortune; he also became a very good friend. He was more than just a manager to me. He was almost a father figure. I had so much respect for him. To this day, we're very close.

"I thought Johnny did a heck of a job. When he came up in '63, he really was a player's type of manager. All the guys on the team liked him very much. As you know, he's a very personable guy. It was hard not to like to play for him. Although I never consciously was aware that I was pitching to make it better for him, maybe I was—but my best years were with Johnny Pesky. In '62 when I was Rookie Relief Pitcher of the Year, it was directly attributable to what Johnny had taught me the year before."

Pesky's confidence in his players paid off. Sometimes he was maybe a little too tough; other times, maybe not tough enough. One time it took Seattle trainer Bud Holmes to give Johnny a bit of a nudge. He respected Holmes, having worked with him for five years in the Detroit system. "He was great, and when I came over to the Red Sox, I brought him with me. Even after I left the Red Sox, he stayed with them. I had him in Seattle. My first year, some of the kids thought I was a little tough. My bark was worse than my bite. The second year, I had all the kids. I'm letting them play a little bit, run around a little bit too much. Bud grabbed me one day, about three, four weeks into the season, and he said, 'When are you going to crack down on your club?' I said, 'Yeah, I've been letting them run a little bit, haven't I?' He said, 'Yeah.' I says, 'Well, we'll have a meeting tomorrow and we'll straighten it out.' That was it. We never had any more problems after that.

"I had some disappointments, too. I loved Earl Wilson. I always had a good feeling about him. He was wild, but he had a great arm. Run. I used to bring him out at 11:30 in the morning to run him. I used to use him as a pinch-hitter. He could hit. He does pretty well in Boston, but Herman traded him for a centerfielder from Detroit and Wilson goes over there and wins 21 the second year, 19 the next year, 18, 19 again.

He's got his thing under control. He's 6'4" and handsome. He really wasn't black. He was this reddish color. He looked more Indian. And, God, was he a great dresser! What a great kid."

Wilson battled racism to make the Sox. Pumpsie Green and Earl Wilson were the first two African-American players for the team, Green coming up just a month before Wilson in 1959. It was a tense time, and players' antennae were up. Even the briefest comment or the smallest of gestures could speak volumes. Wilson recalls Johnny Pesky as sympathetic to him as a player.

Johnny had introduced Wilson to the Paveskovich family when the Rainiers visited Portland, and Earl never forgot it. "I remember when I was sick [in 1982]. I was laying in that Deaconess Hospital and Earl called me up. I guess Radatz told him where I was. So he gets me on the phone and we're talking a little bit, and now he starts to cry. I'm talking to him and, Christ, he was crying. I said, 'What's the matter with you?' He said, 'Oh, I feel bad about this.' I says, 'Earl, please stop. Lookit, I ain't dead yet. I'll be all right, Earl. Thanks for the call.' "

Wilson, interviewed in March 2002, recalls his manager with fondness. "I first knew Johnny in Seattle, Washington. He worked hard and if you didn't plan on working hard, it didn't do you no good to come around Johnny. He's just a good man. As simple and strong as I can put it, he's just a good man. Johnny always found something good about what you did.

"There's always a cloud over your shoulder when you're a young feller, but he just kept telling me I was all right, don't worry about it, I'm going to be here and you're going to pitch every time your turn comes around. That stuff helps; as a matter of fact, it helps a lot. And not only that, he just takes you under his wing. I think he tries to mold you into a good person. Every thing about him, I appreciate.

"I look at guys that you play ball with and then you look at a guy named Johnny Pesky. He was a guy who'd been ridiculed a little bit, too. The Slaughter thing in the World Series, and I think he kind of understood people stepping on you. When I went down to the minor leagues, I didn't have any idea if I'd ever get back to Boston or not. And, matter of fact, it had got to the point where I didn't even care. But Pesky just stuck with me. He'd come in the restaurant and sit down and talk to me. He kinda knocked that feeling out of you that you're not liked or you're not wanted. It was deep. I got a chance to go back to Boston again. It was hope.

"I met Johnny's wonderful wife and family. I was like her son. He did things he didn't have to do. He'd do things because he wanted to help you, or because it was right, or for no reason at all. As long as you've got something to talk about, he's there to listen. Yes, I called him when he was in the hospital for so long; I thought we had lost him. I just wanted him to know that I cared about him. He had his favorites, and I was glad I was one of them. We were like his Seattle kids—Bob Tillman, Dick Radatz. . . . He's just a good baseball man."

There was a reunion in 1999 and about 25 of the players from the '61 Rainiers showed up. It was actually a reunion of both the 1960 Minneapolis Millers and the 1961 Rainiers, since there was such an over- lap of players between the two. Johnny recalled the weekend with pleas- ure. "We had a great time. We were all there for three or four days on Whitby Island—I came walking in about 3 o'clock and they're all sitting around having a drink. It was kind of a rainy day. So I walked in and they all said, 'Hey, John. How are you?' I said, 'OK, now that I've got all of you here, which one of you guys hated me the worst?' They all stood up! Then they all came over and gave me a hug. 'Oh, you little shitass, how are you?' 'You didn't talk to me like that when you were playing for me!' "

Don Gile caught and played first base. He recalls Johnny as a very fair manager, one who took the time to work with the players and encourage them. He doesn't feel Johnny played favorites at all, and gave everyone fair playing time—consistent, of course, with the dictates from the home office. Gile joined the club partway into the season and they did well, leading the league at the halfway point—thereby earning the right to host the all-star game. "Johnny treated us like men," he reports, "with respect, and not like a bunch of kids." He wasn't strict with rules, and the players responded. He found Johnny exceptionally straight- forward—if he had something to say—good news or bad—he'd sit down and explain it thoroughly to the player. He was neither autocratic nor hard to decipher. Given the small coaching staff—it was really just Johnny, Harry Malmberg and Elmer Singleton (who served as sort of an informal player/pitching coach)—it was a close working relationship. Once in a while, Johnny would jump into the batter's box himself and take some b.p. Gile remembers Johnny lining drives to left, center and right—some real shots.

At least Johnny had a coaching staff! This was Triple A, one step removed from the majors—but Johnny hadn't worked with a Triple A club since the Denver Bears in 1955, so having others to help out—and to confer with—felt luxurious.

This was a big club: Gile was 6'6", Radatz was 6'5". Earl Wilson was 6'3". Tillman was 6'4". There were two or three other players on the team that were well over 6 feet tall. They made allowances for their vertically challenged (5'9") manager—when Pesky came out to the mound, they all stood on the grass while he stood on the rubber.

Johnny backed his players up. Gile recalls him as an occasionally fiery manager—when the situation demanded it. There were a couple of times that year, Gile laughs, when an umpire's call went the wrong way. "I would get really irate—and there would come Johnny, irate right along with me."

Pesky served in Seattle for two full seasons during which time he had a few big league coaching offers. "One really had me excited," he admits. "I couldn't sleep." Ruth talked him out of it, arguing that he was lucky to be where he was. The Red Sox had given him good players to work with. "These people have been good to you. Don't get too high on yourself." He took her advice and his loyalty soon paid off. By the end of 1962, he'd been offered the job as manager of the Red Sox. Major league coaching followed—rather than preceded—his stint as manager.

The idea of stability appealed to Johnny's much-traveled son, David. "I was a lot of places when I was young. It was a nice feature of my youth. When he became manager of the Red Sox, the gypsy life sort of abated a little bit. It was in Seattle when we went to Hawaii. They took us on a road trip to play some team out there. I remember some bus trips. Bus trips in the Great Smoky Mountains. I never made the train trips. I was a little too young for that, but I remember some bus trips. Minor league style travel. I might have flown with the Red Sox once or twice, but nothing comes to mind. I don't think I did."

19

Becoming Red Sox Manager

Meanwhile, back in Boston, the Red Sox had been in decline throughout the 1950s, finishing under .500 in 1952 for the first time since the war years.

These were years of Yankee dominance and Red Sox doldrums. Save for 1954 and 1959, the Yanks won every year for 16 years. The Red Sox were not so fortunate—or not so good. Although in 1953 they recovered to 84-69, they were still 16 games behind the Yankees. In the following years, they were:

1954	69-85	.448 and	42 games behind
1955	84-70	.545	12 GB
1956	84-70	.545	13 GB
1957	82-72	.532	16 GB
1958	79-75	.513	13 GB
1959	75-79	.487	19 GB
1960	65-89	.422	32 GB
1961	76-86	.469	33 GB
1962	76-84	.475	19 GB

Not surprisingly, attendance at Fenway had fallen off as well. After the Boston Braves departed for Milwaukee, Boston became a one-team town but even that market monopoly didn't help much. When Ted

Williams retired, the Red Sox lost their last remaining draw—and, in truth, even Ted hadn't been packing them in like he once did. It got so bad that the Bosox even failed to sell out on Opening Days.

Like his team, it seemed as though Tom Yawkey was in a funk, sinking into a sad relationship with crony Pinky Higgins. Higgins benefited from the friendship with his drinking partner/patron, demonstrating remarkable job tenure despite an absence of on-field results. Worse, Higgins was, at heart, an embittered man.

Glenn Stout and Dick Johnson in their comprehensive *Red Sox Century* decry the "country club" that the Red Sox had become. "Tom Yawkey now did little more than 'act like a rich guy and pretend to work,' in the words of one former associate. His familiar old cronies still ran the organization, chief among them Pinky Higgins, protecting the status quo, demanding little from his team, virtually guaranteeing mediocrity. The players took full advantage of him. The Sox didn't even pretend to be capable of challenging the Yankees." Ominously, they add, "Higgins's ongoing role with the club continued to saddle it with a racist reputation, an ever more anachronistic and embarrassing perception." It wasn't until 1959 that the Red Sox had even one black player on the major league team—Pumpsie Green—a full 12 seasons after Jackie Robinson, who the Red Sox had rejected in a sham tryout, began play with the Brooklyn Dodgers.

Mike Higgins first took over as manager for the 1955 campaign and managed through 1962, with the exception of a confusing period in 1959 when Rudy York took over as interim manager, succeeded shortly afterward by Billy Jurges. Jurges managed into 1960, trying desperately to bring a little hustle and discipline to the Red Sox. He quickly lost the respect of the players and by mid-season was gone. In a bizarre twist, the inmates of the asylum voted for their new warden; Joe Donnelly reported in *Sport* magazine that the Red Sox players actually "held what possibly may have been the first election in major-league baseball by a team to determine who it wanted as manager. The players voted for Higgins. Yawkey reappointed him." Higgins resumed the reins, holding on through the 1962 season. He had been a Red Sox player in 1938, 1939 and 1946 and sadly, it was Ted Williams who seems to have recommended Higgins to Yawkey. (1)

Red Sox fans rebelled by staying away in droves. The organization was a foundering ship and a new commander was needed to right it. Yawkey put Johnny Pesky in charge. Finally Pesky was going to get a shot at managing the Red Sox, the team he loved. Arthur Siegel of the *Globe*

wrote that Pesky "may be the first in baseball history to move from clubhouse boy to pilot-house. He was the first home-grown product of the
Sox since Bill Carrigan." Johnny had worn a baseball uniform every year
since 1934, when he was batboy for the Portland Beavers.

The 43-year-old Pesky was also the first member of the Yawkey
regime to work his way up through the Boston farm system to top spot.
There was some irony in Johnny stepping into Higgins' shoes. After all,
Higgins was a former PCL player whose shoes Johnny had shined as a
clubhouse kid in Portland. Higgins once commented: "I was playing third
for Detroit, and Johnny beat out three bunts to me. Next day he came up
before the game and said, 'Remember me? I was your clubhouse boy in
Portland.' I hadn't recognized him, but I told him then he shouldn't be
making an old man out of me with those bunts."

The official announcement that Johnny Pesky was to be the new
manager of the Boston Red Sox was made on October 6, 1962. Just the
week before, the Peskys had sold their home in Lynn. They had been living short term in Revere before they made the move to Swampscott. Ruth
and 9-year-old David had just moved into the rental in Revere the very
night before the news.

Johnny had no advance notice, no idea this was in the offing. "I was
brought into Yawkey's hotel room to get the news from Tom Yawkey and
was stunned. The appointment came like a bolt from the blue. I had no
idea I was under consideration. I was sitting in my hotel room figuring
what I would do at Seattle next year, when I got the call from Mr. Yawkey
and Mr. Higgins. I couldn't sleep all night after getting the news. It was a
story-book thing for me." Johnny had indeed come a long way—from
Vaughn Street to Fenway Park.

The Red Sox had only drawn 733,080 fans in 1962, down 117,509
from the year before—itself a very disappointing year. Declining attendance mirrored the declining fortune of the club in play; for four consecutive seasons, they'd not won half their games. Hiring the popular
Pesky was partly a move to boost attendance. Tim Horgan reported that
literally hundreds of season ticket holders had let the organization know
they would not return if Higgins did.

Columnist Bud Collins reflected the sense that Red Sox fandom had
finally rebelled against Yawkey's drinking buddy: "Mike Higgins' second
managerial term was unacceptable to the people from the moment it
began in June of 1960. It was doomed, just as the first, because Higgins
had a command of inertia that would have made Calvin Coolidge seem
like a Marxist."

Higgins stuck with Don Buddin for five years despite him being the "most erring shortstop in Boston history." After leading the A.L. in errors in '59 and '60, he seemed to stop trying to get to balls—which consequently went through for hits. Pitchers and other infielders almost led a revolt and Higgins was forced to trade him. Eddie Bressoud came in and hit .277 and made great plays. Higgins had said of Bressoud, "He won't hit"—but he easily outhit Buddin both for average and for power.

Hy Zimmerman of the *Seattle Times* wrote that Higgins had only done as well as he did—sixth place—because of the pitchers that came up from Pesky's Seattle Rainiers club—Schwall, Cisco and Earley. Before that, they had a "Venus de Milo pitching staff—no arms."

Higgins seemed to have a stultifying influence, sometimes on individual performers and sometimes on team accomplishments. In 1960, Vic Wertz had 103 RBI and hit .282. By September 8, 1961 Wertz had around 50 RBI but was down to .260 and he was put on waivers, claimed by Detroit. In 1962 Pete Runnels was A.L. batting champ. Dick Radatz was the best reliever. The Red Sox, though, finished tied with Baltimore for 7th place.

There were even suggestions that the growing dissatisfaction extended beyond the fans and some of the players. John Gillooly noted in print that Ted Williams never visited Fenway even once in 1962, despite being around the area most of the summer and despite being on the Red Sox payroll, and that it was because he couldn't stand watching the team. "So Yawkey didn't associate with his beloved Kid all season. Maybe he wants to lure Teddy Boy back by offering him something more appealing than the soporific 1962 Sox." Gillooly was a Pesky pal, and he called Johnny "Kennedy-popular" with the fans.

O'Connell, Higgins and Yawkey had all gone to New York to see the Giants/Dodgers playoff and to choose a new manager. Even though Higgins had a year left on his contract, it was clear that a change was in order. Higgins was replaced after seven years but, unfortunately, was promoted! He was made "executive vice president in charge of baseball." Dick O'Connell's title was "executive vice president in charge of business." O'Connell had clearly been given more power within the organization. Yawkey supposedly wanted someone whose "background and personality will add color to the team." Names batted around included Sal Maglie, Billy Herman, Bobby Doerr, and even Ted Williams. It was probably farm director Neil Mahoney who had first recommended Johnny Pesky. Sportswriter Bill Liston suggested that the Sox' first choice was Yogi Berra, but the Yankees wouldn't let him go. It was then that they settled on Pesky. Johnny had seven years of minor league managing experience and he'd done pretty well the last two of them in the Red Sox system.

He was invited in and accepted the position that evening. Higgins was gracious in his first comments to the public. "The only reason he finished fourth this year [in Seattle] was that I took all his good players," he said. Pesky returned the compliment during this honeymoon period: "I hope that I can become half the man Mike Higgins is. . . . I've talked a lot with Mike and he's really shown me something. He's got some ideas that are great ones and we have to put them across, if we can." There is no question, though, that Pesky was Yawkey's choice and not Pinky Higgins'. And having Higgins stay on, supervising his own successor, would prove to be a poor decision.

Pesky was a popular pick around New England, but every manager knows he is hired to be fired. At a public appearance soon afterwards, Johnny seemed to sense the insecurity of the position, "I hope you all still love me as much a year from now."

Harold Kaese's first column acknowledged the difficulties facing Johnny. "To his credit, the man named manager at 9:30 PM Saturday night by the publicity-unconscious Red Sox, did not resign on the spot," Kaese cracked. "He knows that all the Red Sox need to beat the Yankees next season is a pitcher who can win 20 games, a slugging outfielder, a little power at first base, a slightly better bench, discipline, a better knowledge of certain fundamentals, good physical condition and a determined attitude."

"The way I figure it," said a philosophical Pesky, "the job is mine just as long as I produce. This is the chance I've always dreamed of and if I can't deliver, good luck to the guy who follows me. . . . This is a matter of survival for me. I just can't afford to fail. It may sound a little corny, but I hope I can help Mr. Yawkey. He's been wonderful to me since the time I first joined the Red Sox organization. It's great to be a major league manager, but it's a still bigger thrill to be managing a club you really love."

Johnny indicated he was going to be even-handed as a manager, but no doormat. "I'm no tyrant, but I'm not out to win any popularity contest, either. There are certain things you demand of a player, and if you don't get them, you step on him. I'll never embarrass a player publicly, but he'll hear from me in the clubhouse about his mistakes. And if a player has to be pushed, I'll push him. There was no fooling around at Seattle, and there'll be no fooling around in Boston. Everybody's going to be in condition. I don't mind ball players having a little fun once in a

while, but this is a business, and if they want fun, they'll have to get it in
the off-season. I used to run out everything when I was playing ball, and
anybody who plays for me is going to run 'em out, too.

"I don't want to be a tyrant. But I'll go to extremes to win. There is
only one purpose to being on the ballfield and that is to win. Neither am
I looking to win any Oscars by over-managing. I don't believe in running
out to the mound every five minutes."

This is when Johnny had expressed his appreciation of the Major,
Ralph Houk. "If it hadn't been for Ralph Houk, I'd probably be peddling shoes or doing something else right now. He's the guy who first
got me interested in being a manager." After his first year in Seattle,
Johnny was offered a coaching job in Baltimore by old friend and
roommate Billy Hitchcock, who had just been named manager for the
O's. Sam Mele, another old friend and then manager of the Twins, asked
for and got permission from the Red Sox to offer Pesky a coaching job
in Minnesota. Hy Zimmerman wrote, "Old Needle, who had the Rainiers
in the lead for 78 days and brought them home third in the Pacific
Coast League, turned down both chances. Pesky has long been considered the future manager of the Red Sox, hence his decision to skip the
coaching offers. . . . " (2)

Arthur Sampson wrote during the 1955 off-season that Harvey Kuenn
had really been improved by working with Pesky and Sampson quoted
Johnny: "I certainly got a kick out of working with him and since then I
have decided that I'd eventually enjoy the opportunity of working with
youngsters." Sampson added his own perceptive comment on what it can
take to become a good baseball teacher: "Sooner or later, Pesky will probably get the chance. There are not too many major leaguers qualified to
teach others. Many are natural athletes and for that reason never had to
figure things out. Little guys like Pesky have to study the game to make
the grade. Johnny didn't have the strength or physique to power the ball
out of the park. So he learned to choke his bat a little and poke the ball
to all fields. Not having power to drive in many runs, he adopted other
tactics and became valuable to the team with his ability to get on base
often. In the field, Johnny wasn't blessed with a powerful throwing arm.
So he learned to get the ball away quickly and play the batters smartly."

Sampson concluded: "And there is every evidence that he has the
knack of really teaching."

Soon after his hiring, Johnny was on a three-week visit to scout Sox
rookies in the Florida Instructional League, an involvement which was in
itself a departure for the Red Sox. "I don't want any lazy players," he said.

"Joe McCarthy always said if you have lazy ball players you'll never win. Let them be lazy with some other ball club. I don't want them. You can't slide by in this game. They say this is a challenge, this managing business. It's no challenge. It's a fight for survival. I know that you've got to win in this game or else. You have got to bust your back. I want to be honest with everybody. I'll put the cards right on the table. This is the biggest chance of my life and I'm going to do everything possible to succeed."

Ted Williams himself, in the *San Diego Union* of January 18, 1963 gave his blessing: "What I like most about the situation is that Pesky has come up from the very bottom of the organization and has reached the top of the heap. That's a great thing and the first time it's ever happened."

Back in Portland, old mentor Rocky Benevento agreed, "He's gone right to the top. I knew he would. He always was a hustler. For $500 they got a million-dollar guy."

Pesky set '65 as his target year. He was under no illusions that things could be turned around on a dime. Pesky replaced coaches Sal Maglie, Rudy York and Len Okrie with Harry "Fritz" Dorish (pitching coach) and Al Lakeman and Harry Malmberg. Billy Herman stayed on as third base coach. "The only thing Higgins did was insist that I keep Billy Herman. He wanted Billy to manage. If I didn't have Harry Dorish, I'd have kept Sal Maglie. I knew something about him but I wasn't around him that much as a coach."

Before the season began, as they were preparing rosters, Johnny didn't hesitate to stand up for players he believed in. "I guess when we played, we thought what we did was perfectly all right, but when you're running a club you see it differently. I remember when I started managing, this was very noticeable. You look at a guy. You look at his age and look at his makeup. You look at his body. And this is where you make judgment on these guys.

"I remember one year we had a kid and I'm not going to use his name, but I'm managing now—managing the big league club. Neil Mahoney was the farm director. I wanted to go back to Seattle in '63 because I knew what was coming, but Mr. Yawkey wanted to make a change. Anyway, in those years after the season we always had a meeting about those guys we wanted to protect. This kid here, the Red Sox gave him a lot of money. He played for me. I had him for two years in the Coast League. I just didn't think he could play [in the majors]. I wanted a guy that was nimble [and] I wanted to protect somebody else. In fact, I protected a kid who hit .219 for us. It was Tillman. The catcher—but he hit home runs. This other guy, a second baseman. . . . Well, anyway, to make a long story short, Mahoney said, 'Johnny, are you sure about this?' 'Lookit, Neil. If this kid plays in the big leagues, you can fire me.' "

As it happens, the kid washed out early, and Tillman hit 17 homers and batted .278 in 1964. Johnny had a good feeling about Tillman. "He was big and he could catch and he could throw. That's what I liked."

Johnny never could repress his optimism—a trait which serves him well even into the 21st century—and on the last day of January in 1963 the new manager predicted that the Red Sox might even finish as high as third place.

NOTES

(1) Ted Williams, *My Turn At Bat*, p. 191, 192
(2) *Seattle Times*, October 22, 1961

20

Manager, 1963

Managing the Red Sox may have been Pesky's dream but it had the potential to be a nightmare. For years, management had demonstrated such a laissez-faire attitude towards the players that Boston newspapers routinely labeled the Red Sox the "millionaires" and the "country club." Johnny did not have a strong roster to work with, either. In 1962, the team had finished in 8th place, winning just 76 games.

Some players had done well in 1962. Yastrzemski had knocked in 94 runs, hitting .294. Third baseman Frank Malzone had 95 RBI, with 21 home runs and a .283 average. Lou Clinton had contributed 77 RBI, with 22 homers. Pete Runnels was the A.L. batting champion, with a .326 mark and knocked in 60 runs. Eddie Bressoud had batted .277 but other than that, most of the team was well under .250. The Sox had had some decent pitching, but this was not a well-rounded team—and the proof was in the pudding. Other Red Sox teams had worse winning percentages, but no Red Sox team had finished as low in the standings since Tom Yawkey took over.

The Sox had moved to address some of their bigger needs. There was hope that the off-season additions of Roman Mejias (24 homers, 76 RBI with Houston in '62) and Dick Stuart (16 homers and 64 RBI with Pittsburgh) would pump the team up offensively.

There was hope that the team had improved with their off-season moves, and that bringing in a sparkplug manager like Pesky would reenergize the troops. Johnny was dealing, though, with an immediate superior in Higgins who was not the least bit supportive and may well have wanted to see Johnny fail. Had Johnny just Dick O'Connell and Tom Yawkey to deal with, he would have had more of a fighting chance. Higgins, though, was the fly in the ointment. Al Hirshberg wrote that Pesky was "hired directly by Yawkey, who kicked Higgins upstairs. Higgins didn't want to go upstairs. He would have preferred to continue as manager. Higgins resented [Pesky's] succession to the job, and was determined to get rid of him as soon as possible."

Johnny was fired up to be manager, though, and full of energy. The Boston baseball writers dinner on January 23rd featured "A Salute to Johnny Pesky"—Johnny was always popular with the media. He explained he wouldn't hesitate to juggle the lineup based on performance. "I'll have guys in and out of there faster than you ever saw if they are not producing. I'm not an impatient person, but I'm hungry. I was hired to do a good job and to develop a winner. I want guys on my club who are also hungry. I want 'em to play to win at all times. I'm willing to work twenty-four hours a day if necessary and I expect those players who require extra work to go along with us."

The Peskys moved into an apartment house at 101 Monmouth Street in Brookline, a half mile from Fenway. "It was only a ten-minute walk. I always went to the park early and I always left the car for Ruthie. She had to pick up David from school. When I went home, usually most everybody was off the streets."

Leo Cloutier wrote in the *New Hampshire Sunday News* 12-2-62:

"In the days when Pesky was a member of the Red Sox infield, whenever we used to visit Fenway Park, Pesky always delighted us in going through a ritual which amused us to no end.

Knowing of our friendship with and admiration of Ted Williams, who wore No. 9 on the back of his uniform, Johnny would do a hand-stand. He wore No. 6 and when he'd go through his little acrobatic bit, the inverted figure would look like No. 9. It was always good for a laugh."

"Remember, I'm manager now. Don't expect me to stand on my head for you any more."

Johnny was busy making appearances around New England. On January 20th, he'd spoken at a breakfast in Brookline. He appeared several times that next week at the Red Sox booth at the New England Sportsmen's Show. Eight hundred turned up at a testimonial dinner for Johnny in Saugus, headlined by Frankie Fontaine. This annual dinner (now known as the Johnny Pesky Friendship Dinner) continues even today, in the 21st century. The 2003 dinner was the 51st annual.

Johnny's proclaimed "get tough" policy lifted Sox fans' spirits. He ordered a sliding pit built at the Red Sox spring training facility in Scottsdale. They hadn't had one for years and Johnny said everyone—even the pitchers—were going to practice sliding. He also said he and new pitching coach Harry Dorish were going to have the pitchers run a lot, to keep them strong and in shape. Though now routine, Larry Claflin, writing in *The Sporting News* termed it a "Pesky innovation" to have the following day's starting pitcher keep a chart of the pitches during the game and discuss the results with the catchers and coaches.

Billy Herman returned as third base coach, but in addition to Dorish, Johnny brought in Harry Malmberg as first base coach and Al Lakeman to work with the catchers and the bullpen. Higgins mandated that Herman be kept on, and Johnny found him a "very good coach" but naturally he wanted to bring in his own people. "I wanted guys who would do some work. Harry Malmberg threw batting practice by the hour." One could infer that the older Herman may have coached well, but did not share the same work ethic as Johnny's younger team. "I liked Billy as a person. When I first took the job, Higgins wanted me to keep him. He knew the league and all that. I told Billy once in a while, 'If you've got an idea, go ahead. . . . ' but he never did."

Herman was clearly a Higgins guy. "We were supposed to go to an affair at the Kenmore and I asked the coaches to go with me. Billy said, no, he said his wife was making some dinner, he had something to do. So when we were coming out of the hotel, who drives up but Herman with Higgins? They were out.

"That didn't bother me. They were the same age. They knew each other from before. I'm not a jealous guy. And I liked Billy Herman. Billy Herman was a fine guy, a fine coach. They say he wasn't a good manager, though. They say he'd go out and play cards with guys. I didn't believe in that. That's why you have coaches. Zimmer and Ralph Houk—this is who I learned from. You learn from the good guys. You can't get involved with the players." Of course, Johnny added, "You're not going to ignore them. If you have a problem, you call them in and you shut the door and you talk."

Pesky, with great candor, all but conceded the pennant to the Yankees even before the season began. He did think the Red Sox had a shot at third, which would have been a remarkable improvement. "In all my years with the Red Sox, I was never with a second-division club, and I don't intend to start now," he stated. Pesky and the Sox party flew out of Logan Airport for Scottsdale on February 22.

His stated ambition was for modest but significant improvement. "I'm shooting for a first-division finish," said the new skipper. "I don't think any manager can work miracles in the field. That's up to the ball players. But if hard work and desire can produce victories, I'll be disappointed if the Red Sox don't climb out of the second division. Sure, we've got problems. But who hasn't? We're all starting out even. There's a long way to go before this season ends. My first objective is to make sure that our club is in good condition when the season starts. The Red Sox have been notorious as poor starters." He added that he felt, "Mike Higgins has given me a better ball club than the one he had the last two years." As Jerry Nason pointed out, if Pesky's team could win ten more games than the year before, that would have put the team in third place in '62. Winning just one additional game per month could well put the Sox in the first division.

Dick Stuart had been obtained from the Pirates, along with Jack Lamabe, for Don Schwall and Jim Pagliaroni. Stuart came in with a rep as a poor fielder, but Eddie Bressoud suggested that might be due in part to field conditions at Pittsburgh. Dick Groat said of his former fellow Pirate, "He can make the plays, but has a tendency to dream when he doesn't have a bat in his hands." Stuart wrote an article for the *Globe*, wherein he declared, "As an ex-outfielder, I enjoy playing first base. The reason I enjoy playing first base is because it keeps you in the ball game. This is especially important for any youngster whose mind may wander."

Stuart began spring training with a decent work ethic, "running and sweating with the common ball players," in the words of Tom Monahan. The writers were on the lookout for signs that the country club atmosphere would prevail, despite the hustle the 44-year-old manager brought to Arizona. Pesky told a story that there was "one member of the Red Sox who developed the quaint notion that ballplayers should put out even if they wear B-O-S-T-O-N across the front of their shirts [but] the eager beaver was quickly disabused of the idea when another veteran came to him and straightened him out." This supposedly happened while Jurges was manager, the veteran saying, "Don't try to shake things up. Just take it easy, do your work and you can stay around here a long time. Get overeager, and you'll louse up everything."

Johnny planned to use his much-improved bench and had high hopes in particular for Felix Mantilla who he remembered from '55 when "The Cat" played for Toledo. "What are the substitutes for unless it's to play?" Johnny asked. "I don't want anyone to go stale."

He drove his players hard in Scottsdale, maybe too hard. Johnny set two workouts a day, one at 10 AM and the other at 1 PM. At first, the new regimen was accepted. "Manager Johnny Pesky loves to work his players," wrote one newsman. "And the players, despite aches and pains, are loving it too." Not for long, apparently. He soon abandoned the double workouts but continued to push the players, running them long enough that some players even missed their afternoon tee times at the local golf courses. He set a curfew, though he announced, "I'm not going to hold you to any exact minute." It seems a quaint notion today, but Johnny also stated, "There'll be no swimming. It dulls your reflexes."

"I said, 'Forget your golf clubs.' They were getting through at noon. This was ridiculous. This is the big leagues. We started maybe a half an hour earlier but we didn't get through at noon. We were there about a week and Herman came to me and said, 'Johnny, do you object to golf? The players seem to think you object to golf.' I don't object to golf. I think it's good for them. A lot of times people misinterpret what you're trying to say." At the time, he let reporters know, "I have nothing against golf, but the boys are being paid to play baseball, and if they expect to become expert golfers at the same time, they will have to take up night golfing."

Harry Dorish worked his pitchers, too. "All our pitchers that year were in great shape," remembers Johnny. "Dorish believed in a lot of running to get yourself in shape physically and Higgins didn't like that. I told Higgins that Harry was right. That first year we were getting decent pitching but I guess a couple of them complained to Higgins without my knowledge."

The memories from fifty years earlier may have smoothed over what now appear to be eccentricities in discouraging swimming and golf. If Johnny represented anything, it was a noble effort to overcome the so-called "country club" atmosphere of which the Red Sox have often been accused. And if nothing else, all of the teams Johnny had managed previously came out of spring training strong and ready to play.

Pete Runnels, despite being the reigning A.L. batting champ, had been traded to the Houston Colt .45s for Roman Mejias in a bid for more power. The loss of Runnels was not as bad as it might have seemed—he hit only .253 in 1963 and (in limited service) a weak .196 in '64. Dick Williams joined the team, also from Houston. Ted Williams was in camp, evaluating hitters and was impressed by both Stuart and Mejias. Johnny was similarly taken with Dalton Jones and Tony Horton. Young Rico Petrocelli was in camp, too. Johnny didn't want to rush any of them. For the most part, though, Johnny knew his players from past experience. He had previously managed all but ten of the players on the 1963 roster.

Pesky envisioned Bill Monbouquette, Earl Wilson and Gene Conley as his main three starters, with Ike Delock as number four. Dave Morehead and Bill Spanswick were possible number fives, with Chet Nichols having an outside shot. They gave a look to Jerry Stephenson as well. Radatz remained the core of the bullpen. Sox spring training often features some bizarre situations. Dick Radatz, Sox rookie of the year in 1962, pulled a muscle doing an interview, when he reached for a cigarette in his pocket while talking with Harold Kaese.

Johnny got down and dirty too, personally giving sliding instruction in the newly-built pit. Except for those who had played under him in Seattle, most of the players had never practiced sliding before. "I had the pitchers sliding, too. Higgins didn't understand that. We didn't have the designated hitter then. I even had Radatz sliding. They were having some fun with it. We never had anybody get hurt. I remember in Detroit we had Bernie DeViveiros—he must have been in his 80s—you should have seen him slide. He'd slide on concrete and never get a bruise. He was the instructor there. That's where I learned all this stuff from—then and when I was a kid in Portland."

Mejias seemed to engender the most talk in camp. "There are so many opinions expressed about Mejias," Clif Keane wrote, "that you wonder if he's one of triplets or quadruplets."

Alvin Dark acknowledged that it "takes time for a new manager to get things going his way. Pesky will need two years . . . it takes two years to install a system. All Pesky can do now is take the material he's been given and do the best he can." This involved trying to assemble the sort of team he wanted; coming in fresh, though, Johnny basically had to work with the hand he'd been dealt. It also involved working with the personalities involved. Carl Yastrzemski, for instance, despite having two years under his belt, was still a "victim of over-eagerness" who often threw to the base and not the cutoff man. Stuart's problem was the opposite—inertia. In March, Yaz fired the ball over cutoff man Bressoud's head—trying to cut down a runner going from first to third—and when it didn't work, the Giants ended up with the hitter advancing to second. A little soft drive to right field scored two runs, and this time Stuart didn't even try to cut off the throw in to the plate—which again allowed the hitter to take second base off his single. "Failing to make a cut-off seems like a little thing, but you can see what it can lead to," Johnny angrily said later. "We've practiced cut-offs, so now we're going to practice them some more. We've got to get them straightened out. . . . I hate to see players develop bad habits."

Pesky reiterated that when there's a runner on second and first base was empty, the third baseman is the man to take the cutoff. That way you have a chance to catch the batter trying to stretch a single into a two-base hit, maybe catching him in a rundown between second and first. A few days later, the situation presented itself when Ernie Fazio singled into center. Yaz fired the ball toward the plate low enough to be cut off—but Malzone wasn't the only one who moved in to cut it off. So did Stuart. The two practically collided and the ball nicked off one of their gloves, allowing Fazio second base. No one was covering third at this point, so he scooted over and took the base. That was not a happy day for Johnny.

Some of the bad habits certain Red Sox players had adopted were non-baseball ones. There was one time in Cleveland that year when a player became hungry and asked the clubhouse kid to get him a pizza. The kid brought the pizza right into the dugout. Pesky was aghast. The player had enough sense to become embarrassed and hastily instructed the kid to put the pizza in his locker.

Higgins had always taken the shortcut of writing Yastrzemski's name on his lineup card as "Yas." Johnny dignified Carl with his full last name. "If I can spell Paveskovich," he said, "I certainly can spell Yastrzemski."

Johnny summed up the attitude he brought to managing—and still brings to his work nearly forty years later—"Once you lose your enthusiasm, you've lost everything. I'm not going to lose mine. I'm going to try to keep my guys from losing theirs."

Bill Veeck picked the Red Sox for 7th place. "Boston has improved enough to nose out Cleveland, a statement which Johnny Pesky might not take as an unqualified endorsement." Harold Kaese, the next day, picked the Sox for 5th or 6th, characterizing the new Sox skipper. "First reactions favorable. In one respect, he is already four years and six weeks ahead of Mike Higgins. Pesky was kicked out of a game by an umpire Sunday. Higgins wasn't kicked out until May 9, 1961. What kind of manager is

Pesky? Straightforward, slightly irascible, not fancy. He plays an orthodox, not a Jules Verne or Edgar Allan Poe game . . . Pesky may spend the season in the second division, but he is not likely to spend it sitting on his hands."

While the more relaxed approach of some of the veteran players nagged at him, he reconciled to it and devoted more time to preparing the younger players. "I still want to be called Johnny by you men," he told the assembled players on the eve of the opener. "I want to continue on friendly terms with all of you. But don't expect that friendship to protect you when you mess up a game." He acknowledged that mistakes occur but he would brook no sloppy play, that he'd not cracked the whip during spring training but the regular season was different and anyone thought to be "jaking" would hear from him. "I let them know that if they didn't play solid baseball, I'd consider that a personal matter. If they're doing anything to hurt me when I'm just starting a big league career, they're not going to get away with it."

The *Globe* panel summarized Pesky's progress, on the eve of the opening day game. "Pesky is no martinet, merely a dedicated young manager whose problems lie before him. . . . No manager in Boston history ever carried more well wishes into a seasonal opener than Pesky, a local resident who spent the entire Winter doing public relations for the Red Sox." The opener was in Los Angeles, a night game broadcast back to Boston with the telecast beginning at 11:00 PM Eastern time. Ruth Pesky admitted she fell asleep around the fifth inning. She didn't have her season's pass yet and wasn't sure where she would sit once the team got home, and she foresaw a problem. As the wife of the manager, she realized that perhaps she had to sit apart from the players' wives: "There seems to be some kind of an unwritten rule about that and I'm going to miss the girls." She'd never been one to hold herself above others.

When the team came to Fenway that season, there were seats right next to the dugout reserved for the manager's use. "Ruthie usually came, but David was at the age where he was running around and she didn't want to make a nuisance for the fans around there" so Ruth often gave up her seats.

The Red Sox lost the opener, 4-1, the big blow being Lee Thomas's three-run homer off Monbouquette in the fifth. It was the sixth consecutive Opening Day loss for the Red Sox. "[Thomas] haunted me for two years when he was in the minors," Pesky said in post-game remarks. "He ruined me in the Eastern League and in the Texas League." The Red Sox came back the next day, though, and won under Earl Wilson.

As it happened, the Red Sox got off to a good start, and there was a good spirit amongst the players. On Patriot's Day, they'd played both a morning game and an afternoon 3 PM game, sandwiched around the Boston Marathon. April 20th was the tenth game, played before a Ladies Day "crowd" of 7839. The Tigers had taken a 3-2 lead in the top of the 15th inning at Fenway until Roman Mejias drove home two with a game-winning double in the bottom of the inning. The players rushed out onto the field and were pounding Mejias on the back. "I know it may have looked juvenile," Johnny said afterward, "but we just felt like doing it." Johnny himself got so caught up that he swallowed his chewing tobacco. "That happened to me only once before," he said. "It was in my first year of managing in the minors. I went out to argue about an umpire's decision. I was so excited on the way out, I swallowed the tobacco and got so sick I couldn't argue. But this time I swallowed the stuff and enjoyed it."

Near the end of April, Johnny had become more optimistic and said he hoped to finish fourth, then climb one position per year to take the pennant in his fourth year. It was their best start in a full decade, since the 1953 season under Boudreau.

By May 2, the Sox had moved into first place. Yaz was hitting .388 and exhibiting stellar defense, "Yazzle-Dazzle" in the words of *Globe* writer Harold Kaese. By May 17, a Kaese column was headlined "Sox Tie '46 Home Start"—they were 13-3 at home, which matched the way they'd begun the 1946 season.

With the first ten percent of the season under their belts, Boston was 10-6 and feeling a touch euphoric. Arthur Siegel wrote, "The Red Sox won't start accepting World Series ticket applications before Labor Day." Harold Kaese asked "What's the magic number?" while talking a bit about Pesky getting his revenge against the Cardinals in the World Series.

On May 12, Dave Morehead threw a one-hitter, the one hit being a solo shot by Chuck Hinton in the 1st. The 19-year-old San Diegan—like Ted Williams, a graduate of Hoover High School—was validating Dorish and Pesky's decision to keep him on the club out of spring training. This win put him 3-0 on the young season. Earl Wilson was doing well, too. Asked what the difference was, Tillman said "Strikes," Johnny answered "Maturity" and Wilson himself said "Confidence." He two-hit the Angels as the Red Sox clambered back into first.

Some of the Sox were struggling. Stuart was not hitting well, in fact he struck out in 11 of 16 at bats during one stretch on the road. Demoted from cleanup to sixth in the order, he responded on the 15th with a grand slam and a three-run homer, helping win both halves of a doubleheader in L.A. "Good leadership by Johnny Pesky, who has calmly kept his foot on the accelerator without antagonizing his players," was how Kaese characterized it.

It had been hard to draw more than around 7000 fans but by the 17th the Sox were in first and ticket sales began to pick up. The game that day was delayed 13 minutes due to a large, late-arriving walkup crowd. The turnstiles that day read 24,116.

The standings were so tightly packed that a single loss on May 20 dropped the Bosox from first to fourth place. It was the start of a team slump, where the Sox dropped 5 out of 6 and 12 of 16. The on-again, off-again Stuart went 2 for 27 and Johnny began to muse out loud about putting in Dick Williams to take his place at first. "Every time I look down the bench and see Dick sitting there I get a wonderful feeling. He's a nice guy to have around. Someday he's going to make fine managerial timber." Little did Johnny know, when he'd spoken of attaining the pennant in four years, that it would be Dick Williams who would do so—to everyone's surprise—in the 1967 Impossible Dream year. A versatile utility player, Williams kept three gloves in his locker—a regular fielder's mitt, a first baseman's glove and a catcher's glove.

Johnny finally sat Stuart down after he went another four at bats without a hit, and the slugger actually supported Pesky's move. It took the time off to notice that he was turning his head away from the ball. At the same time, he went to see an optometrist, who found some astigmatism.

In 1963 Yaz was still a little raw—though he really matured this season in particular and wound up leading the league in hitting, while improving in the field. Pitching now became a problem. A May 23 Larry Claflin story in the *Record American* declared, "Pesky Looks to Seattle As Sox Starters Flounder." Local Belmont phenom Wilbur Wood had already pitched 3 shutouts at Seattle and Jerry Stephenson had won his first game there, striking out 10. Conley still had a bad ankle from the basketball season. Ike Delock had complaints of arm trouble. Old teammate Mel Parnell was managing the Rainiers and Johnny kept in touch. On June 2, the Sox gave Delock his outright release and called up Wood. Morehead had lost his fourth straight game. Wood never did catch on in Boston, and certainly not in 1963.

Radatz was pitching wonderfully in relief. He contributed 13 consecutive scoreless relief appearances including one 8 2/3 inning stint against the Tigers on June 11, a 15-inning win against Detroit. That appearance followed just one day of rest, after he'd pitched six innings in a 14-inning win over the Orioles. His string reached to 31 straight scoreless innings, and he sported a 0.92 ERA on the season. He'd won three games in four days, then won his sixth of the year without even throwing a single pitch—the official scorer in Chicago changed his ruling made during a June 2 game and gave the win to Radatz instead of the previously-credited Earley. That same day, June 12th, the Red Sox climbed back into the first division.

Radatz was amazing. The fearsome fireman stood 6'6" and weighed 240 pounds. He'd played for Pesky in Seattle where Johnny converted him to a reliever. One day in '63, Earl Wilson had struck out 12 Yankees and was holding onto a 2-1 lead in the top of the ninth at Fenway, but he'd loaded the bases and there was no one out. "Jesus Christ! Full house. So I go out to Earl and I say, 'How do you feel?' 'All right'—which they always say. So I kind of turned a little bit, and I says, 'The big guy is ready in the bullpen.' Wilson says, 'Well, I am getting a little tired.' So in he comes, Radatz. He takes the ball and says, 'Pop me a cool one. I'll be right in.' The son of a bitch, he struck out the side." The "Yankee killer" struck out Mickey Mantle, then Roger Maris and finally Elston Howard, one after the other, using only ten pitches.

Because the league was so balanced, Johnny said the Sox actually had an "outside chance" at the pennant. Defense and pitching were the team's weaknesses. Performing better than expected were Radatz, Malzone, Schilling, Monbouquette and Geiger. Below expectations to this point were Yastrzemski, Clinton, Conley, Mejias and Tillman. Delock, who was the only player on the team whose career overlapped Johnny's, felt he got a bad shake. There was a little bit of bad feeling going both ways—Pesky felt that Delock had let down on his effort.

On the first day of summer, the Sox were 34-26 when the Yankees came to town riding a seven-game win streak. Monbo won the first game, becoming the league's first 10-game winner. Then New York took a twin bill on Saturday and won the Sunday game as well, when Wilson and Bressoud collided going for a pop fly. Two innings later, after Wilson had been sent out for X-rays, Yaz pulled a calf muscle and had to leave the game, too. Wilson was OK, and able to make his next start on the 26th, but again was involved in an accident, this time crashing into the bunting Sudden Sam McDowell and landing right on the same bad shoulder he'd injured in the collision with Bressoud. Again, he had to leave the game. The Sox took both games from the Indians that day, and Radatz saved both of them. Wilson never pitched as well the rest of the year, though he never used it as an alibi. It was only the following spring that it came out that he had been unable to throw over the top and had altered his delivery.

Fans in Boston had responded to the team, and by this date were averaging 15,000 a game in attendance, up dramatically from around 8,400 the year before. That they were out of ninth place and in the hunt didn't hurt. "When you win," said the rookie manager, "you eat better, sleep better, your beer tastes better and your wife looks like Gina Lollabrigida."

So much of the talk during Johnny's two years as manager centered around Dick Stuart. A streak hitter, he really put up some power numbers (75 home runs in the two years). He led the league with 118 RBI in 1963 and the 114 he banged in the following year was second only to Brooks Robinson's 118. Stuart, though, had a huge ego and enjoyed the spotlight maybe a little too much. His fielding percentage itself was decent, but he really was abysmal on defense—you don't get charged with an error for failing to cut off a ball or back up a play. Known as "Dr. Strangeglove" and "Old Stonefingers" for his shortcomings in the field, Johnny did credit him for his hitting. No one could ever hit as well as Ted Williams, particularly in Pesky's eyes, but he paid Stuart a compliment: "We think of Dick as a Williams type. He doesn't hit as good as Ted, but he does field much better than Esther."

On July 1, the Red Sox finished up a series at Yankee Stadium and Stuart rode the bench. He said he was embarrassed at being benched for the game. "You embarrassed the rest of us Sunday," countered Pesky. On Sunday, Stuart had failed to get to a ball between him and Schilling that his manager thought he should have snared, and was indecisive on another grounder in the same inning, permitting a runner to score. Later the same game, Stuart misplayed a routine Kubek grounder into a three-run error, a ball described as rolling at "slightly less than medium speed." It was the second Sunday in a row Stuart had muffed one. Manager and slugger ended up in a shouting match, and Stuart strode out to centerfield for the entire pre-game workout, where he bounced the ball off the wall for a while, played catch with some fans in the stands and then sat in the bullpen—until he was called in to pinch-hit for Earley in the ninth. He grounded out. "No player is going to tell me how to run my team," Pesky stated. "He claimed I was trying to show him up. But that's not true."

Johnny never benched a player for long, if he felt the team needed him in a game. Stuart was back in the lineup on Tuesday night in Cleveland, because of the smaller left field playing area at Municipal

Stadium. Pesky explained he'd sat Stuart down in part because of all the lefthanders in the Yankee lineup. He was worried that Stuart would have to deal with a lot of ground balls down the line at first and suffer further embarrassment.

Reflecting in 2001, Johnny said, "The only thing I insisted on is that when you hit a ball, you run as hard as you can. That used to irritate me more than anything. I had to run hard, because I wasn't blessed with a lot of ability. Dominic DiMaggio had a lot of ability, but I never saw him loaf."

All in all, Pesky was pleased as punch at mid-season. Dave Morehead had turned in two straight gems—a two-hitter against the Indians on July 2 and a three-hitter versus the White Sox five days later. He'd lost five in a row before that, and gone eight straight starts without a win. Most managers would have feared to stick with a 19-year-old rookie who'd hit such a patch but Johnny knew Morehead from Seattle and felt he just had to pitch to work his way through it. "Johnny's confidence in me was the most important thing," Morehead told reporters after the White Sox victory. "I began to press when I wasn't pitching well. I thought that I might be on my way back to Seattle after each poor showing. So I began to press. I threw too hard. I didn't have my control. It finally dawned on me that Pesky wasn't thinking about sending me back. He never even mentioned it. So I figured I was up here to stay and that gave me the confidence to pitch the way I have lately."

Attendance was up a projected 275,000 over the previous year, the team sat in second place for a day and there was talk of Pesky as a candidate for Manager of the Year. Not in a decade had the Red Sox been seven games over .500 and in third place at the All-Star break. "Did you ever think little John Pesky would be managing in the major leagues?" he asked old friend John Drohan of the *Boston Traveler* one night before a game. The Sox were leading the league in hitting, but pitching was the key. The major disappointment had been Gene Conley, who'd won 15 in 1962 but only had two victories in '63. Johnny hoped that his arm would respond and he could win seven or eight in the second half. It wasn't to be; he was to win only once more that year before retiring from baseball.

Meanwhile, Stuart's ire was not reserved for Pesky alone. There was another flap involving Stuart and the All-Star Game. Johnny was chosen by A.L. manager Ralph Houk to serve as one of the coaches, but Stuart was passed over by Houk. In those days, the players cast votes to select who would represent the league, and Stuart came in second. That might normally get him the nod for the team, but Houk chose his own Joe Pepitone instead. Malzone, Radatz and Yastrzemski represented the Red Sox—along with coach Pesky. Houk had taken every other second place choice except Stuart. He clearly just did not like him. Stuart felt snubbed, and said so in no uncertain terms: "What's the use of the players voting, if Houk doesn't pay any attention to the count? Houk is a busher who never was better than a third stringer when he was a player. What does he know about all-stars?" Johnny sympathized somewhat, rhetoric aside—in 1942 the rookie Pesky was 60 points ahead of Boudreau in batting average but Boudreau was chosen and Pesky didn't make the team. "In those days," wrote Arthur Siegel, "the *Chicago Tribune* ran the polling and was always suspected of juggling the votes so the players with reputations were in the lineups."

A pitcher had to have 162 innings to qualify for the ERA title. Radatz at mid-season projected to 152, but had a 1.42 ERA and was 8-1. The Sox were still a team that won more at home—they were 30-15 at Fenway and 14-22 away. The first game after the break, on the road in Minnesota, Stuart hit two home runs and drove in five in a 7-4 Sox win. The headline: "Radatz 'Tired,' Yields Hit in 3 Innings of Relief." Radatz was 10-1 by July 12. Another *Globe* headline read "Is Pesky Lucky Or a Genius"—he'd rested three of his first-string infielders in the second game of a Bastille Day doubleheader in L.A. and still won—with Chet Nichols on the mound. Stuart was the one infielder who did play. Gary Geiger had helped the team as well. He'd suffered a collapsed lung in 1960. After the '62 season, he needed six blood transfusions to help him with a bleeding stomach ulcer. He had a serious air travel phobia and couldn't sleep at all the night before a flight. Uncertain as to whether he could return, he even had his number taken away from him and given to Dick Stuart, and both Yaz and Mejias were played at center in Geiger's absence. He still fought back and had 10 HR and was hitting just over .300 in center by late July.

The first ejection of the year came on July 17. Lou Clinton was kicked out for slamming his helmet in protest of a close play he'd lost while running to first. In the dugout, Pesky was himself tossed out at the end of the inning by umpire Al Smith. "I was giving Smith the 'choke' sign with my hands at my throat," Johnny admitted. "He had to kick me out. I had it coming to me. But it was a bad call and I told him so." Johnny ran back onto the field to argue some more with Smith, though, then got in an argument with a fan in the stands as he was departing. The Sox won 10-6, and Radatz won #11.

The team then began to slip, gradually. The papers talked about "daffy base-running and other mental lapses" and Pesky held a clubhouse meeting. "I think I'll go back to fundamentals, boring as it may be. This is something the players should have learned five years ago." Fatigue and injuries proved costly. The Sox lost 15 of 20 games and by the end of July were just barely above .500, close to falling into the second division. Despite this, the press had not really reported discord in the clubhouse aside from the occasional run-in between Stuart and his manager. As of August 6, though, the Sox dipped under .500 at 54-55, and they were 15 GB. They just kept sinking. "When Has Club Fallen So Fast?" read one headline. They lost 21 out of 26 games, and in the four week from July 15 to August 11, fell from second to sixth, from 10 over .500 to 6 under, from 5½ GB to a full 20! Kaese recalled Pesky's saying, "I hope you can make me laugh in August like you're making me laugh now." He also reminded readers of the time back in 1960 when Frank Sullivan told his teammates, "Scatter when we get off the plane, men, so they won't get us all with the first blast."

Smatterings of solace cropped up, such as the Sox taking two from the Yankees on August 14, but inevitably the tables seemed to turn. Just two weeks later, New York took two back from Boston in a twi-nighter, winning by 5-0 and 3-0. New York's Jim Bouton even had a no-hitter going into the 9th in game one. As of the next day, August 29, the Red Sox were 62-70 (.470) and 24 GB. The 1962 Red Sox on the same date had been in just about the same sad state: 62-71 (.466) although they were "only" 15 games behind. Pesky was a little stunned by the twin shutouts and said even with the seven-inning second games they played in minor league ball, he could never recall being with a team shut out twice. "Maybe the game is changing. Maybe it's more of a game of pitching and defense than it was twenty years ago. Look at the Yankees, they haven't got a home run, an RBI or a batting leader and they're walking away with the pennant. We've got the batting leaders in most every

He stood up for his players. One time Johnny was tossed by Ed Runge for leaping to Morehead's defense when Runge had accused the youngster of throwing too close to batters. "I never swear on the field, though," Johnny explained, "because I remember there are women and children in the stands." What he had done instead is suggest that Runge's hearing was better than his eyesight.

department and we're down in second division. . . . Sometimes it has a bad effect on the rest of the club. You lose the proper perspective and think of baseball more as a game for individuals rather than the team it is supposed to be."

"Don't Presume Pesky's Return," Harold Kaese wrote on September 6. "Because of the fine first-half record and the . . . attendance gain, we would assume Pesky's return in 1964, but in baseball—especially Fenway Park baseball—it is wiser never to assume anything." Productivity at the plate dropped dramatically. Yaz hit .336 before July 16, but only .285 subsequently. Malzone's first-half average was .326, but only .244 in the second half. Geiger's was off 130 points, Schilling's down an even 100 points. Nixon and Clinton were both down somewhat as well. Bressoud and Tillman were the exceptions, both improving significantly. Bob Holbrook gave Higgins credit for assembling some strong performers—the team could have the league batting champion, RBI leader, the two best relief pitchers in baseball [Radatz and Lamabe] and a 20-game winner, while setting a team record for home runs in one season. There was talent there. The question inevitably becomes how it was handled.

Ted Williams was supportive of his pal, telling the *Globe*: "Pesky has stimulated a lot of interest with a different type of managing. Not that Mike Higgins wasn't a good manager. But Pesky is a fireball, and it makes for improvement."

Tom Yawkey commented, saying, "It hasn't been a dull season, nor has it been a discouraging one. There have been minor mistakes that can be corrected. This club made the summer lively around Boston. . . . This season has been a lot like Stuart. He's exciting and controversial, yet he has done very well. In some ways he's done better than we expected." Stuart was leading the league in home runs, RBI, assists and also in errors with 23—way ahead of the NL leader Cepeda, who had 16. There still remained hope that Boston could plant itself in the first division. They did so on September 2, but only for a day.

Yawkey let it be known that Johnny would be rehired. Though "Pesky ran out of miracles," in Arthur Siegel's words, and 1963 was Pesky's year "on the house", the general feeling was that he had done a decent job. "The first half of the season . . . made Pesky look like a Fenway miracle man. The second half, with a pitching collapse, a hitting collapse and injuries reduced Pesky to a human being. Yet Pesky's refusal to panic weighs well with Yawkey." Looking ahead, Johnny indicated his wish list for next season: an outfielder, a catcher, better pitching (though he had hopes for Morehead and Heffner in '64). It was the lack of speed he saw as the team's main handicap. He didn't take any shots at Stuart, in fact saying, "Dick Stuart has had a fine individual year and he's given us way more help at the plate than any harm around first base."

On September 23rd, Johnny Pesky was rehired for the following year. "Is His Job Enviable?" asked Harold Kaese. Sure, he had another one year contract now. Did that make him lucky, "or is the whole situation so difficult that only an ocean of heartache awaits him?" Kaese rated Pesky's performance as "fair" and believed he definitely deserved the renewal. The loss of Gene Conley hurt badly. To have a 15-game winner secure only three wins was a tremendous blow. In the last 27 games of the season, the Sox maintained—going 13-14 for a near .500 pace. At least they had recovered their equilibrium after that 14-32 slide.

Kaese also pointed out that several players had their best years to date under Johnny. That list included Dick Stuart, Yaz, Monbo, Radatz and Jack Lamabe. On the other hand, the team was not really one big happy family. There was some resentment, he wrote, of both Pesky and Stuart. "Objections to Pesky included his temper, changeable mind, sharp tongue during games, use of his bench, and comments on players which if not printed were carried to them by tale-bearers. The new manager did not show enough authority, therefore did not command enough respect." There must have been some talk of Pesky not getting enough support from the front office, because Kaese said he was in no position to know whether or not that was the case. He also wondered whether or not play would have been improved had Pesky not been left waiting for weeks to know whether his contract would be renewed. In any case, Kaese wished him luck for '64 but said, "I wouldn't be in his shoes for anything."

The final game of the year was rained out. The Sox had finished in seventh place, with about as identical a record to the previous year's as you could possibly get with one more game played (the '62 Sox had two rainouts there had been no need to make up).

| 1963 | 76-85 | .472 | GB = 28 | 7th place |
| 1962 | 76-84 | .475 | GB = 19 | 8th place |

Immediately after that last game was canceled, the team (meaning Pinky Higgins) fired Harry Dorish as pitching coach. Sal Maglie, Mel Harder, Mel Parnell and Bob Turley (who had joined the Sox as a player midyear) were being considered as a replacement. This was a little unfair to Dorish, Kaese pointed out: after all, it wasn't his fault that Conley hurt his ankle playing basketball or developed a sore arm, nor that Stuart's

> Johnny wore #22 as manager. Later as a coach in the years 1975-80, Johnny wore #35. Asked about his choice of numbers years later, he simply said, "I just wanted a double number. I liked the infielders to have single numbers. That's the way I was raised."

poor fielding flustered Earl Wilson to the point of distraction, or that Ike Delock lost his effectiveness, or that teenager Dave Morehead wasn't quite ready. All told, the squad "entered the season with shaky pitching, and came out of it with shaky pitching—but the staff allowed 50 fewer runs than it had in three previous seasons, and had a lower earned run average."

Having to fire Dorish tore Johnny up inside. "Late in the season, we weren't playing very well. About a week before the season was to end, Higgins wanted me to fire my pitching coach and I didn't want to do it. I tried to talk him out of it. I liked Dorish very much. I played with him. He was my pitching coach in the minors. He was just a great kid and a hard-working guy.

"I went there every morning about 10 o'clock just to see if I could change Higgins' mind, and he wouldn't pay any attention to it. He'd sit there and growl and look at the paper. I was almost in tears, I was so upset. I came home that night and Ruthie met me at the door. 'I had to tell Harry he wasn't coming back.' 'And what did you say to Higgins?' 'I didn't say anything.' She says, 'You know what you should have done, Johnny?'—these are her exact words—'you should have told Higgins to stick the job up his ass.' Those were her exact words.

"She says, 'Johnny, this is not you. This man's been loyal to you since you've been managing. This is not right.' I said, 'Well, I can survive this.' She said, 'Johnny, I've been telling you this whole week, I know you're upset—but this guy doesn't want you! How many times do you have to be hit over the head? If you're worried about me and David, well, don't. Don't worry. We wouldn't go back to the minor leagues.' I said, 'Well, you don't know what could happen. This is a job . . . I've been a Red Sox all my life. . . .'

"The general manager runs the ballclub. Higgins didn't want me to come back my second year but we were doing pretty good, drawing real well." Higgins hand-picked Bob Turley as Pesky's pitching coach for '64. The 1958 Cy Young Award winner had joined the Sox in mid-season '63 and logged over 120 innings, though a disappointing 3-11. Johnny saw Turley as a good man, and noted that he'd given good advice to some of the younger pitchers. What he hadn't known at the time was that Higgins has already promised Turley the job as coach. "Ruthie was very upset with what I did with Harry. That's the only thing I resent in my whole baseball life."

Lou Clinton was the position player who'd dropped off the most from 1962. Mejias was a "major disappointment" as were Malzone (only 15 RBI in final two months), Bressoud (not as steady), Chuck Schilling (started well, but inexplicable nosedive) and the catchers collectively (led catchers in throwing ball into center field). Yaz won the American League batting title with .321, and was good in the field. He led in hits and doubles but only managed 14 home runs and 68 RBI and disappointed in base-running. Even Radatz tailed off in the second half, possibly giving cause for some concern. Stuart made 28 errors and set a club strikeout record, but he did hit 42 home runs and knocked in 118 runs and probably helped sell a few more tickets. Hy Hurwitz called him a "miniature edition of Ted Williams in the controversy department."

Being not much older than some of the veteran players, Pesky may have lacked some of the stature of, say, the manager Johnny most admired: Joe McCarthy. The new spirit he brought to his work, though, seems to have been appreciated at the gate. Attendance was up over 200,000, from 733,080 to 942,642—a dramatic increase.

That fall, the Red Sox and the Houston Astros combined resources and entered a combined team in the Florida Instructional League. Johnny visited and saw the players in action, as did Higgins and farm director Neil Mahoney. On the trade front, Pesky said the Sox had a top catcher as their priority. Pesky had been high on Tillman, who he'd managed in Seattle, before the season calling him a "right-handed Bill Dickey." Overrating Tillman could have been one of the biggest mistakes of 1963. Tillman had only batted .225 with just 8 homers and 32 RBI.

Pesky was pumped on Tony Conigliaro, though. He'd played in Florida and had come off a rookie-of-the-year season in the New York—Penn league. Johnny saw him as "built for Fenway Park."

Though there had been little reported in the Boston press about Pesky's problems with some of his players, *The Sporting News* around Thanksgiving indicated that it was actually a serious issue—possibly meriting the characterization "rebellion"—and that Yawkey himself might need to step in. The publication recognized that it was inevitable there be some unhappiness among players, but that what was different here was that it was taking the form of "internal sniping at Pesky, a tireless, dedicated worker." Yastrzemski had leveled some sharp criticisms of Pesky in after-dinner remarks at a local event in Norwood, which were reported by Larry Claflin in the *Record-American*. "The guy makes too many mistakes," Yaz complained. Hy Hurwitz asked if there was a "conspiracy brewing" to get Pesky fired; his story in *The Sporting News* was headlined "Mutiny in Hub? 'Conspirators' Reported Plotting Pesky's Exit." The reports indicated that the "conspirators include members of the press and radio as well as Red Sox personnel" and that on the team side rumors included front office people (presumably Higgins leading the way) right down into the clubhouse.

Years later, Johnny downplayed it. "Stuart was a great hitter. Stuart was all right. I had the best player in baseball in Yastrzemski. I had him at a young age. I'm not one of those managers that breathes down your neck. I left him alone but, jeez, he used to do some things that made you wonder. You'd try to correct them and sometimes I think he kind of resented it, but we got along good after I came back as a coach. He was taking me to dinner and everything. Yaz. I have to say he's one of the best players that's ever played this game. He got better, the older he got.

"That year he'd hit a ground ball and he wouldn't go to first base like I thought he should. That's the only complaint I had with him. I called him in and said, 'Carl, you're the best player on this team. You've got to lead by example.'

"I just wanted Yastrzemski to be the player he became. We became very good friends. A lot of times, he'd hit a ball and didn't run it out. But how can you dislike the best player on your team? If something critical got in the paper, I probably might have said it but I didn't mean it to the point where I'm going to lose this guy. Christ. The guy led the league in hitting the first year I was there.

"Yastrzemski worked as hard in spring training to get in shape as any player I've ever been around. If Fred Lynn had done some of the things that Yaz and Rice did, he'd have been the perfect player. He was a stylish guy, but he did everything easily. Baseball came easy to him. Yaz worked it. He was a perfectionist."

Yaz felt that Johnny had shown him up, talking with the press about his shortcomings. Arthur Siegel suggested that Johnny was done for, in part, because he didn't consult Higgins enough. "I sat in his office day after day," Johnny countered in 2001. "Maybe I was immature about some of these things."

Johnny seemed to be candid to a fault, particularly open in one-on-one talks with members of the media. When asked in 2001 about the comments that indicated some of the '63 players may have been stung by his remarks, Johnny got a little hot. "I resent that. I never criticized a player publicly. Well, that might be with people talking to each other but I would never criticize a player publicly." What he seems to say is that he may have offered something (privately) in person to a reporter ("people talking to each other") but didn't consider that to be criticizing "publicly"—and yet some of those comments inevitably were repeated, and some of them made it into print. Ever the Red Sox loyalist, Johnny will not speak ill of players on the teams he managed close to forty years ago. It would be easy for some to badmouth a few players and excuse shortcomings at this remove, but that is not Pesky's personality.

When players spoke up it created an atmosphere that poisoned the second half of the season. Apparently, Yawkey—down home in South Carolina before the season was over—never intervened or supported his manager. "Any other front office would have promptly put the player in his place," wrote Joe Williams. The Red Sox front office did not. The "ensuing, unbroken silence . . . was interpreted as indifference, if not actual agreement." The cloud of controversy hung ominously over the 1964 Red Sox.

Opening Day lineup:

2B Chuck Schilling 1962—.230
SS Ed Bressoud 1962—.277
LF Yaz 1962—.296 94 RBI
1B Dick Stuart 1962—(PITTS) .228 16 HR, 64 RBI
CF Roman Mejias 1962—(HOU) .285 24 HR, 76 RBI
RF Lou Clinton 1962—.294 22 HR, 77 RBI
3B Frank Malzone 1962—.283, 95 RBI 21 HR
C Bob Tillman 1962—.229
P Bill Monbouquette

21
Manager, 1964

We thought John had done a pretty good job. Old devil booze got the best
of Higgins. The last ten years of his life were just horrendous.

—Dick Radatz

Johnny had started off like a miracle man in 1963. After the All-Star
break, the team floundered and by the time they'd stabilized, it was
too late. The next year was to be a true test of will. One reporter
noted that, "What for Pesky had been an embarrassing position in 1963
became an untenable one in 1964. His direct boss hardly spoke to him,
and then only to make some snide remarks about the failure of the ball
club to do better. His players were divided, some with, some against him."
Yaz "openly criticized him" and was quoted in Joe Donnelly's *Sport* magazine story "Dissension on the Red Sox" as saying, "I resented criticism in
the press coming from the manager. It is a reporter's job to criticize a
player when he does something wrong. But the manager should speak to
the player in private and not discuss it in public print."

Johnny approached spring training with a willingness to compromise.
One 2½-hour workout a day was decreed, an implicit admission that he
had probably over-worked them the prior year. There was no prohibition
on swimming or golf. Bob Holbrook wrote that Johnny was to be congratulated for his willingness to adapt. He showed he had learned from a
year of experience. "Players must be led and not pushed. Pesky was a
pusher who had discovered the folly of such a system."

Pesky admitted, too, "I probably did too much expounding last year, and that may have bothered some of the boys. I think I showed too much familiarity with them. I've cut that down. I had to learn about them and managing in the big league at the same time. If we weren't going to win in '64, I knew I was going to get moved."

Tony Conigliaro was a long shot to take over right field. Yaz was secure, although there was concern about the fallout from his outspoken remarks during the off-season. Pesky made it clear he wasn't going to be a problem, and reported that he and Yaz were "all squared away." Pesky admitted maybe he'd been too frank with a reporter about Yaz' lackluster baserunning. "Yaz got mad because he thought I had held him up to public ridicule . . . My innocent answer was blown up out of all proportions in the newspaper accounts and the headlines magnified them still more." All in all, though, Johnny said that Yaz at 23 was a "kid with great talent. . . . He's a fine boy and nothing about him is either mean or malicious. He has the intensity and drive a manager has to admire. . . . If you can't get along with a potential .400 hitter, you might as well stick your head in a bowl."

The "feud" was played up big by the media, though. Though things had quieted down, at the Baseball Writers dinner in Boston, Yaz made a few brief remarks while accepting an award and thanked Mike Higgins "for all you've done for me" but didn't even mention manager Pesky, who was sitting at the head table. Writer Bud Collins wondered aloud which adjective best described Yastrzemski: impolite, dumb, thoughtless or vicious? It clearly came across as an insult in front of the 700 assembled Boston sports people. Again, Collins noted, the Boston brass did nothing, and neither did Johnny—perhaps hoping the issue would go away once the season got underway, perhaps worried he wouldn't have the backing of Yawkey, O'Connell and Higgins.

"My job is to win games," Johnny stated, "not to go around kissing players to make them happy. Now I've heard that some players were mad at me because I criticized them in front of other players. Well, if they can't take criticism in front of other players, then they shouldn't be in baseball."

Unfortunately, several of the players failed to make comebacks in spring training. Conley had quit basketball, but there were murmurs that maybe he should quit baseball as well. Mejias and Schilling has been disappointing as well. Once again, Johnny announced the first division as the goal and expressed impatience with some of the players' performances. Geiger's bleeding ulcer kicked up again and he had to be hospitalized.

Higgins did make an effort, at least for a while, to work with Pesky. They began to meet once a day during spring training and they talked about player personnel. The year before, perhaps Pesky had worried that going to Higgins would betray uncertainty and a lack of resolve on his part. Higgins may have felt that approaching Pesky would be like back-seat driving and so he stayed away. An issue involving Stuart which cropped up in the spring was resolved quickly, with Higgins backing Pesky.

Pesky perhaps should have fined Stuart but instead tried to smooth things over. Bud Collins retorted sarcastically a few days later, "That really impresses players. There are about five things that impress baseball players—and the first three are money. They don't take Pesky seriously any more, realizing that they'll stay longer than he. . . . Maybe we can get Higgins to come back for a third term as manager. Then we can all go to sleep—until it's post time at Wonderland." (Wonderland is a local dog track.)

Yaz may have learned to be a bit more judicious in his comments. In late February, he commented, "I certainly wouldn't want to say anything that might be detrimental to the ball club. The whole thing was blown out of proportion." Johnny chatted with writers. "I know that if we don't do well I probably will get fired—you expect that in baseball. But there's no plot to get me. I'm sure of that, but I don't like this talk of dissension." Bud Collins painted the ball club as a poor one, having "disintegrated to a frightful state during Tom Yawkey's unimaginative and unaggressive ownership. The Sox are Inertia, Inc., and even Aladdin's genie would get a hernia trying to pull them into the first division."

Collins liked Pesky and said as much. Bob Holbrook liked him, too, but didn't hesitate to speak out against some sportswriters who he viewed as Pesky apologists. There is a clique, he wrote, "which is very much in Pesky's corner. They have painted him as a bright knight in shining armor." Higgins gets a lot of blame, he wrote, and so did Yawkey—but Holbrook felt that both cared vitally about the team. "The real fact is that the team suffered under Pesky last year. It started out as a ball club and wound up as a team ridden with jealousy and dislikes, and the responsibility rested smack on the shoulders of the manager. Nobody else." Holbrook claimed that a number of writers pulled their punches, and in one instance a writer said he wasn't allowed to write what he wanted because Pesky was pals with one of the higher-ups at his paper. Things seemed better in the Arizona desert, Holbrook admitted. "Gone is the cocky pop-off of a year ago. His speech is judicious, his thoughts about players so far have been spoken privately."

"The air is clearer than it has ever been," Johnny said.

This was a very young spring training squad. Five of the players were teenagers. Six others were only twenty. Under the bonus rule of the day, four of the players had to be included on the 25-man roster: Dave Gray, Pete Charton, Tony Horton and Tony Conigliaro. The sum effect of this was that Pesky really only had 21 player slots available to him. There was another change on the roster as well. There were, Roger Birtwell wrote, "two colored players"—Reggie Smith and Jack Gaines. In fact, the Red Sox had five black players at spring training—up from zero only a few years earlier. One thing to keep in mind when evaluating Pesky's performance is that just three years before he took over as manager, Pumpsie Green became the first black player on the Red Sox team. Consequently, the Red Sox suffered from a disadvantage other teams did not face—far fewer African-Americans in their system. Pesky was really impressed with Reggie Smith. "He looks too good to be true. . . . Right now he looks so talented he scares me." Smith was still several seasons away, but he'd caught Johnny's eye.

Stuart livened things up by announcing a target of 50 home runs for the year. Conigliaro was beginning to receive an inordinate amount of fan mail—even before he made the team. One thing Conigliaro did win very early on, though, was the respect of his fellow players for his play and his poise. Clubbie Don Fitzpatrick gave Tony three of Ted Williams' old undershirts—the Red Sox always were known for economizing. "I'll wear 'em till they're in shreds," Tony enthused. Williams himself declared Rico Petrocelli the best prospect, and Tony Horton the best hitter. Conigliaro, he said, was at least two years away. As early as March 8, though, Pesky penned Conig in at right field. Pesky was proven right.

Johnny had a typical old-school pro-veteran bias. Asked how long a kid should spend in the minors, he answered, "I figure three years but then I see some of these kids and I wish I could use them right away. But what can we do with the guys who already have won regular jobs and are entitled to keep their jobs?" In right field, though, Lou Clinton had sunk from .294 down to .232, though his power numbers remained steady. Conigliaro seemed worth a shot. "Tony's Batting Best Since Ted" read a Kaese column header. Tony's parents Sal and Theresa were in Scottsdale and toward the end of March they saw their son put on a show. He hit a homer on the 29th, then the next day hit a double, two triples and a 13th inning home run. Despite fewer at bats than some other Sox, he was leading the team in doubles, triples, home runs and runs batted in. He made ten extra base hits in a row.

"I think Johnny has run a great spring training camp," said Mike Higgins in mid-March. "He has conducted a happy camp and a lively one. He has done the right things all the way down the line and, if some players aren't happy about their situation, let them work a little harder to show they are better than the kids." As it happened, the very next day Pesky had put a lineup of regulars in a "B" game against the Giants, and a number of them spoke up, expressing a feeling they'd been "downgraded." Stuart was one who objected, and Johnny forgot to be judicious for a moment. "He's selfish. I don't know what he has to complain about. After I had been in the major leagues for thirteen years, I had to play five 'B' games one spring. What does it matter which game he played in? I thought the regulars would like an afternoon off."

Kaese mocked the way that Red Sox management—Pesky, Higgins and Yawkey—tolerated this sort of stuff from players like Stuart. Maybe the manager should ask him questions such as "I'm sorry I spoke harshly to you when you loafed on that hit yesterday" or "A right-hander's pitching for them. Would you like to wait for a left-hander?"

Kaese suggested a possible Opening Day lineup for the Red Sox in '64:

Controversy, 1b
Worry, 2b
Discord, ss
Strife, 3b
Misery, lf
Woe, cf
Trouble, rf
Calamity, c
Contention, p

The actual Opening Day lineup was:

2B Chuck Schilling
SS Ed Bressoud
LF Carl Yastrzemski
3B Frank Malzone
1B Dick Stuart
RF Lou Clinton

CF Tony Conigliaro
C Bob Tillman
P Bill Monbouquette

The team won three of sixteen exhibition games, but Pesky remained optimistic. "We have better pitching, our catching is the same as a year ago, our infield can be better and our outfield can be rated stronger." Truth be told, the team had not really changed dramatically. In fact, a few weeks into the season, Bud Collins caustically commented, "Few streaks in baseball history are as imposing as the one Red Sox general manager Mike Higgins has going. Mike has charged through 510 straight days without making a trade." Noting that with the exception of one giddy three-week period at the end of 1962, Higgins had stuck to the commandment "Thou shalt not shake up the ball club." Between November 21 and December 13 of 1962, Higgins pulled off four trades. "But Mike got hold of himself. On Dec. 14, 1962, he set off on his historic streak. He made it all the way through the 1963 season without budging, and he has a chance to keep it going through 1964."

The final Cactus League totals for the Red Sox were 8 wins and 22 losses. Pesky said the Sox would be better in '64, though, because "I'm a better manager."

The '64 Sox visited Yankee Stadium for Opening Day, and recognizing that anything is possible before the season begins, Bud Collins' column was headlined "Until 2 PM Sox Good As Yanks." New manager Yogi Berra welcomed old friend Pesky. "Shake hands, Johnny, and wish him luck," called out a photographer. "The hell I will," Pesky countered as he threw his arm around Berra's shoulders, "We've been good friends, but now you can go to hell. How do you spell Mantle? M-e-n-d-e-l? I wish you luck . . . all bad." It worked, that first day. It was a 3-3 tie in the top of the eleventh, when Tillman tripled with one out [his fourth hit of the day] and Berra walked to the mound to talk with Whitey Ford. The next pitch went wild and Tillman scored what proved to be the winning run, as Radatz held off the Yankees in the bottom of the inning.

Johnny did tighten up clubhouse access to the media. The year before there had been free access. Now, the clubhouse was to be closed an hour and fifteen minutes before the game. "Some writers have trouble getting to the park for the first pitch," wryly noted Kaese, "but others want unlimited access to the clubhouse, and would even set up light housekeeping there if permitted." He predicted the ban would come back to haunt Pesky, moving him "one step nearer the end of the plank."

Tony Conigliaro pounced on the very first pitch offered him at Fenway Park and hit it over the screen for a home run. The Red Sox won their first two games, then began swapping wins and losses and then headed into a four-game losing streak. On April 28, Stuart tied the game in the 9th with a two-run double, but the Sox gave up two runs in the top of the eleventh. In the bottom of the frame, Stu hit a grand slam to win the game. "I needed that to get the grandstand managers off my back," said a relieved Johnny Pesky. As of the end of April, though, the Red Sox were an undistinguished 5-7.

Gary Geiger returned, still a bit weak after a couple of stomach operations. Knowing he needed four or five more days to get his strength back, Johnny yelled down the dugout bench to him, "Hide! Hide—or I'll be tempted to use you." A healthy Geiger could have meant a lot; by May 5 the Red Sox were in sole possession of last place. Geiger was unable to contribute at all and retired on May 13—too weak, and too fearful of flying.

Within a month, rumors abounded that Higgins was finally ready to make a move—he wanted to replace Johnny Pesky with his pal Billy Herman. Herman wasn't the only name that surfaced. Billy Hitchcock's name also came up. Players were reportedly talking about it, too. "There seem to be many people who feel that Pesky is in far over his head," wrote Clif Keane. "But he is a normal, average person, and it's just impossible for anyone other than a messiah to cope with the Red Sox situation. He told a player to bunt not long ago, and the man wouldn't. He has given other signs and had to repeat them several times. Life with Pesky on the Red Sox is very sad at the moment." The player was Stuart, and the *Globe* quoted him as saying "I'm a slugger, not a bunter." He did get hit with a fifty-dollar fine, but it's doubtful that any corrective purpose was achieved. Keane further wrote, "If I were to be asked, 'Can Johnny Pesky manage this ball club?' my answer is 'No, he can't—but who can?'" Herman, maybe, because Higgins would be there to back him up.

A sign Johnny had affixed to the wall inside his office at Fenway read, "When I'm right no one remembers. When I'm wrong no one forgets."

In an April 1964 article out of St. Louis, Bill Fleischman wrote, "Johnny Pesky, with only one year of experience as a major league pilot, has joined an elite group—The Society of Managers Accused of Causing Dissension. Whether the charge is true or false is not the point. Pesky, the Red Sox pilot, is now in the company with John McGraw, Miller

Huggins, Leo Durocher, Billy Southworth and a lot of others, including Oscar Vitt."

Pesky did have a little good fortune once in a while. The Red Sox were in extra innings at home against the Twins and found themselves with Radatz batting with two outs and the bases loaded. Radatz was never known for his hitting (he only had two hits in 1963) but Pesky chose not to take him out in favor of potential pinchhitter Schilling, reasoning that the law of averages dictated that any hitter would be more likely to make an out than a hit, and he wanted Radatz in to pitch the 12th. Radatz worked a 3-2 count and then fisted a bleeder into short right that won the game. Yastrzemski was known to be tight with his money but after The Monster had two hits in one week earlier in the season, he had bet Radatz five dollars he wouldn't hit another one all year. Radatz was ready to collect, but Yaz balked, "Sure, I made the bet, but I'm not going to pay him for a lucky hit like that. He's the worst hitter in the league." Radatz now had three straight hits, and Higgins was beginning to sweat his record of twelve straight. "I'm seeing the ball better," Radatz laughed.

It was a good stretch. Radatz pitched four games in a row, including both halves of a doubleheader. On May 19, the Red Sox were down 3-0 but scored four in the ninth to win it. Dalton Jones' pinch double with the bases loaded was the big hit. After 31 games, Stuart was batting just .233 and had hit only two homers. It sure didn't look like he was going to make the 50 he'd predicted and the fans began to give him a "raspberry diet." Still, Pesky kept him in the lineup.

On May 24, Stuart broke out of his slump in the eighth inning with a grand slam to boost the Sox to a 6-2 win in game one of a doubleheader. With the score tied 1-1 in game two, Stuart hit one over the net. The Sox won the game 3-1, and reached .500, 18-18. That same day, though, Conigliaro's hand was broken by a Moe Drabowsky pitch.

Two days later, Tom Yawkey showed up in Boston for the first time that year. Fortunately for Johnny, the Sox had won nine of their last twelve and won again the first day Yawkey was back, 3-2 in the 9th as Earl Wilson pitched and scored the winning run. Birdie Tebbetts remarked, "I'm happy for Johnny Pesky. When we were training in Arizona, he was worried about the first month of the season. He feared a bad start might wreck the whole season. But the Sox seem to have survived that first month and are playing good ball." Stuart was on a streak; he homered seven times in nine games.

Higgins finally made a move, trading Lou Clinton for Lee "Mad Dog"

Thomas, halting his tradeless streak at 536 days. On June 15, the trading deadline, the Sox dropped two to the Orioles, but were still in 5th place, still at .500 (29-29) and home attendance was actually up 10,000 over the prior year. The "team is not solid, but it isn't a dull club," wrote Arthur Siegel. He credited Pesky with truly creating a team with spirit and said the players respected him, "recognizing his boyish eagerness to win and his willingness to gamble on their ability to hit in the clutch. On the other hand, he has learned restraint."

Pesky had a chance to get Lou Brock in June but the front office wouldn't lift a finger. Brock went to St. Louis instead, hit .348 there and helped the Cardinals win the world's championship. It was reported that Ruthie talked Johnny out of resigning, when he realized no one upstairs was going to give him any help.

Asked about this story in 2001, Johnny replied, "That was Higgins. I wanted to get Brock. I thought we were going to make the deal. Brock was just a young player. I would never have resigned. They would have had to fire me. One thing in baseball—you never resign. You just get fired. When you're a manager, you're responsible for all this. You're going to get criticized no matter what you do. I had a general manager who wouldn't make any moves with me. If the manager doesn't have a rapport with the general manager, you're going to have some problems. O'Connell was my favorite of all the general managers. Higgins and I never hit it off."

The concern was always there, not far below the surface. As Johnny checked into the team's hotel in Chicago, he asked the desk clerk if there was any mail for him and was told there was not. "That's good," he cracked, "I haven't received my release yet." And he laughed, something he hadn't done that much in recent months.

Stuart was again passed over for the All-Star Game, despite leading the league in runs batted in. Al Lopez preferred Joe Pepitone, and didn't hesitate to offer the Sox slugger a little public advice: "Stuart should hustle more. He would be a better ballplayer if he did." That must have been music to Pesky's ears, though he kept mum. Yaz was not doing well in the first half of the season, hitting just .260 around the end of June. Tony C had come back, but then crashed into the left field grandstand wall, spraining his back and hurting his knee and hand. On the 27th, Pesky sent up Russ Nixon to pinch-hit and he banged a two-run homer off Tommy John in the 9th to win the game 3-2 over the Indians. It was his first home run of the year. "That Nixon made me look so good that I told him to take the wife and kids out for a steak dinner on me."

At the midpoint of the season, the Sox were leading the league in hitting with a .264 average but were 19th in the majors in pitching, with only Kansas City pitchers faring worse. "Second Half Tumble Feared" headlined one article. Pitching was no better under Turley than it had been under Dorish. Kaese even suggested that one of the reasons Turley had been hired—despite having no coaching experience whatsoever—was that he had a two-year contract as a player and this was a way of getting value for the second year.

Conigliaro got hurt yet again in late July, having his forearm fractured by a Pedro Ramos pitch. It was the fourth time Tony had been hit that year. Bill Liston wrote that "Conigliaro is the type of hitter who crouches way over the plate and he is going to be hit a lot." It was a bad day all the way around: Tony had already lost $250, the result of having broken curfew the night before. It was an innocent overnight with family friends—a fine family who Pesky knew personally—but that wasn't the point. He hadn't had permission. "I'm not going to be a watchdog," Johnny said, "but I'm going to stick by the rule that I established. Last year one of the mistakes I made managing this club was making threats and never following through." Pesky had typically warned players in advance when a bed check was going to be made, apparently a common practice in sports at the time. For this particular road trip, though, the players were advised there would be no advance warning. Pesky had the backing of Higgins and Yawkey. They were close enough to the first division that they wanted to tighten things up. "Johnny Pesky's strict curfew rule should make line-drive batters of the Red Sox," opined Jerry Nason's fictional pundit. "He doesn't want them hitting it up."

As July closed, Boston was 52-52, having climbed back to .500. The modest accomplishment lasted but 24 hours as the Sox promptly dropped seven in a row and twelve of thirteen. Yaz lost nine pounds in nine days and lamented, "I'm tired, really beat."

Tensions grew as Bressoud and Turley had words, possibly stemming from the shortstop's fear he was trade bait. Turley supposedly said something about Bressoud's fielding being to blame for the pitching woes. Johnny said he'd look into the rumors of trouble but reassured Bressoud that he was not going to be traded. "The trouble with our team certainly isn't the shortstop," Pesky said. "But I also told him that I would trade my own brother if I could make a deal that would better the ball club."

The Sox were in free fall. They won only seven games in all of August, dropping 22, and replicating the second-half struggles of '63. "I can't stand this," Johnny moaned. "I never used to take the game home with me, but this has been a real nightmare and I'll never know why I don't have an ulcer. It's humanly impossible for us to have played as badly as we have in spots. Now, I'm waking up at 6:30 in the morning and can't get back to sleep. And my appetite has soured. . . . I keep dreaming in my sleep that the Red Sox have runners on first and third with no one out and then can't score any runs. It's nightmarish." He took everything on his own shoulders: "I feel that I'm not doing enough to help the club. Somebody probably should take a poke at me; maybe that would shake things up."

Would Johnny be back for a third year or not? Will McDonough quoted a top official in the regime as saying, "Johnny is in solid with Mr. Yawkey." Where they hadn't spoken that much in 1963, in Johnny's second year "they are constantly in communication with each other both at home and on the road." Johnny had come across as more confident. But the Red Sox were 21 games behind, with just a .444 winning percentage as August came to a close. Pesky began to worry out loud that he wouldn't be back as field boss. "I came up through the Red Sox organization and want to stay with them," Johnny offered. "If they don't want me to manage then I'd gladly take some other position in the organization."

September saw a couple of high-profile benchings. On the 1st, Pesky benched Stuart for the first time all year, but announced in advance that it was just for two days. Stuart, nonetheless, blew his stack. When he came back, though, he played distinctly better. Dick Radatz talked about Pesky and Stuart: "Johnny had sort of a love-hate relationship with Dick Stuart. Stuart was sort of a funny guy. To the ballplayers, he was funny. I'm sure to a manager like Johnny, he wasn't too funny. He was a good power hitter, a helluva hitter. And he was just a big old lazy first baseman. He'd tell you, don't ask me to make any spectacular plays over there. I'm just getting paid to do one thing and I do it very well, and that's to hit balls out of this bandbox. That's what he did. Johnny didn't particularly care for that, but he was such a good hitter. He was just lazy, that was all. He could have been a lot better if he'd wanted to."

Yaz himself got benched late in the year. He was well off his 1963 pace but still did rank 8th in the league for average. His power was way down, though, with only 15 home runs and 62 RBI at the time to go with his .296 average. Benched for "loafing" in not running out a grounder to short, Yaz was not pleased, claiming he'd told the manager he'd had a virus for four days, but didn't want to take himself out of the lineup. Pesky, under pressure, was curt. "I never loafed when I played, and I played when I was sick on many occasions." Pesky had benched

1963's RBI champ and then the 1963 batting champ, albeit very briefly in both instances. Both were embittered by their respective benchings.

Clif Keane told Angels' manager Bill Rigney that he thought Pesky was done. Rigney replied with a question: "Who is going to manage the Red Sox? The manager or the players? I understand that the players have a lot to say about the management over there, and have had. You can't manage under those conditions."

Keane himself placed some broader blame on the style of Sox management over the years. "Do Pesky and Mike Higgins ever sit down and discuss these situations? They should, every day if possible. Before every game at Yankee Stadium, Joe McCarthy lunched with Ed Barrow. Clark Griffith talked with his Washington managers, Bucky Harris and Joe Cronin, every day—by telephone, if the club was on the road. A manager needs advice and moral backing, and there are times when he needs a shoulder to cry on. Looking back over the years, a lack of rapport between Red Sox management and general managers is noted. A fine thing, when nothing is much more essential to continued success."

Attendance had really fallen off. On Monday, September 14, the Red Sox drew just 2056 to Fenway, an all-time low for a home night game.

As Johnny sweated out the last two weeks of the season, there were rumors that Doerr would be brought in to replace him, or Mace Brown. Birtwell predicted Billy Herman would be named the new manager, and Maglie reinstated as pitching coach. Pesky would be offered a job as a special assistant, he guessed. A press conference was announced four days in advance and Pesky was left to stew and suffer in the interim. "The latest development gives Mike Higgins . . . a victory and top-control in the Red Sox organization" wrote Arthur Siegel. Siegel termed it a "coup in Fenway Park palace politics." Pesky didn't consult Higgins enough, didn't ask for advice, and Mike's feelings were hurt. That was the word. "And Pesky talked too much. He made explanations when silence was the order. He expressed his innermost feelings and that was regarded as panic."

Everyone thought he was in solid with Mr. Yawkey but Higgins still had a hold on Yawkey, got the OK and fired Johnny. "I'm at home, about a week or so to go in the season, and Higgins called and invited me to have breakfast with him at 9 the next morning. I said, 'No, I'll have a cup of coffee.' I knew what he was going to tell me, and he said, 'We decided to make a change.' I said, 'OK, you're the boss.' There's nothing I could do. I didn't raise hell or anything. I just took it nicely and left there."

On October 1, only 306 customers—the smallest crowd in Fenway Park history—saw the Sox snap a six-game losing streak with a 4-2 win over Cleveland. Box seats were $3.00 and bleachers $1.00. Third base coach William Jennings Bryan Herman was handed the managerial job, and a two-year contract, surprising no one. It was Higgins who had hired Herman, back in 1960.

Though the Red Sox under Yawkey had quite a tradition of taking care of their own, Higgins said of the departing manager, "At the present time there is no opening for him in our system."

Respected manager Frankie Frisch spoke up, saying that giving Pesky just two years to turn things around wasn't adequate. The future Hall of Famer didn't pull any punches. "Boston isn't a good club, and a manager needs at least four years to develop his players." Pesky shouldn't have been fired; he "should get the manager of the year award for all he's put up with." Singling out Yaz in particular, Frisch said his obvious ill feeling was "stupid. What a way to act. No team can win with a bunch of Humpty Dumpties."

Others spoke up for Pesky, too. Columnist Jerry Nason said the player material was the problem, and an ongoing one for the Red Sox in recent years. "It should be fairly obvious after seven or eight seasons that a pattern for failure has been established as a yoke for whatever manager assumes the risks. Even the most ardent Red Sox partisan can't help but recognize that this ball team represents more of a breakdown in procurement than of field managing."

Fired with just two games to go, Johnny was reported as "disappointed but not downcast" and also "not bitter at the Red Sox." Herman had to manage without coaches those last two games—Malmberg had already left town and Turley and Lakeman were both told not to come in. His team won both games, the last two games of the season. It was not a harbinger of anything better to come, however. The '64 Sox finished in 8th place, 27 GB with a .444 mark. Under Herman, they did distinctly worse. They dropped to 9th place—40 GB and only won 38.3% of their games losing ten more games than they had under Johnny—an even 100 losses in '65.

Years later, J.P. said that he knew he had taken over a "bad ball club. I knew it was a bad club when I took over, but you don't say no to a major league managing job. But if you don't have the horses, you don't win. And if you don't win, you get fired. You don't like it, but there's nothing you can do about it.

"There were never any harsh words between Higgins and me. Someone asked him, 'Why don't you get a couple of players for Johnny?' and he's supposed to have said, 'I'm not going to get that Polack any players.' He's supposed to have said that, but I'm not sure if I believe that. I don't think he was that kind of guy. I'm not a Polack, anyway; I was a dignified Austrian."

Looking back, Johnny confesses, "My managing experience was probably the low part of my life. The general manager and I didn't hit it off and it was just a matter of time."

There were a number of post-mortems from the press. Clif Keane wrote, "Pesky never really had a chance. Yawkey, in effect, was kicking the late Higgins upstairs after Higgins had failed dismally as a manager. Higgins didn't want Pesky to manage the club, and Higgins had some back-stabbers in the press to make it more difficult for Johnny." Johnny told Keane, "I had the club for two years, and Higgins made one trade for me. He got me Lee Thomas from the Angels. I used to give him a list of names, and he'd shrug his shoulders. It hurt me. I had Carl Yastrzemski on the team and he was young and I used to talk to him a lot, but he liked Higgins and that was it."

Gillooly clearly was one of those who felt Pesky got a raw deal. "Pesky Fired Before He Was Hired" headlined one of his columns that reminded that Pesky never had the full right to choose his coaches (Higgins insisted on Billy Herman at third and Turley to replace Dorish). Herman was a Damoclean sword hanging over Pesky's head. Gillooly had nothing against Herman. A near teetotaler, he wasn't that kind of buddy to Higgins. But he was a "'foreign agent' whose loyalty had to be to Higgins," Gillooly wrote, "Pesky has been treated like a shoe-shine boy during his managerial regime here. . . . "

Roy Mumpton differed in the *Worcester Gazette* of January 1, 1965, writing "I'm not among those who feel Pesky got a bad deal from the Sox. He wasn't nearly the manager his friends had hoped. But he was always a class guy. His cheerfulness was contagious."

Just four months after Johnny was fired, the Boston Baseball Writers' Association held their 26th annual dinner in February 1965. A number of awards were presented—to Dick Radatz as Fireman of the Year, to Bob Tillman as most improved player, and Felix Mantilla as comeback-of-the-year. Larry Claflin reported, though, that the "biggest ovation of the night went to Pesky, who was seated in the audience. Toastmaster Tim Horgan called on Pesky to take a bow and a prolonged ovation broke out with many fans standing. Later, when Conigliaro received his rookie of the year award, he said: 'I want to thank the man who made this possible— Johnny Pesky.' Again the crowd broke into a noisy demonstration which left little doubt that the eighth-place finish of the Red Sox under Pesky had not destroyed his popularity in Boston."

Pesky later said he shouldn't have been quite as friendly with the ballplayers. "You can't be too nice a guy in this business. You have to be tough. Being tough doesn't mean you lose friends. Look at Tony Conigliaro. I kept after him and kept after him, and I fined him a few times, because I know if that kid takes the proper attitude he'll be another Joe DiMaggio. He never resented it. At the Baseball Writers dinner in January he got up and said he owed all his success to me, that if it hadn't been for me he'd still be in the minors. A class kid. If a few others had been that way, maybe things might have been different.

"I wish I could have survived another year. I knew what was coming. Petrocelli. Dalton Jones. The pitching. I remember Will McDonough was with me on a trip to Baltimore in July. We met coming into the lobby almost simultaneously and we went in to breakfast together, and he said, 'This is not the kind of club you like, is it, Johnny?' I said, 'No, it isn't.' We had breakfast and I told him how I felt.

"If you're the manager and you don't win, a change is made. Some guys have a terrible time accepting it. It gets to them physically. I understood. If you don't win, you're gone. It's like when you're a player, if you don't produce, someone takes your place. It's as simple as that. This will go on as long as baseball is played."

22

Johnny Pesky in Pittsburgh

A fter all the press and pressure that attends managing the Boston Red Sox, it must have been a relief to head for the relative anonymity of Pittsburgh. Pesky passed four years with the Pirates, three of them serving as first base coach for the major league team and the fourth as skipper of the Columbus Jets, the Bucs' Triple A club. In Pittsburgh, Johnny served under Harry Walker, the same Harry Walker whose RBI hit drove in Enos Slaughter and won the 1946 World Series.

Boston had been Johnny's hometown for over twenty years, and it's a city where there has always been more scrutiny by the media than in any other baseball market—and more criticism. In Johnny's playing days, coverage was pretty well confined to the print media but when he returned as manager, the broadcast media had evolved. Mercifully, radio and television confined their reporting to play on the field, and sports talk radio had not yet uttered its birth yelp. Nevertheless, the pressures on Johnny Pesky, an adopted but adoring son of New England, had to have been intense.

To head for the spring training home of the Pirates in sleepy Fort Myers and then to a coaching position with a National League team which no longer visited Boston must have seemed strange, but comforting. He wasn't being paid as well, but he was doing okay and he was in baseball—at the major league level. And the Pirates were a good and very interesting club.

They'd been World Series champs as recently as 1960, when they battled the Yankees into the seventh game and won it on Bill Mazeroski's
"walk-off" home run.

The next year, 1961, Pittsburgh plunged to sixth place, 18 games out
of first, but they were beginning to come back. Johnny enjoyed some
competitive baseball. 1965 and 1966 were good years, with Pittsburgh
placing third both seasons—they won 90 games in '65 and were only
seven games out. In '66, they finished with 92 wins and were only three
games behind. Better to be in Pittsburgh than Boston those two years!
The Red Sox under Billy Herman were fully 40 games out of first in
1965—losing 100 games and finishing three games out of the cellar. In
1966, they were only a half-game out of last place—the only possible satisfaction being that the Yankees were the ones at the very bottom.

Of course, 1967 was another matter indeed. It would have been a
wonderful year to be associated with the Red Sox in any capacity—'67
was the Impossible Dream year where the team unexpectedly rose from
the depths to win the pennant. In Pittsburgh, the Pirates dropped off to
a mediocre 81-81 record, a 9th place finish 20.5 games from the top.

Johnny Pesky, sporting #4, was now a first base coach and it could be
argued that he had apprenticed in first baseman's hell—with Dr.
Strangeglove the reigning demon. In truth, first base coaching isn't the
hardest job in the world. You don't bear the entire responsibility for the
team on your shoulders, as Pesky had while managing the Red Sox. You
don't have to suffer like a third base coach who's sent a runner home
from third, only to see him cut down at the plate.

The way the Pirates used their first base coach also made for a more
relaxed environment for Johnny. The team had a lot of veteran players.
Roberto Clemente and Bill Virdon had both been on the team since 1955
and Mazeroski since 1956. First baseman Donn Clendenon had been with
the Pirates since '62, though 1965 proved his best year—.301 with 184
hits and 96 RBI. Willie Stargell and Bob Bailey had begun in 1963, the
year both Jim Pagliaroni and Manny Mota joined the team.

Johnny was a hitting instructor, too, but these were experienced players and they didn't really need a lot in the way of instruction or counsel-
ing. Though able to help a bit here and there with comments, Johnny
basically just pitched in and did what Walker or any of the players might
ask of him. He still believed his gung ho approach would inspire his
ballplayers. "One thing that I found out, even in the minor leagues,
you've got to set by example. By that I mean, when you show up at the
ballpark. Your eating habits. How you conduct yourself in the clubhouse

and on the field." He threw a lot of b. p., hit to the fielders and helped keep things moving along nicely.

Johnny didn't work that intensely with any one player. "You do more of that now than you did in those years," he explains. He was asked to try to keep up Clemente's self-confidence. "I used to tell Roberto that he was as good as Ted Williams and that was something from me. Williams was a god to me and I was putting Roberto in the same class with him. I saw him make plays that were just about impossible, and I was forever praising him and he loved every second of it. Great kid. A wonderful player. Probably as good a player as ever played the game. He could run, hit, throw, hit home runs. I had Stargell out a couple of times for extra hitting, but Clemente didn't need it. He was just so good. When you talk about Clemente, you're talking about Mays . . . He was a hell of a player."

In 1965, Johnny's first year of coaching at first base, the Dodgers won the pennant, with the Giants just two behind. Pittsburgh had made a race of it, finishing just one game ahead of Cincinnati. Clemente had 194 hits and a league-leading .329 average. A decade later, after Johnny had returned to the Red Sox fold as first base coach, he was asked who were the three best hitters he'd ever seen. He named Ted, Joe DiMaggio and Roberto Clemente.

When Johnny returned home to Greater Boston after the 1965 season, Higgins had been let go by the Sox—the same day Morehead threw a no-hitter at home—and Dick O'Connell took over as GM. Boston reporters were still asking for Pesky's views on the Red Sox. Jack Denty of the *Salem News* wrote at the end of November, "Looking back after a year at Pittsburgh, Pesky—not naming names—commented that 'I could name ten of them who should have been traded off the team. A good major league ball player of today must have a combination of speed and great desire. And these ten haven't got that combination.'" He did predict good things for the Sox under O'Connell.

Higgins comforted the culprits who complained Pesky had been "too tough" on them, but Johnny would not be drawn into criticism of Higgins, though be did break into a grin and said he wanted to thank Higgins for what he had done for him. "I am now with a great organization. They pay me a nice salary and I just received a $1200 check as my share of the Pittsburgh World Series money for finishing third in the race. And I'm pleased that they have asked me to return again as a coach next year."

A Gillooly column suggested, though, that Johnny's "heart is still chipped because the Red Sox made him walk the plank after he rose from cabin-boy to captain. His happiness with Pittsburgh is only a pretense; I'll bet the first thing he reads [at Pirates spring training in Florida] is the dispatch from the Red Sox Arizona gymnasium."

The 1966 edition of the Pirates was pretty much the same as the year before, with Matty Alou taking Virdon's place in center and Jose Pagan joining them as a utility infielder. They played to the very same 92-70 record as in 1966, but that put them in third place, just three games out—behind LA & SF.) "That second year, we really should have won," says Johnny.

Johnny rated Willie Stargell very highly. "Stargell was just one of the guys, a great strong guy. He loved to play. I used to love to see him get on the bus. He'd say 'Ho Ho'—he'd never miss the bus, never complain. He'd go midway back the bus and go to sleep . . . Nothing bothered him. Mazeroski was a great kid. Great player. I got very friendly with him. Used to hit ground balls to him. When he got his hands on the ball, you were out."

Clemente had 202 hits and 11 triples, and a total of 342 bases, second behind Hank Aaron with 119 RBI and fourth in the league with his .317 average. Matty Alou led the National League with his .342 mark. Pesky gave Harry Walker credit for Alou's unforeseen success, "Harry Walker really helped him. Harry liked that opposite field."

In 1967, the team slipped. They only won half their games (81-81), which dropped them to sixth place. The Cardinals ran away with it, 10 1/2 games ahead of the second place Giants—and, of course, they beat the Red Sox in a seven-game World Series.

Clemente led the NL in with 209 hits and 324 TB. His 110 RBI put him just one behind Orlando Cepeda. His .357 average bested everyone. Maury Wills joined the team, after eight seasons with the Dodgers, and hit .302.

In '67, Walker was fired and Danny Murtagh came in to finish the season. Morale was poor. "We were going so bad. My oldest brother died and I went back home for four or five days. When I got back, we were all still living at the hotel. Clyde King and Smitty [Hal Smith] came down and said, 'Glad to see you, Johnny. We hate to see you come back to this situation.' We'd lost something like six or seven in a row."

After the season, Johnny was dumped as coach, as was the whole coaching staff. Pesky signed on as manager of the Pirates AAA team, the Columbus Jets in the International Association.

In October 1967, Johnny settled into a lower box V.I.P. seat at Fenway and watched the Red Sox Impossible Dream team battle the St. Louis Cardinals in the World Series.

1968—COLUMBUS

Johnny began work with the Columbus Jets in the spring of 1968. "I enjoyed that year. We were in the race all year."

Here Johnny was again, managing—but despite Columbus being a Triple A club he had no coaches to assist him. Johnny was manager and third base coach, and gave all the signals. One of the players would coach first. "We had a kangaroo court. I had three guys. One was the judge and two were the lawyers. We didn't even have a pitching coach."

The Jets finished in second place (82-64), one half-game behind the International League leader Toledo Mud Hens, 83-64 This was a team with a lot of talented players; it's no surprise that later editions of the parent club did so well. The '68 Jets included several players on the N.L. East leading 1970 Pirates: Richie Hebner, Al Oliver, Freddie Patek, and Manny Sanguillen. Johnny said, "They were all quality players, and you could see that, but they needed that year down at the Triple A level."

Faith in your player was still a Pesky hallmark. Johnny had Dock Ellis come in for the eighth inning of an 8-2 game (Jets on top.) Ellis retired the last two batters, but in the ninth he gave up a double and two singles before striking out the side. A while later in another game, Ellis came in again for the eighth, the Jets having tied it up in the top of the inning. He walked the first two Rochester Red Wings. After a sacrifice bunt moved the runners over, he intentionally walked a batter to load the bases. He lost that game on a two-run single. Four days later, the Jets had lost five in a row, and had an all-night bus ride awaiting them. They were up by a run. In the eighth inning, one on and one out, Ellis was called back in again and he got out of the inning. In the ninth, he gave up two straight singles to the first two batters—the potential tying and winning runs on. But Pesky left Ellis in. "At the risk of losing a ball game," Pesky confessed. "I wanted Dock to know I was still with him. If I had taken him out, it might have destroyed his confidence, and he might not have been worth a quarter to us the rest of the season."

It was no surprise that when both Dock Ellis and Freddie Patek graduated to the Pirates, they said, "We hated to leave Pesky."

Gerry Finn of the *Springfield Republican*, writing in 1975, commented that Johnny had a "genius for taking the crude ingredients out of raw material and replacing them with finesse and expertise" and cited the '68 Columbus club as the prime example. Johnny downplays his success, saying, "Oh, I suppose I've helped a couple of guys get where they are. But they had to have something to develop in the first place. I've never said I was responsible for anyone making the major leagues. Maybe, just maybe, I got them there quicker." Alumni from Columbus included Manny Sanguillen, Richie Hebner, Fred Patek, Dave Roberts, Dock Ellis and Al Oliver—and the latter might be the "classic example of Pesky's approach to handling men."

"When we left spring training in '68, everyone knew that Oliver was a star of the future. The team brass was concerned with his personality and behavior. He had a short fuse, so they told me to 'pet' him.

"Well, that was all right for a while. But when he started breaking helmets in the dugout because he was batting below .200, that petting stuff vanished. I tapped him thirty dollars for each helmet he smashed. Then one night after he struck out with the bases loaded, he stormed into the locker room and tore off his uniform. That corked me. The next day I brought him in for a meeting. I also brought a bat with me. He was a strong guy.

"I know what he was doing wrong at the plate. So, I told him a couple of things. First, I straightened him out on his tantrums. Then, I suggested he choke up on the bat. He looked puzzled until I showed him something from a Ted Williams instruction book. I read it out loud . . . 'if a pitcher's tough, go up a little on the bat.' That convinced him. In two weeks he went from .190 to .280."

Pesky also remembered an interchange with Sanguillen. "One time we were in Richmond and we were behind about 5-2 or something in the middle innings. We had two outs and then Manny Sanguillen swung at a bad ball. I said something to him in the dugout, and he thought I was mad at him. 'My god, Manny. How can you swing at a pitch like that?' He started to say something but then he thought better of it. About two innings later, he hits a three-run homer and he's back in the dugout, he's putting his gear on, sitting alongside of me, and he said, 'Any time you want to get mad at me, you can.' I said, 'Manny, I wasn't mad at you. I just want you to get better. When you're at the plate, you've got to watch the ball. You can't hit the ball unless you see it.' "

The season went down to the final day, with the team missing by just that half game. Columbus played one game less, and could have tied had they had the chance to make it up. "We lost by percentage points. Toledo played one more game than we did and they won it. In those years, we didn't make those games up."

In October, Johnny resigned as manager of the Jets. A day later he announced he was taking a job in broadcasting—with the Boston Red Sox. Johnny called Harold Cooper and said, "I've got a chance to go to the big leagues. Radio and TV."

23

Broadcaster, 1969–1974

Even though I'm a native New Englander, when you start a new job it's very difficult to get accepted, especially in Boston. I was able to take advantage of Johnny's presence when he wasn't so fortunate. That was the season—1983—when Johnny was so ill. He had that reaction to yeast, as it turned out, and was losing weight. They didn't know what was wrong with him. He was on the coaching staff but after hitting fungoes he didn't have the strength to stay during the game so he used to come up to the radio booth—it was my first year—and Johnny used to stay and do color, and he really helped me get established and get accepted. You know Johnny—when he likes you, the whole world knows it.

Johnny, you really were very instrumental in my career and I thank you.

—Joe Castiglione, at the 50th Annual
Johnny Pesky Friendship Dinner, 2002

I was born in Melrose, Mass. When I was 19, I was at Norwich University and interning for Joe Castiglione. When I was there, Johnny Pesky made me feel very much at home. Johnny Pesky was a name I'd heard my dad talk about, and it was really like an honor to have him welcome me. It was kind of like showing up at the Vatican and having the Pope welcome you.

—Don Orsillo, Red Sox broadcaster

BROADCASTER, 1969–1974

Here was a new challenge, another side of baseball—the media. Johnny had been a clubhouse kid, a player, a coach, a manager—now he became a broadcaster. Concomitant with his tenure in the booth, Johnny would also help create the first Red Sox marketing department. But they still couldn't keep him off the field. He began to moonlight as hitting instructor near the end of his six years of broadcasting.

Johnny signed on with WHDH, Channel 5 in Boston. He was to be an analyst with Ken Coleman and Ned Martin, working on both the television and radio broadcasting teams. When WHDH lost the rights, Channel 4 (WBZ) picked up the contract—and Pesky, too. Johnny served in the booth from 1969 through the 1974 season.

Larry Claflin mused in print "Pesky . . . will make no attempt to insult our intelligence with lies or deceit on the air." Pesky confessed to the *Lynn Daily Item*: "It was worse than hitting against Bob Feller with 60,000 people watching." A perfectionist, Johnny had Ruth tape the broadcasts at home and then he would listen and critique himself. He took weekly elocution lessons from Mrs. Ann Wood of Roxbury, learning not to run his words together, to vary his choice of words, to say "got to" instead of "gotta" and so forth. He also admitted, "My wife Ruthie is teaching me to score. You'd be surprised how few players know how to score a game."

Ironically, Johnny could have had a position working as coach for Ted Williams, when Ted became manager of the Washington Senators in 1969. Ted told the *Herald*'s Joe Fitzgerald about it in 1994. "Hell, I'll tell you something about Johnny Pesky you don't know. When I became manager of the Washington Senators [in 1969] I said to myself, 'How did I get into this spot?' I never wanted to manage. So one of the first guys I call, someone I want to have with me in the worst way, was Pesky. I say, 'Johnny, I know nothing about the infield.' And he tells me, 'Ted, I'd love to, but I've got an obligation to the Red Sox.'

"I tell him, 'Dammit, Johnny come with me! How much are you making?' I guess you'd say I was interfering with another club at the time. Anyway, he tells me, so now I offer him more and the sonofagun is *still* saying no. We finally get up to offering manager's pay but it made no difference; Johnny had given his word and, damnit, he was sticking to it. Oh, he's a great guy."

But Johnny Pesky was Mr. Red Sox and his loyalty to that organization won out. Even out of uniform, it kept Johnny in baseball and in the hearts and minds of New Englanders.

Along with Mel Parnell, he was one of the first "color men" in broadcasting. During radio broadcasts, Ken Coleman would do six innings and Ned would do three. Then Johnny or Mel would pop in. The Red Sox were also televising about fifty games a year and for those games Johnny would be on television for the whole game and Coleman would do the first three and last three on TV, going over to do the middle three on radio, as Ned moved over to do the middle three on television.

Ken Coleman says, "One of the joys of my broadcasting life was working with Johnny. Johnny would get excited. He was a Red Sox guy, somewhat of a cheerleader, I guess you could say. You wouldn't expect anything else from Johnny Pesky. The Red Sox were his life. He loved the team and was very much at home in the clubhouse and on the field because he played for so long. He's a gregarious guy and he liked being around the players."

Nevertheless, Johnny was never that comfortable in the booth. He chafed under the relative inactivity of the broadcaster, and told reporter Ed Cahill, "I can't get used to sitting around all day while we're waiting for a night game or loafing around at night following a day game. For the first time in my life, I am working extremely short hours. As a player, manager and coach, I used to get some work each day to keep in shape."

Looking back a quarter of a century later, Johnny will simply say, "I was never really comfortable there. I was terrible on play-by-play. I could talk about what was going on, on the field. My bag was in rain delays! Telling stories about guys like DiMaggio and Williams."

Johnny was a real fan, though nothing like the rabid "homer," the great Boston Celtics broadcaster Johnny Most. Bill Liston, writing in the *Herald Advertiser* indicated that "the only rap which might have been directed at his radio and TV work was that the former Red Sox star and later manager always looked on the bright side of things." Pollyanna Pesky? Hardly a scathing condemnation of the man, it was part and parcel of Pesky's positive personality. Build up your young players, and don't speak ill of the organization.

Clif Keane later wrote: "As a TV man, he was a great player and coach. Good grief, those times when Coleman would say to Pesky: 'Well, this young right-hander, Joe Blow, what's he like, Johnny?' And Pesky would say: 'Well, Ken, he has a good arm, Ken and he has a sinker, Ken, and if he can get that sinker on the black, Ken, he'll be a good pitcher, Ken. I'll say one thing, Ken, he's got guts, Ken.' Pass the aspirin."

Johnny concedes that he was no critic. "I could have been, hell, I'm no softie. But I always put myself in the ballplayer's place. Joe McCarthy used to say to me: 'Johnny, be careful what you say about ballplayers. You may wind up on the same team with a guy you rap someday.' So I didn't rap anyone, and here I am back with the Red Sox where I belong."

A few years later, Keane softened his assessment: "Pesky wasn't all that bad. On rainy days with fill-in anecdotes, he was very good. The new men will be more glib, but Johnny was a Red Soxer from his shoes to his smooth black hair, every inch of him, every moment he was on the air."

Darrell Johnson had been catcher on the Denver Bears team in 1955, when Johnny served as Ralph Houk's coach. Now the positions were reversed as Johnson selected Johnny Pesky as one of his coaches. Johnny was still working as a broadcaster, as he did throughout the year, but the two spent a lot of time together. Late in 1974 Johnson had gone to Pesky to ask him about helping Rick Miller and in the next four games, Miller went on a tear, collecting seven hits.

Rick Miller expressed appreciation for Johnny's assistance: "He was a broadcaster when I first met him, in spring training but he'd been a manager, a coach, a player—he wasn't your typical broadcaster. The Red Sox wanted me to be the leadoff hitter in 1975. They wanted me to change my swing and be more of a singles hitter, hit the ball on the ground and get on base for the other guys. So we worked on that. We spent a few weeks together. It's an ongoing process. You can't just change your swing overnight. I think I hit over .300 for the month.

"He really cares. He's a joy to have around. He worked with Jim Rice, to make him a better outfielder. Jimmy hit the heck out of the ball, but he wasn't a very good outfielder. There was a lot of hard work, and Johnny hit a lot of line drives off the Wall for him—even while we were taking batting practice. Johnny would be out there with him every day. Whatever we asked him, he was there to help us. When I wasn't playing every day, he'd give me extra work in the outfield—just to get a good workout. Just to run, to shag fly balls, to stay in shape. We'd play little games amongst ourselves, the extra outfielder. He was there for anybody who wanted help or advice—or just a shoulder to lean on. I don't want to get too mushy, but I'm sure nobody has a bad word to say about him. Johnny helped me change my swing and it took hold. It helped me a lot in my career."

Once Channel 38 won the bid to assume the TV broadcast rights for Red Sox games, both Ken Coleman and Johnny were going to be replaced. It was no secret that the station wanted to bring in a new team. Sportscasting was not Johnny's forte. "I think I belonged on the field,"

Johnny Pesky the Disc Jockey

Presaging Johnny's later career as a broadcaster, he did a stint in the off-season of 1950 as a disc jockey for dawn to dusk radio station WBMS in Boston, helping host the daily Monday-Saturday 60-minute show "Million Dollar Ballroom" with Bill Stewart. The show ran from 2 to 3 every afternoon. "It's a hit. It's the Johnny Pesky Show!" says the announcer and then Benny Goodman's "Big John Special" kicked off the hour.

Pesky's career could have taken another direction, just as Mickey McDermott (or Tony Conigliaro) might have developed his singing career. "If I do well enough, I hope to make this a permanent thing. The days of a major league player are numbered and I want to be prepared for the future. I like radio and George Lasker, owner of WBMS, has given me this opportunity to get started."

There was no particular sponsor, at least at first. They tried to sell automobiles and TV sets. Johnny played records—he made the selections personally—it was planned to evolve into an all-request format, where listeners would write in to Johnny with what they wanted to hear. Some early choices were "Stardust," "Oh Babe," "Some Enchanted Evening," and "My Heart Cries for You." "I play all kinds of records," he told the *Lynn Item*. "Whatever the listeners request. My favorite is Glenn Miller. He's the best. Tommy Dorsey's good, too."

Walt Dropo was DJ Johnny's first on-air guest. *The Sporting News* (Dec. 27, 1950) reported that they "discussed the effect of the Korean crisis on major and minor league ball; praised Lou Boudreau, new Red Sox acquisition; promised Boston fans an improved home team next year, and reviewed American League prospects for 1951." Guests included Frankie Fontaine and WCOP's Sherm Feller, as well as ballplayers Birdie Tebbetts, Sam Mele, Mickey Harris, McDermott and Eddie Waitkus.

Johnny knew the bench jockeys would give this disc jockey a hard time. "A few years back, they gave me the business when I was named Governor Bradford's aide. 'Umpire, don't call a strike on him,' they yelled, 'he's the Governor's aide!' I can just hear what they'll say next season, 'Mr. Announcer, will you please play a hill-billy song for me? Will ya, huh? This is WBMS striking out, etc.'"

"Sure, I was nervous," he admitted, "especially when it came to reading commercials, but there aren't 35,000 fans watching me when I'm on the radio. They can hear me but they can't see me if I boot one." Of his wife, JP said, "She said I was better than she thought I'd be. I worry about my batting average all summer. Now I have a Hooper Rating to think about all winter."

Johnny maintains today. Critics agreed, one writer indicating that Pesky had been "miscast" as a broadcaster and that "although a knowledgeable baseball man, Pesky never quite clicked" in the role. Where Johnny belonged was in coaching and instruction, and he certainly felt more comfortable with a bat than with a microphone.

Johnny was officially named first base coach and batting instructor by Johnson on November 13, 1974.

Tom Yawkey almost certainly put in a word on Johnny's behalf. Claflin termed this typical of Fenway "intrigue," but it was probably just Yawkey wanting to find a position for Johnny Pesky. In fact, the flip side of the 1975 pennant victory is that Darrell Johnson got to keep his position into 1976. Had the team bombed in '75, there was every possibility that "the move to bring Pesky back as manager [would have swept] Boston like a tidal wave."

When Johnny first came back as coach, the Red Sox official scorebook magazine noted, "Thousands of fans are pleased to see #35 out there in the first base coaching box at Fenway Park, but no one is happier about being back in uniform than Johnny Pesky, himself." Johnny was ecstatic, "This is great! This is the part of the game that I've always enjoyed the most, the teaching part. . . . "

His work with Miller impressed a number of players. Soon Burleson, Evans, Lynn and others began to come out early, too. Johnny preached that there is no magic formula for making a good hitter, and that improvement came from within the hitter himself. But there was a role for an instructor. He recognized that his talents would be limited as far as helping hitters with power, but he was more than willing to employ new technologies to assist him in instruction. In particular, Johnny embraced the use of video tape. When a player was in a slump, he could now use this visual aid to dissect a slumping hitter's swing and correct the problem.

Pesky's main teaching strength may well have been his flexibility and openness. "What worked for one player might not work for another." Harry "The Hat" Walker did "a lot of good things, but he seemed to want everyone to hit in his style in a crouch and not everyone can do that. I'm a closed stance guy, but Wally Moses had much success teaching his open stance style. The key is patience. I know I've got a lot more patience with hitting than with any other part of the game."

Johnny's list of successful pupils would make a Harvard professor turn crimson: Richie Hebner, Al Oliver of the Pirates, and Freddie Patek. When he visited future MVP and rookie-of-the-year Fred Lynn at Pawtucket, Lynn was hitting only .267. "I got him to move his hands away from his body more, and once he got comfortable with that, he wound up hitting .320."

Professor Pesky was back with the Red Sox and on the field of play. He was content.

NOTE

As it happens, Johnny turned down a big league manager's job in Pittsburgh to continue broadcasting for the Red Sox. Shortly after he turned down the Pirates job, he received Darrell Johnson's offer to coach first.

"I turned down the Pittsburgh job in '74 because of Dick O'Connell. Harding Petersen called O'Connell and asked for permission to talk to me, and of course Dick allowed him. I flew into Pittsburgh and met Petersen at the airport. "Petersen says, 'The job is yours if you want it,' and I said, 'For how long?' and he said, 'We only give managers one year at a time.' Jesus. I was looking for a three-year deal and I'd have settled for two. Ruthie said, 'Johnny, do what you want to do.' I said, 'Pete, O'Connell's been very good. I've got to be loyal to him. The guy's given me a decent job'—I was doing radio and TV at the time. I was never comfortable there, but I worked with two great guys—Martin and Coleman. He said, 'Well we hire our managers one year to the next.' I said, 'Well, if it'd been a couple of years before, I might have taken a chance on that'—I knew the talent.

"He said, 'Well, Johnny, go home and think about it.' I asked, 'When do you want an answer?' This is on a Saturday. He said, 'Well, Monday or Tuesday's fine.' I said, 'I'll call you tomorrow.' So I went home and Ruthie says, 'What do you want to do?' I said, 'Dick has been good to me. Dick put me in a good spot.' And she said, 'You'd like to go, wouldn't you?' I said, 'Yeah, I would. I'm not going to do it, though, because I have too much respect for O'Connell. This thing's going to get better here. I think I'll just stay here and keep my mouth shut.'

"I met [old friend] Joe Sanchez. We were going out that night. We had a little cigar group, maybe 10, 12 guys. We'd have dinner and smoke a cigar. He knew I'd gone to Pittsburgh. I said, 'You know, Joe, Goddamnit, it's very tempting.' He hadn't opened his mouth. I said, 'I think I'll just call Mr. Petersen and tell him I'll stay with the ballclub.' He said, 'That's the punchline I wanted to hear, John.'

"I was really gambling that I'd eventually get back on the field—which I did."

24
Coach, 1975-1984

After Darrell Johnson anointed Johnny as first base coach in 1975, he served a succession of managers for the next ten years. Johnny was thrilled to be back on the field. It was obviously good for the Red Sox as well—as soon as he took over as first base coach, the Red Sox won the pennant and went to the World Series! It was his first World Series since 1946, a 29-year hiatus.

Pesky predicted in February that the key to Sox success in 1975 would be Rick Wise (who did have his best year, 19-12, as it turned out): "If Wise can come back from his arm and shoulder problems like we're expecting, then the Red Sox definitely will be in business. He's the key."

Johnny worked particularly closely with rookie Jim Rice, as he did throughout Rice's career. Had Rice not had his hand broken by a Vern Ruhle fastball during the last week of the season, forcing him to miss the entire World Series, the Sox may well have won it all. Even without the Boston strongman, they fought down to the seventh game.

It was a great Series and Johnny Pesky was standing in the first base coach's box when Carlton Fisk hit his dramatic twelfth inning home run to win Game Six. "I patted him on the ass going around first base and I was at home plate when he got there. That was a hell of a thrill."

To which Johnny immediately adds, "Fisk should have never left this club. You've got to blame Haywood Sullivan for that. Didn't even send a goddamn contract. Made him a free agent! Fisk could have still signed with the Red Sox, but he got pissed off at the general manager. He made Fisk a millionaire. If we had had Fisk the next three or four years, we might have been in a couple more World Series. That's how important he was. The good clubs always have a good catcher."

When the '76 season began, Johnny embarked on another sideline: he became one of "The Window Boys" working as a radio and TV spokesman for JB Sash and Door, a Boston area outlet for windows and doors. Sal Bertolami grew up in the area and loved Johnny Pesky as a player. One of the company's salespeople suggested a ballplayer as a spokesman and they settled on Darrell Johnson, manager of the team that had just won the pennant the year before. "We had set up to do the ad with him and all of a sudden in '76, the Red Sox lost ten games in a row. He backed off because he was getting pressure from the media and he didn't want to be selling windows while the Sox were losing. So our sales-person said, 'Well, what about Johnny Pesky?' and as soon as he mentioned Johnny Pesky it brought back all my childhood dreams of being a ballplayer and I was ecstatic.

"We went into the clubhouse with the little Sony tape recorder. I had written the ad myself because I was familiar with the product, and John and I did it with this fellow being there, and that's how it all started. The ads started to become popular. I can tell you that Johnny Pesky was absolutely the perfect person. He gave our company that credibility that we were looking for."

The ads moved to TV and anyone who's watched Red Sox baseball for the last 25-plus years knows that Sal and Johnny say, "We're the Window Boys."

It was the day-in/day-out coaching that Johnny always loved the most, and for a full decade he was in his element, interrupted only by a serious illness in 1982. Every day Johnny put on his Red Sox uniform and worked with the players—in spring training, on the road and at home in Fenway Park. These were good times. Johnny had in Dick O'Connell a G.M. who truly valued Johnny's work, a succession of three managers (Darrell Johnson, Don Zimmer and Ralph Houk) who wanted him on the field, and the opportunity to work with a number of players and help them develop their potential.

During this period, Pesky worked with Jim Rice and Wade Boggs, and a stream of other players, some of whom made it and some of whom did not. In the clubhouse and on the field, traveling with the ball club, knowing he was helping make a difference, this truly was Johnny in his element. Johnny's tenure as coach was a long one; a decade is a long time in major league baseball. Only four other coaches in the century-plus of Red Sox baseball have experienced such longevity: Del Baker (1945–8; 1953–60), Tom Daly (1933–46), Walt Hriniak (1977–88) as hitting coach, and Paul Schreiber (1947–58) as pitching coach.

"Jim Rice insisted on me," Johnny explained, "and I went with him every place. Even after workouts, he'd be out in leftfield, especially in spring training. He'd watch film and I'd ask, 'Well, what kind of a swing was this? What was that pitch?' I might point out something on the film. I'd say, 'Now when you go to the plate, don't be a dummy. You're not a dummy. God was good to you, He gave you a great body, and all you've got to do is put the ball in play. Pick the ball up. Pick the ball up and hit it. Try to get to know the strike zone. If you know the strike zone and you've got some contact, you're going to hit!'"

Wade Boggs was very appreciative of Johnny's help. "Johnny was an infield instructor when I first broke in, along with Eddie Popowski. At 3:00, Johnny would give me 50 balls to my right, 50 balls to my left, 50 double plays and then 50 slow rollers coming in. He would hit me about 200, 250 ground balls a day. It seemed like the more and more that Johnny and I worked together, the better I got. One of my superstitions was that the only person that could hit me fungoes was Johnny Pesky. That went on for about . . . probably about 10 years." Johnny joked with Wade, "Boggsie, you got the Gold Gloves with the Yankees!" Asked about it later, Boggs commented, "Well, that was all the ground balls that paid off. If you don't like Johnny Pesky, you don't like Americana. In my opinion, Johnny Pesky is one of the greatest human beings I've ever met."

"I liked most of the managers. Kasko treated me very, very well. Kevin Kennedy treated me well. Butch Hobson treated me well. Joe Morgan. I was hoping he would ask me to coach, but he didn't. So I didn't say anything. He had his own mind and rightfully so. I love Joe Morgan, though. I thought he should have never gotten fired. That was a tragedy. Hobson should have stayed back in the minor leagues for a couple more years. It would have been better for him, because he hadn't had enough experience. He wasn't ready. I thought he was, but I was wrong. Hobson right now, though, would be excellent. Don Zimmer won more games than any manager we've ever had around here—well, except for Cronin. In those years, they didn't change managers as quickly. Zimmer, I've got to put him on the top of my list. He's baseball night and day. Kasko. Kennedy. And Jimy Williams. I was very fond of Jimy Williams. He showed me something, with the kind of club that he had."

Midway through the 1976 season, Darrell Johnson was let go and Don Zimmer named manager. Zimmer both managed and served as third base coach, though in 1977 he planned to manage from the dugout. Johnny hoped to be able to stay on, and he would have been glad to coach third for Zimmer. "Toward the end of the season I asked him for a crack at the job but I didn't hear anything," Johnny said. "I told Zimmer I don't care if I picked up the baseballs and towels. I just wanted to remain with the Red Sox. I just love it here."

In November 1976, Pesky was the first coach rehired by Don Zimmer, and the only coach Zimmer kept. It was during the Zimmer years that Johnny stopped throwing batting practice, after he got hit in eye by a ball when he failed to get fully back behind the protective screen. Johnny was in his 60s and Zimmer said "No more." A quarter of a century later, though, Johnny's still adept with the fungo bat. "I haven't thrown much," he said early in the 21st century. "Even ten years ago, I could throw a little bit, but now I can't throw the ball across the street. Luckily I haven't gotten fat. I remember when I first got married, Ruthie's mother said, 'When you stop playing, Johnny, you're going to get big and fat.' Well, I haven't, and I won't."

Zimmer's years as Red Sox manager were difficult ones, despite winning 97 games in 1977, 99 in '78 and 91 in '79. The counter-culture had established itself in the Boston clubhouse and Zim's run-ins with the "Buffalo Heads" (Bill Lee, Bernie Carbo, Ferguson Jenkins, Rick Wise, and Jim Willoughby) were legendary. Bill Lee, in particular, clashed repeatedly with Zimmer, constantly taunting him with disrespectful—occasionally cruel—comments, most notoriously terming his manager a "gerbil." Lee played to a younger generation of sportswriters covering the team; they ate it up and printed Lee's every utterance regardless of how flip or caustic. Boston's a tough market and writers often cater to a cynical crowd. It's surprising Zimmer lasted as long as he did, though the team did well enough in 1978 to have earned a tie at the end of the regular season in 1978, before Bucky Dent's home run punctured Red Sox pennant hopes for good.

Johnny was in Boston for this fated 1978 playoff game, one of two players in uniform for both American League single-game playoffs: the 1948 game against Cleveland and this '78 game against the Yankees. The Red Sox lost both. Bob Lemon was the other player.

Zimmer stayed two more years after '78, but was let go with just a few days to go at the tail end of the 1980 season. Johnny recalls how he felt when the beleaguered manager was terminated. "Zimmer—that broke my heart when he got fired. I don't know what happened there. Sometimes ballplayers have a tendency to run up to management and create a scene. To me, Don Zimmer was as good a manager as we've ever had here." Johnny was asked to step in and close out the season as interim manager.

JOHNNY AS INTERIM MANAGER, 1980

Johnny Pesky was once again manager of the Red Sox, albeit in an interim capacity for the last four games of 1980. But then it seemed that all Red Sox managers were interim managers. Although the list of "permanent" replacements was long and diverse, Pesky's name was not on it.

The "troika" of Red Sox ownership was Haywood Sullivan, Buddy LeRoux and Jean Yawkey. Mrs. Yawkey was a Zimmer supporter, and favored retaining him. But attendance was plummeting. As Zimmer had left the mound one day after changing his pitcher, he faced a crescendo of boos and raised his arms over his head to acknowledge he'd heard them. In a gesture unusually demonstrative for her, Jean Yawkey stood up in her owner's box high atop the stadium and applauded Zimmer. She simply didn't think the Red Sox failures of 1979 and 1980 were his fault—and she was probably right.

Zimmer had won 411 games and lost 304, a .575 winning percentage which only Joe McCarthy topped (among managers who oversaw 300 or more games.) He truly had been made the scapegoat and Jean Yawkey was outvoted. "I'm not blaming Zimmer for anything," Sullivan announced. "In his seven years here as a coach and manager he's never given anything but 100 percent. I don't think we could ever find a more dedicated baseball man." Nonetheless a change was needed. Leigh Montville called Zimmer "the public punching bag [who] always bounced back."

When Johnny Pesky was named interim manager, he spoke out: "I resent people saying we have a country club atmosphere. We're not a country club and there has always been discipline here. Zimmy had a great way with players and his coaching staff. He seemed to know how to handle guys, yet he knew when to back off. Maybe I'm going overboard, but if you don't have feelings about people, what the heck are you doing here?

"Discipline today has to come from within a player. The manager can't quite be the same as it was when you could fine a guy $200 and tell him not to do it again. Nowadays, you have to fill out a letter in triplicate and file a report with Mr. [Marvin] Miller. Zimmer did a good job. But Boston is a tough place to manage. . . . "

The final two games of the year were a doubleheader on October 4. The Red Sox were playing the last-place Blue Jays and had to play 26 innings only to lose both games (the first game ran 17 innings.) The Red Sox finished tied for 4th place, 19 games out of first. It was their lowest position in the standings since 1968, when they had also finished fourth. Pesky's record as interim manager, picking up the pieces, was 1-3.

"It's very discouraging, boys," Johnny summed up to the media. "I don't see how Zimmer put up with it all year." The Red Sox had been 3rd in hitting, but 11th in pitching. Johnny amplified his remarks, in the process again indicating his sympathy for ownership: "I want to say that I still have a great admiration for this ball club. And it's a damn shame that what has gone on this year had to happen to people like Mrs. Yawkey, Sully and Buddy. If somebody had come up to me and said we'd lose 77 games this year, I'd hit them in the mouth. Some things you can foresee. But not this. It still burns me."

Haywood Sullivan said the top priority was "getting back the respect of the fans of New England." The new manager they settled on was "The Major"—Ralph Houk. Johnny did retain his position as coach, working again with Houk for the first time since 1955 in Denver. Houk's tenure was a decent one, by managerial standards—four years—after which he was replaced by John McNamara.

Johnny liked Johnson and admired Zimmer, but he says, "My favorite was Ralph Houk. I told Ralph I wanted to be the new Frank Crosetti. Crosetti had more than twenty opportunities to manage but he said, 'No, I'm happy with the Yankees.'"

Managing is tough, and more so today. "I think it's tougher now than ever before," J.P. said in 2001. "The years I managed we never had to go on the radio with a show every day. Now even the general manager has a show. You've got to be very careful. I'm glad I didn't have to do that because I probably would have said something and got myself in hot water. You have to be honest, but the most important thing a manager has to do is to protect his players."

In 1982, just a couple of weeks after the World Series, Johnny Pesky became very ill and began to lose a lot of weigh quickly, thirty pounds in just two weeks. He dropped as low as 128 pounds and told *Globe* writer Leigh Montville, "I looked at myself in the mirror and couldn't believe it. I looked as if I belonged as the skinny man in the circus. My bones were sticking out all over. I looked as if I were one of those pictures from a famine or something."

Johnny was worried it was cancer but there was no family history and the doctors quickly ruled that out. He spent five weeks in Deaconess Hospital and then ten days in another hospital. "It was all he could do to walk," remembers Ruthie. Finally, Dr. Charles Trey of Deaconess diagnosed the illness as celiac sprue—an allergy to wheat and related foods. He cannot eat anything with gluten in it—nothing made with wheat, rye, barley or oats. It's a hereditary disease, something he'd had in a dormant form all his life, but it chose this time to kick in. There are about 130,000 people in the United States with the disease—celiacs, they are called—and they all have to read labels very carefully. Many vegetable soups, for instance, contain wheat flour. Frozen chicken is often treated with a flour-based product. Celiacs have to be careful in restaurants as well.

"I'm not exactly Tyrone Power," Johnny says, "but I looked like Bela Lugosi." It took him a long time to recover his strength. The whole 1983 season, Johnny really just visited the clubhouse when he could, but wasn't really able to work. He never traveled with the team. "It was awful," he recalls. "I'd sit at home, and we were playing lousy, and I'd be cursing at the television set. Those West Coast games! Two o'clock in the morning and I'd be alone in the room, yelling at some stupid umpire!"

In 1984, though, Johnny was able to return and put in another full season as dugout coach. The Major was happy to have him back. It was to be Houk's last year as manager and Johnny's swan song as a coach.

Lou Gorman had taken over as Red Sox general manager to begin 1984, and after the season, he hired John McNamara as team manager. McNamara elected not to bring Pesky back in '85. He had his own ideas who he wanted on the coaching staff. Both Johnny and Tommy Harper were moved to new positions as special assistant to the general manager, and Johnny held that title through 1992, when he became Special Assistant for Player Development. In 2000 he became a special assignment instructor, along with Charlie Wagner.

"Gorman wanted me to become an assistant to the general manager," Johnny explained, "but I said, 'Lou, I can't sit in an office with a shirt and a tie on.' " Johnny feels that he wasn't being fully utilized. After his coaching years, he's never been able to contribute as much as he believes he can. Under Gorman, Johnny became a roving instructor, reporting directly to the GM. "I like him, but I don't think he used me the best he could. I'm a jock. I belong on the field." Gorman, though, valued

Johnny's work: "I had him go look at kids that we had in the system. I sent him to the minor league clubs to look at some of the top prospects, work with some of the infielders. If we had a trade going on that would involve an infielder, I'd send him to take a look at the kid—on the major league level or on the Triple A level."

Johnny worked at special assignment tasks and continued to do some off-season work in the marketing department. He traveled a fair amount—he went down to Winter Haven, went down to Lynchburg, Pawtucket. He visited various clubs in the Red Sox farm system and worked with the younger prospects there—in the process meeting another generation of future ballplayers on their way up. He did this for several years, right through the end of the 1980s.

1986 was another great year in Red Sox history, though ultimately another frustrating one. This time, the Red Sox had the World Championship in their grasp but for a ball that didn't come up on the bounce and eluded poor Bill Buckner—who'd done about as much as anyone on the team to get the Sox into the Series.

MANAGING AGAIN AT PAWTUCKET, 1990

As a 70-year-old special assistant to the general manager, Johnny was surprised when Lou Gorman asked him to take over the reins at Pawtucket mid-way through the 1990 season. Other than those four games as interim Red Sox manager in 1980, it had been 22 years since he'd last managed—for Columbus in 1968. "We had a problem in Pawtucket," Lou Gorman explained. "Our manager there, Ed Nottle, had been there for a number of years and had done a good job for us. But I think he thought he had a chance to manage the big league club for us. When we extended Joe Morgan's contract earlier this year, Nottle seemed to lose his enthusiasm. He stopped having workouts and the players weren't progressing."

Johnny thus became the oldest manager in organized baseball at the time.

Old friend Sam Mele took advantage of the occasion to poke a little fun at Pesky and Pawtucket. He got some stationery from a nursing home in the area and wrote to Mike Tamburro, the Pawsox president, thanking him for "getting an old guy out of the home to manage." Mele's letter added that the home would send a van to McCoy Stadium to pick Johnny up after games and would "keep the light on in case he stays out late."

Johnny was surprised at what he found in Pawtucket. "They had a manager down there that just didn't want to do anything. You've got to make preparation." I go down there and the first three or four days I saw terrible baseball. I said, 'Ah, shit.' We won one and we lost one, and now we go to Rochester. I think they ripped us in the first game pretty good, but the next three games we had a pretty good chance to win all three of them but we wind up blowing them on stupid little things. So the last day, when the game was over the last night, I told the clubhouse kid, 'Shut the door, I have something I want to tell the players.' So I said, 'Lookit, there's something wrong here. Goddamn it. You guys can't be that bad. There's enough guys here that we like and should be doing much better, but there's a reason here, there's something wrong. Now we're going back to Pawtucket tomorrow and I want everybody in uniform at 1 o'clock.' They said, 'OK,' so I said, 'Grab your sandwiches,' and we got on the bus to Pawtucket.

"They were all there waiting for me. I explained to them, I said, 'OK, lookit. Pitchers aren't fielding their position. They're not getting over. Cutoff men. Outfielders are watching guys run the bases instead of going to the ball' and all this sort of thing. Just little things. So I did a drill with the pitchers. I did just a quick one, a refresher, and then I did it with the infielders and the outfield.

"The next day I brought the infield back and I got alongside of them and told them, now, this is what I want you to do. When you catch the ball, so many times you're hurrying too much when you don't have to. Especially when you've got a good arm, you use your arm. Naehring was there. Cooper was there. Mo Vaughn was there. John Flaherty and Phil Plantier in the outfield. They were good players.

"The third day I brought the outfield out. I'm in the outfield and I'm running alongside of them and I say, 'Look, the ball's hit down the corner, the shortstop's going to be the cutoff man. I want you to get to the ball. Get to the ball. Get the ball and throw it to the cutoff man. I don't care if he's five feet in front of you or fifty feet in front of you—you give him the ball.' I said, 'When the runner sees that, he stops. We're giving these people four or five outs an inning. We're never going to win a game!'

"The next day I bring the pitchers out and I worked their asses off. They'd start, now, kind of kidding around, they think they're getting to know me a little bit so they're bullshitting with me pretty good. A couple of them are fooling around with our drill, so I said, 'OK, now you, you go down and stand in the coach's box. Until we get this done right, you're staying out there.' I said, 'Boys, that's my penalty box.'

"So now I get these three guys back on the mound and I says, 'You ain't gonna leave here until you do this right. Just catch the ball and give it to the catcher. Don't be in such a hurry. They've got to run ninety feet and all you've got to do is run ten.' We kind of turned things around.

"I lost Naehring in about a week; Joe Morgan needed him. There was a good-looking catcher, John Flaherty; we should never have traded him. Goddamn. Good hitter, good thrower. He went over to San Diego. I was always partial to the young players. Our pitching wasn't as good as it could have been. I wish I'd have gone a month earlier. We might have had a shot."

The club went 32-41 under Johnny, but Paw Sox P.R. executive Bill Wanless notes that "Johnny had no real decent pitchers to work with—and therein lay the problem." Lou Gorman says that Pesky wanted to go back the next year but "at that point in his life, I thought maybe he'd be better doing special assistant things—coming to the big league camp, working with some of the young kids." Lou realized that sometimes Johnny's recommendations had to be put in perspective. "He was such a very positive guy. He was never a negative guy. If he had any faults, he would be overboard in his judgment of players. He rates everybody high. You'd have to interpolate his judgment because he liked every player. When I sent him to Pawtucket, I thought we had 19 prospects! I thought he would just do it for a couple of weeks, but he had such enthusiasm, it was like he was thirty. He's that kind of guy and I love that positive attitude in him."

It was Johnny's last stint. From 1991 forward, he's been a Special Assistant for Player Development, keeping as active as he can and contributing what he can, working with the younger players in spring training and throughout the regular season with the two Red Sox minor league clubs within relatively easy driving distance, at both Pawtucket and Lowell. Johnny has long been the unofficial ambassador for the Red Sox, an elder statesman representing the team and ready to help out in any way he can.

Johnny has been a fixture at Red Sox Fantasy Camps since they began. Dave Mulvey, a Fantasy Camp regular, first met Johnny at camp in 1988 and hasn't missed a year since. "Johnny is famous down there for his fungo bat, whether you're playing on his team or against them. It's like a third leg for him. He'll go on the sidelines and he'd start hitting fungoes to you out in the outfield. I grew up in Pawtucket and we started talking about that. Some of the coaches didn't really care a whole lot. They were just there. But Johnny was always very active. He'd coach fielding and hitting. He'd be giving you tips all the time. People were constantly coming over and asking him for help. He'd be standing there by the batting cage and you wouldn't know if he was concentrating on the hitter or not. He'd be standing there with the fungo bat, hitting fly balls out to the guys in the field, and all of a sudden, boy, he'd drop his bat and he'd jump in the cage, 'Naw. That's not how you do it. You do it like this.' The campers loved it. Johnny is always one of the more active pros down there. He really plays it up pretty good down there. He really likes to get involved.

"Our last game of the week, we play against the pros. Special rules. They only get two outs. I was pitching the one inning, starting the game. Up comes Johnny. Back then he was about 70. I figure I can get him out. I threw him my best 60-mile-an-hour fastball. He absolutely smoked the ball right up through the middle on me.

"His favorite thing when people are in the clubhouse is to just set up a stool and start telling stories. All of a sudden, there's liable to be twenty people sitting there. They'll literally have to say, 'Come on Johnny, let's break this up. We've got to get people out there.' He would just sit there and tell stories for hours and hours and hours. It really was just about the highlight of the camp. One time he looked over at me and said, 'Boy, Dave, I love telling these stories. Some of them are even true.' Everybody cracked up.

"He's been telling me now the last five years, 'I think this is going to be my last year.'

"All he wanted was just to sit on the end of the dugout bench during the games. Hit some fungoes beforehand. I think in the back of his mind he's probably hanging on as long as he is, hoping that maybe he can get that one last year—when Duquette's gone or Williams is gone, or whoever—and maybe the next administration would let him do that. I think maybe if he could get that one last year in, he might retire. Really, his only job in his life has been baseball, other than when he was in the service. He just lives it."

Johnny says of Fantasy Camp, "It's just a bunch of old timers. You have to be 30 or over. We have some guys in their seventies who play. One year we had a son who was in his sixties and his father who was deep in his eighties. They have a kangaroo court that Radatz and Bell do. It's really something. Everything they get from the kangaroo court, they send it to the Jimmy Fund. A lot of times you get a couple of rich guys down there and if they get a pretty good pot, they match the pot."

Dave Mulvey notes that Johnny gets fined often (as do most

people)—fined for sitting down while coaching, for example. "It adds up!" Johnny laughs.

"It's a lot of fun," Johnny enthuses. It's baseball, and Johnny Pesky thrives on anything that lets him put on his Red Sox uniform and enjoy the company of other men. Every winter he looks forward to this very first breath of spring, which precedes formal spring training.

25

The Late 1990s

While Lou Gorman was G.M., Pesky talked with him almost every day. During the Kevin Kennedy years, Johnny was always welcome on the field and in the dugout at Fenway. It was a nice way to continue to contribute to the big league club. There was a sharp contrast between Gorman—who clearly sought Pesky's judgment and utilized him productively—and Gorman's successor Dan Duquette, who gave no feedback and who left Johnny wondering if anyone was even reading his reports. One gets the impression that Duquette's implied message was "don't call me; I'll call you." And he never did.

From '92 through '96 when Hobson and Kennedy were managing, Johnny wasn't officially a coach, although he was on the field. When Butch Hobson replaced Joe Morgan in 1992, Johnny sat on the bench during games, but because of a league rule limiting the number of coaches, he was not officially a coach. He'd often suit up, hit fungoes and then head upstairs. "People just assumed he was a coach, maybe even since Babe Ruth was with the team, which wasn't true but made a good story." (1)

In April 1997, a media firestorm broke out when Johnny Pesky was "banned from the bench." When the story broke, it sounded like another ill-considered episode in a string of public relations blunders. Johnny Pesky, who'd been with the Red Sox since 1942, suddenly banned from the bench for no good reason? An arbitrary move by a new Grinch-like general manager who sneered at tradition? It was front-page news in the

Boston Globe. Dan Shaughnessy opened the page one story, "In the latest cold, cowardly, corporate move of the Dan Duquette regime, 77-year-old Red Sox lifer Johnny Pesky has been told he's not welcome in the Boston dugout anymore. 'It hurts me quite a bit to be honest with you,' Pesky said last night from his home in Greater Boston."

Mo Vaughn was "angry" and said, "How can you let No. 6 not be around the kids? He does nothing but help them. He likes to be there for them. Johnny Pesky gave his heart and soul to the Boston Red Sox. He should be here with us, on the road with us, talking with us . . . if anybody should be here, it's him." Spokesman Kevin Shea and field manager Jimy Williams both characterized it as a decision of the organization, not of any one man. VP John Buckley noted, "Johnny Pesky has a longstanding commitment from the Red Sox organization to be paid for the rest of his life." He added, "We're looking to have him refocus his role in the community, which is of major importance to the Red Sox."

When the Red Sox opened at home a few days later, Gordon Edes reported that the club and Pesky had agreed to have him as low profile as possible, presumably not to detract from the Opening Day festivities. "Officially, the 77-year-old Pesky is happy that that Red Sox will no longer allow him to hit fungoes before home games, or sit in the dugout, as he had for the last three years," Edes wryly noted. The Red Sox told him he's welcome to visit triple A Pawtucket and single A Lowell Spinners, "but otherwise, his only link with the big league club is to conduct clinics and make other public appearances."

Johnny had no warm feelings for G.M. Duquette. He never felt welcomed but, then again, Duquette left a lot of people feeling underappreciated. The new G.M. was a couple of generations removed from players of Johnny's era and had his own ways of doing things. One might not blame him for thinking that some of the old-timers were just hanging around the ballpark taking up space—or, worse, confusing younger players by offering outdated theories. Johnny was still sending in reports from his work in the field, evaluating players but his reports were sent in longhand, not via e-mail, with the language and style of days gone by, not using the latest lingo. Johnny mailed in the reports but never received any feedback. Were the reports just getting tossed in the trash on arrival? How do you know, if you don't get feedback? There is something very poignant about a veteran who loves the game so much, who is out there sincerely looking at players and trying to help them out even as age begins to catch up with him, who has so much to offer, but does not feel valued.

This all could have been true. But over the years Duquette has indeed shown a reverence for Red Sox tradition, going out of his way to bring back players such as Carlton Fisk, Dwight Evans and Luis Tiant into the fold. True, these are the players who Duquette himself followed as a fan when he was young. On his watch, too, the Red Sox Hall of Fame was initiated and the graphics used on tickets and team publications reflected a respect for tradition. Would someone with this degree of respect for Red Sox history go out of his way for no apparent reason to order Johnny Pesky—Mr. Red Sox—off the field, in a move sure to provoke negative reaction? Something about the notion just didn't compute.

There was the initial thought that Pesky had perhaps become too close to Kevin Kennedy and perhaps Jimy Williams was concerned to keep him a little further away from the players. "Why should that have anything to do with it?" Johnny asked, quite reasonably. "Yes, we were close. But would I be disloyal? They could fire me tomorrow and I would never have anything but respect for them." He added, "I like Jimy Williams very much; he's a great kid. I hope he has success."

Understandably Johnny felt hurt. The fact that the story broke in the first place was probably due to his mentioning it to newspapermen. Johnny is well aware of the power of the media, and has always had a considerable number of friends in the press and broadcast end of the business. Duquette never responded, perhaps to his credit. Were the Red Sox concerned that Johnny was getting too old and might suffer a stroke on the field? Was there some concern for Johnny, or about his health, or the team's insurance liability? Not at all, according to team medical personnel. What really happened here?

Neither Jimy Williams nor Dan Duquette would answer the question directly. The real story may have begun under manager Kevin Kennedy. Kennedy did let Johnny travel with the team, work out on the field and sometimes sit on the bench during games. In his second year as Red Sox manager, it was supposedly Kennedy—not Duquette—who told Johnny: "No more road trips."

Johnny was said to have sometimes nodded off on the dugout bench during the game. At least one person who had regular business in the clubhouse has suggested that Johnny was a little set in his ways and that there was also some sense that he was just "in the way." Sometimes, he may have been a little too free with his opinions. He might be sitting next to a young player on the bench—perhaps the teacher in him leads to his always preferring to spend time with the youngest players—and when an aggressive batter at the plate would swing at a pitch at the ankles, Johnny might comment, "Goddamn it! He's got to learn to take a pitch once in a while!" That candid comment might get back to the batter, and supposedly a couple of more veteran players complained to Kennedy near the end of the 1996 season. The stage was probably set well before Jimy Williams was brought on board to replace Kennedy.

Jimy Williams was more of an old-time baseball guy and really liked Johnny Pesky. But Pesky wasn't really necessary and Williams wasn't about to buck a decision that had already been made; there was no percentage in that for a new manager coming on the scene. Jimy used to like to hit fungoes himself before the game; it was both a way of keeping active and also creating a barrier between himself and the media. He was working and not approachable. A couple of times in spring training his first year, there'd just be too many people hitting fungoes and Williams would almost have to elbow his way in. In some ways the ban on Pesky suited him, too.

Lou Gorman, though, doubted it was either the players ("the players seem to love him—he was so well-liked.") Jimy Williams commented, "I like Johnny Pesky a lot. He's been tremendous with me. I've enjoyed many conversations with him, this year as well as other years. I respect his ability and evaluation of players. He has great work ethic. Loved to hit fungoes, ground balls . . . loves to be around baseball players. I have tremendous respect for Johnny Pesky. He loves the Red Sox. He's been an influence on young players. He teaches and talks with young players. It doesn't matter what level they're playing at. He likes to be around baseball players that like to play. I spent five good years with Johnny Pesky. I'm the lucky one."

For Johnny, even though he felt hurt, this may have offered an outcome that was not as bad as it might seem. Appearances count, and Johnny came off looking good. He was portrayed as a martyr embodying old-time baseball traditions against a heartless, clueless G.M. who ran him off the field. In a way, he got out looking better than had he held on and held on, fading away and maybe embarrassing himself in some fashion.

And all's well that ends well. Johnny has remained vital. He dressed with the teams at Pawtucket and at Lowell. Manager Arnie Beyeler of the Spinners had nothing but good things to say about Johnny and the contributions he offered some of the young prospects. Johnny will often attend Red Sox home games and spend the game upstairs watching from one of the Red Sox executive boxes. He doesn't nod off, or show any signs at all of lack of energy. The idea that some players resented Pesky's candid comments seems more plausible than the notion that Duquette unreasonably and arbitrarily decided to prohibit him from suiting up before the game. If correct, one has to credit parties such as Duquette and Jimy Williams for not being explicit; their choice to forego comment may have spared Johnny further hurt.

Johnny's record of 205 hits as a Red Sox rookie stood for 55 years. It was tied and broken on Johnny's 78th birthday, September 27, 1997, and Johnny couldn't even watch the game on TV since it was a Fox broadcast from Toronto, blacked out in favor of another game. Johnny listened on radio, and afterwards called the man who broke his record, Nomar Garciaparra, at the team hotel to congratulate him. Nomar had three hits that day—a home run, a double and a single, ending the day with 207. "I'm so proud of that kid," Johnny told Gordon Edes. "I got goosebumps listening to it." For his part, Nomar said, "It's real nice to know that Pesky had the record before, knowing Johnny and what a great individual he is. I wish he was here to share it with me. He's always pulling for me, he was such a good influence. The kind of person he is, it means more to me, breaking something like that."

Johnny realizes he's near the end of his years, but longs to stay active. "There's only one other guy who did the same things I did, but for the Cardinals. [George Kissell was coach for the Cardinals from 1969–1975.] Now he just sits in the dugout and goes everywhere. He's got his name on the uniform and travels with the team. He's older than I am. His health is good. When your health is good, you can do a lot of things.

"I know in a couple more years I've got to get off the field. Age is starting to tell on me a little bit. I hate to give in on it, but what the hell—it's happened. I don't want to get to be a pain in the neck. So far my memory is decent. I'd hate like hell to be a pain in the neck. This guy's hanging on, and all this. I'm sure they're saying it now."

The Red Sox continue to take care of Johnny financially. The checks just keep coming, even though Johnny readily admits he hasn't signed a contract in ten years. "I'm inclined to believe that when O'Connell was here, he took care of a lot of us. He took care of Charlie, Pop and me."

When Johnny worked in the front office all those years, others had a pension but he did not. "I think Mrs. Yawkey set up something for the rest of my life. I've never signed a contract [but] I'm doing better financially than I was as a player. That's one of the reasons I never wanted to leave the Red Sox."

Johnny does get money from Major League Baseball. "That helped me a lot! I have a pension from the Red Sox, but I haven't done anything with it. If I take my pension, then my salary stops. The major league pension I had to take, because I needed the money. I put David through college and got him a car. Ten, fifteen grand to me was a lot of money. If I was a Hall of Famer, I'd go to just two card shows a month and I'd make as much money as I did when I was playing."

When the sale of the team took place in 2002, and the Yawkey era officially ended, Johnny officially retired from the old Red Sox. New principal owner John Henry called Johnny at home and invited him to spring training. He's been made welcome at Fenway ever since.

"I've had a very interesting life. It's been a good life, really. It could have been financially better, but I have no complaints. For the type of player I was, I wasn't paid handsomely, but I was paid adequately. We paid our bills. There's no such thing as the good ol' days. Who gives a crap? Today's a good day! Tomorrow might be even better. That's the way you have to look at it."

Johnny has always been a very sociable man; he clearly enjoys people and they enjoy being with him. He can always be found chatting with fans, whatever field he's on. There are also a couple of long-established rituals he faithfully follows. One is the annual Johnny Pesky Friendship Dinner, held a few days before spring training. In the early 1950s, a group of fourteen or fifteen of Johnny's friends from the Lynn area put together a dinner at Hawthorn's in Lynn on the eve of Johnny's departure for Spring training. It's an all-male event attended by about 300 men, a vestige of another era—though an event as tame as can be. Dick Flavin needled Needlenose at the 51st Annual Friendship Dinner in late January, 2003, saying, "For 51 years people have been getting together to celebrate the fact that Johnny Pesky is leaving town."

The 50th dinner was held, as have been the last several, at Nandee's on Market Street in Lynn. A large ice sculpture of Johnny's number "6" graced one end of the hall, and the head tables were full—a sold-out event.

Johnny also has had his own "breakfast club" for the last ten years or so. Every morning, at the Bickford's down the road from his house, he gathers with a diverse groups of friends at 7 AM. One of Johnny's oldest friends in Boston—shipbuilder Joe Sanchez—attends. Joe was one of the original fourteen or fifteen guys at the first Friendship Dinner. Manufacturers rep Buzz Martin is a veteran breakfast club member as are Bob Grant, the Assistant Clerk of Courts in Salem, and Earl Weissman, a Beverly attorney who met Johnny back in 1948. Jordan Goldman, an accountant—whose father used to idolize Johnny—joined the group more recently.

Late in 2001, concerned about Ted Williams' health, Johnny sat in the back seat of Dom DiMaggio's car while Dominic and Dick Flavin shared the driving. Dom was heading for Florida, as he does each winter. Ted was seriously ill, and the three decided to drive down to visit. It was a wonderful visit, enjoyed by all three, and written up in a very warm *Boston Globe* story by Dan Shaughnessy as "the ultimate road trip." David Halberstam later crafted his book *The Teammates* around the road trip. The visit was a tonic for all involved. Johnny almost teared-up when first seeing the gaunt, thin Williams. But Ted seemed to come back to life, drawing strength from the camaraderie of his visitors. They enjoyed talking and had a wonderful time. "I had such a good feeling," Johnny told Shaughnessy. "Dom, me, and Teddy. It's like we were kids again, you know?" Train trips aside, the old teammates may have become much closer in later years than they ever were while actually in uniform, but they'd shared so many experiences over the years that the "four from the Coast"—DiMaggio, Doerr, Pesky and Williams—formed a quartet that we'll almost certainly never see again.

NOTES

(1) *A Red Sox Journal*, Spring 1997

26

Mr. Red Sox

On Opening Day April 1, 2002, Johnny was introduced by P.A. announcer Ed Brickley as a "Boston legend." He lined up with the rest of the Red Sox team and coaches on the first base line in pre-game introductions and when the 2002 Super Bowl Champion New England Patriots team threw out the first balls, one of them flipped a ball to Johnny. It was the start of a wonderful season for Johnny Pesky, a season he could not have foreseen just three months earlier.

In 2001, it looked as though Johnny Pesky's years with the Red Sox were going to end in disappointment, leaving Mr. Red Sox feeling discarded and disrespected. For a man who spent so much of his life as the personification of the Boston Red Sox to feel unwanted at Fenway was bordering on the tragic. Johnny's love for the Red Sox now seemed unrequited. He still wanted to contribute, to make a difference, to feel useful but Duquette's reign left him only feeling empty.

Although the management in Pawtucket and Lowell welcomed his leadership and let him know it, a courtesy acknowledgement by G. M. Duquette, a query about a prospect, a note of thanks for his inspiration and work as ambassador would have meant a lot to Pesky. Those courtesies were not forthcoming.

Pesky knew time was passing him by, but he still had his health, still had his faculties and enough wisdom to know that the truths about baseball are eternal—that baseball can't just be reduced to a computer model. After more than seven decades in the game, Johnny knew in his heart that he still had something to offer to players young enough to be his grandchildren.

Fortunately, the John W. Henry leadership group understood and valued the importance of tradition to Red Sox Nation. Larry Lucchino had a natural instinct for the appeal of nostalgia, manifest in his development of Camden Yards during his tenure in Baltimore. Tom Werner revered Fenway Park even from his college days in Boston, and had honed in Hollywood an appreciation for just how viscerally people respond to the sense of continuity that binds baseball fans to the sport they love. Public relations man Dr. Charles Steinberg was a master of his craft, always providing the right touch and striking the right note in the public arena. Like so many Red Sox teams before, they needed Johnny Pesky.

The new group needed to forge a sense of legitimacy with the Red Sox fan base, and one move among many was to welcome back Johnny Pesky. It was a feel good/can't lose proposition and one they embraced effortlessly, to Johnny's considerable pleasure. They made an old ballplayer feel wanted again.

Much to Johnny's dismay, the role they had in mind for him was that of consultant. "I told Bresh [Dick Bresciani], 'Jesus. It makes me sound like a pompous ass. Just make me out an instructor.' "

Johnny understood that his role was marginal. He never wanted to overstep his bounds. But now he felt welcome once more. His locker is the last one on the left as you exit the clubhouse, and all the players give him a nod, poke a little fun at him, banter a bit—and he gives it right back. His enthusiasm and love for the game help engender a more positive feeling in the clubhouse and that is no small matter. And Johnny Pesky felt loved by the players. It brought a renewed sense of dignity and acceptance.

Trot Nixon told Karen Guregian of the *Boston Herald*, "This is where he belongs, right here at Fenway." Nomar Garciaparra, with whom Johnny had worked more closely, spoke more bluntly, "It means a lot to us to have him back. We missed him. I was sad when they wouldn't let him dress up. I thought that was absolutely wrong. I honestly think he should be out there [in the dugout] throughout the games. There should be a grandfather clause or something. I mean, here's a guy who's given so much to the game, and still wants to be around it. Why don't we give him the respect to be able to go out there? I think he deserves to be out there. He just wants to be out there and support us."

Lou Merloni chipped in, "It's great having a guy like him around, in uniform, in the clubhouse, and out in the field for batting practice hitting ground balls. He's always been there for us with words of encouragement, and we enjoy being around him."

Nomar elaborated, "I listen to him, and listen to his stories That's what it's all about. When you see guys like Johnny Pesky . . . it teaches guys what it means to put on this uniform. There's a respect when you go out, and when you put the uniform on for what you represent. It's not only yourself, but the people in the past who have worn the uniform. Great people like him." (1)

In 2002, Johnny made it to every single home game at Fenway. "I went down to Pawtucket early in the season and never did get back there. They claim I went 'big league' on them," Johnny chuckles. Number 6 accompanied the team on one road trip—to Seattle and Minnesota, and brother Vincent came up to visit when the team was in Seattle. All in all, it was a season to enjoy—except for the fact that the Red Sox fell short once again.

The Red Sox royal, complete with his fungo bat scepter, was back in his Fenway castle.

Should Johnny Pesky have been in the Hall of Fame? He had the fourth highest batting average ever for a shortstop [through 1991, anyway].

[re: Hall of Fame.] "They take your ten best years. That's the way they're supposed to do it. Now I can't even get into the old-timer's group [Veteran's Committee]. Jesus Christ, when you look at my stats compared to Reese or Rizzuto, they're better. A lot of guys would say, 'I got screwed.' But this doesn't bother me. I grew up in the Depression years.

"Rizzuto was a good player. A lot of people say that his stats weren't appropriate for the [Hall of Fame]. If you compare us for ten years, my stats were better. I don't resent that he got more [attention and consideration by virtue of being in New York.] I heard they talked about me in the Veterans' Committee and said, 'Good player, but . . . ' I said, 'Don't worry about it. That doesn't worry me.' I wish I could have had maybe two or three more years. If I hadn't gone into the Navy, I'll guarantee you . . . I might not have got 200 hits but I would have got anywhere from 180 on up. I was still young. I lost my 22nd, 23rd and 24th birthdays. I was 25 from I came back. And I got to 30 real quick. Those middle infielders back then didn't play ten or twelve years.

"I wasn't the greatest player but my peers thought I was a decent player, and that's good enough for me."

"It was fun," Johnny said. "Joe Cochran and all the kids around the clubhouse treated me like royalty. I was in my element. I was very, very happy. I couldn't ask for anything more. I felt more like part of the ball club than I have for 6 or 7 years. I talked to Grady [Little] a lot. He'd come down and visit with me. I was paying a lot of attention to Shea [Hillenbrand], about his fielding. He made such an improvement. You don't like to put too much in a young player's head. But Shea was so good. He'd ask questions and you'd try to answer them. He only made one real mistake, when he threw the ball blindly one time and the guy went to second and eventually scored. When he came back off that trip, he came in the clubhouse and of course he run into me and he says, 'Johnny, I thought about you.' I says, 'Well, listen, they tell me Babe Ruth threw to the wrong base. All the great players . . . this game is not perfect.' He works so hard and he's such a great kid."

In late May, 2003, though leading the Sox with runs batted in, Hillenbrand was traded to the Arizona Diamondbacks for pitcher Byung-Hyun Kim. A trade of Hillenbrand had been rumored all winter and spring, but never triggered. Just when everything had gone quiet, Johnny appeared at a book signing for *The Teammates* by David Halberstam at the Charles Hotel in Cambridge. Someone in the audience asked Johnny what he thought of the Sox so far that season, and he said he felt good about it, but then declared that if Hillenbrand was traded, "I'll quit. I've got my letter all ready for Mr. Lucchino." A reporter was present and the remark appeared in the next day's *Globe*. Within 24 hours of that, Shea was sent west and Johnny was on the spot.

"I was damn near tears," Pesky told Gordon Edes. This was a young player he'd worked with a lot, more on the defensive placement of his feet while in the field than anything to do with his batting. Johnny reached Shea by phone, and the young protege assured the veteran that it might be a good trade for both teams. "Shea thanked me for all the patience I'd had with him," Pesky told Edes. "I told him that I considered him like my own son. He said, 'You've been very good to me.' I was gulping like a damn schoolgirl." It was a loss because in some ways Hillenbrand was like Pesky. "He made himself a player," Johnny explained. A hard worker, the kind of player Johnny had been, and admired. Shea told Johnny not to quit, and Johnny thought better of the impulse. Besides, as Gordon Edes wrote, crediting Johnny's writer friend Maureen from Lynn, "Just what job would he quit from? How do you quit being Johnny Pesky?" This is the same Johnny Pesky who, asked to name his favorite book in 1982, replied, "the *Boston Red Sox Media Guide*."

On Johnny's birthday in 2002, the Red Sox asked him to take out the lineup card before the game. "Grady says, 'Here, you take the lineup card.' We won that night. The players were great. Baerga and Manny, and of course Nomar's my pet. They all are. Pedro. I hadn't done that for a long time. I felt like a big wheel that night. The people were very kind to me."

Is the day ever going to come when Johnny will hang up his spikes for good? "I'm sure when I get to be 85, that'll be it," he says. "I'll just retire and become a fan. If Jimmie Reese did it in his 90s, I can do it 'til I'm 85, 86." Of course, it doesn't take but a moment until one begins to realize that any designated date might provide a little flexibility. "When I was 75, I said, 'When I'm 80, I'm gonna get out.' When I was 80, that went to 82. Now I'm 82, now I put it to 85. If your health is good, you can do it. I think that's kept me going."

Johnny Pesky would never be a Connie Mack; he loves to put on the uniform. He loves being out on the ballfield with a fungo bat in his hand—even if he's no longer as active with it as he once was. He loves sitting in the clubhouse with baseball preparation going on all around him, where some of the younger Dominican players will come by and give him a good-natured hug and call him "Papi."

This is an humble man who wants nothing more out of life than to be around ballparks with baseball players. He doesn't want to be some executive assistant with a sinecure on the Sox. He wants to be field level. In a uniform, not in a necktie. And even if it's just hitting out a dozen grounders before a game or swapping a few stories or tossing off a few gibes and one-liners to the ballplayers as they pass by, he's welcomed— and loved—by the clubhouse staff and by the players, and by the fans. He fits in, no longer a major cog perhaps, but still a crucial cog.

After all, how do you stop being Johnny Pesky?

NOTES

(1) Karen Guregian, "The Pesky Poll," *Boston Herald*, June 2, 2002

JOHNNY PESKY MAJOR LEAGUE CAREER STATS

YEAR		G	AB	R	H	2B	3B	HR	RBI	BB	SO	AVG	OBP	SLG	OPS	FA
1942	BOS	147	620	105	205	29	9	2	51	42	36	.331	.375	.416	791	.955
1943	military															
1944	military															
1945	military															
1946	BOS	153	621	115	208	43	4	2	55	65	29	.335	.401	.427	827	.969
1947	BOS	155	638	106	207	27	8	0	39	72	22	.324	.393	.392	785	.976
1948	BOS	143	565	124	159	26	6	3	55	99	32	.281	.394	.365	759	.951
1949	BOS	148	604	111	185	27	7	2	69	100	19	.306	.408	.384	792	.970
1950	BOS	127	490	112	153	22	6	1	49	104	31	.312	.437	.388	825	.974
1951	BOS	131	480	93	150	20	6	3	41	84	15	.313	.417	.398	815	.961
1952	BOS	25	67	10	10	2	0	0	2	15	5	.149	.313	.179	492	.917
	DET	69	177	26	45	4	0	1	9	41	11	.254	.394	.294	688	.952
	Tot	94	244	36	55	6	0	1	11	56	16	.225	.372	.262	634	.953
1953	DET	103	308	43	90	22	1	2	24	27	10	.292	.353	.390	743	.991
1954	DET	20	17	5	3	0	0	1	1	3	1	.176	.300	.353	653	.000
	WAS	49	158	17	40	4	3	0	9	10	7	.253	.298	.316	614	.979
	Tot	69	175	22	43	4	3	1	10	13	8	.246	.298	.320	618	.979
Career		1270	4745	867	1455	226	50	17	404	662	218	.307	.394	.386	780	.964

INDEX

A

Abel, Larry 67
Aitkenhead, "Airtight" Andy 44, 45
Alexander, Dale 60
Alevizos, John 79
Alou, Matty 242
Andres, Ernie 43
Avila, Bobby 185

B

Baker, Del 18, 255
Barrett, Marty 103
Bartell, Dick 96, 128
Barwick, Bill 66
Batts, Matt 122, 145, 158, 161
Bauer, Hank 129
Becker, Joe 24
Bell, Billy 68, 69
Bell, Gary 263
Benevento, Dick 3, 19
Benevento, Richard "Rocky" 17–19, 24, 201
Benza, Al 179, 180
Berger, Wally 24
Berra, Yogi 125, 170, 198, 229
Bertolami, Sal 254
Beyeler, Arnie 268
Boone, Ray 151, 163, 166
Boudreau, Lou 58–61, 86, 125, 142–156, 211, 216, 250
Bouton, Jim 217
Brecheen, Harry 42
Bresciani, Dick 273
Bressoud, Eddie 198, 203, 206, 209, 213, 221, 228, 233
Broadbent, Dick 87
Brock, Lou 232
Broeg, Bob 92, 96
Brown, Bobby 139
Brown, Mace 68, 235
Bubalo, John 3, 27
Buckner, Bill 89
Buddin, Don 198
Burleson, Rick 251
Burwell, Bill 41–3
Busby, Jim 167

C

Camilli, Doug 177
Castiglione, Joe 246
Center, Pete 83
Cepeda, Orlando 242
Chandler, Spud 56, 57
Cisco, Galen 187, 188
Clemente, Roberto 240, 241
Clinton, Lou 187, 203, 213, 216, 218, 221, 227, 228, 231
Cobb, Ty 85, 112

Cochrane, Mickey 16, 18, 145
Coleman, Joe 65, 66
Coleman, Ken 247–249, 252
Collins, Eddie 45, 51, 52, 55, 61, 62, 68, 75, 77
Combs, Earl 141
Conigliaro, Tony 80, 221, 225–238, 250
Conley, Gene 208, 212–215, 219, 225
Cooper, Scott 261
Cronin, Joe 41, 45, 48–53, 75, 76, 81–87, 92, 96, 100, 102, 106, 108, 117, 120, 143, 155, 156, 235, 255
Culberson, Leon 91–95
Cuyler, Kiki 121, 125

D

Daly, Tom 71, 255
Dark, Alvin 138, 208
Delock, Ike 153, 208, 212, 213, 220
Dickey, Bill 55, 72, 221
Dillinger, Bob 125, 126
DiMaggio, Dominic (Dom) 1, 14, 24, 49, 53–57, 60, 62, 64, 68, 74, 76, 83–85, 90–92, 94, 97, 102, 118, 121, 124, 126, 135, 136, 138, 144–149, 151–153, 215, 271
DiMaggio, Joe 24, 105, 114, 124, 126, 135, 143, 147, 238, 241
Dobson, Joe 52, 68, 110, 114, 115, 121, 137
Doby, Larry 102, 148
Doerr, Bobby 14, 24, 25, 49, 52, 57, 60–62, 67, 74, 76, 78, 81, 82, 84, 85, 90, 93–95, 100, 102, 103, 109, 110, 112, 114, 117, 121, 129, 135, 136, 138, 139, 141, 142, 145, 147–152, 161, 172, 198, 235, 271
Doherty, Ed 54, 75
Dorish, Harry 190, 201, 205, 207, 211, 219, 220, 233, 237
Dropo, Walt 136–142, 145, 152–157, 161, 250
Duquette, Dan 263, 265, 266, 269, 272
Dykes, Eddie 92

E

Earley, Arnold 188, 189, 191, 214
Easter, Luke 148
Ellis, Dock 243, 244
Embree, Red 86
Erautt, Ed or Joe 16, 32, 99
Evans, Dwight 251, 267
Evers, Hoot 128, 145, 154, 155

F

Fazio, Ernie 209
Feller, Bob 54, 57, 81, 86, 100, 103, 104, 115, 147, 190, 247
Ferriss, Dave 74, 84, 96, 105, 110, 121, 123
Finney, Lou 49, 60
Fisk, Carlton 253, 254, 267
Flavin, Dick 270, 271
Ford, Whitey 229
Fowler, Dick 78
Foxx, Jimmie 49, 52, 82

Franciskovich, Bill 70
Frederick, Johnny 25, 39
Friend, Owen 161, 162
G
Galehouse, Denny 116
Garciaparra, Nomar 60, 269, 273, 274
Garver, Ned 149
Geary, Huck 42
Geiger, Gary 213, 216, 218, 225, 230
Gile, Don 179, 187, 193, 194
Goldman, Jordan 270, 271
Gomez, Lefty 21
Gonzales, Mike 92, 93
Goodman, Billy 108, 114, 136–140, 146, 147,
    151–153
Gordon, Joe 18, 30, 56, 61
Gorman, Lou 76, 259, 260, 262, 265, 268
Gowdy, Curt 148
Grant, Bob 270
Gray, Dave 227
Green, Pumpsie 192, 196, 227
Greenberg, Hank 141, 161
Gregory, L. H. 20, 21, 24
Gremp, Buddy 65
Grieve, Bill 129, 130
Griffith, Clark 111, 166, 235
Groat, Dick 206
H
Haefner, Mickey 88
Haney, Fred 18
Harder, Mel 219
Harper, Tommy 259
Harridge, Will 113
Harris, Bucky 235
Harris, Mickey 68, 102, 103, 105, 110, 121, 123, 250
Hatfield, Fred 143, 152, 155–157, 161–163, 165
Hebner, Richie 243, 244, 251
Held, Woodie 170, 172
Henrich, Tommy 56, 58, 129
Henry, John W. 270, 273
Herman, Billy 191, 198, 201, 205, 230, 235–237, 239,
    240
Herzog, Whitey 170, 172
Hickey, Jackie 128
Higgins, Mike "Pinky" 24, 93, 94, 188, 196–199, 201,
    204–209, 218–222, 225–233, 235–237, 241
Hillenbrand, Shea 275
Hitchcock, Billy 42, 111, 115, 200, 230
Hobson, Butch 255, 265
Hoderlein, Mel 166
Holcombe, Ken 156
Honochick, Jim 154
Horton, Tony 208, 227
Houk, Ralph 129, 169–172, 200, 205, 215, 216, 249,
    254, 258, 259
Howard, Elston 213

Hriniak, Walt 255
Hubbard, Cal 132
Hudson, Sid 79
Hughson, Tex 49, 84, 102, 105, 110, 121
Hutchinson, Fred 159, 163, 165
J
Jeter, Derek 141
Johnson, Bob 18, 49, 51
Johnson, Darrell 170, 171, 249, 251–256
Johnson, Earl 37, 100. 121
Johnson, Ernie 29, 32, 34–36, 43
Jones, Dalton 205, 231, 238
Jones, Murrell "Jake" 101, 105
Judnich, Walter 58, 81
Jurges, Billy 196
K
Kaline, Al 163–166
Kasko, Eddie 255
Keeler, Wee Willie 106
Kell, George 78, 130, 154, 155, 159
Keller, Charlie "King Kong" 81
Keltner, Ken 128
Kennedy, Bob 69
Kennedy, Kevin 255, 265, 267
Killebrew, Harmon 167, 168
Kinder, Ellis 110, 116, 117, 121, 122, 130, 137
Kiner, Ralph 137
Kirsch, Donnie 25, 168
Kissell, George 269
Klein, Chuck 106
Klinger, Bob 91, 92
Kramer, Jack 81, 110, 117, 121, 127
Kuenn, Harvey 159, 161–166, 200
L
Lakeman, Al 201, 205, 236
Lamabe, Jack 206, 219
Landis, Kenesaw Mountain 32, 47
Larsen, Don 170
Lemon, Bob 256
Lenhardt, Don 153, 155–157
Leovich, Johnny 22
Lepcio, Ted 151, 152, 154
Lewis, Buddy 103
Lipon, Johnny 155, 159
Little, Grady 275, 276
Littlefield, Dick 137
Lolich, Mickey 7, 181
Lopat, Eddie 147
Lopez, Al 232
Lucchino, Larry 273, 275
Luck, Eugene "Bucky" 180, 182
Lynn, Fred 222, 251
Lyons, Ted 60
M
Mack, Connie 22, 139, 276
Maglie, Sal 198, 201, 219, 235

Mahoney, Neil 188, 189, 198, 201, 205, 236
Malmberg, Harry 174, 187, 193, 201, 205, 236
Malzone, Frank 203, 209, 213, 216, 218, 221, 228
Mantilla, Felix 207, 237
Mantle, Mickey 213, 229
Manush, Heinie 38, 39, 41, 43, 60, 165
Mapes, Cliff 125, 129, 147
Marchildon, Phil 84
Martin, Buzz 270
Martin, Ned 247, 248, 252
Martinez, Pedro 276
Masterson, Walt 123
Mays, Carl 24, 25
Mazeroski, Bill 242
Mazur, Al 40–42
McCarthy, Joe 106, 108, 109, 111–113, 115, 116, 120, 121, 123, 127, 134–138, 147, 175, 201, 221, 235, 249, 257
McCormick, Frank 96
McDermott, Mickey 110, 121, 123, 149, 250
McGinnis, William "Mac" 30
McHale, John 163, 164, 173, 175, 180
McLeod, Don 20, 21, 24
McNamara, John 258, 259
McPhail, Lee 169
McQuillen, Red 103
Mejias, Ramon 203, 208, 211, 213, 216, 221, 225
Mele, Sam 113, 115, 123, 200, 250, 252, 260
Merloni, Lou 273
Metkovich, George "Cat" 82, 127
Miller, Rick 249, 251
Milnar, Al 58
Mitchell, Dale 126, 162
Mize, Johnny 143
Monbouquette, Bill 208, 210, 213, 219, 228
Montgomery, Bob 188
Morehead, Dave 208, 211, 212, 215, 217, 218, 220
Morgan, Joe 255, 260, 262, 265
Moses, Wally 101, 251
Mullin, Pat 164
Mulvey, Dave 262, 263
Muncrief, Bob 59
Murtagh, Danny 242
Musial, Stan 49, 61, 143
N
Naehring, Tim 261, 262
Newhouser, Hal 105, 136
Nichols, Chet 208, 216
Niggeling, Johnny 60
Nixon, Russ 218, 232
Nixon, Willard 137
Nottle, Ed 260
O
O'Connell, Dick 75, 76, 198, 204, 225, 232, 241, 252, 254, 269
Oliver, Al 243, 244, 251

O'Neill, Steve 136, 137, 139, 140, 142–147
Orsillo, Don 246
Osborne, Bobo 177
P
Pagliaroni, Jim 206, 240
Paige, Satchel 31, 102, 114
Parnell, Mel 59, 115, 116, 121, 122, 127, 130, 135, 137, 138, 142, 146, 212, 219, 248
Partee, Roy 93, 95
Pasquel, Bernard 76, 77
Patek, Freddie 243, 244, 251
Paveskovich, Jakov 7, 8, 9–12, 34
Paveskovich, Marija Bajama 7–12, 22, 35, 36, 45, 62, 63, 69, 103, 123, 127
Paveskovich, Vincent 3, 8–12, 15, 19, 21, 34, 36, 45, 73
Paveskovich, Antony 8–12, 47, 50
Paveskovich, Anica (Ann) 8–12, 16, 50, 70
Paveskovich, Danica (Dee) 8–12, 17
Paveskovich, Milica (Millie) 8–12
Pellagrini, Eddie 33, 48, 49, 75, 79, 80, 100, 121
Pepitone, Joe 216, 232
Perry, Gaylord 185
Pesky, David 160, 181, 183, 185, 194, 197, 204, 210, 270
Pesky, Ruth Hickey 64, 70, 71, 73, 80, 84, 87, 97, 143, 148, 156, 157, 160, 181, 183, 185, 194, 197, 204, 210, 220, 221, 247, 252, 259
Petersen, Harding 252
Petrocelli, Rico 208, 227, 238
Piersall, Jimmy 144, 153, 154
Popowski, Eddie 33, 179, 255, 269
Posedel, Bill 25
Priddy, Gerry 113, 152, 153, 161, 162
R
Radatz, Dick 187–193, 195, 198, 208, 212, 213, 216, 219, 221, 224, 231, 237, 263
Ramos, Pedro 233
Raschi, Vic 130
Reese, Jimmie 276
Reese, Pee Wee 42, 43, 48, 273
Reiser, Pete 184
Reynolds, Allie 122, 150
Rice, Jim 222, 249, 253–255
Richards, Paul 169
Richardson, Bobby 169, 172
Rigney, Bill 171, 235
Rivera, Pablo 180
Rizzuto, Phil 42, 61, 100, 118, 122, 125, 128, 273
Robinson, John 122
Rolfe, Red 56, 112, 154, 159
Rommel, Ed 58, 59
Rosar, Buddy 78, 136
Rosen, Al 162
Rowe, Preacher 42
Runge, Ed 217

Runnels, Pete 167, 168, 198, 203, 207, 208
Ryba, Mike 52
S
Sain, Johnny 65, 68
Sanguillen, Manny 243, 244
Scarborough, Ray 106, 143
Schilling, Chuck 213, 214, 218, 221, 225, 228, 231
Schmidt, Milt 87
Sanchez, Joe 252, 270
Schoendienst, Red 90
Schreiber, Paul 255
Schwall, Don 187, 188, 206
Sewell, Luke 132
Shea, Kevin 266
Sievers, Roy 167
Simmons, Al 128
Slapnicka, Cy 35
Slaughter, Enos 89, 91–97, 102, 192
Smith, Al 216
Smith, Hal 242
Smith, Paul 187
Smith, Reggie 227
Snyder, Jerry 168
Southworth, Billy 18, 208
Staller, George 179
Stargell, Willie 240, 242
Steinberg, Dr. Charles 273
Stengel, Casey 127, 129, 135, 139
Stephens, Gene 153
Stephens, Vern 42, 61, 77, 108, 109, 112, 114, 117,
    118, 123–126, 130, 133–152, 154, 159, 161
Stephenson, Jerry 208, 212
Stepovich, Mike 22
Stewart, Ed 130
Stobbs, Chuck 121, 130, 136
Stuart, Dick 204, 206, 208, 209, 211–215, 218–222,
    226–234
Sullivan, Haywood 253, 257, 258
Summers, Bill 80, 126
T
Tabor, Jim 49, 52, 61
Tamburro, Mike 260
Tebbetts, Birdie 112, 136–138, 141, 165, 231, 250
Terry, Ralph 171
Terwilliger, Wayne 167
Thomas, Lee 210, 231, 232, 237
Throneberry, Faye 153
Throneberry, Marv 169, 170
Tiant, Luis 267
Tillman, Bob 179, 187, 188, 193, 194, 201, 202, 211,
    213, 221, 228, 229, 237
Trout, Dizzy 155
Trucks, Virgil 135, 158, 159
Turley, Bob 219–221, 233, 236, 237
Tyce, Joe 189
U

Umphlett, Tom 167, 187
V
Vander Meer, Johnny 50
Vaughn, Mo 261, 266
Veeck, Bill 209
Vernon, Mickey 85, 167
Virdon, Bill 240, 242
Vollmer, Clyde 136, 137
W
Wagner, Charlie 39, 52, 54, 61, 68, 76, 259, 269
Wagner, Hal 84
Waitkus, Eddie 250
Walker, Harry 90, 91, 93, 95, 97, 239, 240, 242, 252
Wanless, Bill 262
Weissman, Earl 270
Wells, Leo 42
Werner, Tom 273
Wertz, Vic 145, 198
White, Hal 111
White, Sammy 153, 154
Whitman, Dick 32
Widmar, Al 178
Wight, Bill 143, 155, 156
Williams, Dick 208, 212
Williams, Jimy 255, 263, 266–268
Williams, Ted 1, 14, 19, 21, 24, 25, 44, 48–57, 60–68,
    72–91, 94, 96, 99, 101–107, 112–117, 121–130,
    134–141, 143–147, 150, 151, 153, 161, 184, 187,
    190, 195, 196, 198, 201, 204, 208, 211, 214, 218,
    221, 227, 241, 244, 247, 271
Williams, Wade W. 16, 20, 22–24
Willoughby, Jim 256
Wills, Maury 242
Wilson, Earl 187, 188, 191, 192, 194, 208, 210, 211,
    213, 220, 231
Wilson, Jack 34
Wise, Rick 253, 256
Wood, Jake 180, 181
Wright, Tom 136, 167
Wynn, Early 104, 110, 111
Y
Yastrzemski, Carl a/k/a Yaz 62, 203, 208, 209,
    211–213, 216, 218,219, 221, 222, 225, 226, 228,
    231, 233, 234, 236
Yawkey, Jean R. 83, 257, 269
Yawkey, Tom 27, 30, 55, 61, 62, 86, 99, 111, 117, 122,
    130, 131, 142, 143, 156, 173, 196–199, 201, 203,
    204, 218, 221, 223, 225–227, 231, 233–237, 251,
    257
York, Rudy 74, 76, 82, 84, 85, 90, 99, 101, 102, 196,
    201
Yost, Eddie 167, 168
Z
Zarilla, Al 124, 136, 137
Zimmer, Don 205, 254–258
Zuber, Bill 58

ABOUT THE AUTHOR
~

Bill Nowlin has co-authored six previous baseball books and over 100 articles on baseball—almost every one of them tied to the Boston Red Sox. His first writing on the Red Sox was in 1957 at age 12, for a self-produced neighborhood newspaper. After a forty year hiatus, he took up where he left off with 1997's book *Ted Williams: A Tribute*, coauthored with Jim Prime. He is a co-founder of America's premier roots music label, Rounder Records, based in Cambridge, Massachusetts.

For more information on Rounder Books, please visit our website at www.rounderbooks.com

Please also visit author site, www.billnowlin.com

THIS BOOK WAS SET USING QUARK XPRESS, UTILIZING THE MINION & CAXTON FAMILIES OF TYPE, BOTH OF WHICH WERE INSPIRED BY CLASSICAL OLD-STYLE TYPEFACES OF THE LATE RENAISSANCE; AND THE APTLY NAMED FENWAY, A SWASH TYPEFACE BASED ON THE BOSTON RED SOX'S FENWAY PARK SIGNAGE.

DESIGN BY WINDHAVEN PRESS & BILL NOWLIN.